BOCKSTAEL

D1563930

Beach Nourishment and Protection

Committee on Beach Nourishment and Protection

Marine Board
Commission on Engineering and Technical Systems
National Research Council

NATIONAL ACADEMY PRESS
Washington, D.C.   1995

National Academy Press • 2101 Constitution Avenue, NW • Washington, DC 20418

NOTICE: The project that is the subject of this report was approved by the Governing Board of the National Research Council, whose members are drawn from the councils of the National Academy of Sciences, the National Academy of Engineering, and the Institute of Medicine. The members of the panel responsible for the report were chosen for their special competences and with regard for appropriate balance.

This report has been reviewed by a group other than the authors according to procedures approved by a Report Review Committee consisting of members of the National Academy of Sciences, the National Academy of Engineering, and the Institute of Medicine.

The program described in this report is supported by cooperative agreement no. 14-35-0001-30475 between the Minerals Management Service of the U.S. Department of the Interior and the National Academy of Sciences and by interagency cooperative agreement no. DTMA91-94-G-00003 between the Maritime Administration of the U.S. Department of Transportation and the National Academy of Sciences.

Printed in the United States of America

Cover: Anna Maria, Florida, beach nourishment project. Photo courtesy of Aero Photo, St. Petersburg, Florida.

Acknowledgments

The committee gratefully acknowledges the contributions of time and information provided by:

Ms. Cheryl Ryder, Environmental Specialist, Florida Department of Environmental Protection

Dr. Walter Nelson, Florida Institute of Technology

Dr. Timothy Kana, President, Coastal Science & Engineering, Inc.

Mr. J. Thomas Jarrett, Wilmington District, U.S. Army Corps of Engineers

Mr. Millard Dowd, Charleston District, U.S. Army Corps of Engineers

Mr. Robert W. Lindner, Baltimore District, U.S. Army Corps of Engineers

Mr. David V. Schmidt, Jacksonville District, U.S. Army Corps of Engineers

Mr. Michael Kieslich, Galveston District, U.S. Army Corps of Engineers

Mr. Adrian J. Combe, New Orleans District, U.S. Army Corps of Engineers

Dr. Donald K. Stauble, Coastal Engineering Research Center, U.S. Army Corps of Engineers

Mr. Jeff Gebert, Philadelphia District, U.S. Army Corps of Engineers

Ms. Monica Chasten, Philadelphia District, U.S. Army Corps of Engineers

Mr. John G. Housley, Headquarters, U.S. Army Corps of Engineers

Preface

BACKGROUND

Beaches are essential storm barriers. They protect natural and developed areas and provide valuable recreational resources. But beaches are dynamic, often eroding in winter and accreting in summer, moved by waves, currents, and wind. Many beaches are naturally eroding, their shoreline position moving shoreward over time. Various strategies are used in an effort to manage shorelines to satisfy socioeconomic needs. Fixed structures, such as seawalls, groins, and shore-parallel breakwaters, have been used for many years to create a barrier between land and sea. But they can interrupt the alongshore flow of sand, exacerbating erosion problems in some instances and creating new ones in others. Beach nourishment, which involves the addition of sand in designed contours to extend a beach and the nearshore shallows seaward, has grown in acceptance as a shore protection and beach restoration measure in the United States, Europe, and Australia.

The use of beach nourishment has encountered strong opposition as well as ardent support. Proponents consider the management of littoral sand resources the preferred solution to shoreline erosion. They view beach nourishment as technically and economically sound when projects are well planned and well executed. Opponents often view beach nourishment as little more than building temporary sand dikes to protect against an advancing sea. Some projects have performed well, and others have not, or they have failed to meet public expectations. The mixed results have stimulated considerable controversy. The technology has been challenged with respect to perceived inadequacies in project location, prediction, design, monitoring, cost-benefit analysis, sand placement and distribution, cost-share allocations, and the understanding of complex shore processes. Contributing to the controversy are perceptions about project performance that are based on anecdotal information rather than technical performance criteria.

Section 309 of the Water Resources Development Act of 1990 (P.L. 101-640) has stimulated considerable public interest in beach nourishment by raising the question of linking federal participation in the planning, implementation, or maintenance of any beach stabilization or nourishment project with a state's establishment or commitment to a beachfront management program. Further, the requirement for a cost share for shore improvements, based on the Water Resources Act of 1986, has raised the stakes for states and municipalities, which now have a much more direct interest in the cost and performance of shoreline projects.

Given the overall experience with beach nourishment and the growing interest and reliance on it, an assessment was needed to establish an improved technical basis for decision making about the use of beach nourishment in shore stabilization and management and in the design of beach nourishment projects in which the federal government is involved.

THE NRC STUDY

As a result of its deliberations and informal discussions with the U.S. Army Corps of Engineers (USACE), the Marine Board of the National Research Council's (NRC) Commission on Engineering and Technical Systems determined that an improved technical basis for decision making could be established by exploring the engineering, environmental, economic, and public policy aspects of beach nourishment. Important factors meriting assessment include improvements in the understanding of shore processes; definition of the appropriate role of beach nourishment in shore management; and enhancements and improvements in predictive capabilities, project monitoring, and performance evaluation. The NRC convened the Committee on Beach Nourishment and Protection under the auspices of the Marine Board.

Committee members were selected for their expertise and wide range of experience and viewpoints. The principle guiding the constitution of the committee and its work, consistent with NRC policy, was not to exclude members with potential biases that might accompany expertise vital to the study but to seek balance and fair treatment. Committee members are experts in coastal engineering, coastal geology, economics, ecological preservation and response to coastal change, development of beach areas for both public and private uses, and federal and state coastal land-use planning. Academic, industrial, government, scientific, engineering, and public perspectives are reflected in the committee's composition. Biographies of members are provided in Appendix A.

The committee was assisted by the Federal Emergency Management Agency, the National Oceanic and Atmospheric Administration, the U.S. Geological Survey, and the USACE, all of which designated liaison representatives. The Minerals Management Service provided information and commentary useful to the committee.

The committee was asked by the NRC to conduct a multidisciplinary assessment of the engineering, environmental, economic, and public policy aspects of beach nourishment to provide an improved technical basis for judging the use of beach nourishment and protection technology in shoreline stabilization, erosion control, recreational beach creation, dredged material placement, construction of coastal storm barriers, and protection of natural resources.

Included in the scope of the study are:

- measures of beach nourishment project performance;
- methods for designing and predicting the engineering performance of beach nourishment projects;
- engineering, economic, and environmental requirements for monitoring the performance of beach nourishment projects and developing project monitoring methodology;
- the potential for improving beach nourishment projects in conjunction with hard structures and other systems, and appraisal of the technical and policy implications;
- the potential environmental impacts of beach nourishment; and
- economic issues, including the costs of design, construction, and maintenance and the accuracy of prediction, the costs and benefits of beach nourishment relative to other shoreline management alternatives, and a determination of who benefits and who pays.

All elements of the beach nourishment system—the borrowing of fill, the transportation of fill to the placement site, the placement of fill, and the possible integration of beach nourishment with hard structures—are within the scope of this study.

The committee reviewed available data and literature and conducted site visits to determine the state of practice of beach nourishment. The committee also solicited data and views and met with expert practitioners and researchers in federal, regional, and local government agencies; researchers and practitioners in the coastal engineering community; and members of professional societies. In addition, the committee visited beach nourishment projects in Florida (on both the East and West coasts), Maryland, Delaware, and Southern California, and individual members visited other locations. Case studies of specific projects are cited in Appendix B. Appendixes C through I provide technical descriptions and analyses of prediction, design, economic analysis, construction, environmental considerations, and monitoring.

REPORT ORGANIZATION

This report was prepared for policy and project decision makers; members of the coastal and civil engineering communities concerned with beach nourishment and shoreline protection; scientists and engineers concerned with prediction, design, construction, and maintenance of beach nourishment projects; and the general public. Understanding the role of beach nourishment requires an understanding of physical processes as well as their socioeconomic and environmental effects.

Chapter 1 introduces the beach nourishment concept, discusses regional differences in physical processes, and frames the issues associated with project decision making.

Chapter 2 identifies and discusses management issues.

Chapter 3 discusses the roles and responsibilities of federal agencies relative to shoreline protection and the application of beach nourishment.

Chapter 4 describes and assesses the state of practice in design and prediction.

Chapter 5 describes environmental issues, assesses monitoring capabilities and needs, and discusses improvements in the state of practice.

Chapter 6 discusses physical, economic, and environmental monitoring in the planning, design, and performance assessment of beach nourishment projects.

Chapter 7 presents the committee's conclusions and recommendations.

Contents

APPENDIXES

BOXES, TABLES, AND FIGURES

Boxes

Tables

Figures

Beach Nourishment and Protection

Executive Summary

The nation's beaches—transition zones between land and sea—provide a measure of protection to the shore from damage by coastal storms and hurricanes. Their effectiveness as natural barriers depends on their size and shape and on the severity of storms. Beaches are also highly valued as recreational resources. Visiting beaches has become synonymous with coastal recreation. Beach amenities are an important factor in the commercial and residential development of most upland areas behind beaches. In the past, development of coastal areas often began behind dunes or in back bay areas, which provided substantial buffers between buildings and the sea. However, modern development of beach areas has predominantly occurred in close proximity to the beachfront and has often resulted in the replacement of dune systems with buildings. This practice has increased the exposure of buildings to damage from natural forces. Most beaches are naturally eroding when observed over long enough time spans to average out large seasonal variations. The existence of buildings relative to an eroding shoreline results in a reduction in beach width, adversely impacting both natural storm protection and the recreational quality of affected beaches.

A number of engineering approaches have been used to counteract the effects of erosion by stabilizing or restoring beaches. Traditional protective measures have included "hard" structures such as seawalls, revetments, groins, and detached breakwaters. These structures can reduce flooding hazards, armor the coastline, reduce wave attack, and stabilize the beach. None of these shore protection structures, however, adds sand to the beach system to compensate for natural erosion. Beach nourishment stands in contrast as the *only* engineered shore protection alternative that directly addresses the problem of a sand budget

1

deficit, because it is a process of adding sand from sources outside the eroding system. The result is a wider beach that improves natural protection while also providing additional recreational area. Beach nourishment serves as a sacrificial rather than fixed barrier. The sacrificial nature of beach nourishment projects and public misconceptions about how beach fill projects are supposed to perform have been the source of much controversy.

Although proven engineered shore protection measures exist, there are no quick, simple, or inexpensive ways to protect the shore from natural forces, to mitigate the effects of beach erosion, or to restore beaches, regardless of the technology or approach selected. Available shore protection measures do not treat some of the underlying causes of erosion, such as relative rise in sea level and interruption of sand transport in the littoral systems, because they necessarily address locale-specific erosion problems rather than their underlying systemic causes. Further, all shore protection and beach restoration alternatives are controversial with respect to their effects on coastal processes, effectiveness of performance, and socioeconomic value. Beach nourishment, the subject of this report, has received widespread national attention in the print and broadcast news media and in the federal government.

Most coastal engineering practitioners consider beach nourishment a technically sound engineering alternative when properly designed and placed in an appropriate location. Beach nourishment projects in some locales have performed better than predicted, whereas others have performed more poorly than predicted. In some cases, often as a result of inappropriate or uninformed perceptions about project performance, public expectations have not been met even when design performance criteria were achieved. The adequacy of beach nourishment design methodology has been a source of controversy. Some of the criticism has stemmed from a perception that coastal geological factors have been undervalued or neglected. As a result of questions about actual project performance, the use of beach nourishment has encountered strong local, regional, and national opposition. Opponents often view the sacrificial aspect of beach nourishment as little more than building sand castles to protect against an advancing sea. The controversy over the technical merits of beach nourishment has been exacerbated by national concerns over the economic effects of beach restorations, the appropriate way in which to account for flood protection benefits derived from a beach nourishment project or program (a series of beach nourishment projects) in the National Flood Insurance Program, and the role of beach nourishment in federal disaster assistance. The suitability of beach nourishment as an engineering alternative in shore protection has thus been fundamentally challenged.

Advancing the state of practice of beach nourishment requires an improved understanding of project location, complex shoreline processes, prediction, design, cost-benefit analysis, sand placement and distribution, cost-sharing allocations, and monitoring. This report provides technical descriptions and analyses of these critical areas. In so doing, it addresses six basic questions:

- Does beach nourishment work?
- How should success be measured?
- Is beach nourishment economically justified?
- How can beach nourishment applications be improved?
- What is the appropriate role of fixed structures with respect to beach nourishment?
- What is the role of beach nourishment in flood protection and disaster assistance?

The report addresses these questions to improve the technical basis for public policy decision making. The inducement of shore development that might result from a beach nourishment project or program is an important public policy issue, but it is beyond the scope of this report except with respect to identifying an economic valuation methodology and monitoring program that would provide the technical basis for decision making. Major conclusions and recommendations are presented here in summary format. Chapter 7 contains the committee's complete conclusions and recommendations.

DOES BEACH NOURISHMENT WORK?

Beach nourishment is a viable engineering alternative for shore protection and is the principal technique for beach restoration; its application is suitable for some, but not all, locations where erosion is occurring. Beach nourishment can provide protection from storm and flooding damage when viewed within human time scales (decades not centuries) in those situations where its use is technically feasible, provided that:

- erosion rates are effectively incorporated into project design and, ideally, the erosion cause is reduced;
- state-of-the-art engineering standards are used for planning, design, and construction; and
- projects are maintained according to design specifications.

Further, to provide valid predictions, uncertainties must be realistically accounted for in design, construction, and maintenance. Beach nourishment may not be technically or economically feasible or justified for some sites, particularly those with high rates of erosion. Government authorities with responsibility for coastal protection should view beach nourishment as a valid alternative for providing natural shore protection and recreational opportunities, restoring dry beach area that has been lost to erosion.

HOW SHOULD SUCCESS BE MEASURED?

There is no single measure of successful beach nourishment projects because projects usually serve several objectives. Further, a project may be successful in meeting some but not necessarily all objectives that led to its implementation. Project sponsors should establish the *specific performance criteria* that will be used and how performance will be measured and assessed as an essential element of the design process for each project.

The immediate measures of success that should be quantified and reported are dry beach width, volume of sand remaining after storms, poststorm damage avoidance assessments, and flood protection capability. Subaqueous sand volumes should also be measured because they contribute to protection from storm waves and to recreational value.

Realization of projected economic benefits and reduction of shoreline retreat should also be measured, although the effects are more likely to occur over a longer term than the other performance measures. Effective project performance from an engineering perspective may or may not result in the changes in economic conditions desired by local sponsors of projects because socioeconomic conditions can change over the life of a beach nourishment program.

IS BEACH NOURISHMENT ECONOMICALLY JUSTIFIED?

Assessing and Allocating Costs and Benefits

Beach nourishment projects result in economic benefits in a variety of forms and to a variety of recipients. Cost-share ratios for projects in which there is federal involvement do not necessarily describe the actual distribution of the benefits or adequately account for the impact of navigation projects on nearby and down-coast shorelines. All benefits that accrue from a beach nourishment project should be assessed and quantified, and cost sharing should more accurately account for the spread of benefits to the various recipients. The federal share needs to appropriately incorporate any adverse erosion impacts of federal navigation projects on nearby and downdrift shorelines.

Cost-Benefit Analysis

The theory and methodology for conceptualizing and measuring costs and benefits are well developed but are not systematically applied for the valuation of beach nourishment projects. Social costs and benefits are not always fully represented in decision making about whether to undertake a project and which of the alternative project designs and implementation strategies to select. Federal procedures for calculating costs and benefits are overly restrictive, and they need to include the full range of potential costs and benefits; that is, the full complement of recreation benefits and the beneficial effects to adjacent beaches outside the project limits are to be appropriately accounted for. The U.S. Army Corps of Engineers (USACE) rules governing its cost-benefit analyses, and the choices among alternative project design and implementation strategies, need to account for the true social costs and benefits in decision making. Federal policy should recognize the storm damage reduction and recreation values to the total area affected, including the benefits of sand being transported to adjacent areas outside a nourishment project's boundaries. To improve the technical basis for assessment of costs and benefits, the USACE could conduct postconstruction economic evaluations to identify and measure the wide range of costs and benefits that actually result from beach nourishment projects and programs. To present state-of-the-art economic valuation methodology more effectively and to provide an improved basis for policy analysis and decision making, the USACE should incorporate and consistently apply an up-to-date economic valuation methodology, especially for measuring nonmarket benefits such as recreation.

In the committee's view, physical interactions between the costs and benefits of adjacent federal navigation and beach nourishment projects have not been effectively correlated. The erosion mitigation and nourishment needs of beaches affected by navigation projects have not been adequately recognized or accommodated in the planning and implementation of navigation projects, in order to minimize disruption of the littoral system. To conserve and use sand resources optimally, the USACE should modify its policies to require that beach-quality sand dredged from federal navigation projects be placed in the littoral system from which it was removed rather than offshore. The cost of offshore disposal is greater than has been estimated in the past, when only the direct cost of offshore disposal was considered. The USACE should modify its cost-benefit procedures to accurately account for the economic value of sand and to consider the cost-benefit relationships between federal navigation and beach nourishment projects. A navigation project should be "charged" the cost of any sand budget deficit that it might impose on adjacent shorelines and the littoral system.

Improving Cost-Benefit Analysis

The USACE could improve the basis for economic evaluation of beach nourishment projects by reassessing the categories of costs and benefits that merit inclusion in project evaluation, incorporating uncertainties in assessing costs and benefits both with and without the project, investigating behavioral responses stimulated by beach nourishment projects and associated policy issues, considering the coupling of projects with local growth and land-use plans to increase the net benefits of projects, and designing incentive-based financing schemes. Postconstruction economic surveys to identify and quantify the full range of cost-benefit components should also be conducted to establish a more complete and accurate measure of the actual costs and benefits.

HOW CAN BEACH NOURISHMENT
APPLICATIONS BE IMPROVED?

An up-to-date design methodology and certain technical improvements are needed to advance the state of practice in beach nourishment project design, construction, and maintenance. The great diversity of conditions, the mix of coastal processes, and the resulting major regional differences make it neither practical nor desirable to establish a national standard design for beach nourishment projects. Each project must therefore be designed to satisfy the conditions of its location. However, project design is hampered by limitations in our understanding of coastal processes and substantial uncertainties in numerical evaluations of shoreline change. A more complete understanding of the underlying causes of beach erosion at project sites and an ability to model and evaluate coastal processes quantitatively are needed to improve project design.

Differences exist in the planning and design methodologies employed by the USACE field offices. Although some of these differences are necessary to accommodate regional differences in beaches, others have resulted from local modifications of the agency's design methodology and have not realistically employed the state of the art. Where they have not, uneven effectiveness and less-than-optimum project design have resulted. The USACE should develop and implement a consistent methodology for beach nourishment design while retaining sufficient flexibility to accommodate regional variations in physical conditions.

The *Shore Protection Manual* published by the USACE is technologically outdated; yet it remains the de facto standard for coastal engineering, including the design of beach nourishment projects, throughout most of the world. Engineers in private practice in the United States are compelled to continue using it because of strong legal constraints and liability considerations even though the USACE no longer uses the manual as its design standard. The USACE should publish detailed and comprehensive state-of-the-art engineering guidance on the design of beach nourishment projects.

The updated design methodology should establish procedures for innovative sand placement and corrective action to accommodate the significant spatial alongshore variation, high erosion or accretion, that routinely occurs in nourished beaches. Design profiles should be based on natural profiles at the site that are suitably adjusted for nourishment grain size. Analytical and numerical models should be used to estimate end losses that will be caused by spreading of sand to adjacent beaches. Safety factors should be developed to account for variability and uncertainty, including the possibility of erosional hot spots, and should be appropriately applied to both design volumes and advanced-fill volumes. Fill volumes should be adjusted to account for rock outcrops and seawalls in order to provide sufficient volume to nourish the entire profile from the berm or dune to the seaward limit of the active profile and to avoid underestimating fill requirements. Sediment performance characteristics should be included in the design analysis. The first renourishment time interval could be shortened to allow for uncertainties in alongshore erosion rates; erosional hot spots can then be corrected before the design performance criteria are violated, and overbuilding of those areas in which the beach is widening through accretion can be avoided. All these methods should first be used in conjunction with overfill and renourishment considerations and then as a substitute for these methods as more experience is gained with actual project performance.

Management and Public Policy

Public Involvement

Public involvement in project development is not always adequate. This situation has contributed to misunderstandings and controversy over project costs, benefits, and performance. Project sponsors should establish public information and involvement programs as an integral component of the beach nourishment project at all stages. The public involvement programs should continue for the life of the beach nourishment program to update the interested and affected populations periodically on individual project performance and future plans and actions. The public involvement programs ought to address design expectations for beach behavior; adjustments in profile associated with construction techniques; uncertainties with respect to design, prediction, future environmental conditions, and storms; the replenishment program and interim corrective actions that may be needed; and project costs.

Availability of Nourishment Material

Increasing demands for sand, both for nourishment projects and for other uses, will make it increasingly difficult to predict the price at which sand will be available in the future. This uncertainty is of particular concern to beach nourishment programs because of the need to plan for a series of renourishment projects over a long time and because of the difficulties in predicting costs and benefits over a program's life.

If public sand sources that are free to publicly funded beach nourishment projects in a state become insufficient to provide sediment of appropriate quality for the planned life cycle of a nourishment program, sand sources outside that state's jurisdiction will become more important. Competitive bidding for resources mined from federal waters on the continental shelf outside state waters and the use of sand from foreign commercial sources will lead to substantially higher, and highly uncertain, future costs. Mechanisms do not currently exist to contract forward for federal continental shelf resources, and involved federal and state agencies need to investigate possible arrangements in order to help sponsors contract for long-term sand commitments. When sand sources for renourishment cannot be identified with certainty, the nourishment program must consist of a series of individual projects, and each project in the series should then be made economical.

Project Scope

Beach nourishment projects are often undertaken without due consideration for their relationship to and impact on other portions of the littoral cells that often cross political boundaries. Further, most projects encompass only a portion of an area that can be considered a littoral geographic region or littoral sediment cell; yet actions within a littoral cell generally affect other areas in the cell and sometimes in adjacent littoral cells. The typical arbitrary proscription of project length does not adequately account for uncertainties of performance, and all parties need to recognize this real-world constraint in planning and design. Beach nourishment programs should be planned as part of an overall regional beach management plan in which all involved participants undertake appropriate action to ensure that the process used for planning, design, and approval of projects achieves this objective.

Economic analyses commonly show that a broad range of potential projects produces positive and comparable cost-benefit ratios; yet a single project width that provides maximum net benefits is typically selected as the federal National Economic Development (NED) plan. However, selection of a plan larger than the NED plan would provide a safety margin against uncertainty and variability in project design and performance, often without a significant change in the cost-benefit ratio while significantly increasing the margin of safety. The federal government should modify its policies to allow for the selection of a project larger than the NED plan as long a positive cost-benefit ratio is provided and is within the financial capability of the local sponsor. A sensitivity analysis of both the advanced-fill and the design beach should be performed for each prospective project in order to identify the scope of a more inclusive project that would reduce the risk of excessive damage.

Borrow Areas

Careful consideration needs to be given to the effects of borrow sites located within the closure depth (the water depth at which no appreciable movement of sediment by wave action occurs) of the beach profile or at a shoal site on adjacent beaches that normally feed the downdrift beaches and are critical to the success of the nourishment efforts. The impacts of creating a local depression in the sea bottom on offshore sand movement from the nourished beach and the quality and quantity of sand are particularly important. Borrowing sands within closure depths should be done mainly as a sand bypass operation designed to mitigate the effects of any geographical feature or structure that interrupts the littoral movement of sand.

Timing for Federal Beach Nourishment Projects

The 10- to 15-year-long federal planning process for new beach nourishment projects and the 5 to 6 years required to activate previously authorized federal projects add years of uncertainty regarding storm damage, creating burdens for local sponsors. The federal approval process should be streamlined and delays minimized through contracting of technical services outside the USACE. Further, action to remove the institutional constraints that effectively block use of provisions of the Water Resources Development Act of 1992 would enable local governments to undertake the planning process for authorized projects to reduce schedule slippage. The federal approval process should be streamlined to permit more timely decision making and project funding. Federal laws and rules should be modified to enable federal funding for locally constructed federal projects upon approval of preconstruction engineering and design by the Assistant Secretary of the Army for Civil Works rather than after a project has been completed.

Commitments for Long-Term Program Maintenance

The long-term financial commitment required to maintain a beach replenishment program effectively, although generally recognized by involved communities, is not always incorporated into the planning process. The 50-year life cycle for a typical USACE beach nourishment program is rarely, if ever, paralleled by similar long-term planning by the public and local project sponsors and may not be backed by dedicated sand resources for the projected life of the program or for supplemental renourishments that may be necessitated by severe storms or other factors. A planned beach nourishment program should be characterized as such only when long-term planning and commitments to maintain it are in place.

Emergency Maintenance and Contingency Plans

Although severe storms that exceed design levels can create the need for rapid emergency restoration of a beach or dune system, contingency plans for emergency repair are not common. Procedural delays caused by locating appropriate sources, obtaining permits, and contracting for construction can further jeopardize endangered buildings. Project sponsors should develop contingency plans for emergency repair as an integral element of each beach nourishment program. Emergency-use borrow sites should be identified and the permits obtained and held in reserve. The contingency plan should also establish expedited procurement procedures to identify and secure the proper dredging equipment.

Environmental Planning and Monitoring

Most beach nourishment projects are inadequately monitored following construction; monitoring of the physical environment and the performance of the fill material is often too limited and of insufficient duration to quantify project performance adequately. Consideration of beach nourishment effects on biological resources has been limited, especially at sand borrow sites. The consequences of those changes have not been well defined. Beach restoration projects should be planned so as to avoid significant long-term degradation of the biological resources that are affected by construction activities, with emphasis on monitoring resources and habitats of greatest concern, including borrow areas. The effects of dredging and discharging the dredged material should be considered, and, where feasible, construction projects should incorporate a design that would enhance biological resources of concern. A monitoring program should be required for all beach nourishment projects and programs to support these objectives and should be factored into the life-cycle cost of every project. Monitoring should be appropriate to the scope of the project and sufficiently robust to permit evaluation of changes in the physical and biological conditions. Design of the monitoring program should recognize how the data will be used in making project-related decisions, and data should be analyzed and used in a timely manner in decision making.

Improving the Technical Basis for Decision Making

A better understanding of the physical and biological processes associated with beach and littoral systems is needed in order to minimize the effects of uncertainties and to accommodate regional differences in physical and biological processes. A more complete understanding is also needed of the following factors: the natural variability of beach profiles and their response to natural processes, physical processes with respect to closure depths, sand characteristics (i.e., grain size, shape, density) and their effects on project performance, process-based cross-shore sediment transport models related to profile changes, and the causes of erosional hot spots. An intensive research monitoring study for a few large-scale beach nourishment projects should be undertaken by a third party under federal sponsorship in order to test the validity of and improve predictive methods and design assumptions. The costs and economic benefits of projects and their overall effects on economic development should be assessed.

Design and prediction are constrained by insufficient directional wave and erosion data needed for verifying the adequacy of design and providing insights for improving the design methodology. The erosion data that are available are uneven and of varying usefulness. The USACE should require the collection, analysis, and dissemination of directional wave data for major beach nourishment projects in which there is a federal cost share. A uniform, national, reliable data base on historical erosion rates is needed to improve project design and prediction. The USACE, the National Oceanic and Atmospheric Administration, and the U.S. Geological Survey should establish the needed data base and standardized rates of erosion and accretion on time scales of a decade for all U.S. shorelines that are subject to significant long-term change.

WHAT IS THE APPROPRIATE ROLE OF FIXED SHORE PROTECTION STRUCTURES?

No device, conventional or unconventional, creates sand in the surf zone. Any accumulation of sand produced by a structure is at the expense of an adjacent section of the shore. This fact distinguishes structures and other devices from beach nourishment, which addresses the basic problem in coastal erosion—the shortage of sand. Traditional structures have a proven track record upon which to base decisions regarding their suitability. They are capable of providing effective shore protection and of mitigating the effects of erosion when appropriately designed, sited, and constructed. However, the use of traditional shore protection measures without adequate attention to their effects on physical processes within local littoral cells has contributed to a widespread but technically inaccurate public perception about the relationship of fixed structures to beach erosion. Misconceptions about traditional shore protection structures have resulted in prohibitions on their use in a few coastal states, to the detriment of beneficial applications of the technology. The use of unproven alternatives for shore protection should be approached cautiously. In particular, the data on which to base the suitability of nontraditional structures are limited. Evaluation of any beach protection system is expensive because of the size of any meaningful experiment, and it is time consuming because of the need for testing under the full range of climatic conditions.

Fixed Structures

The performance of some beach nourishment projects can be substantially enhanced by the use of fixed (hard) structures when they are appropriately designed and placed at suitable locations: to anchor project ends, to protect specific locations (e.g., inlets), to provide a reserve capability to prevent flooding and wave attack where dunes cannot or do not exist, or to reduce wind-blown losses to the land. Structure design and associated beach fill need to be carefully planned and implemented because structures rearrange and control the movement of sand rather than increase the volume of sand within the littoral system. Agencies with proscriptive laws, regulations, and management plans for the shore should modify them to allow the use of fixed structures in conjunction with beach nourishment projects where project performance can be significantly improved, out-of-project negative effects are acceptably small or can be mitigated as necessary, and beach access or use is not impaired, all with due considerations for costs and environmental impacts. Each fixed structure used in conjunction with a beach nourishment project should be filled to the upper limit of its holding capacity if its function is to retain sand. When a beach nourishment project is not maintained, the adverse effects of any structures should be mitigated or the structures removed.

Nontraditional Shore Protection Devices

Nontraditional shore protection devices have been offered or installed as solutions to shore erosion problems, often without the benefit of objective laboratory or field evaluations. In general, these devices are intended to interfere with wave-driven sand motions and to "trap" in shallow water sand that otherwise would not be available to the littoral system. Many nontraditional devices have shown no real capability for shoreline protection over the long term. Some nontraditional devices that involve large concrete structures placed near the shore may cause unfavorable conditions that are difficult and expensive to correct. At the same time, technical innovation should be encouraged in the interest of advancing the state of practice. A methodology for assessing the suitability and effectiveness of nontraditional shore protection devices is needed. The USACE should develop such a methodology in the form of a performance demonstration specification that any interested agency or private buyer could use. However, nontraditional devices should not be substituted for beach nourishment where nourishment is justified without a successful demonstration of the device under the recommended performance demonstration specifications or a similar procedure developed objectively by qualified engineers acting in a third-party role.

WHAT IS THE ROLE OF BEACH NOURISHMENT IN FLOOD PROTECTION AND DISASTER ASSISTANCE?

Flood Protection

Beach nourishment projects located seaward of upland buildings reduce storm damage relative to the level of protection that would exist otherwise. The damage reduction attributable to a beach nourishment project can be approximated by using existing risk analysis methodologies. It should be noted, however, that the level of protection is not absolute because of significant uncertainties about the frequency of storm conditions that may compromise project performance. The level of protection can be reduced rapidly during a major storm and is also progressively diminished when a previously nourished beach is not maintained by subsequent renourishment. In addition to uncertainties that affect performance, there are uncertainties about the continuing financial means and political will to continue a renourishment program when not formally required to do so; the long-term availability of beach-quality sediment resources is another concern. In view of the uncertainties that can affect the level of shore protection, it is not prudent to lower or eliminate construction or building location standards that are based on prefill hazard assessments or to alter dune protection setback requirements in a beach nourishment project benefit area. For the same reasons, the Federal Emergency Management Agency (FEMA) should not alter (i.e., remap) its Flood Insurance Rate Maps to show a widened beach stemming from a beach nourishment project designated as an "engineered project."

The increased level of protection that is provided by beach nourishment projects and programs reduces risk and supports a reduction in National Flood Insurance Program premiums. Unlike the more permanent effects of lowered construction standards, premiums can be adjusted to accommodate subsequent changes in the level of protection. A reduction in owner contributions to flood insurance might be viewed as a subsidy because there are few economic incentives for owners to invest insurance premium savings in further flood hazard mitigation measures. Yet owners also contribute, primarily through taxes, to the local cost share of beach nourishment project construction and maintenance. FEMA should reduce premiums to accommodate decreased risks where an adequately designed, constructed, and maintained beach nourishment program is in place.

Disaster Assistance

The definition of an "engineered beach" currently used by FEMA to qualify for payment of sand losses from a beach nourishment project does not, in the committee's opinion, provide sufficient specific criteria to define the engineering adequacy of proposed beach restoration projects. The agency's definition of and requirements for an engineered beach consist of technical criteria, monitoring requirements, and measures to foster accountability for project performance. The design level of storm damage reduction should be used as the technical basis for certification. FEMA should establish a standard risk factor for each major coastal region and apply this factor when qualifying a beach nourishment project or determining an engineered beach status. The capacity of an engineered beach to provide storm protection should be assessed periodically and sources of emergency renourishment material identified in advance. Sediment losses to an engineered beach caused by a storm that results in a presidential declaration of disaster should, in the committee's opinion, be eligible for public assistance reimbursement to ensure timely restoration of beach or dune dimensions to protect against subsequent storm damage.

1

Introduction

This chapter describes the U.S. shorelines, regional differences, and major historical efforts to control the eroding shoreface and introduces the concept of beach nourishment as a shore protection measure. It also discusses the issues of beach nourishment project performance and public perceptions of beach nourishment.

THE CHANGING SHORE

Beaches form the barrier between the land and the water along most of the coastline of the United States. They are susceptible to movement and reshaping—even temporary disappearance under the worst conditions—by combinations of winds, waves, and currents. In the public's perception, beach visitation has become synonymous with ocean recreation. Living at or near a coastline, particularly one with a sandy beach, is highly prized. The result is a marked escalation in coastal population growth and in the value of land in many coastal areas (Culliton et al., 1990; Edwards, 1989; Houston, 1995). At the same time, some beaches are recognized as having significant environmental value as habitats for a wide range of marine life, including threatened or endangered species. The high value placed on the shorefront for economic and recreational purposes, and more recently for environmental considerations, has resulted in great public interest in protecting the shorefront.

The expenditure in the United States for shore protection and restoration is small in comparison to the economic value of beaches. Travel/tourism is the largest industry in the United States, and by far the largest employer. The increase in tourist-related jobs in the past year is more than the increase of jobs in all manufacturing industries in the United States, and beaches are a key element of tourism. Forty percent of Americans list beaches as their preferred destination for vacations, and 85 percent of tourism revenues are spent in coastal states (Houston, 1995).

The United States has spent about $15 million per year for the past 44 years to help protect the nation's beaches. In contrast, federal subsidies of $134 million and $53 million, respectively, per year were paid for wool and mohair production. To put this in context, compare the production of wool and mohair ($60 million and $13 million, respectively, per year, although no longer strategic materials) to tourism, with worldwide revenues of $2.9 trillion and which provided the United States with a $17 billion trade surplus in 1992.

The United States spends about $15 million per year (in federal dollars) to protect beaches. A number of other countries, notably Spain, Germany, Japan, and the Netherlands, spend proportionally and in actual dollars much more, from twice the dollars in the Netherlands to 100 times in Japan (Houston, 1995). The Dutch adopted a coastline preservation public policy that favors periodic sacrificial nourishment, reportedly because of its cost efficiency, flexibility, and minimal environmental impact.

Natural forces change beaches considerably; they change seasonally in response to storms and over long time scales. Some changes are more visible than others. For example, beaches may change drastically in width and elevation during storms, and they may effectively disappear for extended periods during hurricanes and other extreme storms. Sand generally moves offshore from the beach during these storms, but much or all of it often returns to the visible beach during the spring and summer when waves are not as high. Sand also migrates along the shore, transported by oblique waves and alongshore currents. As a result, inlets tend to migrate as well, except where the inlet position is fixed or stabilized, usually by jetties (Mehta, 1993; Rose et al., 1878; Silvester and Hsu, 1993).

The coastlines of the United States can be divided into regions that are eroding at a significant rate, those that are stable or have negligible erosion rates, and a few that are accreting. Significant erosion rates (averages of up to several meters per year) are not constant but are strongly influenced by sand supply variations and even more drastically by major storms. Moreover, just as mountains continue to erode under all conditions, beaches are subject to continuing processes that tend to remove material. If these processes are not matched or exceeded by supply processes, erosion is inevitable regardless of subsidence or sea-level changes (Amos and Amos, 1985; McConnaughey and McConnaughey, 1985; Perry, 1985). The erosion is aggravated by the gradual subsidence of the coastline as a result of geological processes, by human interference with natural processes, and by the global rise in sea level (Boesch, 1982; NRC, 1987, 1992). Among human activities that aggravate erosion are the construction of dams that impound sediment that would otherwise reach the shore and the stabilization of naturally migrating inlets with jetties, which interfere with alongshore sediment transport (Bruun, 1989a,b; Herbich, 1990, 1992a,b; Mehta, 1993; Silvester and Hsu, 1993).

Shore Protection

The history of public and private shore protection measures to reduce net erosion and the movement of beaches and barrier islands is marked by "hard" structures that were intended to have long service lifetimes when appropriately maintained. These measures have included bulkheads, seawalls, breakwaters, revetments, jetties, and groins. Hard structures are used less often today because of problems related to restricted beach access, enhanced erosion, and cost of maintenance. The method of choice has evolved toward beach fill with periodic renourishment. This approach is popular largely because it preserves the beach resource and occasionally serves as a response to criticism about the effects of hard structures, discussed later (Charlier et al., 1989; USACE, 1994). Beach nourishment creates a "soft" (i.e., nonpermanent) structure by adding sand to make a larger sand reservoir, which pushes the shoreline seaward. A wide beach is effective in dissipating wave energy as a result of its increased interaction with the waves, its larger surface area, and its greater bulk. The destructive force of storm waves thus falls on the beach rather than on upland structures, although extreme elevations of sea level produced by strong winds and low-pressure systems (which produce storm surge) and high astronomical tides may cause direct wave impact on structures lacking fronting dunes.

The beach nourishment concept is not new. The first documented beach nourishment project in the United States was at Coney Island, New York, in 1922-1923 (Farley, 1923).

Although major beach nourishment projects have been constructed for decades in the United States, Europe, and Australia, stabilization of shores using this approach is controversial. Many beach nourishment projects have performed successfully with respect to design criteria, but others have not met expectations. Some failures can be traced to inappropriate sites or inappropriate application of the technology; others can be attributed to gaps in knowledge concerning both the wave forces and coastal processes. Nearshore processes are complex, and scientific understanding of them is far from complete. There is also serious uncertainty concerning data interpretation, particularly regarding the natural movement of sand onto and off beaches in response to wave energy and water-level variations (such as storm surges) and the shore protection benefits of sand just offshore.

Disagreements over the suitability of beach nourishment as a shore protection measure have polarized the debate with respect to both public policy and technical issues. Critics regard nourishment as little more than building sand castles that will be wiped away by the next storm and as a public subsidy of shorefront property owners. Others see management of the littoral sand budget as preferable to beach erosion, wave damage, flooding, and potential economic losses or to the use of hard structures. Proponents urge that beach nourishment is a sound, cost-effective approach when properly engineered, constructed, and maintained. To them, beach nourishment projects are formidable barriers against the destructive potential of the sea. Both sides in the debate have found evidence and rationale to support their positions.

The need to provide a sound basis for evaluating the suitability of beach nourishment as a shore protection measure is becoming increasingly urgent. Federal, state, and local agencies and private property owners, all of whom collectively bear the cost of beach nourishment projects, need objective estimates of long-term costs and benefits. Current federal laws requiring state and local cost sharing for projects and well-defined state coastal management programs highlight limitations in the technical basis for decision making in this area. In addition, the United States public needs guidance in these matters.

Beach Nourishment Issues

Like hard shore protection structures, beach nourishment has a finite life, which depends on the intensity of the destructive forces of nature and, occasionally, of human activity. A nourished beach will generally require renourishment over time to maintain its design function. This is inevitable, as are repairing potholes in streets and highways, painting bridges, and replacing telephone poles. Beach nourishment does not remove the physical forces that cause erosion, wave damage, and flooding; it simply mitigates their effects. If the environment is benign, the intervals between renourishment will be long, with obvious cost reduction benefits. If the background erosion rates or the ferocity or frequency of storms become great enough, it may not be possible to justify the continued costs of nourishment. In this case, the alternatives range from constructing hard protective structures to retreating and abandoning shore development.

Coastal flooding caused by storm surge and wave runup may be a dangerous and costly reality. In many locations, natural or constructed sand dunes are an effective barrier to flooding and to serious erosion of the shore and damage to upland structures. Sand dunes, stabilized by vegetation and protected by a broad fronting beach, can limit damage from major storms. When beaches are eroded and dunes depleted after a storm or series of storms, coastal landowners and some federal and state agencies may want to rebuild the protective structures as rapidly as funds are available.

On the other hand, various groups object to the nourishment of beaches. Objections of some groups include concern for endangered species, particularly sea turtles along the South Atlantic and other coasts. They fear that life and reproduction cycles may be detrimentally affected by the construction activities associated with renourishment. Other critics object to the technical and economic validity of constructing projects that they believe have relatively short and unpredictable useful lifetimes.

Coastal engineers believe that in some cases the performance of a beach nourishment project is enhanced by the construction of hard structures as part of the design (see Chapter 4 and Appendixes C and D). However, some sectors of the scientific community and the public believe that such structures are detrimental to the shorefront. In some states, laws or regulations restrict or prohibit the construction of seawalls, groins, and other hard structures. Then beach nourishment is the only legally acceptable shore protection measure, provided that environmental restrictions are satisfied. Shore modification is restricted under federal regulation; natural beach migration is typically allowed to continue unimpeded for national seashores and large portions of the coastline that form undeveloped barrier islands. However, exceptions exist.

The federal interest in protecting the shore and coastal development from erosion and flooding is centered with the U.S. Army Corps of Engineers (USACE) and the Federal Emergency Management Agency (FEMA). The management and research aspects of shore protection are conducted by the Coastal Engineering Research Center of the USACE, the National Oceanic and Atmospheric Administration (NOAA), the U.S. Geological Survey (USGS), and the Minerals Management Service (MMS).

The USACE administers the federal shore protection program. Between 1950 and 1993, it invested $403.2 million, or about $9.4 million per year (in 1993 dollars), in 56 specifically authorized shore protection and beach erosion control projects covering a total of 364 km (USACE, 1994). A total of $327.9 millon, or about $7.6 million per year, was spent on initial and periodic beach renourishment (USACE, 1994). The general location and number of major shore protection projects with beach nourishment components are shown in Figure 1-1.

FEMA is concerned with the protection of coastal property subject to damage from storm-related flooding. As an example, after a December 1992 storm, FEMA provided $600,000 to two eligible communities (Avalon and Sea Isles, New Jersey) for beach renourishment. In addition to providing assistance to the states when there is a presidential declaration of disaster, FEMA administers the flood insurance program that insures private property owners from damages cause by coastal flooding and erosion losses. NOAA supports and subsidizes state coastal zone management activities and is responsible for the protection of marine life resources. Research is conducted by the USACE, USGS, and MMS. The USGS conducts nationwide basic and applied coastal and marine research on a wide range of geological framework and coastal processes studies; its annual budget is about $35 million. The USACE's annual research budget averages $18 million. Other federal agencies with related interests are the U.S. Fish and Wildlife Service—sedimentation effects on shores and wetlands; the MMS—sources of sand in federal waters needed for beach nourishment projects; and the

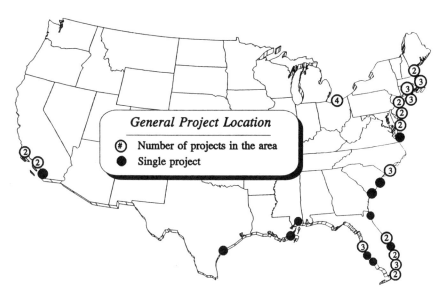

FIGURE 1-1   General location and number of USACE major shore protection projects with beach nourishment components in the lower 48 states.   There is also a beach nourishment project in Homer, Alaska (Adapted from USACE, 1994).

U.S. Environmental Protection Agency—the impacts on water and sediment quality and on the marine habitat. These agencies are mirrored in coastal state governments.

In an attempt to reduce federal inducements and subsidies that encourage increased development of barrier islands, Congress established the Coastal Barrier Resources System (CBRS), with passage of the Coastal Barriers Resources Act (CBRA) of 1982 (P.L. 97-384). Subsequently, the CBRS was greatly expanded, with passage of the Coastal Barrier Improvement Act (CBIA) of 1990 (P.L. 101-591). In 1982 the U.S. Department of the Interior began to review U.S. shores to identify undeveloped coastal barriers for inclusion in the CBRS. Once included, areas may no longer receive direct or indirect federal financial assistance for new construction or substantial improvements. The intent of both the CBRA and the CBIA is to discourage development in CBRS areas because coastal barriers are deemed inherently hazardous areas for long-term habitation or development. To date, just under 600 CBRS units have been included, from Maine to Florida along the Atlantic coast; from Florida to Texas along the Gulf coast; in Puerto Rico and the Virgin Islands; and in Ohio, Michigan, Wisconsin, and Minnesota on the Great Lakes.

PHYSICAL ELEMENTS

The Beach

The physical characteristics of beaches are diverse, ranging from ill-defined edges of broad, sandy islands to narrow ribbons of sand overlying coral or rock, including those that consist principally of pebbles or cobbles. Thus, a precise or universal physical definition of a beach is not practical. For purposes of this study, "beach" is defined in terms of its mobility. The landward edge of a beach, which in this broad definition often includes backing dune fields, is set by the maximum shoreward movement of water during a severe storm. The seaward extent is determined by the point at which substantial shore-perpendicular motion of sand ceases. Both these limits depend on storm intensity during the period of observation. Because of possible larger storms, the limits remain conceptual rather than strictly definable points. The extent of a beach in the alongshore dimension is set by large features that substantially inhibit or prevent the free travel of sand along the shore. These features may be natural, such as an inlet, headland, or submarine canyon, or of human origin, such as a jetty, a large groin, a breakwater, or a dredged navigational channel.

Regional Differences

Coastlines differ significantly in their morphology (structural form), geological setting, and climate. These characteristics require different approaches to both engineering and economics. Following are descriptions of U.S. coastal features.

Pacific Coast

Along the Pacific coast, the coastal lands are well above sea level and with reduced impacts of worldwide sea-level rise because of tectonic uplift of the coast. Mountains are typically near the shore, and rivers tend to be short and discharge directly into the ocean with few large estuaries or embayments. Dunes are rare, and barrier forms are limited to an occasional large spit. The continental shelf is quite narrow, limiting significant increases in water level produced by strong onshore winds. Sand sources are predominantly rivers and soft seacliff erosion, with only a small contribution from shells or other biogenic sources (Good and Toby, 1994; McConnaughey and McConnaughey, 1985). There are relatively few constructed harbors in sandy shores, and the greatest human contribution to coastal erosion stems from flood control measures that trap sand in river basins, mining sand from these basins and beach and dune deposits, stabilization of naturally eroding seacliffs, and construction of jetties and groins that retard the alongshore movement of sand. Large swells from the Southern Hemisphere are common in California in summer, and winter storms from the North Pacific are energetic.

Great Lakes Region

The Great Lakes are nearly tideless but are subject to large annual changes in water level that are driven by variations in rainfall and evaporation. Much of the shorefront is backed by erodible cliffs. Beaches are found where glacial moraines provided a supply of sand, but much of the shore is covered with cobbles or fine cohesive sediments. When lake levels are low, erosion of sandy shores may be minor for as long as a decade. During periods of high water levels, property damage may be extreme. Lake levels are partially regulated but still fluctuate significantly and cause shoreline damage at high stages. Dunes are extensive but highly localized, and there are no barrier islands, although there are a few prominent spits. The lakes are large enough to produce destructive waves and storm surges but seldom the low swell that is beneficial in returning sand to the beach following a storm. Extensive seawall construction has removed some of the cliff material as a sediment source, and the jettied harbors have severely disrupted the natural alongshore transport of sand.

Gulf Coast

The Gulf coast has extensive barrier island/dune systems composed of fine sand. It enjoys a relatively benign wave climate except during hurricanes, which cause large storm surges over the broad shallow continental shelf, allowing coastal flooding and the penetration of large waves well inland of the normal position of the ocean edge. The Mississippi delta is naturally unstable and changeable, in part owing to subsidence and the formation of channels that transport sediments to deep water. The west coast of Florida is predominantly sandy, with a long segment of low-energy beaches with fine sediments (muds). The Panhandle section of Florida, Alabama, and the contiguous coastline of Mississippi have extensive beaches of white quartz sand. The shore is typically low lying and particularly susceptible to coastal flooding. Astronomical tides are modest in range, but meteorologically forced water levels can be large. Storm-surge water levels have been as high as 7 m during hurricanes.

Atlantic Coast

The Atlantic coast can be conveniently divided into three sections. In the north (from northern Maine to Long Island) the coast is rocky, tide ranges are large, winter storms are typically severe, and beaches are restricted to local protected areas. In the central section (the Atlantic coast of Long Island to the Carolinas) are long stretches of barrier islands, most with extensive dunes. Virtually the entire section is fronted with sand beaches. Astronomical tide ranges are moderate to large. Potential inland sources of sand are typically trapped in estuaries and bays, and the beaches and barrier islands are largely derived from glacial moraines in the northern end of the section. Toward the southern end of this reach, biogenically derived sand begins to appear (Amos and Amos, 1985; Khalequzzaman, 1994; Perry, 1985; Williams, 1989). The winter months are marked by frequent storms, often severe, out of the northeast. Summers are benign with an occasional hurricane making landfall or a close approach, causing local flooding and erosion. Where coastal development is high (e.g., in New Jersey), significant shore modifications include the stabilization of many inlets by construction of jetties. They often cause accretion on one side and erosion on the other side of the inlet, depending on the dominant wave direction.

The third section, from Georgia south to the Florida Keys, is also marked by long stretches of barrier islands with extensive coral reefs in the southernmost area. Astronomical tide ranges are small. Shell and coral are the principal sources of sand. Hurricanes cause much of the erosion, wave damage, and flooding, and the occasional penetration by a northeaster in the winter adds to the damage. The entire stretch of coast is only slightly above sea level and is therefore prone to flooding. In general, the wave climate is much less energetic than along the sections to the north due to sheltering by the Bahama Islands. Southern Florida is marked by many stabilized inlets that contribute significantly to beach erosion.

Arctic Coast

The coast of Alaska facing the Beaufort and Chukchi seas is icebound for most of the year. Its narrow spits and barrier islands of sand and gravel are occasionally overwashed during autumn storms. In many reaches there are near-shore echelon bars in relatively shallow water. Some sections are backed by eroding bluffs faced by narrow beaches. Tide ranges are small, and the local sea level is dominated by wind. The shelf is shallow and wide, and storm surges up to 3.7 m have been observed. The Arctic coast experiences some of the highest erosion rates in the world during the few ice-free months. A major beach nourishment and protection plan has been developed for Barrow, Alaska.

Hawaii and Midocean Island Coasts

Hawaii's beaches are formed from both calcareous (coralline and shell sources) and dark detrital siliceous grains from the weathering of basaltic lava. The distinctive black sand beaches found on the southern part of the island of Hawaii are glass grains formed during the explosive contact of molten lava flow into the ocean (Moberly et al., 1965). Because of the typically severe wave climate on the windward coasts, beaches are often formed landward of protective fringing coral reefs. The background erosion rates for the beaches are strongly influenced by the level of protection provided by the reefs, which cause large waves to break well offshore. Human impacts on the reefs, ranging from the effects of water pollution and turbidity on the growth rate of coral to the blasting of deep channels to allow vessels into the lagoons, can significantly affect beach lifetimes (Moberly and Chamberlain, 1964). The midocean islands have small tide ranges, and their steep slopes cause only modest storm-surge effects, although wave runup may be large on windward shores.

Definitions

Shore protection terms have specific meanings for coastal engineers, but the public often uses them loosely. For example, "beach nourishment" is the engineering practice of deliberately adding sand (or gravel or cobbles) to an eroding beach. But the term is often loosely applied to individual projects (one-time placements of sand) and programs (a series of beach nourishment projects). The terms as used in this report are defined in Box 1-1.

Long-Term Uncertainties

The typical beach nourishment program, consisting of a series of projects, is based on analyses that assume that coastal conditions will remain reasonably constant over the program's lifetime, on the order of 50 years. Of course, uncertainties are associated with any of these assumptions. One of the biggest uncertainties is the availability of nearby sand for the life of the program. The longevity of beach fills depends largely on using sand of suitable size and composition, and an affordable program depends on nearby sand deposits. For some factors, experience indicates that the variability is small or predictable (e.g., the rise in relative mean sea level over the project lifetime). Other factors may vary sufficiently to have major impacts on the long-term success of the project. Some are associated with major climate changes. A shift in world weather patterns could significantly change the frequency and intensity of storms, thus changing the renourishment interval from the original predictions upon which the project was based.

A reduction in the ozone layer and the subsequent increase in ultraviolet radiation and skin cancers could change attitudes about beach use and thus impact recreational demands. Some apparently unrelated human act that is similar to the local subsidence associated with the removal of hydrocarbons and ground water in a coastal region or to the reduction in sediment availability through shore or upland alterations far from the project (e.g., the construction of dams) could significantly affect the viability of the project. Further, the program plan is predicated on the continuing ability and willingness of the funding agencies to pay for subsequent nourishment activities.

BOX 1-1
Terms Used in This Report

Beach—The shoreface extending from the foot of a dune (or other upland structure) to the seaward limit of sand movement by waves. This includes both the subaerial and subaqueous portions of the shoreface.

Beach nourishment—The deliberate addition of sand to an eroding beach or the construction of a beach where only a small beach, or no beach, previously existed.

Shore protection—Structures or sand placed at or on the shore to reduce or eliminate upland damage from wave action or flooding during storms.

Shore protection structures are shore parallel, such as breakwaters or seawalls, or shore perpendicular, such as groins or jetties. The principal function of shore-parallel structures is to intercept waves impacting the beach or upland assets. The principal shore protection function of perpendicular structures is to influence the alongshore distribution of sand by waves and currents.

Beach nourishment project—The placement of sand on a beach to form a designed structure in which an appropriate level of protection from storms is provided and an additional amount of sand (advanced fill) is installed to provide for erosion of the shore prior to the anticipated initiation of a subsequent project. The project may include dunes and/or hard structures as part of its design.

Beach nourishment program—A plan for conducting a series of beach nourishment projects at a specific location, typically over a period of 50 years. The program would be based on establishing the technical and financial feasibility of beach nourishment for the site and would include plans for obtaining funding and sources of sand for its duration.

Sand source—A resource of appropriate sand that can be economically used for beach nourishment. The sand must meet requirements for size distribution and cleanliness, and its removal and transfer must not create unacceptable environmental effects. The source may be on land, offshore, in a nearby inlet, or in a navigational channel, a shoal, or other area in which sand accumulates.

Sand bypassing—The deliberate transfer of sand along the shore around a barrier such as a jettied harbor entrance or inlet. In the case where sand accumulates preferentially on one side of an inlet, this action may result in nourishment of the beach on the eroding (receiving) side.

Monitoring—The systematic collection of physical, biological, or economic data or a combination of these data on a beach nourishment project in order to make decisions regarding project operation or to evaluate project performance.

Evaluation—The process by which a project's performance is determined relative to criteria developed for this purpose.

Erosion—A volumetric measure of the amount of sand removed from a beach by waves, currents, or other processes.

Recession—A linear measure of the landward movement of the shoreline.

Geographical Scope

The committee's investigations of were generally limited to conditions in the United States and to the coastal protection methods used here. When possible, other countries' technology was compared with U.S. practice, although it must be recognized that physical conditions, laws, motivations, and methods of economic analysis often differ. The technology of beach renourishment appears to diffuse rapidly; the experience of other countries is included here when appropriate.

REFERENCES

Amos, W. H., and S. H. Amos. 1985. Atlantic and Gulf Coasts. New York: Alfred A. Knopf.

Boesch, D., ed. 1982. Proceedings of the Conference on Coastal Erosion and Wetland Modification in Louisiana: Causes, Consequences, and Options. FWS/OBS-82/59. Washington, D.C.: U.S. Fish and Wildlife Service.

Bruun, P. 1989a. Port Engineering, Volume 1: Harbor Planning, Breakwaters, and Marine Terminals. Houston: Gulf Publishing Co.

Bruun, P. 1989b. Port Engineering, Volume 2: Harbor Transportation, Fishing Ports, Sediment Transport, Geomorphology, Inlets and Dredging. Houston: Gulf Publishing Co.

Charlier, R. H., C. De Meyer, and D. Decroo. 1989. "Soft" beach protection and restoration. Pp. 289-328 in E. M. Birgese, N. Ginsburg, and J. R. Morgan, eds., Ocean Yearbook 8. Chicago: University of Chicago Press.

Culliton, T. J., M. A. Warren, T. R. Goodspeed, D. G. Remer, C. M. Blackwell, and J. J. McConough III. 1990. 50 Years of Population Change Along the Nation's Coasts, 1960-2010. Rockville, Md.: National Oceanic and Atmospheric Administration.

Edwards, S. F. 1989. Estimates of future demographic changes in the coastal zone. Coastal Management 17:229-240.

Farley, P. P. 1923. Coney Island public beach and boardwalk improvements. Paper 136. The Municipal Engineers Journal 9(4).

Good, J. W., and E. S. Toby. 1994. Coastal natural hazards policy in Oregon: a critique and action plan. Pp. 685-697 in M. P. Lynch and B. Crowder, eds., Proceedings of the 13th International Conference of the Coastal Society: Organizing for the Coast. Gloucester, Mass.: The Coastal Society.

Herbich, J. B. 1990. Handbook of Coastal and Ocean Engineering, Volume 1: Wave Phenomena and Coastal Structures. Houston: Gulf Publishing Co.

Herbich, J. B. 1992a. Handbook of Coastal and Ocean Engineering, Volume 3: Harbors, Navigation Channels, Estuaries and Environmental Effects. Houston: Gulf Publishing Co.

Herbich, J. B. 1992b. Handbook of Dredging Engineering. New York: McGraw-Hill.

Houston, J. R. 1995. Beach nourishment. Shore and Beach 63(1):21-24.

Khalequzzaman, M. 1994. Factors influencing coastal erosion in Delaware. Pp. 419-428 in M. P. Lynch and B. Crowder, eds., Proceedings of the 13th International Conference of the Coastal Society: Organizing for the Coast. Gloucester, Mass.: The Coastal Society.

McConnaughey, B. H., and E. McConnaughey, eds. 1985. Pacific Coast. New York: Alfred A. Knopf.

Mehta, A. J., ed. 1993. Beach/Inlet processes and management: a Florida perspective. Journal of Coastal Research, Special Issue No. 18, Fall.

Moberly, R., Jr., and T. Chamberlain. 1964. Hawaiian Beach Systems. Report No. HIG-64-2. Honolulu: Hawaii Institute of Geophysics, University of Hawaii.

Moberly, R., Jr., D. Baver, Jr., and A. Morrison. 1965. Source and variation of Hawaiian littoral sand. Journal of Sedimentary Petrology 35(3):589-598.

NRC. 1987. Responding to Changes in Sea Level: Engineering Implications. Marine Board, Commission on Engineering and Technical Systems. Washington, D.C.: National Academy Press.

NRC. 1992. Coastal Meteorology: A Review of the State of the Science. Board on Atmospheric Sciences and Climate, Commission on Geosciences, Environment, and Resources. Washington, D.C.: National Academy Press.

Perry, B. 1985. A Sierra Club Naturalist's Guide: The Middle Atlantic Coast. San Francisco: Sierra Club.

Rose, T. F., T. T. Price, and H. C. Woolman. 1878. History of the New Jersey Coast. Philadelphia: Woolman and Rose.

Silvester, R., and J. R. C. Hsu. 1993. Coastal Stabilization: Innovative Concepts. Englewood Cliffs, N.J.: Prentice-Hall.

USACE. 1994. Shoreline Protection and Beach Nourishment Projects of the U.S. Army Corps of Engineers. IWR Report 94-PS-1. Fort Belvoir, Va.: Institute of Water Resources, Water Resources Support Center, U.S. Army Corps of Engineers.

Williams, S. J. 1989. International Geological Congress Field Trip T219: Geomorphology and Coastal Processes Along the Atlantic Shoreline, Cape Henlopen, Delaware to Cape Charles, Virginia. Washington, D.C.: American Geophysical Union.

2

Management Strategies for Shore Protection

This chapter appraises management strategies for shore protection and, in particular, examines public issues. Legal constraints, uncertainties, and the economics of the three basic strategies for addressing shoreline erosion are discussed.

THE DECISION PROCESS

Each beach nourishment or other shore protection program begins in a beachfront community that perceives a problem. The loss of a recreational beach, damage to private buildings or public facilities, flooding, or loss of tax revenues can all be symptoms that shoreline changes are affecting the utility, safety, or social or economic well-being of a community. The community must then decide how to respond. In some cases, the aftermath of a severe storm results in pressures to act quickly, but often the problems are chronic and discussions continue for years before an action plan evolves.

Assuming that the shore erosion and recession cannot be eliminated, three broadly defined strategies are available to a community:

- construct a structure, such as a seawall or groin, to limit the continuing damage or threat of damage;
- initiate a program of periodic renourishment of the beach to provide the desired level of protection, perhaps in conjunction with hard structures; or
- abandon or move buildings or other facilities that are damaged or endangered by continuing erosion.

In practice, protection achieved through installation of hard structures, beach restoration, and selective removal of buildings and infrastructure have all been undertaken in varying degrees. Restoration of severely eroded beaches is accomplished by removing hard structures that interrupt littoral drift, providing measures for sand to bypass such structures, replenishing the lost sand, or a combination of these three measures. Reestablishing a beach that provides recreational opportunity as well as shore protection from storm damage is becoming the management option preferred by many communities. Abandonment was the choice in some locations following the 1962 Ash Wednesday storm that caused extreme damage to many Atlantic coast communities (New Jersey State Highway Department, 1962; Shore and Beach, 1962a,b,c). In Nags Head and Kitty Hawk, North Carolina, the retreat option is being implemented through the gradual removal of individual buildings—buildings are removed by owners or they are destroyed in relatively small storms. Abandonment or retreat may not be a politically viable option regardless of technical merit, except following a severe storm. It is not uncommon for upgraded redevelopment to follow destructive coastal storms even before shore protection is fully restored.

As described in the following sections, the appropriate option for a particular location and set of circumstances often depends on engineering and economic analyses. Both initial costs and continuing costs differ for the three options, and opportunities to share these costs vary with the federal and state governments. There are local perceptions of the relative importance of maintaining a recreational beach in addition to actual economic impacts. Each of the options has different long-term consequences, with potentially widely diverging effects on the character and economy of the community, the region, and the nation.

If a federal interest is involved in the region impacted by erosion, federal involvement is often sought early in the decision. "Federal interest" is conditioned by the ownership of land or facilities adjacent to the beach by public entities or from public access to a recreational resource, the economic return (as measured by the increase in national economic development benefits), and the disaster outlays and insurance payouts associated with federal disaster assistance and flood insurance programs. Thus, only in the case of completely private ownership of a continuous strip of property with no public access is the federal government excluded from participation in shore protection projects. Further, the federal government could participate in the cost of the abandonment or movement option for privately owned structures under the Housing and Urban Development Act of 1987 (commonly known as the Upton-Jones Amendment), although this enabling authority was rarely used and has now been rescinded by subsequent legislation.

An important but often inadequately addressed component of beach nourishment programs involves the inclusion of diverse interested and affected parties to ensure that their concerns are accommodated. This inclusion is necessary in order for these parties to accept "ownership" in project goals and objectives (see NRC,

1992, 1994). Local public support is fundamental to program initiation and implementation because the public is directly affected by erosion and storm hazards, responses to these hazards, and local cost-sharing responsibilities. Public support is also important with respect to the authorization and funding of federal cost sharing for shore protection works. Significant debate is often associated with public discussion of beach nourishment as a shore protection measure. Recognizing that beach nourishment is complex and controversial and that public support is essential, an open planning and implementation process is an important way to ensure that all pertinent interests and concerns are identified and addressed by decision makers.

Congress may be requested by a local sponsor (city, county, state, or regional authority) to direct the U.S. Army Corps of Engineers (USACE) to undertake a reconnaissance study of the problem area. The advantage of this arrangement from the perspective of the local sponsors is that the federal government assumes all the costs of the study. (However, the costs of any follow-on feasibility study must be shared 50-50 by the federal government and the local sponsor.) One disadvantage is that the process is slow, and several years may pass before a final recommendation is made. Alternatively, a local sponsor, sometimes in partnership with the state, may engage a private firm to study the technical and economic options. In either case, the result is a preliminary evaluation of the problems and solutions. The technical feasibility of each of the three options is then assessed, and preliminary estimates are made of the costs and benefits. Several states have legal impediments to hard structures as solutions, thereby reducing possible options to relocation or nourishment. Following this preliminary study, the local sponsor, utilizing the appropriate political process, decides on the preferred approach. This report focuses on beach nourishment as the preferred alternative. Included in the analysis is the potential for beach nourishment program enhancement using hard structures.

Erosion and storm hazard problems that are critical to public safety, or that have resulted in high exposure to risk from storm damage, often result from decisions made decades ago. One example is the continuing serious erosion problem associated with a seaward bulge in the shoreline at Wrightsville Beach, North Carolina. The bulge was created in 1966, when Moore Inlet was closed and filled as part of a hurricane and shore protection project (USACE, 1977, 1982, 1989). The anomalous shape of Wrightsville Beach results in wave energy being concentrated along the bulge and wave breaker angles on the bulge transition that vary from normal breaker angles. These conditions alter the normal rates of sediment transport and cause increases in sediment transport away from the bulge in both the north and south directions. Without continued nourishment, the natural tendency would be for Wrightsville Beach to assume a convex (inward) shape between Masons and Masonboro inlets, with the resulting shoreline near the center of the island eventually moving several blocks inland (USACE, 1989).

A natural shoreline rearrangement is Assateague Island, a barrier island in

BOX 2-1
Beach Erosion Following the Breaching of Assateague Island

Following the breaching of Assateague Island in 1933, local residents were determined to preserve the inlet to stimulate the local economy. Jetties were built to stabilize the inlet. This action resulted in changes to the physical processes affecting the shoreline to the north and south of the new inlet. Sand built up on the north side of the inlet at Ocean City, while sand starvation associated with jetties caused Assateague Island south of the inlet, now a 53-km barrier island, to retreat dramatically landward, with a substantial reduction in width over much of its northern section. Ocean City's southern end became wide, so much so that residents did not like the long walk to the water. Subsequently, many hurricanes and storms caused considerable erosion of the Ocean City beachfront in the 1940s and 1950s. The great 1962 storm, which attacked the shoreline with storm surges and waves over five high-tide cycles, literally moved the beach onto the main road that paralleled the beachfront. Sand was 1.2 m deep on top of the road. Although the USACE moved this sand back to the beach and conducted emergency beach fill operations using sand that had been transported to back bay areas, the resulting beach was narrower than before the storm. The north jetty continued to trap sand, providing a substantial beach in front of the boardwalk and an opportunity for commercial recreation facilities at the southern end of the island. The recreational quality of the beach was sufficient to support continued economic development of Ocean City. Ultimately, erosion continued to the point at which beachfront structures north of the inlet area were severely threatened with erosion hazards and the potential for storm damage. Finally, the contribution of the Ocean City economy to the state's tax revenues was so substantial that the state became the principal local sponsor and cost-sharing partner for the ongoing beach nourishment program for the entire beachfront. Meanwhile, the massive ebb-tide shoal that has built up around Ocean City Inlet is providing some protection for Assateague Island as an offshore buffer that shields the northern extremities of the island from the full impact of storm waves. The ebb-tide shoal is looked on as a source of sand for renourishment of the Ocean City beach by project proponents. The National Park Service, which operates the Assateague Island National Seashore, considers the shoal as natural protection that should not be removed.

southern Maryland and Virginia that was created when an inlet formed during a hurricane in 1933. Public response to the complex Ocean City, Maryland—Assateague Island sand-sharing relationship and erosion problems set in motion a series of events that culminated in an ongoing major beach nourishment program and controversy over rights to use sand from the Ocean City Inlet ebb tide shoal (Box 2-1).

On the Pacific coast, beaches tend to be narrow bands below bluffs of varying heights. These bluffs provide considerable natural protection against the sea. In Oceanside, California, some beachfront residences are located below the bluff

line on the beach and thus are more vulnerable to wave-induced damage from severe episodic storms
than are those built well landward of the bluff. Such situations are found throughout the nation's seacoasts. Rather than fault past decisions, those made today with respect to shore protection are likely to affect and constrain the hazard mitigation responses of shorefront communities for decades and thus must be understood in that context.

Faced with a diminished beach and declining demand for rental units and commercial establishments, beachfront communities may perceive beach nourishment projects as a means to reverse declining local economic trends associated with a decline in recreational activity. The potential for such reversals is exemplied by the economic revitalization of Miami Beach. Following completion of the beach nourishment project during 1982, investment in new and updated facilities substantially increased tourism there. Increased building density immediately adjacent to the beach often resulted as older buildings were replaced by much larger ones that accommodate more beach users (see Wiegel, 1992). Such development is in itself an incentive to maintain the beach in order to sustain revenues derived from recreational activities and tourism and to protect the investment from erosion and storm damage or loss (Stronge, 1994). Unlike the National Flood Insurance Program discussed in Chapter 3, no zoning or construction standards are imposed by the federal government as a condition for implementation of beach nourishment projects. However, state and local restrictions may apply.

Because sand moving along a beach does not respect city, county, or state boundaries, one community's activities can negatively or positively affect neighboring communities. In general, a single large shore protection program is cheaper overall than several smaller ones done separately. There are irreducible costs associated with the preparation of study reports, information dissemination meetings and similar activities, equipment mobilization, permitting, and other factors that may result in economies of scale for regional approaches to shore protection problems. Not the least in importance, the combined political power of larger entities has great impact on state and federal agencies and legislative bodies. For these reasons, some regions find that it is in their best interest to collaborate in formulating and implementing shore protection strategies.

An example of regional planning developed over the past decade is the experience of San Diego County in Southern California. The county has a north-south coastline of about 40 miles that stretches from the Orange County border at Dana Point to the international border with Mexico. The actual shoreline is considerably longer. The area is topographically complex, with rocky headlands, a large spit, a major harbor, several rivers (most of which flow only periodically), long unbroken stretches of beach, easily erodible seacliffs, and several coastal lagoons. The entire county has three natural major littoral cells that function as systems but that have little apparent interaction with each other. Only one of these cells is contained within a single community; the largest embraces many jurisdictions. Acting jointly, the communities began by forming a shore erosion task force, which determined that beach nourishment was the solution of choice. They subsequently formulated a long-term plan that includes consideration of costs, funding sources, and the preservation of sand sources for future needs. It precludes independent action by a community—action that would be detrimental to the overall region and the objectives of the plan (San Diego Association of Governments, 1995).

PROJECT FORMULATION AND DESIGN

Once a program of beach nourishment is selected as the primary approach to shore protection, the process of creating a project—the first element of the program—begins. The local sponsor (designated in the reconnaissance study phase, as described above), together with the appropriate federal and state agencies, defines the project. The definition process includes a determination of the project boundaries and a preliminary assessment of the desired configuration of the designed beach, including the type and location of structures if they are being considered in the design. The configuration would include consideration of beach width for recreational activities as well as for dissipation of wave energy, and it would consider berm or dune height, as appropriate, for protection from wave attack and flooding. The end products of this phase are a designed beach configuration, identification of the sand source for construction of the beach, and the placement of sufficient sand seaward of the designed beach to account for erosion and other losses prior to the next renourishment.

The design of the beach follows the methodology described in Chapter 4 and Appendix D. In general, designers use whatever is known about the performance of the natural, or existing, beach as a starting point. Because of the need to determine average or "background" erosion rates, the amount of sand lost over a long enough observation period is of particular interest. The designers then predict the response of the beach that will meet the desired characteristics to an assumed climate of storms that might be anticipated over the planned interval before the next renourishment. Prediction typically involves both simple analytical models based on general beach performance and more detailed computer models specific to the site (see Chapter 4 and Appendix C). Because the predicted performance of the beach depends on the quality and type of sand available for nourishment, the design must include identification of sand sources that can be used economically. Placement of the sand on the beach is an element of the design and is usually dictated by the minimum-cost construction technique for this site and the sand source. Placement, as discussed below, affects the near-term performance of the beach but in the long term is not expected to be significant to performance. Except for the rare case where the nourished beach is naturally contained between headlands or large structures forming a pocket beach, the

FIGURE 2-1   Ocean City Inlet, Maryland, ebb-tide shoal. Photograph by Steve Underwood.

FIGURE 2-2   Oceanside, California, beach and bluff. Photograph by Wayne Young.

action of waves and currents will spread (diffuse) the placed sand along the shore, resulting in losses of the sand to areas outside the defined project. In a long project these losses may be a small factor in the overall performance of the beach fill. In a short-length project they can be important in the design and in the prediction of performance, except for projects at pocket beaches.

Public Expectations About Design Performance

A public dialogue on alternative responses to the erosion problem always precedes the emplacement of a replenished beach. Each project involves important public issues that must be understood and accepted by project sponsors and community leaders. Through analysis of the dialogue, beach nourishment can be evaluated as a shore protection alternative. For example, a community needs to know the reliability and reasonableness of cost and beach durability estimates, possible secondary effects on the community's quality of life, and possible economic and environmental impacts. Experience with public issues of beach replenishment on the U.S. Atlantic, Gulf, Pacific, and Great Lakes coasts provides a basis for identifying the issues critical to communities, both with "first-time" beaches and those with multiple nourishment projects.

Part of the controversy associated with beach nourishment projects is related to public perceptions about the value of beach nourishment as a shore protection measure. These perceptions vary and, as will be shown later, may or may not correlate with scientific data and engineering principles. To gain a better understanding of the state of practice, including insights into public perceptions about beach nourishment projects and programs, the committee addressed inquiries to federal, state, and local beach managers. The responses generally suggested that public understanding at the local level was better than the committee expected with respect to specific projects and economic potential. But there was less appreciation of the importance of renourishment issues that could impact decision making about the long-term viability of a beach nourishment program. Public understanding of beach nourishment beyond the areas of public involvement and more complete news media coverage of local projects and programs are probably less well developed than indicated by the responses to the committee's inquiry (see Box 2-2).

All beach nourishment project designs are based on assumptions that contain some element of uncertainty. The contributions to risk resulting from these uncertainties are discussed later in this chapter. A survey conducted by the committee (see Box 2-2; the survey background paper is listed in Appendix B) revealed that the public is sometimes ill informed about these risks and uncertainties and even about the behavior of the beach fill itself. The responses to the committee's survey questions indicate that:

- Public expectations for the performance of beach nourishment projects,

Box 2-2
Indication of Level of Public Understanding

The following indications of public awareness of specific beach nourishment issues were recorded in response to the committee's inquiry about the public understanding at the time of initiation of a beach nourishment project:

YES	NO	Issue
32	5	The objectives of the nourishment project included protection from erosion and flooding as well as provision of a recreational beach.
31	4	There could likely be improvement in the tourist industry.
29	8	The cost-sharing agreement for the project.
28	9	There is an expected lifetime of a nourishment project, and that renourishment may be required after only a few years.
28	8	There is a need for a long-term financial commitment for renourishment.
27	11	Monitoring of a project is needed to determine its performance and effectiveness.
26	8	There could be an increase in the values of residential properties.
25	11	There could be increased requirements for public access to the beach.
21	14	The nourishment project may have been an alternative to the construction of a seawall.
18	14	There could be an increase in property taxes as a result of increased property values.
18	19	The losses of sand volume during initial readjustment could be quite large if a major storm occurred.
17	19	There is the likelihood of an initial readjustment phase for the nourished beach, during which time there would be some loss of sand from the subaerial beach.
12	19	There could be broadly applied and selective increases in property taxes to help defray the costs of beach nourishment.
11	19	There might be an intensification of shorefront development.

how these expectations were formed, and the public's understanding of technical aspects of project performance have all factored into public debate over the efficacy of beach nourishment as a shoreline protection measure. The committee's questionnaire included a series of yes-no questions (Box 2-2) intended to ascertain the level of understanding of important technical and policy issues at the time of project initiation. Although the sources of information are secondary and largely governmental, it is believed that public representatives and officials could, based on their public involvement experiences, provide reasonable, if not complete, indications of public understanding.

• Responses to the questions suggest that the interested and affected publics were generally well informed about many aspects of beach nourishment projects with respect to the technical and policy issues. However, lack of public understanding was reported to have the potential to stimulate controversy over project performance.

Lack of public understanding was indicated for three economic factors that could potentially affect long-term support for beach nourishment projects, depending on how they ultimately affect property owners and business:

— there might be an intensification of shore development,

— there is potential for broadly applied and selective increases in property taxes to help defray the costs of beach nourishment, and

— there could be an increase in property taxes as a result of increased property values.

• A second area in which public understanding could be improved is in the awareness of visible performance of beach nourishment projects. The two factors that were reported were:

— the likelihood of an initial readjustment of the nourished beach during which there would be some loss of sand from the subaerial (dry) beach and

— sand loss during initial readjustment could be quite large if a major storm occurred.

• These responses suggest that the manner in which fill is placed and the expected initial performance may not be effectively conveyed to or understood by the public in some projects. In particular, the questions and responses suggest that the practice of placing sand on the visible beach where its movement can be observed by the public, regardless of technical soundness, exposes technical performance to cursory assessment based on visual observations rather than empirical data. The degree to which public understanding could be improved with respect to technical issues through various public awareness and involvement measures was not addressed in the questionnaire. Also not examined were public perspectives with respect to alternative fill placement techniques, such as placing fill in the nearshore area rather than on the beach.

In many project designs the fill material is placed primarily on the beach face, resulting in a wide subaerial beach with an unnaturally steep seaward face for two reasons: (1) the cost of material placement on the beach face is low compared with that of a carefully contoured placement, and (2) it can reduce the threat from flooding. The designer anticipates that much of this material will be moved seaward to form the more gradual slopes found in nature. Having borne some portion of the cost of this project, a public that is not well informed sees only that a large fraction of the acquired beach width has disappeared rapidly.

There are slower losses from the ends of the project and losses of sand because the selected source contains some sand that is too fine to remain on the beach. The beach will continue to erode, of course, as it did naturally. The public needs to know that this erosion is an expected part of the project design. In a few projects all the fill material is placed offshore to reduce construction costs, and the design beach width is approached only slowly if the waves move the sand shoreward. Again, if public expectations do not include this delay, the project may be viewed as a failure.

Beach nourishment projects that require local participation in the costs benefit from public participation in that local, state, and federal officials discuss not only bond bills, beach-use tax, hotel-room tax, and other taxes to fund the sponsor's part of the costs but also beach access and other issues as the studies progress.

Although public understanding may be well developed at the beginning of a beach nourishment program (see Box 2-2), public perceptions and support for beach fill initiatives are influenced by the visible response of a beach fill to storms. Further, storms often have considerable media value; a costly beach fill can result in additional public interest and news media coverage. The media generally report the visual results of a storm but often fail to note that designers expected and planned for significant movement of sand off a beach during a storm. Nor do the media report on the return of sand during fair weather following the storm. How well a beach fill performs with respect to design criteria for the storm that was experienced and the storm damage prevented as a result are more realistic indicators of project success than how much sand moved off the dry beach.

Media coverage of beach fill performance at Ocean City, Maryland, is a case in point. A dune and berm were constructed as oceanfront storm damage barriers in 1990 and 1991. Severe storms occurred during the following two winters. The sequence of storms included an event on January 4, 1992, with a recurrence interval of about once every 10 years and an event on December 11, 1992, with a recurrence interval of about 5 years. Although each storm was less intense than storm criteria with a 100-year recurrence interval that the design had allowed for, each resulted in appreciable adverse effects on the project. Designed storm damage reduction levels were restored by using additional fill in both 1992 and 1994, and the beach was rehabilitated by mechanical redistribution of sand in 1993. The considerable commitment of resources ($12 million) that was required to reestablish levels of protection was offset by the fact that damage to oceanfront property was notably slight despite the severity of the storms. The project prevented damage to buildings and infrastructure of an estimated $93 million (Houston, 1995). An extensive data collection program has monitored the physical effects of these events on the project, providing essential information to enable technical analysis of how actual performance compares with projections made in the design process

(Leatherman et al., 1987; Grosskopf and Behnke, 1993; Grosskopf and Stauble, 1993; Kraus, 1993; Stauble and Grosskopf, 1993).

The collection and analysis of data needed to assess project performance relative to design criteria necessarily take considerably longer than the immediate judgment that the public desires. The Ocean City project has attracted widespread news media attention owing to its visibility, scale, and the large investment of federal and state funds. Damage prevented has limited news value, especially to the broadcast news media. In the absence of damage to buildings, news coverage has focused on apparent storm impacts on the beach and dune. Much of the sand that had moved off the beach was later determined through site surveys to still be present in the designed project profile, just seaward of the visible beach (Stauble and Grosskopf, 1993). To engineers and beach managers, the project responded well in protecting developments backing the beach. However, among the general public, many perceived that it fell short of its promise because of so much apparent loss of fill immediately after expensive construction.

The Ocean City, Maryland, situation is particularly important because the public perceptions generated from it are formed not only locally but also nearby in the nation's capital. Locally, an extensive public awareness and education program was mounted to involve residents and beach users in the decision-making process. Through public education it was explained that the sacrificial nature of beach nourishment is an essential element of such projects. As a result, there is strong and continuing local and state-level support for the project and planned renourishment program. However, members of the public outside the local area generally lack this background and depend on news media coverage, which has ranged from accurate technical reporting to sensationalistic live reports from the beaches during the height of the storms.

Improving the basis for informed decision making could be accomplished by mounting a two-pronged program to enhance public awareness and facilitate public involvement. This would lead to a broader recognition of the uniqueness of each beach fill initiative by establishing the criteria for judging a specific project or program. Most important, however, the public needs to learn about the concepts inherent in a shore protection *program* in order to understand its continuing requirements. That is, once a beach nourishment project has been undertaken, it must, with very rare exceptions, be followed by further renourishment at intervals measured in years rather than decades. The public typically assumes that once beach nourishment becomes the preferred option, the next project will be another nourishment. However, this option would be exercised only if nourishment continues to be technologically and economically viable. If conditions change at some future time, it may become desirable to install a hard structure or to abandon the site. Each of these options involves substantial costs to the locality. The public is currently not well informed about these possibilities and the potential costs.

Legal and Regulatory Constraints

Under typical congressional authorizations that enable the USACE to undertake studies of potential coastal projects, each study is independent and narrowly prescribed. Thus, for the two major classes of studies, navigation and shore protection projects, the planning and, most particularly, the calculation of cost-benefit ratios, are independent of each other. This restraint has resulted in some instances of dredged material from a navigation project that is suitable for beach nourishment being hauled to sea and dumped when beaches in the vicinity could benefit from nourishment. The resolution of this problem lies jointly with the USACE and Congress. The USACE could identify to Congress potential synergism between navigation and shore protection activities when the studies are first considered for authorization. Congress could then allow sufficient latitude in its authorizations, so that the USACE districts, which are locally responsible for both navigation and shoreline protection, can consider the best possible use of scarce beach-grade material and can develop the most effective combined solutions.

Federal policies over the past decade have placed limits on the degree to which the USACE can consider recreational benefits in determining cost-benefit ratios for beach nourishment projects. (This issue is discussed later in this chapter.) Regulations discouraging modifications to national seashores have prevented shore protection measures in some locations. There are, however, exceptions. Shore protection projects were constructed on the Indiana Dunes National Lakeshore in Indiana, the Cape Hatteras National Seashore in North Carolina, Perdido Key in Florida, and Assateague Island in Maryland.

Laws and regulations governing the protection of the environment, water quality, and endangered species all have significant impacts on beach nourishment projects. Limitations on construction typically exclude construction in certain seasons—spawning seasons for grunion in Southern California and the nesting season for sea turtles on the Atlantic and Gulf coasts, for example. Clearly, there are short-term environmental impacts associated with both removing the sand from the source and depositing it on the beach. In some cases, these disruptions may be similar to those caused by the rapid erosion and deposition associated with major storms. In most cases for which studies have been conducted, beach fauna appear to recover relatively rapidly from each of these disturbances, thereby avoiding long-term negative impacts (Nelson, 1985, 1989). In the past, most emphasis was on beach impacts, with less attention paid to the recovery of offshore sand source areas and associated biota. Because these source areas may recover slowly or suffer severe dislocations as a result of mining operations, they require more thorough monitoring and analysis.

Many otherwise acceptable sand sources, including some harbor areas, may not meet federal or state water- or sediment-quality standards and cannot be used on beaches. In most cases, the cost of remediating the sediments would make use of these sand reserves economically unattractive. Although high turbidity levels occur in surf zones naturally under storm conditions, turbidity levels have been restricted in some areas, particularly in Florida. Turbidity regulations may be more stringent when adjacent beaches are used for recreation or when turbidity can result in significant negative biological impacts.

UNCERTAINTIES, RISK, AND THE MEASUREMENT OF SUCCESS

The assessment of beach fill performance is complicated by considerable uncertainties of varying magnitudes. They are discussed below.

Primary Uncertainties

The primary uncertainties are:

- the actual severity and frequency of storms compared with design assumptions,
- the variability in erosion for a given storm climate,
- the continuing availability and quality of sediment sources, and
- the stability of public policies and priorities.

Severity and Frequency of Storms

There is a basic underlying variability in weather and the resulting wave conditions. This necessitates a statistical approach to design and economic analysis of beach renourishment projects. However, superimposed on this weather variability is the possibility of regional climate shifts. Time scales for such events are on the order of a decade (or several decades), after which the average intensity of storms changes significantly from the preceding epoch. Seymour et al. (1984) describe the type of climate variability that has been documented for the Pacific coast. Such variability is independent of longer-term world climate changes, such as global warming and associated sea-level rise. In addition, there is great variability in the recovery of a beach from a given storm event.

Sediment Sources and Quality

Uncertainties exist with respect to the sources and quality of sediment available for a beach nourishment program because of geological conditions, environmental considerations, competing uses, limitations of available volumes, changes in public policies or priorities, and shifts in the economics of obtaining suitable sediment.

Public Policies and Priorities

Substantial uncertainties exist with respect to public and private priorities, which are reflected in major policy shifts or in the willingness to pay for projects and programs. Because of the length of programs—spanning two generations and many political generations—it is difficult to predict how future generations may perceive and value a beach nourishment program.

Secondary Uncertainties

Variations in rainfall influence sediment supply in certain locations where rivers discharge directly into the ocean. This aspect of weather, which can vary independently from intense ocean storms, is subject to the same short- and longer-term variability as the ocean storms. Subsidence caused by ground water or hydrocarbon removal can result in locally significant increases in relative sea level that are not necessarily predictable from previous sea-level records. Changes in building codes or state or local laws and regulations cannot be predicted. For example, a state may make the repair of a damaged seawall or other hard structure illegal after initiation of a program that incorporates this structure as an integral part of the design.

Risk

Any method devised for dealing with shore protection problems entails risk. Moving a building landward carries the risk that a severe hurricane will destroy it even in the new location. Hard structures may fail by overtopping during storms that exceed their design conditions. Beach nourishment projects—or programs— run some risk of failure, largely because of the uncertainties described above. There are no guaranteed solutions to wave damage and flooding for any structures built near the ocean's edge. The Federal Emergency Management Agency attempts to employ a standard actuarial approach to risk assessment to establish insurance rates, but regional variations in both storm severity and beach response, coupled with the small size of the experience base, make the statistics relatively unreliable. Formal risk assessment techniques have not been applied to shore protection. That is a research area that might well be explored profitably.

Measurement of Success

Establishing measures of successful performance is made even more difficult by the existence of a large number of interested parties, often with disparate viewpoints, objectives, needs, and ideas. Because these factors vary by location and circumstances, it is useful to identify the needs that beach nourishment programs are called on to meet and the effects they are expected to mitigate. Each of

TABLE 2-1 Examples of Major Objectives, Criteria, and Approaches for Evaluating Beach Nourishment Projects and Programs

Objective	Criteria for Success	Measures of Performance
Provide, enhance, or maintain a recreational beach	A viable (acceptable width and carrying capacity) recreational asset during the beach-going season, usually expressed as dry berm width.	Periodic survey of beach width using quantifiable observation techniques. Assessment of a number of beach visits. Aerial photography useful.
Protect facilities from wave attack	Sufficient sand, gravel, or cobbles remaining in a configuration suitable to block or dissipate wave energy prior to its striking facilities. Protection possibly including hard structures in the solution.	Evaluation of structural and flooding damage following storms that do not exceed the limit for which the project was designed.
Maintain an intact dune or seawall system	No overtopping during a storm that does not exceed design water-level and wave-height limits.	Verification of stabilization of the shoreline position.
Create, restore, or maintain beach habitat	Seasonal extremes in erosion not exceeding the design profile. Structures, if allowed, remaining intact. Postfill erosion rates comparable to historical values.	Profile surveys to establish that the amount and configuration of the sediment meet or exceed the design profile.
Protect the environment	Sediment extent and condition and the vegetation of the backbeach or dune meeting environmental needs.	Observations of habitat characteristics and condition.
Avoid long-term ecological changes in affected habitats	Return to prenourishment conditions within an acceptable time period.	Periodic monitoring of faunal assemblages of great concern.

these areas has separate and unique objectives; even the methods of measuring the level of success (or failure) differ. The diversity of viewpoints is illustrated in Table 2-1.

Determining where a project fits in a continuum of values between successful performance and failure is highly subjective for any of the objectives illustrated in the table. Generic criteria that would define success have not been standardized even for the specific interest areas listed above. Specific criteria can be established in advance that would provide benchmarks for measuring performance. Such criteria, well documented and promulgated among the many interested parties in advance, can alleviate many of the misunderstandings that occurred in the past in some beach nourishment programs.

Each beach nourishment project or program has a lifetime expectation that is a statistical average based on predicted conditions that will affect the project site. That is, a program is designed with an average interval for planned renourishments. The actual interval will vary based on the conditions actually experienced. A beach nourishment program is considered an overall success with respect to this dimension of performance if the average interval is met, even if one or more of the project intervals are shorter than the design average. For example, the interval could be shortened by the occurrence of greater than statistically anticipated storm severity or frequency. However, provision must be made for monitoring and evaluating the project in order to measure its success.

PAYING FOR BEACH NOURISHMENT

A principal public policy issue regarding the use of beach nourishment is the appropriate cost shares for federal and nonfederal contributions to proposed projects. A related issue is whether the direct beneficiaries of a project contribute a fair and appropriate share of the costs. Indeed, there is a perception by some that beach nourishment is a government "gift" to a wealthy segment of the population. This issue may be the primary underlying factor that stimulates criticism of many projects. A review of the current cost-sharing determination procedures is necessary to assess the validity of this criticism.

Authorization for the USACE to conduct beach erosion control projects is provided by Congress on a project-by-project basis. The USACE undertakes various types of projects that result in the placement of sand on beaches. Box 2-3 summarizes the authorities that determine the guidelines and cost-sharing arrangements under which the USACE does its beach nourishment work. Excerpts from the acts pertaining to the placement of sand from channel maintenance projects on beaches are included in Appendix I. Of the nourishment projects conducted under the authorities noted in Box 2-3, the 65/35 (federal/nonfederal) cost-sharing arrangement prescribed in the Water Resources Development Act of 1986 (e.g., at Ocean City, Maryland) has stimulated concern that the federal share is too large or is directed away from other public disaster assistance or socioeconomic needs. Although such concerns are not unique to beach nourishment projects, the appropriateness of cost-sharing arrangements associated with nourishment projects in which there is federal involvement is an important policy issue.

A recent (1995) proposal by the Clinton administration to the Congressional

---

BOX 2-3
Summary Description of Acts Affecting Beach Nourishment

River and Harbor Act of 1968—Section 111, as amended by Section 940 of the Water Resources Development Act of 1986. Authorizes the USACE to take corrective measures for erosion and attendant damage to adjacent shorelines that result from a USACE navigation project if the corrective measures are determined to be economically justified. Work conducted under this authority is rather limited because it is usually associated with older navigational work that has resulted in increased shoreline erosion.

Public Law 84-99—Authorizes the USACE to investigate and repair federally authorized and constructed hurricane and shore protectionprojects when these projects are damaged by floods or unusual coastal storms. Work conducted under this authority is 100 percent federal.

Public Law 94-587—The Water Resources Development Act of 1976, as amended by Section 933 of the Water Resources Development Act of 1986. Authorizes the USACE to place sand dredged from navigation inlets and channels onto adjacent beaches if the additional cost of placing it on the beach compared with other placement or disposal alternatives is shared on a 50/50 basis. It also authorizes the use of dredged material from navigation projects to serve the requirements of shore protection that are being provided by (1) a small beach erosion project that was authorized under Section 103 of the River and Harbor Act of 1962 or (2) an emergency project authorized under Section 14 of the Flood Control Act of 1946 to protect *public facilities* from shore erosion.

Public Law 99-662—The Water Resources Development Act of 1986. Established a cost-sharing arrangement of 65/35 (federal/nonfederal) for projects whose purpose is hurricane and storm damage reduction and a 50/50 share for the separable cost of recreation-oriented projects.

Public Law 102-580 The Water Resources Development Act of 1992. Authorizes the Secretary of the Army to enter into agreements with political subdivisions in a state to place sand on beaches but requires the political subdivision rather than the state to make any required payments.

---

public works subcommittees redefines the future work of the USACE as that of "nationally significant missions." If enacted, the cost share for water resources development projects would change from 65/35 to 25/75 (federal/nonfederal), and the cost-benefit ratio would be at least 2, up from the present 1. Federal participation in shore damage reduction projects would be eliminated on the basis that such projects are local (not national or interstate) and thus should be paid for with nonfederal dollars. The proposal would also increase funding for planning assistance to states, beneficial uses of dredged material, and programs to improve the environment, all of which could be used on some facet of shore protection problems.

One way to reconsider the cost-sharing arrangement is to determine the distribution of benefits of nourishing an eroding beach and to set cost-sharing ratios that reflect the percentage of benefits anticipated from a project. The current USACE practice of economic analysis is to determine whether the federal share of the cost of construction and maintenance of a project is equaled or exceeded by the National Economic Development benefits that accrue from the project. The USACE does not now consider the total range of benefits or to whom they would accrue. Increases in property values, rental demands, retail sales, service industry jobs, and activities commonly associated with resort beach vacations like charter fishing, sailboat rentals, and golfing all may result from improving or reestablishing a beach. This potential benefit to the local economy, and especially the direct property value benefits derived by waterfront property owners, is not directly factored into the cost-sharing arrangements on a project-by-project basis.

Just as each nourishment project has physical conditions that are unique, each project has economic and social conditions that are unique. The distribution of financial benefits derived from nourishing a diminished beach can be different for each project. For example, a project may cost $20 million to construct and provide $20 million in storm damage reduction benefits but may also result in $50 million in other economic benefits. The issue to be examined is whether the total distribution of benefits realized from a nourishment project should be the basis for determining the cost-sharing partnership ratio.

ECONOMIC ISSUES

Although scientific and technical issues are the principal focus of this study, economic, regulatory, and management considerations also are vitally important. This section discusses some of the economic issues inherent in evaluating beach nourishment projects. Economics is popularly taken as a synonym for commercial activity, but this usage is misleading. Economics is really concerned with how society allocates its resources (natural and human) to produce goods, services, and amenities and with the relationship that the resulting allocation bears to society's preferences. Economists are concerned with all goods, services, and amenities (including the provision of natural environments that have value to society), whether they are supplied by private firms or the public sector or are produced as intentional or unintentional byproducts of production (externalities).

It has long been recognized that the private sector, on its own, does not always produce a socially optimum configuration of goods, services, and amenities because of market imperfections, such as externalities (spillover effects whose costs are not privately borne) and public goods (goods that can be jointly consumed by many individuals and are appropriated by none). This point is one of the long-standing justifications for government intervention and certainly a factor in beach nourishment.

Beach nourishment projects are nearly always public decisions, often with large percentages of federal funding. The criteria by which proposed public

projects and government regulations are evaluated have become more comprehensive and more stringent over time. Although not always achievable, the intent
is to determine whether a given project or a given regulatory action is "worth it"
to society (Joint Economics Committee, 1969; Haveman and Weisbrod, 1975;
Freeman, 1993). In addition, there has been increasing interest in the distribution
of the costs and benefits (i.e., who pays and who benefits).

The field of economics has developed rapidly over the past two decades and
has established the theoretical underpinnings and methodology for measuring
social costs and benefits (Just et al., 1982). As with any other empirical discipline, however, its practical application is often hampered by data limitations and
uncertainties over outcomes. Applications of cost-benefit analysis typically focus
on those categories of effects that are expected to be the most significant. Additionally, depending on the regulatory, political, or statutory environment, some of
the costs or benefits may be systematically ignored in the decision making.

Costs and Benefits of Beach Nourishment Projects

A common mistake in thinking about the value to society of public projects
is to confuse economic impacts and cost-benefit effects. Impact measures are
dollar measures of market transactions (e.g., beachfront rentals, hotel and restau-
rant revenues). Cost-benefit measures reflect society's well-being and are measures of the value to society of what is obtained, over and above the value of what
must be given up to get it. (A more complete explanation is given in Appendix E.)

The obvious costs of a beach nourishment project are the costs of labor,
materials (including sand), depreciation of capital, and management services, all
of which could alternatively have been used to produce something else of value to
society. It is important that these costs are the true opportunity costs of the
resources. Sand in the nearshore system within state waters has historically been
free to beach nourishment projects. As a consequence, sand for nourishment
projects has not always been charged at its true social cost. However, as beach-
quality material from upland sources, federal waters beyond state jurisdiction, or
foreign sources is required over time to maintain nourishment programs, programs will likely incur increasing resource costs.

The obvious benefits from beach nourishment projects—and the ones currently allowed when federal participation is planned—are storm damage reduction and recreational benefits (by current policy, if at least 50 percent of the
project costs are covered by storm damage reduction benefits, the remaining
benefits may be recreational benefits). It should be noted here that travel/ tourism
is the largest industry, employer, and provider of new jobs in the United States,
providing a trade surplus only slightly exceeded by agricultural exports. Beaches
are the leading tourist attraction in the country (Houston, 1995). A brief review of
empirical attempts at assessing the benefits of beach nourishment projects is
provided in Appendix E.

Storm damage reduction benefits are currently measured as the difference in expected losses in property values owing to storm damage with and without the beach nourishment project. The problems of measuring these effects are considerable; they depend on both predictions of storms and projections of damage under different scenarios. Areas already highly developed have much larger gains from storm damage reduction because the amount of capital (both private and public) at risk is comparatively large.

Recreational benefits are only slightly more straightforward to measure. Current USACE guidelines allow travel costs or contingent valuation methodologies to be used in assessing recreational benefits. Descriptions of the methodologies for measuring nonmarket benefits are found in Appendix E. These methods depend on survey techniques to estimate the value (consumer surplus) associated with current beach use for individual beach users, whether one uses revealed preferences techniques (e.g., "travel cost models") or hypothetical questioning techniques (e.g., contingent valuation). But the methodology for measuring recreational benefits has undergone considerable theoretical and empirical development over the past several years (see Freeman, 1993; Bockstael et al., 1991), and current procedures used by the USACE should be updated in light of the new literature.

Despite these developments, there are always both data limitations and forecasting difficulties. In the beach nourishment case, the problem is one of valuing a change in the *quality* of the beach, and this requires estimating the effect on demand and therefore on consumer surplus of that quality change for current users, as well as of predicting the number of additional users that may be attracted by the increase in quality. The problem is further complicated if the attraction of new users further alters the quality of the beach experience by altering the level of congestion.

There are potentially other, less obvious costs and benefits from beach nourishment projects. At one time, labels such as "indirect" or "secondary" were given to these other effects, but these distinctions are not at all clear. Perhaps a better nomenclature would be "unintentional," because these effects are "by-products" of a project. Whether intentional or not, decision makers concerned with making the best use of public funds would presumably want to consider those cost-benefit effects expected to be of significant magnitude for any given project.

One such unintentional effect might be the change in the amenity values of living near a beach when the nature of that beach is changed by a project. This change would be an effect other than storm damage reduction and recreation, both of which were already "counted" above. These cost-benefit effects include changes in scenic amenities, wildlife-watching opportunities, privacy, or congestion, any of which could improve or deteriorate as a consequence of a beach nourishment project.

A change in the market value of an adjacent property in response to a beach nourishment project will be a reflection of the present value of all the project's benefits expected to accrue to the property owner into the future. However, using changes in property values to determine changes in amenities is not altogether straightforward (see Appendix E). Additionally, care must be taken to avoid double counting. For example, estimates of recreational benefits based on established empirical methodologies are likely to capture the recreational benefits accruing to adjacent property owners as well as to visitors to the area, but a recreational component of benefits will also be captured in the change in adjacent property values. Another drawback to using changes in market values to measure benefits is that they will reflect individuals' expectations of future states of the beach, expectations that might be misinformed.

Another external effect of a beach nourishment project might be "out-of-project" sand deposition or other effects at beaches beyond the official extent of the project. Under present USACE regulations, such benefits may not be included in the cost-benefit analysis, even though they can be estimated with the same precision as the within-project protection benefits.

Unintentional effects might also include beneficial or deleterious environmental effects, described in Chapter 5 of this report. Methodologies for measuring the value of environmental changes to humans are being developed, although most depend on a clear understanding of the (possibly long-term) biological and ecological consequences. These methods for measuring the cost-benefit effects of environmental changes have been developed for use in natural resource damage assessment under the Comprehensive Environmental Response, Compensation, and Liability Act of 1980 (also referred to as CERCLA and Superfund) and the Oil Pollution Act legislation (Kopp and Smith, 1993). In other settings, decision makers often consider the environmental effects in physical terms and produce their own trade-offs with other costs and benefits to society.

Frequently, the argument is made that a beach nourishment project stimulates increased economic activity and new economic development in a coastal area and that these economic effects should somehow be counted in the benefits of the project. Economic activity, per se, is not a measure of well-being. The appropriate measures are the increased profits and income generated. But these are the categories of benefits that need careful counting because for the most part they tend to cancel out on a regional or national scale. A gain in profits or incomes from increased tourist demand in one region is likely to be offset to a large extent by losses from the resulting decreased business someplace else in the United States. An exception is when such gains are generated by new tourist demand from a foreign source. For example, foreign tourists spend $2 billion a year at Miami Beach. The Miami Beach fill has been in place since the late 1970s at a cost of $52 million. The capitalized cost of the fill is about $3 million per year. Thus, the fill provides about $700 annually in foreign revenue for each $1 invested in beach nourishment. This amount is a remarkable return considering that agricultural subsidies do not result in much more than $1 in revenue per $1 in subsidy. Nationally, foreign revenues from tourism total about $80 billion per year, and in view of the fact that beaches are the number one U.S. tourist attraction, benefit calculations should include expected returns from foreign tourists (Houston, 1995).[1] Federal guidelines (e.g., WRC, 1983) tend to label these "indirect" or "secondary" benefits and prescribe their omission from cost-benefit calculations to avoid adding them up nationally only to find the net effect is approximately zero. Foreign tourism clearly is not an "indirect," or "secondary," or regional benefit. Of course, these local gains are critical to the cost-benefit analyses undertaken by the locality proposing a beach nourishment project in order to determine whether local support of the project is justified. Yet counting local benefits while ignoring losses in other regions for U.S. tourism is inappropriate for federal cost-benefit analysis.

Increased profits and income may not be the only local consequence of increased economic activity and new development, and the consequences might not all be desirable, as many localities are discovering. State and local growth controls and land-use management strategies are becoming more prevalent, especially in coastal areas of the United States, where the largest percentage of land is already developed. The reason for the control measures is that local governments have come to recognize some of the negative externalities associated with development. Development places infrastructure burdens on a community, changes the nature of the surrounding community, adds to congestion, and reduces open space and natural environments that people value. Assessing the value to society of any particular development activity is exceedingly complicated because it requires identifying the true benefits (in increased profits and incomes) net of transfers from elsewhere and the true costs in terms of these local externalities.

It is unreasonable to expect beach nourishment project planners to assess this complex pattern of effects, especially because the problem of land-use management and growth control is far broader and more pervasive than beach nourishment. But it is equally unreasonable to ignore the ramifications and attempt to add economic development measures to the cost-benefit analysis. A more reasonable approach may be to encourage localities to develop rational land-use management plans and require that all public actions, including beach nourishment projects, be consistent with these plans. Some states are further along in developing such plans than others.

---

[1]The reader should bear in mind that, while it is true that foreign tourism generates local economic benefits that are not offset by losses elsewhere in the United States, the proper measure of these benefits is the increase in producer's surplus, not the increase in tourist spending.

Special Features of the Beach Nourishment Problem

Time Horizon

Beach nourishment projects provide two kinds of public goods: changes in local amenities and reductions in risk of property loss. Like other public investment projects (e.g., dams, highways) beach projects both incur costs and generate benefits over decades, and the stream of costs and benefits is uncertain. The temporal nature of a project's impacts poses special problems for valuation, including extrapolating future costs and benefits, accounting for behavioral responses to the project, and evaluating the effects of uncertainty associated with random future events.

Valuation first requires the choice of a rate at which to discount future costs and benefits. A dollar spent (or received) now is not the same as a dollar spent (or received) 10 years from now. For several reasons, the appropriate choice of a discount rate for public projects is not a commercial market rate of interest, but the social rate of discount, which is an elusive concept. The federal government currently uses 7.75 percent for public investment projects of this sort, although there continues to be much debate over the level of this discount factor.

A second problem, uncertainty about the future stream of costs and benefits, is even more troublesome. Much of this report examines the nature of this uncertainty. For the purposes of the economic evaluation of a proposed beach nourishment project, however, some information about likely outcomes is necessary. Simple expected values or averages are not useful because both the public and the private sectors tend to be averse to risk. For example, knowing with certainty that over the next 20 years renourishment of a beach will cost $3 million (present value) is likely to be preferred to a 50/50 chance of its costing $1 million or $5 million. Information about projected costs and benefits should include as much about the underlying probability distributions as possible, certainly not just the means of those distributions, in order to reduce the level of uncertainty in cost-benefit analyses.

As explained elsewhere in this report, a beach nourishment program incorporates a series of beach renourishment projects over a long time horizon or life cycle of a program. This fact poses difficulties in predicting benefits as well as costs, because of both uncertain project performance (under unpredictable weather events) and future markets for necessary inputs. Sand is the most important input, and with demand for sand increasing, it is difficult to predict the cost of sand a decade or more into the future. Outer continental shelf sand resources, for example, are allocated by competitive bidding (except for sand to be used on public projects, which is allocated by negotiated agreements), which in itself is likely to be an efficient allocation mechanism, but currently no institutions will contract forward for these resources. Because of the need to estimate long-term costs of the complete life cycle of a renourishment project, institutions for efficiently allocating sand resources are well worth further investigation.

Alternative Scenarios

Cost-benefit analysis makes sense only when defined in terms of comparisons. That is, when the costs and benefits of a project are assessed, they are assessed relative to a best guess of what would happen in the absence of the project. Defining the alternative scenario to a beach nourishment project can be problematic because there is no status quo but an ever-changing situation.

Consideration of alternative public actions is an essential element of the planning and design stages of a project. Presumably, decision makers would want to take into account all of the above considerations in selecting a preferred design for a beach protection project, and at that point the costs and benefits of the preferred design could be compared with the alternative of no public action at all. This choice provides the process internal consistency, if the same congressionally mandated criteria used to determine whether a project can be accomplished with federal funds are used to select the best design. However, this process is costly and may often be infeasible. In the absence of a federally funded project, localities may undertake projects on their own, or private individuals may pursue individual protection strategies. The possibilities are dictated by the regulatory environment (e.g., hard structures are prohibited in some areas) and by the wealth of the local community.

Financing and the Distributional Implications of Beach Nourishment Projects

Two of the most commonly invoked justifications for public-sector intervention in the economy are the existence of public goods and externalities. The latter arise when the actions of one individual have significant but uncontrollable effects on the welfare of others. Classic examples of this are air, water, and noise pollution. Beach protection projects have associated externalities, both potentially positive and negative. What happens along one stretch of beach can have effects up and down the coast.

Public goods are particular kinds of goods whose consumption is not appropriable by a single user. Unlike a slice of bread, a bicycle, or a gallon of gas, a public good can be used by a number of people simultaneously without its value to any one individual being reduced (e.g., national defense). Both storm damage reduction and recreational use are public goods generated by beach nourishment projects. Some goods are local public goods whose public good nature extends over only a small geographic range. Storm damage reduction, in particular, tends to be a local public good in the sense that the benefits accrue to individuals in the near vicinity. These local public goods should be balanced against the larger public costs of disaster relief when localities or states fail to maintain or replenish beach nourishment projects at appropriate intervals. Clearly, the attendant public costs associated with monitoring and maintenance efforts by recipients of public funds for beach nourishment must be considered as well. Except where the beach is particularly renowned, recreational benefits may also accrue largely to area residents. Other effects of beach nourishment projects, such as environmental effects, may have broader appeal or concern. The preservation of endangered and threatened ecosystems or species is important to individuals even when they never visit the natural system.

Beach nourishment projects are associated with both positive and negative externalities, arguing for public-sector coordination and regulation. The projects are also quasi-public goods, a point that argues for public provision. But for a variety of reasons, the federal government has become involved in beach nourishment project planning and construction, and federal cost-sharing policies accompany this involvement. As a result, those who pay a large portion of the costs do not necessarily receive the benefits. This mismatch is not rare among public programs, although society sometimes decides to finance this kind of public project by beneficiary charges. Yet beach nourishment projects are generally supported by public funds, not user charges, and cost sharing takes place between federal and more localized governments.

The financing scheme affects those who benefit and those who lose from the project, but it will also affect the total net benefits generated by the project. A project's total net benefits depend on whether financing is tied in any way to use or incidence of benefits. Recreational benefits differ depending on whether beach access fees (e.g., for parking, entrance) are charged to help finance the project. Higher fees may reduce use of the beach. Likewise, financing schemes that require contributions from local property owners based on increased property values may affect the amount and type of private investment. Pricing schemes that require property owners or investors to share liability for storm damage or renourishment projects may alter long-term liability costs.

The present arbitrary scheme for cost allocation is unrelated to who receives the benefits, in general, requiring only a cost-benefit ratio greater than unity for approval. However, the federal procedure for cost-benefit analyses, which consider only storm damage reduction and limited recreation benefits, clearly does not take into account local indirect or secondary benefits that may greatly exceed the federally acceptable benefits. Recognizing the fact that public actions can cause private-sector reactions suggests that projects may well be coupled with public policies designed either to regulate private activities or to provide the "right" incentives. One possible policy is the negotiation of cost-sharing ratios related directly to the benefits accruing to each sponsoring agency.

The above considerations suggest that careful evaluation is necessary of those cost and benefit elements included in cost-benefit analyses of beach protection projects and to the possible options available for financing projects.

PUBLIC SUPPORT FOR BEACH NOURISHMENT

Decision makers faced with determining whether to support beach nourishment as a shore protection measure could mount a public awareness campaign to improve the basis for informed decision making. Such a program could include the following topics.

Purpose of Beach Replenishment

The problem of shore protection being addressed by sand replenishment is created by the presence of shorefront property and infrastructure on an eroding beach. Replenishment in a developed area, whether for storm damage reduction or improvement of a recreational beach, would not be required in the absence of buildings or if the buildings were moved back from the retreating shoreline. In the absence of buildings or public infrastructure, beach erosion or shoreline retreat generally creates no problems for development or for the quality of recreational beaches. Unless there is a natural obstruction or an obstruction of human origin, beaches experiencing erosion simply move landward, in response to the forces of waves and currents, while retaining their general shape and size.

Commitment Required for a Replenished Beach

Replenishing a beach is the first step in a long-term continuous program of nourishment to mitigate erosion losses. A long-term realistic financial commitment is needed on the part of government at all levels. It is important for the public to understand that funding is not guaranteed beyond the first emplacement. In effect, a typical 50-year USACE nourishment program constitutes permission only to *request* project-by-project funding from Congress for the next 50 years when it is technically and economically feasible. A contingency arrangement for near-term funding of renourishment to restore designed features is prudent because storms may remove sand at much more rapid rates than estimated in design documents, and emergency or special funding from federal sources may not be available when needed. If such a commitment were not in place, there might be a period of time, perhaps extended, when a beach that eroded more rapidly than expected could furnish less-than-design storm damage reduction and recreational benefits.

Gauging the Realism of Cost Projections

The assumed rate of loss of a replenished beach determines the long-term costs, the long-term sand volume requirements, and even the long-term feasibility of beach replenishment as an alternative for managing an eroding shore. Cost estimates for beach replenishment are not precise, because the need for replenishing a beach is controlled by the frequency and magnitude of storms rather than the statistically derived frequency and severity on which the design is based. Predictions of costs, including the future cost of money and of sand volumes, need to account for such uncertainties through the use of error bars and probability estimates. Even when the predictions in published design documents do not reflect the vicissitudes of storms, planners and the public need to recognize that uncertainties exist in long-term costs, and they should plan accordingly. In general, beaches have a longer renourishment cycle on low-energy coasts (e.g., south Florida) and will have a shorter renourishment cycle on exposed higher-energy coasts (e.g., the mid-Atlantic states). Replenished beaches with high preproject erosion rates will likely also suffer continued high erosion rates.

A useful though not precise measure of predicted beach life span is the nourishment interval—the assumed time between nourishment operations that are required to replace erosion losses and to bring the beach back to its design width. In recent Gulf of Mexico and Atlantic coast beach nourishment projects, replenished interval estimates have ranged from 2 years (Sandbridge, Virginia) to 10 years (Panama City, Florida). An examination of the actual nourishment intervals of neighboring replenished beaches, when such beaches exist, is one way to determine whether nourishment interval predictions are reasonable. A recent report (USACE, 1994) analyzes beach fills for the past 44 years and clearly shows that, in the aggregate, cost projections for beach fills have been fairly accurate. On average, actual costs have been 4 percent less than estimated costs. The volume of sand used was about 5 percent greater than estimated.

Visible Beach Versus the Underwater Beach

Two major purposes of beach replenishment are the creation of a storm barrier and the creation of a recreational beach. In both cases, the retention of a subaerial beach is important. Storm damage reduction is afforded by the beach and, when present, the dune. If one or the other is lost by offshore or lateral sand removal, storm damage reduction is greatly lessened. Sand on the underwater profile, in the absence of dry beach and dune, contributes less to protecting the community from storms than the subaerial portion would. This is especially so in combating the effects of storm surges. However, the underwater profile is essential to maintaining the dry beach. Without it the beach would simply move seaward to build an equivalent profile.

An important measure of the quality of the recreational beach is dry beach width at normal high tide. When dry beach disappears at high tide, the recreational benefits are significantly reduced. Because of the importance of the subaerial beach, storm damage and monitoring reports need to note clearly the evolution of the subaerial replenished beach. Although reports noting only the percentage of sand remaining in the entire system (including the underwater shoreface) are useful to engineers and scientists for understanding the fate of replenishment sand, they are not well understood by the public. Statements such as "96 percent of the sand remains in the system" need to be augmented by an explanation of how the behavior of the beach provides protection to the development and public infrastructure.

Use of Hard Structures

The use of groins, seawalls, or jetties in replenished beaches combines "hard" (i.e., concrete, rock, steel, wood) and "soft" (i.e., sand) stabilization solutions with the advantages and disadvantages of each. The life span of replenished beaches can in some cases be significantly increased by the use of hard structures in the replenishment shoreline reach. However, downdrift erosion problems may arise from the use of groins, which will necessitate the use of sand redistribution techniques. This is discussed further in Chapter 4.

Cost-Sharing Responsibilities

Solutions to shore protection problems always involve significant costs. In most cases, the local sponsoring body is responsible for raising a share of these costs. The public needs to understand that these costs will continue beyond the initial project, may come due sooner than anticipated if the storm climate is worse than predicted, will escalate with inflation, and may increase as sand sources become more distant or are otherwise less desirable.

Gauging the Success of a Replenished Beach

Project or program success is likely to vary across the range of objectives that a beach fill is intended to serve. Even when shore protection benefits are achieved, economic benefits may or may not occur as projected. In some cases, a beach fill may be only partially successful with respect to planned physical performance but may nevertheless stimulate considerable economic activity. Such economic results may be seen as either a benefit or disbenefit, depending upon individual points of view.

In order to provide a common framework for determining a project's performance, the criteria by which a project will be judged with respect to goals and objectives should be established through a public involvement process. Although considerable effort is probably necessary, establishing a consensus-based framework for project evaluation would provide the common ground necessary to facilitate decision making.

REFERENCES

Bockstael, N. E., K. E. McConnell, and I. E. Strand. 1991. Recreation. In: J. B. Braden and C. D. Kolstad, eds., Measuring the Demand for Environmental Quality. New York: North Holland.

Freeman, A. M. 1993. The Measurement of Environmental and Resource Values. Washington, D.C.: Resources for the Future.

Grosskopf, W. G., and D. Behnke. 1993. An emergency remedial beach fill design for Ocean City, Maryland. Shore and Beach 61(1):8-12.

Grosskopf, W. G., and D. K. Stauble. 1993. Atlantic coast of Maryland (Ocean City) shoreline protection plan. Shore and Beach 61(1):3-7.

Haveman, R. H., and B. A. Weisbrod. 1975. The concept of benefits in cost-benefit analysis: with emphasis on water pollution control activities. In: Cost-Benefit Analysis and Water Pollution Policy. Washington, D.C.: The Urban Institute.

Houston, J. R. 1995. Beach nourishment. Shore and Beach 63(1):21-24.

Joint Economics Committee, U.S. Congress. 1969. The Analysis and Evaluation of Public Expenditures: The PPB System. Washington, D.C.: U.S. Government Printing Office.

Just, R. E., D. L. Hueth, and A. Schmitz. 1982 (with new edition forthcoming). Applied Welfare Economics and Public Policy. Englewood Cliffs, N.J.: Prentice-Hall.

Kopp, R. J., and V. K. Smith. 1993. Valuing Natural Assets: The Economics of Natural Resource Damage Assessment. Washington, D.C.: Resources for the Future.

Kraus, N. C. 1993. Guest editorial: the January 4, 1992 storm at Ocean City, Maryland. Shore and Beach 61(1):2.

Leatherman, S. P., R. G. Dean, C. E. Everts, and E. Fulford. 1987. Shoreline and sediment budget analysis of North Assateague Island. Proceedings of Coastal Sediments 87:1460-1471.

Nelson, W. G. 1985. Physical and Biological Guidelines for Beach Restoration Projects. Part I. Biological Guidelines. Report No. 76. Florida Sea Grant College, Gainesville.

Nelson, W. G. 1989. An overview of the effects of beach nourishment on the sand beach fauna. Pp. 295-309 in Proceedings of the 1988 National Conference on Beach Preservation Technology. Tallahassee: Florida Shore and Beach Preservation Association.

New Jersey State Highway Department. 1962. Sea Isle City Disaster Survey—Part One. April 4. Trenton, N.J.: New Jersey State Highway Department.

NRC. 1992. Coastal Meteorology: A Review of the State of the Science. Board on Atmospheric Sciences and Climate, Commission on Geosciences, Environment, and Resources. Washington, D.C.: National Academy Press.

NRC. 1994. Restoring and Protecting Marine Habitat. Marine Board, Commission on Engineering and Technical Systems. Washington, D.C.: National Academy Press.

San Diego Association of Governments. 1995. Shoreline preservation strategy for the San Diego region. Shore and Beach 63(2):17-30.

Seymour, R. J., R. R. Strange III, D. R. Cayan, and R. A. Nathan. 1984. Influence of El Niño on California's wave climate. Pp. 577-592 in Proceedings of the 19th International Conference on Coastal Engineering. New York: American Society of Civil Engineers.

Shore and Beach. 1962a. East Coast Atlantic storm: preliminary report, Weather Bureau, Department of Commerce. Shore and Beach 30(1):4-5.

Shore and Beach. 1962b. The March storm and Ocean City, Maryland: preliminary report, The District Engineer, U.S. Army District, Baltimore, Maryland. Shore and Beach 30(1):7-8.

Shore and Beach. 1962c. The March storm: New Jersey and Delaware. Shore and Beach 30(1):9.

Stauble, D. K., and W. G. Grosskopf. 1993. Monitoring project response to storms: Ocean City, Maryland beachfill. Shore and Beach 61(1):23-33.

Stronge, W. B. 1994. Beaches, tourism and economic development. Shore and Beach 62(2):6-8.

USACE. 1977. Masonboro Inlet, North Carolina, South Jetty: General Design Memorandum. Wilmington, N.C.: Wilmington District, U.S. Army Corps of Engineers.

USACE. 1982. Feasibility Report and Environmental Assessment on Shore and Hurricane Wave Protection: Wrightsville Beach, North Carolina. Wilmington, N.C.: Wilmington District, U.S. Army Corps of Engineers.

USACE. 1989. Wrightsville Beach North Carolina Renourishment Report and Supplement to the Environmental Assessment and Finding of No Significant Impact (EA/FONSI). Wilmington, N.C.: Wilmington District, U.S. Army Corps of Engineers.

USACE. 1994. Shoreline Protection and Beach Nourishment Projects of the U.S. Army Corps of Engineers. IWR Report 94-PS-1. Fort Belvoir, Va.: Institute of Water Resources, Water Resources Support Center, U.S. Army Corps of Engineers.

Wiegel, R. L. 1992. Dade County, Florida, beach nourishment and hurricane surge protection. Shore and Beach 60(4):2-28.

WRC. 1983. Economic and Environmental Principles and Guidelines for Water and Related Land Resources Implementation Studies. U.S. Water Resources Council. Washington D.C.: U.S. Government Printing Office.

3

The Federal Role in Beach Nourishment

This chapter introduces the federal agencies concerned with shore protection, especially as it involves beach nourishment. The roles of five agencies are specifically described, and the accreditation of beach nourishment for insurance purposes is explored.

The federal government is involved in coastal management and coastal hazard reduction through a variety of programs that are primarily carried out by three agencies: the U.S. Army Corps of Engineers (USACE), the Federal Emergency Management Agency (FEMA), and the National Oceanic and Atmospheric Administration (NOAA). Two other agencies, the U.S. Geological Survey (USGS) and the Minerals Management Service (MMS), have smaller but significant roles in beach nourishment issues. The degree to which these agencies should subscribe to or use beach nourishment to stabilize or protect beachfront communities is an unresolved question. The answer may vary among the agencies, depending on how they define or envision successful achievement of their missions: to prevent and mitigate storm damage, manage coastal resources effectively for the long term, and enhance a recreational beach and the local recreational economy.

THE U.S. ARMY CORPS OF ENGINEERS

The USACE is the agency designated by Congress to protect the nation's shores from the chronic effects of erosion and coastal flooding. The USACE's shore protection role is an extension of its longstanding civil works mission. In response to a request from the state of New Jersey for beach erosion control assistance in 1930, Congress enacted Public Law 71-520, which authorized the

USACE to undertake comprehensive shore erosion studies in cooperation with state agencies. As a result, the Beach Erosion Board (BEB) was created to address more thoroughly the growing problems of beach erosion and storm damage that were threatening the prosperous new beach recreation tourist industry. The BEB's early efforts to protect beaches relied mostly on constructing groins to trap sand and constructing bulkheads to halt erosion. However, research in the 1930s suggested that any fixed line of defense against waves should have a reasonable expanse of sand in front. "In the 1940s, the BEB urged local interests to construct projects large enough to protect areas extending headland to headland or inlet to inlet and recommended artificial nourishment of the beach" (USACE, 1991). Until the late 1940s, the assistance provided by the federal government through the USACE was primarily of a planning or technical advisory nature in the development of beach erosion control projects. The most common practice for controlling beach erosion at that time was construction of hard structures such as jetties, groins, and seawalls. In many older beach resort communities, such as Atlantic City, Miami Beach, and Ocean City, Maryland, extensive groin fields were constructed as the accepted means to halt loss of the beach. This approach was relatively successful then because the coast did not have nearly the extent of development it has now. The solution to an erosion problem along a short length of coast may have been a hard structure, even though it often moved the problem to an undeveloped downdrift beach area.

Following World War II, society turned more and more to beaches for recreational opportunities, resulting in community growth along the nation's shores. This trend has continued and has accelerated since the 1970s (Culliton et al., 1990). The proliferation of beachfront residences, often constructed where the primary dune had once been, resulted in more demand for erosion relief from the federal government. In response, the USACE's approach to beach erosion shifted away from hard structures and toward the replenishment of sand that had been lost along the beachfronts of resort communities. Coastal engineers began to recognize, and imitate, in their beach erosion control designs the natural protective features of a wide berm and fronting primary dune (USACE, 1994). The BEB was replaced in 1963 by the Coastal Engineering Research Board (CERB) and the Coastal Engineering Research Center (CERC). Both organizations continue today. The CERB's research initiatives are carried out by the CERC (Holmes, 1993). The increasing body of knowledge and continuing refinement of the science and practice of coastal engineering resulting from university and USACE research have improved both our understanding and the quantification of the forces that affect beach size and shape and the changes that beaches undergo. In turn, our ability to predict sediment behavior on beaches and therefore to design successful beach fill projects has improved considerably in the past two decades.

The USACE conducts beach erosion control work under several different authorities. Under one of these, Section 111 of the River and Harbor Act of 1968, mitigation can be undertaken for detrimental erosion or accretion that results from federal navigational works. For example, the 1993 beach fill at Folly Beach, South Carolina, was constructed under this authority because it was determined that stabilization of the Charleston Harbor entrance channel by jetties was increasing erosion at this downdrift location. Another authority is legislation to initiate site-specific studies and projects proposed as a part of biennial public works authorization bills. If approved, these studies and projects follow a multi-year investigation prior to implementation of nourishment.

Presently, the USACE places sand on beaches via two distinctly different initiatives. The first is site-specific beach nourishment projects that are the product of congressional authorization and involve lengthy planning, design, and construction elements. The analysis and engineering for this type of work may be conducted by the local USACE district office; the Dade County, Florida, and Ocean City, Maryland, projects are examples. The other option is the placement of beach-quality material from the construction or maintenance of navigation projects, generally from the dredging of inlets, channel, and harbors. Such placement under current procedures is the addition of sand to the beach system and is not an element of a designed beach nourishment project, although the placement location may also be the site of an authorized beach nourishment project. The sand that is supplied to the beach may be compatible with the sedimentary system, but it may not have the size or weight that will ensure long residence in the system.

The case studies reviewed by the committee (see Appendix B) indicate the degree of investigation and design that the USACE is currently conducting in the construction of beach nourishment projects. The USACE believes that nourishment is usually the most cost-effective way to reduce the threat of coastal storm damage and avoid the high costs of severe coastal storm damage.

The design of federal shore protection projects by the USACE follows the concept of the optimization of net benefits accrued rather than a defense against storm hazards associated with a specific hazard benchmark. The required economic optimization is related to a set of design storms to evaluate the cost effectiveness of design alternatives. Designers prepare a planform that will protect either the buildings behind the dune line or the shore protection structures from damage from a storm meeting these criteria. The defined events are chosen to reflect realistic combinations of the various parameters that are descriptive of historic storms that have impacted the location of interest. For tropical storms, the storm should encompass the range of durations, maximum winds, radius to maximum winds, pressure deficits, track, etc., that have impacted the area. For extratropical storms (northeasters), duration, stage hydrograph, and maximum wind speeds are appropriate descriptors. Frequency relationships are then assigned to the set of storms and their damages. Storm criteria vary substantially among projects.

THE NATIONAL OCEANIC AND
ATMOSPHERIC ADMINISTRATION

The upsurge in development along our nation's shores in the 1950s and 1960s prompted the federal government to initiate action to protect the shores from the environmentally damaging effects of development. These effects resulted from improper construction standards for high-hazard zones and improper location of construction (such as the placement of buildings in the primary-dune zone), which caused numerous and costly property losses and casualties from severe coastal storms. The Ash Wednesday storm of 1962 that devastated much of the eastern seaboard is an example of the kind of shore protection problem that was developing when the new coastal communities were exposed to the meteorological rarity that hits the coast perhaps only once or twice a century (Podufaly, 1962).

The Coastal Zone Management Act (CZMA) was signed into law in 1972. It established a national program to assist the states in comprehensively managing the nation's precious coastal resources through wise management practices. NOAA administers the CZMA through a partnership with coastal states that elect to participate. Currently, 24 coastal states and 5 island territories have developed federally approved coastal zone management programs. They involve 94 percent of the nation's 150,000 km of shoreline (Department of Commerce, 1994). Among the programmatic elements that the CZMA identified as important is coastal hazard reduction. In its *1994 Biennial Report to Congress on the Administration of the Coastal Zone Management Act*, NOAA (1994) stated:

> The CZMA declares a national policy for minimizing the loss of life and property caused by inappropriate development in areas prone to erosion and coastal flooding. NOAA seeks to achieve this goal through state coastal management programs, and has placed increasing emphasis on improvements in this area through the Coastal Zone Enhancement Program. NOAA assists states with technical assistance in the area of coastal hazards through various activities, including participation on mitigation teams, information sharing, and, in limited cases, by using discretionary funding to conduct post-storm research for use in coastal hazard planning efforts.

It went on to say:

> NOAA assists state efforts in coastal hazards planning and mitigation by working with the FEMA on post-hazard mitigation teams, and exercising its responsibilities with other federal agencies. Interagency Hazard Mitigation Teams identify and evaluate areas having significant hazards; review existing land-use regulations, building codes/construction standards, communications and utilities networks, and existing hazard-mitigation programs and authorities; recommend actions to prevent damage from future events; and coordinate actions to implement the team's recommendations.

The federal role in coastal management involves NOAA working closely with states to solve their coastal hazard problems. NOAA has identified improved land-use planning as well as appropriate construction siting and design as the most effective means to mitigate erosion and coastal storm hazards. However, although 24 states and territories (90 percent of the participants in the Coastal Zone Management Plan) identified coastal hazards as a priority for coastal management enhancements, only two states reported on in the 1992-1993 CZMA biennial report include coastal engineering projects as part of their coastal management improvements. It is important to remember that NOAA's management initiative is achieved through approved state activities.

THE FEDERAL EMERGENCY MANAGEMENT AGENCY

FEMA is responsible for coordinating planning and response activities arising from all types of disasters (see Box 3-1). Such disasters include coastal hurricanes, extratropical storms, tsunamis, and damage from northeasters (i.e., coastal storms along the U.S. East coast), which can devastate low-lying coastal communities. FEMA works with state and local governments to develop disaster mitigation and response strategies, assists state and local governments following a disaster by assisting in damage and needs assessments and in immediate response, urges improved mitigation of potential hazard losses through projects and programs, and manages the National Flood Insurance Program (NFIP). FEMA reorganized in 1994 and formed four new management initiatives: (1) mitigation; (2) preparedness, training, and exercise; (3) response and recovery; and (4) operations support. The mitigation mission and FEMA's role in the NFIP are discussed below.

Along with traditional FEMA mitigation activities, such as improvement of construction quality and moving buildings out of a floodway, the questions addressed in this report are the mitigation potential of beach nourishment and the ability to quantify the mitigation benefit, the proper level of credit that these benefits receive within FEMA programs, and FEMA's appropriate level of participation in beach nourishment as a mitigation activity. FEMA has always considered a wide variety of cost-effective mitigation techniques, with an emphasis on nonstructural techniques. Because there are many widely varying uncertainties associated with beach nourishment project design and prediction (see Table 4-1, for example), accurate protection levels and mitigation benefits resulting from a project are difficult to determine. Beach nourishment offers coastal hazard mitigation benefits (see Box 3-2) in addition to other activities, such as improved construction standards and retrofitting old construction, activities that FEMA has promoted in beach areas. Erosion of a beach is addressed directly by the replacement of sediment lost from the beach and by placing fill so that the shoreline is advanced seaward. The beach erosion process is moved back in time so that an earlier sequence of shoreline change can be repeated (O'Brien, 1985), thus miti-

BOX 3-1
Federal Disaster Assistance Programs for Shore Protection

The Robert T. Stafford Disaster Relief and Emergency Assistance Act (administered by FEMA) authorizes the President to provide assistance to individuals and state and local governments to help in response and recovery from a disaster. Following a disaster declaration by the President, public assistance grants may be made available if the impact of the disaster on public facilities and services is beyond the capability of state and local resources. These grants are divided into two separate major categories: (1) emergency work to save lives, protect public health and safety, and protect improved property and (2) permanent work to restore, repair, and replace damaged public facilities. For a sponsor to be eligible for a public assistance grant, the damage must be the result of the disaster, cannot be eligible for aid from any other federal agency, and the damage must not be due to negligence. Restoration of facilities is based on their design and condition as they existed immediately prior to the disaster, plus any upgrades required by applicable standards. Although not listed in the act as a public facility, beaches serve as flood protection works and are thus eligible for disaster assistance.

Replacement of sand eroded from a natural beach is not eligible as permanent work. An improved beach is considered an eligible public facility if it was constructed by placement of sand to a design and if a maintenance program involving periodic renourishment is established and followed. More typical of emergency or temporary measures, these projects include dune augmentation and placement of sand in a simple dune or berm shape with no foreshore deposition. Nearly all these projects were not funded for repair because they lacked a maintenance program. A few projects have qualified as improved and maintained beaches, and they have received funding to replace the sand eroded by the disaster. As a condition of this grant, the sponsor of the project must restore the beach to its full design section, with the cost of replacing the sand loss prior to the disaster the sponsor's responsibility as part of maintenance.

At this time, FEMA is considering the reasoning behind the regulations for applying the Stafford Act criteria. It has been indicated that some communities may be adopting maintenance programs for sand placements that are not properly designed and are not true beach nourishments. Given that any coastal storm with a recurrence interval greater than 5 years has a good chance of resulting in a declaration, this could result in FEMA playing a major role in subsidizing substandard projects and, in effect, promoting inadvisable coastal development. In addition, there is a growing opinion that a properly designed maintenance program should include preparations for extreme events that can be anticipated statistically; thus, the repair of a project associated with almost any erosion episode should be considered routine maintenance.

gating the erosion hazard to coastal communities. Additionally, storm wave energy is dissipated on the beach rather than on or in close proximity to the foundations of shorefront buildings. The dissipation of energy seaward of the construction setback lines also lessens the velocity of wave runup, which can attack building foundations. Whether, to what degree, or how the NFIP should recog-

---

BOX 3-2
Potential Hazard Reduction Contributions of a Beach Nourishment Project

- Returns beach to earlier erosion sequence, although does not halt erosion.
- Widens buffer zone for dissipation of wave energy between water and shore-front buildings.
- Serves as a barrier to overwash, potentially reducing flood elevation to some extent.
- Adds sand to the overall sediment budget, mitigating background erosion trends for downdrift beaches.
- Can be repeated when needed or discontinued owing to changing conditions.

---

nize these hazard reduction benefits has stimulated considerable public and congressional debate. The technical basis for decision making on these issues is discussed below.

The National Flood Insurance Program

Program Overview

The NFIP is both a financial protection and a hazard mitigation program. It extends and provides benefits to entire populations residing in coastal floodplains as well as to floodplains in interior regions of the country. Federally underwritten flood insurance is available (within prescribed limits) at a reasonable cost for buildings in floodplains for which privately underwritten insurance would either be unavailable or not affordable by most residents. Financial protection is provided in the form of flood insurance for homeowners and businesses located in interior and coastal hazard-prone areas. FEMA conducts detailed surveys of floodplains to determine levels of hazard. The hazards are then designated flood hazard zones on floodplain area maps. The objective of the hazard mitigation component is to improve structural integrity and survivability against anticipated flood-related damage. For structures to qualify for federally backed flood insurance, community zoning laws must meet certain requirements, and new and rebuilt structures must be designed and constructed in accordance with standards that are appropriate to the hazard zone in which a structure is located (see Box 3-3).

For nourishment projects to be considered for possible benefits under the NFIP, a level of protection needs to be established. FEMA and other interested agencies must have quantified information regarding the level of protection that will be provided by the project. In the process of risk assessment and reduction associated with beachfront construction, it is imperative that the extremes of

---

BOX 3-3
Coastal Floodplain Hazard Zones

Area of special flood hazard—An area that may be designated as an *A zone* on a Flood Insurance Rate Map (FIRM) and that is defined as "the land in the flood plain within a community subject to a one percent or greater chance of flooding in any given year" (the base or 100-year flood) (44 CFR 59.1).

Coastal high-hazard area—An area that may be designated as a *V zone* on the FIRM and that is defined as "an area of special flood hazard extending from offshore to the inland limit of a primary frontal dune along an open coast and any other area subject to high-velocity wave action from storms or seismic sources" (44 CFR 59.1). High-velocity wave action includes breaking waves 3 feet high or higher.

---

physical forces be quantifiable, including the likelihood of various extreme combinations of storm waves, tides, and storm surge, and that the resulting vulnerability of beachfront structures be ascertained. When FEMA is provided with accurate and reliable data concerning the beach and dune dimensions necessary to prevent damages from at least a 100-year-level storm, risk assessment is much more accurate, and construction standards and insurance premium rates can better reflect the risks at a site. The calculated level of protection also provides a target for nourishment dimensions, advanced-fill parameters, and poststorm response needs. These considerations relate to projects other than USACE projects, although USACE does not necessarily provide for 100-year protection. See Appendix H for USACE design procedures.

NFIP Planning Basis

The NFIP uses an event defined as the *base flood* (also referred to as a *100-year flood*) as a specific benchmark for program administration. A base flood has a 1 percent chance of being equaled or exceeded in a particular year (44 CFR 59). Although a 100-year flood is a statistical rather than an exact description of a particular storm, the base-flood concept is used for planning. Detailed studies are conducted of coastal floodplains to identify base-flood elevations and to develop Flood Insurance Rate Maps (FIRMs). These maps become the quantified benchmarks for program planning and measuring response to NFIP policies and regulations. The detailed studies result in identification and designation of coastal high-hazard zones. They define different degrees of hazard in the 100-year coastal floodplain.

For V zones (see Box 3-3), the NFIP is concerned with "the inland extent of a 3-foot breaking wave, coincident with the location where the stillwater depth during the 100-year flood decreases to less than 4 feet" (FEMA, 1986). For A zones, the stillwater-based flood elevation is the principal concern because the A-zone portion of the 100-year floodplain is by definition not subject to high-velocity wave action. A zones include contributions from waves less than 3 feet high (FEMA, 1986). The essential coastal hazard data used to identify zone boundaries include:

- 100-year stillwater elevation for the base flood,
- topographic data, and
- land-cover area.

Additional data used to identify erosion and runup include:

- bathymetry,
- storm meteorology, and
- wave characteristics.

Also of interest are data on previous coastal flooding and historical erosion trends associated with severe storms (FEMA, 1989). The NFIP recognizes differences in shore conditions on a regional basis. In determining coastal base-flood elevations, FEMA includes wave heights in some areas and wave runup in others. It is appropriate in some cases to include both in the calculation of the base-flood elevation.

Of particular concern with respect to shore protection is the current practice of establishing risk zones in beach communities without high erosion hazard provisions. This practice does not accurately portray the damage risk to buildings because beach erosion can be episodic owing to meteorological cycles that may produce several years of stability followed by several years of stormy conditions that dramatically alter the beach geometry. Thus, the mapping could provide estimates of risk that are either too large or too small. Remapping to update FIRMs for coastal communities involves surveys of individual locations every 5 to 8 years. As a result, the period between the original photography for base maps and the adoption of new maps may be so long that the new maps, when published, inaccurately depict the physical condition of an eroding shore. In some cases, the same topographic data may be used in several successive studies with no updating to reflect changes in the beach and dune geometry.

Program Management Issues

The National Research Council (NRC, 1990) previously reported that more stringent criteria and management could be applied to improve NFIP effectiveness in reducing erosion hazards. It recommended:

- measures to delineate better the areas in which the federal government would offer flood insurance,
- comprehensive state or local management programs guided by minimum standards for all areas experiencing significant erosion,
- changes in flood insurance rates and availability to reflect erosion and economic risks more accurately, and
- changes to make more viable the relocation or demolition of buildings threatened with immediate collapse owing to erosion.

In contrast to calls for more stringent management of coastal floodplains to reduce erosion and storm damage risk, other public and political calls have been made to relax or eliminate regulatory and policy standards when storm hazards have been reduced through beach nourishment. There have also been calls to reduce other governmental restrictions or requirements based on erosion conditions that have been mitigated. Florida, South Carolina, New Jersey, and Michigan have adopted provisions to recognize beach nourishment in the calculation of erosion rates and the establishment of baselines. For example, under the 1990 Beachfront Management Act of South Carolina, the erosion baseline is moved in a seaward direction based on the nourishment design after 3 years of satisfactory project performance. The design must meet comprehensive and prescriptive criteria addressing postfill erosion rates, profile equilibration, minimum fill density (115 m^3/foot alongshore), minimum length (9 km), minimum design level (a storm with a 10-year recurrence interval), and design life. Additional requirements include monitoring, maintenance, and funding commitments. Under the Florida Beach and Shore Preservation Act of 1989 (Florida Statutes, Chapter 161:909-928), erosion rates are adjusted such that "no erosion shall be considered to have occurred during that portion of the project life" for "Authorized Beach Restoration Projects." These projects must meet similar design and maintenance criteria (Florida DNR, 1989; South Carolina General Assembly, 1990; South Carolina Coastal Council, 1991).

Congress, in examining possible refinements to the NFIP, expressed concern that credit was not given to the diminishment of coastal hazards and the reduction or elimination of historic erosion trends as a result of beach nourishment programs. On September 23, 1994, President Clinton signed into law the Riegle Community Development and Regulatory Improvement Act of 1994 (P.L. 103-325), Title V of which includes NFIP reform provisions. In addition to previous concerns with evaluating the effect of beach nourishment on mapped flood hazards, FEMA is now responsible for administering mitigation assistance grants for technically feasible and cost-effective mitigation plans that can include beach nourishment activities. This legislation also requires FEMA to prepare a report to Congress that assesses the full economic impact of mapping erosion hazard areas under the NFIP.

There is a public perception issue as well. Flood insurance underwritten by the federal government for buildings in beachfront areas is seen by some to be subsidizing the development of barrier islands; beaches; and more particularly, the investment properties of affluent individuals with shorefront homes. FEMA (1994) reports that overall post-1985 buildings in V zones as a class are not subsidized—collected premiums have exceeded claims paid. Construction prior to adoption of the FIRMs and of floodplain construction standards is subsidized to some extent, as are structures that are exposed to the increasing coastal hazards associated with continuing erosion and shoreline retreat. Whether development on barrier islands and in close proximity to barrier beaches should be allowed also is strongly debated.

Relating Beach Nourishment to the NFIP

The policy issues hinge on how well beach nourishment projects can provide long-term protection by reducing or mitigating coastal hazards and whether this protection is temporary or permanent. Once this protection is established, it is possible to assess how these benefits can be reflected in the administration of flood insurance. The options for addressing beach nourishment projects in the NFIP range from no official recognition through intermediate measures (e.g., requiring nourishment projects as a precondition for issuance of insurance and economic incentives to sustain and maintain projects) to ultimately reduce insurance premiums and constructions standards. In the latter case, a related question is whether any cost savings by reducing insurance premiums or constructions standards should be applied to further hazard mitigation measures or whether the savings should be passed directly to owners of protected properties for discretionary use. The answer to this question is as much a political determination as it is a managerial and technical one. The nature and uncertainty of coastal hazards and the effectiveness and ability to sustain mitigation measures argue for a conservative insurance management approach.

THE U.S. GEOLOGICAL SURVEY

Since its creation in 1879, the USGS has been the nation's leading earth science research organization. The USGS's basic authorization for surveys, investigations, and research is included in an act of March 3, 1879 (43 U.S.C. 31). USGS scientists conduct both applied and fundamental studies as part of the agency's mission to investigate, collect, analyze, monitor, and disseminate critical information about the nation's energy, mineral, water, and land resources. With this knowledge, society can develop economically and environmentally sound plans to manage the earth's resources and address issues.

To address the need for fundamental geoscience information and improve our scientific understanding of the earth and its processes, the USGS has initiated the National Marine and Coastal Geology Program. The program includes a wide variety of research and mapping activities under themes of environment, hazards, resources, and information. Current studies address a wide variety of coastal and marine issues at research centers in Woods Hole, Massachusetts; St. Petersburg, Florida; and Menlo Park, California. They are being done in collaboration with appropriate federal, state, and local agencies and university scientists. Results from marine geological investigations of critical issues affecting the nation are providing objective scientific information to managers and planners working in coastal and offshore regions.

National Marine and Coastal Geology Program

With a program budget of $35 million and a staff of 250 scientists and support personnel, 27 studies are being conducted nationwide in four theme areas:

Environmental quality and preservation research addresses the geological issues that influence the long-term quality and preservation of marine environments. Specific issues addressed include pollution and waste disposal, fragile environments, marine reserves and biological habitats, and geological records of environmental change.

Natural hazards and public safety research is conducted to better understand the frequency and distribution of catastrophic events and the geological processes acting in the affected coastal regions. Specific issues addressed include coastal and nearshore erosion and offshore earthquakes and landslides.

Natural resources research aims to provide an understanding of the distribution of geological resources in our marine and coastal realms and of the processes that control their composition, origin, and availability. Specific resources addressed include energy resources, marine mineral resources, and freshwater resources. Most germane to the topic of beach nourishment are the delineation and assessment of marine sand resources for use as fill materials.

Information and technology activities provide reconnaissance seafloor mapping as well as information management and dissemination services. Specific activities include systematic mapping of the seafloor, development of a marine and coastal information bank, and maintenance of technology and facilities.

The primary strategy employed within each theme is a series of regional studies that develop a description and understanding of marine and coastal geological systems. Other complementary avenues of research include fundamental studies, catastrophic events studies, long-term observations, and assessments.

Most studies average 5 years in duration from initial data collection through completion of final reports and information transfer. A brief description of the Louisiana study (Williams et al., 1992) is provided as an example:

Louisiana is experiencing the most rapid and widespread coastal erosion and wetlands deterioration and loss of any region in the United States and possibly in the world. Long-term rates of barrier island retreat average 4 m/year; as much as 30 meters has been eroded during a single storm, such as Hurricane Andrew in 1992. Eighty percent of the loss of tidal wetlands in the conterminous United States—an estimated 75 km^2/year—is occurring in Louisiana, which contains nearly one-half of the U.S. coastal wetlands. Since 1986, the USGS, in cooperation with Louisiana State University, has undertaken comprehensive coastal studies of the Mississippi River deltaic plain to assess the rapid coastal erosion and wetlands loss taking place and to better understand the natural and man-made processes responsible.

The information base amassed from this study includes digital shoreline and nearshore hydrographic data spanning the past 140 years, high-resolution geophysical profiles, a dense array of sediment samples and 12-m-long vibracores, a long-term record of storm effects on the barrier coast, and analyses of tide-gauge records documenting the rapid (>1 cm/year) sea-level-rise record over the past 50 years.

Offshore seismic and vibracore data collected as part of the geological framework element of the Barrier Erosion Study have been used to locate and delineate deposits of sand in the nearshore inner-shelf region. A total of 44 sand-body targets, classified into seven major classes of sand bodies (buried distributary channel, relict tidal-inlet channel, relict recurved spit, flood-tide delta, ebb-tide delta, linear shoal, and relict beach ridge) have been identified.

The total volume of mostly fine-grained sand resources in the study area is estimated to be nearly 4 billion m^3, with 70 percent confined to three deposits—Ship Shoal, Cat Island Pass, and Barataria Pass/Grande Terre. The Ship Shoal sand body, containing 1.2 billion m^3 of high-quality quartz sand is particularly attractive as a source of fill for beach nourishment and is being viewed favorably for barrier restoration projects being undertaken by the Louisiana Federal-State Wetlands Task Force.

Through objective analysis of information from the Barrier Island study, a clearer and more complete scientific understanding of the processes of land loss is emerging. Results of these studies are finding immediate application in the design of coastal restoration projects by the Wetlands Task Force.

THE MINERALS MANAGEMENT SERVICE

As economical offshore sand and gravel deposits suitable for beach nourishment become harder to locate, sources beyond state waters become more attractive. The U.S. Department of the Interior's MMS is charged with administering those minerals (including sand and gravel) found in federal waters. Under the terms of the Outer Continental Shelf Lands Act (OCSLA) as amended by P.L. 103-426, the MMS may negotiate with any person for OCS resources for use in a program of shore protection, beach nourishment, or coastal wetlands restoration by a governmental agency. Fees based on the assessed value of the resource may be negotiated, except that no fee may be assessed in the case of the federal government.   ·

Any federal agency that proposes to use OCS sand must enter into a memorandum of agreement with the Secretary of the Interior detailing the potential use of the resource prior to that use. The cognizant congressional committees also are notified.

The sand and gravel found in OCS waters are also used by the construction industry, and the OCSLA requires that they be treated as other minerals that might be mined on the OCS: the MMS is responsible for activities associated with leasing, exploration, development, production, and royalty management. The leases are granted on the basis of competitive bidding. The MMS is also responsible for preparing documents for the National Environmental Protection Act process to ensure that no environmental degradation is caused by OCS mining.

With increasing demand for suitable sand and diminishing nearshore resources, the MMS is working cooperatively with 10 Atlantic and Gulf coast states on projects to identify and assess OCS sand resources for coastal restoration and shore protection needs (see, for example, Conkwright and Gast, 1994).

An MMS study of particular interest to the beach nourishment topic is "Wave Climate Modeling and Evaluation Relative to Sand Mining on Ship Shoal, Offshore Louisiana." This study, awarded in July 1994, is using numerical modeling to examine the current and wave fields around Ship Shoal, an offshore geological feature located in the central Gulf of Mexico, adjacent to Louisiana barrier islands. Ship Shoal is being considered as a source of clean quartz sand for beach replenishment along the rapidly deteriorating Isles Dernieres. The model will be used to help predict the resultant effects on the wave and current field in this area, using scenarios involving various degrees and quantities of sand removal from the shoal. Specifically, the study involves (1) numerical modeling of wave energy transformation and decay across the inner shelf encompassing Ship Shoal and the nearshore adjacent Isles Dernieres, (2) development of a nearshore sediment transport model along the Isles Dernieres, and (3) quantification of changes in (1) and (2) due to removal of various sediment quantities based on likely scenarios of sand removed.

EROSION HAZARD REDUCTION PROGRAMS
OF FEDERAL AGENCIES

Previous sections described the approaches that the USACE, NOAA, and FEMA use to protect shores, reduce coastal hazards, and manage erosion. It is challenging to identify a consistent holistic federal approach to shore protection. There are opportunities for federal agencies to coordinate more closely to develop a position that better complements the objectives of each other. An examination of the ways in which nourishment can help achieve the management goals of each agency follows.

Technical Premises for Protecting Natural Beaches

Beach management and regulatory programs administered by NOAA, FEMA, and most state agencies are based on the premise that beaches are subjected to long-term erosion and communities are becoming progressively more vulnerable to storm damage. The distance between beachfront buildings and the water is an essential factor in protection. There are two reference lines on a developed beach: the shoreline and the line of construction. The dune, when present, and dry beach must fit between them. Cross-shore dimensions of a natural beach are a function of wave energy and sediment supply. When the sediment supply seaward of the line of construction is diminished, the shoreline moves toward the line of construction. The first beach feature to disappear is the berm, followed by the dune, whose location on the beach depends on an adequately wide berm to dissipate wave energy. The berm, or active, unvegetated portion of the dry beach, is the direct product of waves and currents. The berm may retreat to the toe of the dune during a storm. If the dune is unable to migrate because construction is located close behind, the dune becomes narrower until it eventually disappears. The buildings that may once have been safely located landward of the primary dune become located in the dune zone as the dune migrates in a landward direction. Ultimately, the buildings may be effectively seaward of the dunes and vulnerable to direct attack by storm waves. In the long term, however, the beach features do not disappear but are translated landward.

Construction setback lines, erosion rate based or otherwise, have been established in some states in an effort to reduce damage in areas subjected to shoreline retreat. Destruction of dunes and conversion of beaches for development eliminate or reduce the natural storm and erosion protective benefits that an entire coastal community relies on during periods of high tides, storm surges (on the Atlantic and Gulf coasts), waves, and currents. Construction landward of a primary dune and naturally wide berm remains relatively safe from the impacts of coastal storms if those beach units are of a dimension that would naturally be present at that particular shorefront location. However, in erosion-prone areas, buildings built landward of the natural dune 10 to 20 years ago often occupy middune or back berm locations today, as long-term erosion continues the shoreline regression. This continuing landward migration of the beach and the resulting diminishment of the berm and dune width increase the risk of storm damage to waterfront buildings. Thus, construction standards for zones in which a structure was originally built may become insufficient at that same location as the risk of damage increases over time due to beach erosion seaward of the building.

Program Planning

FEMA and USACE programs to reduce damages differ because they have different missions, and different planning criteria apply. Successful beach nourishment projects provide area-wide direct physical protection to shores. The level of protection in the design process varies among projects based on analyses of costs and benefits. The NFIP provides financial protection for construction in hazard zones and attempts to mitigate the expected risks to individual buildings. That program is primarily concerned with the base-flood elevation and the associated effects of wave runup and wave height in the coastal hazard zone insofar as these forces threaten individual buildings. The differences between the two programs need to be understood in order to relate the performance of beach nourishment projects to FEMA's objectives for mitigation of coastal hazards.

Correlating Beach Nourishment Project Performance with Coastal Floodplain Hazard Mitigation

FEMA is reluctant to assign hazard reduction benefits to a temporary form of hazard reduction. This reluctance has been reinforced by the continuing controversy over technical issues, the physical performance of beach nourishment projects, and the economic benefits derived. As a result, determining the appropriate relationship between beach nourishment and flood insurance is neither simple nor straightforward. The differences in planning concepts used by the USACE and FEMA in the administration of their programs provide no direct correlation between the protective benefits of beach nourishment projects and the hazard mitigation aspects of the NFIP. The capability of beach nourishment projects to reduce hazards to meet NFIP objectives varies significantly among projects. Therefore, the contribution of a beach nourishment project to the mitigation of NFIP coastal hazards must be determined on a project-by-project basis.

ACCREDITING BEACH NOURISHMENT PROJECTS TO QUALIFY FOR FLOOD INSURANCE BENEFITS

Accreditation is an acknowledgment by a certifying entity, such as FEMA or a state coastal regulatory agency (NOAA-approved), that a project is capable of performing to design specifications and has therefore effectively reduced an existing hazard. Certain minimum criteria may be required in order to qualify for accreditation of certain programs. Accreditation of hazard protection projects to qualify for NFIP benefits is not a new concept. For example, dikes and levees on interior river systems that have met construction, maintenance, and level-of-protection criteria acceptable to FEMA have resulted in reduced flood hazard determinations for buildings constructed on the floodplain (44 CFR 65.10). These types of projects differ significantly from beach nourishment projects in that they

are designed to provide protection from a 100-year flood with no physical degradation or reduction in the level of protection; a beach nourishment project is
designed to be sacrificial. Nevertheless, the accreditation program used by FEMA
and associated reductions in hazard determinations have set a precedent for considering a similar NFIP response for shore protection by beach nourishment
projects under which the project would receive favorable actuarial treatment or
other relief from requirements that govern coverage under the NFIP. The accreditation concept, as currently applied in the NFIP, does not address the larger issue
of whether flood insurance should be made available or be continued in areas
where residential or commercial structures are physically located on a beach
rather than behind a dune line. Under these conditions, the risk may be too high
from an actuarial perspective to justify flood insurance, regardless of construction standards. Requiring a beach nourishment project as a precondition for the
issuance of insurance may be a reasonable option; however, existing statutes
require that the NFIP provide insurance regardless of the actuarial risk. Recent
congressional debate on insurance availability for beachfront property indicates
that risk in these areas is acceptable for now but deserves further study.

Level of Protection

The NFIP requires a rational basis for determining construction standards
and premium rates. Establishing a level of protection for a coastal floodplain
subject to wave attack, or overwash as a result of storm surges, is difficult. As
discussed previously, the NFIP 100-year base-flood elevation is often not the
same design storm benchmark used for USACE beach nourishment projects.
Further, beach nourishment projects are often designed to have less protection
than a 100-year storm. Nevertheless, the presence of an effectively designed and
maintained beach nourishment project for such a storm can increase the level of
protection within the coastal hazard zones mapped by FEMA in one or more of
the following ways:

- by preventing waves or wave runup from reaching the V zone,
- by reducing wave runup in the V zone,
- by reducing the height of waves that reach into V zones as a result of
  episodic erosion or because of high flood elevations, and
- by providing a buffer between the open ocean and the V zone on existing
  maps.

The actual reduction of risk provided by the beach fill varies considerably
over the life of the nourishment project as the advanced-fill dimensions are
reduced through erosion. Long-term protection depends on program performance
and the commitment to maintain the project through renourishment. Standards or
criteria used for accreditation must consider minimum protective berm dimen-

sions and advanced-fill requirements in terms of berm width and height seaward of the line of construction in order to maintain the level of protection that lies landward of the advanced-fill section. Thus, maintenance of the advanced fill in accordance with the program's planned renourishment cycle (and on an exceptional basis as needed) would be a fundamental consideration for accreditation of a project for flood insurance purposes. Because V zones generally extend beyond project boundaries, it is also appropriate to consider hazard mitigation benefits that may accrue to shorefronts downdrift of project boundaries. Another important consideration is that shorefront property remains exposed to the potential for flooding regardless of the presence of a beach nourishment project. This situation results from the potential for flooding caused by an anomalously large storm or an underestimation of the base flood, either of which could result in a breach in protective dunes or other shorefront protective structures, storm tidal surges in back bay areas, or a combination of both. As a result, beach nourishment projects can mitigate but do not eliminate either the coastal flooding hazard or the potential for damage from waves, depending on the severity and character of the storms. This fact merits attention when considering setback requirements and construction standards.

ADDRESSING BEACH NOURISHMENT IN THE NFIP

Specific alternatives that could be considered in the management of accredited beach nourishment sites within the NFIP include:

- basing construction standards, premium rates, or both on the risk reduction potential of the program at the expected least-protective dimensions of the fill (in effect, relocating the hazard potential zones owing to the relief provided by the fill);
- basing construction standards, premium rates, or both on the determined median fill dimension that would provide a median risk reduction potential over the project life;
- establishing the alternatives of an option for a beach nourishment program as a precondition for the issuance or continuation of flood insurance or the setting of higher insurance rates;
- maintaining construction standards and premium rates at levels appropriate to base-flood elevations determined prior to beach nourishment;
- evaluating protective benefits of beach nourishment programs, maintaining rates, and allocating any savings to funding at the local, regional, or national levels for coastal hazard mitigation projects;
- providing grants or funding to design nourishment projects, conduct site-specific erosion analyses, or monitor project performance;
- establishing a federal entity to provide technical assistance to states or

communities in carrying out technical work when the USACE is not involved in the project; and
- contributing supplemental funding to existing beach nourishment projects to increase the level of protection or life span of the fill.

Understanding the differences between a federal and a commercial insurance program is essential to beach restoration decision making. Unlike commercial insurance, the federal government relies on premiums to fund the basic flood insurance program rather than on earnings from invested premiums. When owners' contributions to flood insurance are reduced, the reduction could be considered a subsidy because there are few economic incentives for owners to invest construction cost or insurance premium savings in further coastal hazard mitigation measures.

Although nourishment may be an effective tool at some locations for combating beach loss for a reasonable period, economic conditions may change over time so as to undermine continuing financial support for project maintenance. Abandonment of a nourishment program could result in progressively increasing exposure to erosion hazards for new and old construction alike and the ability of NFIP funds to pay claims for coastal flood damages.

FIRMs are created to reflect the flood hazards that exist. At issue is whether the maps should be revised to reflect mitigation of flood hazards provided by beach nourishment projects. FIRMs delineate the flood risks for a given area in order to provide construction standards appropriate to the risk at that site. Consideration of lower construction standards at a site that has been protected by nourishment must include potential project performance over time. The physical life expectancy of new construction in a beach area may well be 100 or more years, whereas the life expectancy of a beach fill project without renourishment may be less than 10 years. The design life of beach nourishment programs today is on the order of 50 years, and in many cases the financial and sand resources needed to sustain projects are based on expectations that the resources will be available, rather than on the allocation of mineral resources or financial arrangements to ensure that funds are generated and held in reserve for the planned renourishments. Should any of these needs not be met, a building constructed today landward of the nourished beach may well become exposed to prenourishment conditions at some point during its useable life (Davison et al., 1992, 1993).

Construction Standards

Prior to the NFIP, some dwellings in the coastal floodplains were constructed so as to reduce flood or wave impacts. Most buildings adjacent to the beaches and many buildings landward of them were below 100-year base-flood elevations. Examples of construction that mitigated coastal hazards include some two-story homes on New Jersey's barrier islands dating from the 1920s and 1930s. The principal living areas were on the second rather than the ground floors. Construction that mitigated wave impact damage included the placement of buildings on pilings at elevations above anticipated storm surges and associated waves. During the Ash Wednesday storm of 1962 that ravaged the Atlantic coast, such residences on pilings that were of sufficient dimensions and were driven to adequate depths survived the event. At the same time, virtually all other shorefront buildings that were below the flood elevation on some barrier islands, including many behind seawalls, were destroyed, along with their protective seawalls (Podufaly, 1962). This experience provides the basis for the construction standards required by the NFIP and by some state and local regulations or ordinances regarding new construction or substantial reconstruction in zones or locations deemed vulnerable to flood or wave impacts.

Required construction standards usually include pile specifications, elevation requirements, and attachment specifications. Adherence to these standards results in hazard reduction to the property to which they are applied as well as to surrounding properties. Secondary damage may result if one building fails and the debris impacts adjacent buildings during a storm that includes high storm surges. Vulnerability to these impacts decreases when beaches have been widened, but, as noted earlier, the time duration of a single nourishment project may well be less than the physical life of the structure.

There are pressures for relaxation of construction standards in response to hazard mitigation benefits provided by a beach nourishment project. The appropriateness of construction standards needs to be considered in the full context of coastal floodplain hazards, including uncertainties associated with coastal storms, beach nourishment project performance, time scales, and economic effects. The principal economic leverage available to ensure sound construction is the availability of affordable flood insurance and federal disaster assistance. Relaxation of construction standards in response to hazard mitigation benefits of uncertain duration could potentially undermine the NFIP's leverage to hold communities accountable for sound floodplain management practices and property owners accountable for construction that reduces risk.

With respect to the argument that reducing construction standards could serve as an incentive for maintenance of a beach nourishment project, the fact that beach nourishment projects and flood insurance serve different objectives must be considered. There is no guarantee that a local community will meet its obligations to maintain a beach nourishment program. If the NFIP were to accept lower construction standards, it would thus become hostage to the uncertainties of local sponsor support without the means to force retrofits of buildings to meet more stringent standards. Even if retrofitting were politically feasible, it might not be practical or even possible for some buildings. Faced with such a situation, the only choices open for the NFIP would be to accept the greater liability or to cancel flood insurance for the affected area. Thus, any short-term savings to property owners achieved through relaxation of construction standards need to be balanced against the long-term implications of increased exposure of buildings to severe episodic storms and increased liability for risk that would be incurred by the NFIP.

Setback requirements are usually established at the state or local level to separate land areas that are appropriate for construction from the dune and beach zones. These requirements serve to preserve the protective and recreational values of the dune and beach. Setback lines are usually established as fixed-reference features such as the landward toe of the primary dune or as a line a certain distance from a reference location (e.g., the mean high-tide line or the +3-m contour line). In recent years there has been a trend toward using the average annual erosion rate as a multiplier for moving the setback line landward in an effort to preserve the cross-shore geometry over time. Stabilization or progradation of the shoreline through nourishment of the beach could potentially move the setback line or the reference feature farther seaward following nourishment unless their locations were fixed at the prenourishment project locations.

Premium Rate Adjustments

An alternative to lowering construction or zoning standards is a reduction in flood insurance premium rates. This concept is used by FEMA in its relatively new Community Rating System program. The program was developed to provide an incentive for communities to conduct a variety of activities or institute building practices that help reduce flood hazards. Credit is given in the form of premium reductions throughout the entire community when these endeavors are carried out. However, details of implementation of long-term project viability remain to be developed. Acceptable criteria through accurate monitoring of project performance will relate to the reduction of risk that is directly attributable to a project.

Annual premium rates are established relative to the risk of damage that is determined for a particular property. The risk level is associated with the hazard zone and the base-flood elevation at the site when the building was initially constructed or when the community began participating in the NFIP. Recent NFIP reform provisions call for FEMA to prepare a report to Congress that assesses the full economic impacts of mapping erosion hazard zones (E zones). If the mapping of E zones is eventually mandated by Congress to designate beach areas with a determined average annual erosion rate, a subheading, E_m, could be included to designate erosion that has been mitigated, at least temporarily, through beach nourishment. Considering the fact that beach nourishment can reduce damage potential, reflection of this benefit in the annual premium rate merits consideration.

An alternative to rate reductions in which savings accrue directly to property owners (and are effectively lost to the NFIP) would be funding technical assistance to communities in support of floodplain management activities or of enhancing the performance of beach nourishment projects, sponsoring local beach nourishment projects to reduce the NFIP's risk in hazard-prone coastal areas, and funding emergency fills to restore a project's shore protection benefits after a severe storm. This approach would enhance NFIP objectives for predisaster hazard mitigation and FEMA's postdisaster restoration of community services and damaged buildings while returning the benefit to NFIP participants on a programmatic rather than individual basis.

A STRATEGY FOR REDUCING COASTAL HAZARDS

Federal shore protection programs undertaken by the USACE, the FEMA-administered NFIP, and the NOAA-administered CZMA are based on different agency missions. These programs also use different planning factors to mitigate the effects of erosion and reduce coastal hazard potential. Understanding the differences in missions and in the manner in which protection benefits are determined is necessary to establish whether and to what degree the buffer provided by the beach nourishment project mitigates the hazards as defined by these agencies.

The actual level of protection provided by a beach nourishment program changes during the renourishment cycle and during storms. It is difficult to quantify the actual level of protection that is provided and to relate it to flood insurance program concepts and coastal hazards management plans for uses in estimating how much of the individual program objective has been realized. However, the design section of the fill plan is the minimum section for which the USACE calculates the benefits to be derived from the fill (see Figure 4-6). At any instant of time, the actual section is somewhere between the design section and the advanced-fill section.

The USACE, FEMA, and NOAA could work more closely in developing a comprehensive federal approach to mitigating coastal hazards and determining the role of beach nourishment at any given site. Given the uniqueness of each beach community, the answer may lie in the development of comprehensive beach erosion and hazard mitigation management plans for discrete reaches of the shoreline. A comprehensive plan for a beach town or a region encompassing a geomorphic or littoral compartment could include improved construction standards, removal of some or all dwellings from particularly hazardous locations, and the use of beach nourishment to reduce the hazard potential. Federal involvement in placing material on the beach through the USACE could be predicated on an assessment that considers a cost-effective, long-range management plan for the proposed nourishment area. Inclusion in the plan of the full range of management options and goals that the USACE, FEMA, and NOAA are attempting to accomplish is appropriate.

Criteria could be established for accrediting beach nourishment programs by FEMA that would either allow for development within certain limits or would disallow accreditation for situations that increased exposure or risk in the coastal floodplain. NFIP responses that could limit exposure and risk to the insurer include:

- an approved beach nourishment program that includes a frontal dune (where appropriate) with restrictions that preclude further development of high-erosion-risk zones;
- no remapping of hazard areas;
- no reduction in construction standards as they pertain to shore protection;
- a dedicated funding commitment for the life of the program for all planned and emergency renourishments;
- a requirement that sand sources be available and dedicated (including sand rights) to the program for initial placement, all planned renourishment, and a reasonable number of contingency replenishments;
- a requirement for alternate or secondary sources of sand should physical conditions reduce sand from sources that are dedicated to the program;
- a requirement for a contingency plan that would restore an adequate design level of protection for the subaerial beach following storm losses;
- a requirement for a program to perform as designed within some acceptable level of uncertainty; and
- a requirement for long-term monitoring with dedicated funding covering the full program.

REFERENCES

Conkwright, R. D., and R. A. Gast. 1994. Potential Offshore Sand Resources in Northern Maryland Shoal Waters. Maryland Geological Survey, Coastal and Estuarine Geology File Report 94-8. Unpublished.

Culliton, T. J., M. A. Warren, T. R. Goodspeed, D. G. Remer, C. M. Blackwell, and J. J. McConough III. 1990. 50 Years of Population Change Along the National's Coasts, 1960-2010. Rockville, Md.: National Oceanic and Atmospheric Administration.

Davison, A. T., R. J. Nicholls, and S. P. Leatherman. 1992. Beach nourishment as a coastal management tool: an annotated bibliography on developments associated with the artificial nourishment of beaches. Journal of Coastal Research 8(4):984-1022.

Davison, A. T., C. P. Ulrich, and R. J. Nicholls. 1993. Accreditation of beach nourishment projects: an issues discussion. Shore and Beach 61(4):9-15.

Department of Commerce. 1994. 1992-1993 Biennial Report to Congress on the Administration of the Coastal Zone Management Act, Volume II. Washington, D.C.: U.S. Department of Commerce.

FEMA. 1986. Coastal Construction Manual, FEMA-55. Washington, D.C.: Federal Insurance Administration, Federal Emergency Management Agency.

FEMA. 1989. Guidelines and Specifications for Wave Elevation Determination and V Zone Mapping. Third draft report. Washington, D.C.: Federal Insurance Administration, Federal Emergency Management Agency.

FEMA. 1994. National Flood Insurance Program: Flood Insurance Rate Review. Washington, D.C.: Federal Insurance Administration, Federal Emergency Management Agency.

Florida DNR. 1989. Rules and Procedures for Coastal Construction and Excavation. Pp. 909-928, Chapter 16B-33. Tallahassee: Florida Department of Natural Resources.

Holmes, C. M. 1993. Introduction of Coastal Data Collection Theme. Paper presented at the 58th Meeting of the Coastal Engineering Research Board, June 1993, Atlantic City, N.J.

NOAA. 1994. 1994 Biennial Report to Congress on the Administration of the Coastal Zone Management Act. Washington, D.C.: National Oceanic and Atmospheric Administration.

NRC. 1990. Managing Coastal Erosion. Water Science and Technology Board and Marine Board, Commission on Engineering and Technical Systems. Washington, D.C.: National Academy Press.

O'Brien, M. P. 1985. Beach stabilization by sand replenishment. Shore and Beach 53(1):15.

Podufaly, E. T. 1962. Operation five-high. Shore and Beach 30(2):9-17.

South Carolina Coastal Council. 1991. Regulations for Permitting in Critical Areas of the State's Coastal Zone. Charleston: South Carolina Coastal Council.

South Carolina General Assembly. 1990. South Carolina Beach Front Management Act. Columbia: South Carolina General Assembly.

USACE. 1991. History of the Coastal Engineering Research Center, 1963-1983. Vol. I, WES Library History Series. Vicksburg, Miss.: Coastal Engineering Research Center, U.S. Army Engineer Waterways Experiment Station, U.S. Army Corps of Engineers.

USACE. 1994. Shoreline Protection and Beach Nourishment Projects of the U.S. Army Corps of Engineers. IWR Report 94-PS-1. Fort Belvoir, Va.: Institute of Water Resources, Water Resources Support Center, U.S. Army Corps of Engineers.

Williams, S.J., S. Penland, and A.H. Sallenger Jr., (eds.). 1992. Louisiana barrier island erosion study. Atlas of Shoreline Changes in Louisiana from 1853 to 1989. USGS Misc. Inv. Series. No. I-2150-A. 107 pp.

4

Beach Nourishment Project Design and Prediction

A sound technical basis for beach nourishment design and prediction is important because beaches are dynamic systems that typically experience significant short- and long-term changes. Further, placement of sand during nourishment rarely follows the cross-section profile that would occur naturally. Indeed, the constructed profiles are expected to change significantly during the first several years following construction or renourishment. The constructed profile may not follow the exact design prediction because the coastal processes were different than the available data revealed at the design stage or environmental conditions subsequent to project construction or renourishment varied substantially from the predictions supported by the data.

A sound technical basis for design and prediction is necessary for:

- determining costs and benefits,
- decision making on whether the project is economically viable and whether it merits implementation,
- forming the ground rules for assessing project performance,
- evaluating project performance,
- validating assumptions,
- identifying design deficiencies,
- identifying and developing design refinements and corrective action regimes,
- decision making on whether and when to proceed with renourishment,
- evaluating design and prediction procedures, and
- improving the design process.

THE DESIGN PROCESS

Various methods exist for beach nourishment design and prediction that are complementary in the overall process of establishing optimum project characteristics. The design and prediction process is inherently iterative. Candidate designs are identified and evaluated at a preliminary level in which the performance of the project is predicted by using simple, rapid, relatively inexpensive methods. These performance characteristics are then compared with the design objectives of the project. The design is then refined until the performance predictions using the simple methodology confirm establishment of an optimal design. For sites without complex boundaries (straight beaches without terminal groins, inlets, or headlands), simple prediction tools are expected to allow quantification of time to renourishment to within approximately 30 percent of actual project performance, in the committee's estimation. Once the preliminary design is established, more detailed and comprehensive predictive methods are employed to "fine tune" the preliminary design. The advantages of employing this two-stage approach include a check of both the simple and more detailed methods, a more rapid convergence to the final design than if only the detailed methods were employed, and a better perspective of the interrelationships among the overall project characteristics. If the predicted volumetric losses based on the simple and detailed methods differ by a considerable amount (more than 50 percent), the bases for the results obtained by both methods need to be reviewed. This chapter enumerates, in a general manner, the important design parameters and the prediction capability. Detailed discussions of prediction and design are presented as Appendixes C and D, respectively.

NOURISHMENT OBJECTIVES AND CONSTRAINTS

The usual nourishment objectives are to provide a wide beach that will reduce storm damage from flooding and waves and increase recreational benefits. For those projects that include federal funding, there is a requirement to identify a design as determined by federal guidelines. This requirement involves detailed calculations of storm damage reduction benefits expected to accrue from several designs and from a considerable number of storm scenarios. Projects funded entirely by nonfederal sources may be limited by the amount of available funds, and the objective then becomes placement of material to provide the greatest longevity and maximum dry beach width for the dollars available.

SIGNIFICANT PROCESSES IN DESIGN

The purposes of a beach nourishment project are to increase the dune and berm dimensions and to advance the shoreline seaward to reduce storm damage and widen the recreational area. In addition, ecological advantages may accrue if the prenourished beach was not wide.

Sand placement at a beach nourishment site during project construction or renourishment may or may not correspond to the natural profile of the beach at the time of placement. In the United States, use of a construction rather than a natural profile is the normal placement practice (see Appendix D). The sand can be placed either on the beach, immediately seaward of the beach (e.g., as a bar or mound), or a combination of the two.

Where the initial placement of sand does not follow the natural cross-section profile of the beach, it is important for all parties interested in a project's performance to recognize that substantial changes in the profile are both normal and anticipated. It is also important to monitor and measure these changes to determine whether they conform to predictions and to provide a basis for design refinements and corrective action that may become necessary to accommodate site-specific conditions.

Although other, less significant processes are present, the two most dominant relevant to design and performance are *profile equilibration* and *alongshore spreading (or spreading losses)* of sand from the project area to the adjacent shorelines (referred to as "alongshore equilibration"). *Profile equilibration*, a process leading to an *equilibrium profile* or *equilibrated profile*, refers to the tendancy of a beach to take a characteristic shape or form in response to the integrated action of the local wave climate, as well as to the character and quantity of sediment available. Further discussion is provide later in this chapter (see Figure 4-1). The time scales of these two processes are disparate: profile equilibration occurs in a few years, whereas the alongshore equilibration varies in duration and is related to project length, sediment grain size, and wave environment. For example, a reasonably long project (i.e., alongshore length) may require decades before 50 percent or more of the sand volume is transported to the adjacent beaches. Profile equilibration is usually treated as if it occurs instantly in evaluating performance at the preliminary design level, distinguishing its expected short-term effects from the longer time scale associated with alongshore equilibration.

Profile Equilibration

The most frequent placement is as an extension of the natural berm at a fairly steep slope (steeper than equilibrium) at the seaward limit of placement. A second type of placement is completely subaqueous in an offshore mound. These two types of placement are shown in Figure 4-2. Use of a mound relies on the expectation that the material will provide wave height reduction and eventually move ashore and widen the beach. This placement method is usually less costly and may allow use of finer material than should be placed on the subaerial beach. Profile equilibration is the process by which the beach takes its natural form in

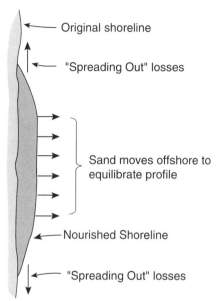

a) Plan view showing "Spreading Out" losses
and sand moving offshore to equilibrate profile

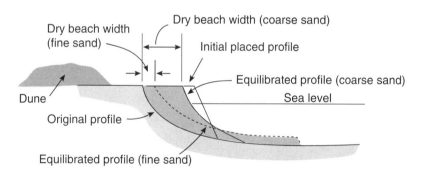

b) Elevation view showing original profile, initial placed profile, and
adjusted profiles that would result from nourishment project with
coarse and fine sands

FIGURE 4-1   Sand transport losses and beach profiles associated with a nourished beach.

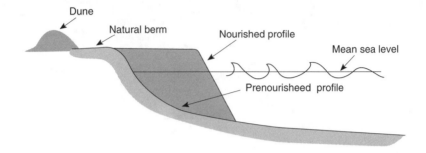

a) Usual method of nourishment with added material placed as
   seaward extension of the natural berm where waves will distribute
   sand to an equilibrium profile seaward of the original profile

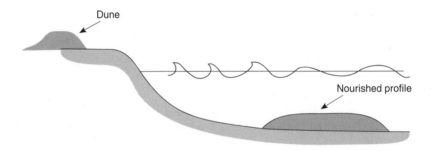

b) Placement of nourishment material in an offshore mound with expectation
   that it will move on shore by wave action to nourish the profile

FIGURE 4-2   Two placement methods for beach nourishment material.

response to the physical forces that are present. A significant advantage of the
beach placement option is the initial additional dry beach widths over the time
required for profile equilibration to occur.

During initial construction and renourishment, sand is usually placed along
the shoreline at slopes steeper than equilibrium. The steeper slopes allow easier
documentation of the volumes of materials placed, and they also provide a temporarily wider beach during the equilibration phase. Under the mobilizing action
of waves, the sediment will be transported seaward, gradually approaching an
equilibrium profile. The equilibrium profile as generally used by designers of
beach nourishment projects is defined as the natural form that the beach would
take for a given volume of sand of a particular grain size under the prevailing

wave environment. The equilibrium profile is affected by the presence of structures or natural features such as headlands that affect physical processes at a project site and that would have to be accommodated for in estimates of the profile. The equilibrium profile is an approximation; therefore, local variations to that profile would need to be accounted for. The profile is dynamic during the course of a year because of seasonal variations in the wave climate. For planning and design, these variations are accounted for in an average or baseline for the site. The physical changes that occur at the site are more pronounced near the shoreline. Physical changes to the seafloor decrease with distance offshore because the wave action in deeper water is diminished near the bottom and less sand is suspended in the water column. The extent of sand movement is determined through various measurement techniques (see Appendix H).

The term *closure* is a volumetric measure that is applied to a position offshore at which changes in profile elevations are so slight as to be difficult to measure accurately within the limits of existing monitoring technology. There may be some sand movement past closure, but it does not normally result in measurable elevation changes (Hallermeier, 1981). *Depth of closure* is an approximate and straightforward reference for the seaward extent of measurable sand movement and is typically used by designers to analyze the degree of profile widening that would be associated with any given volume of sand placed. Although depth is not the only factor associated with the movement of sand, designers believe that there is a reasonable correlation between closure and the depth of closure that fosters this practice. A strong correlation has been observed in some major projects being monitored (Kraus, 1994), but further monitoring and analysis are needed to validate the correlation scientifically.

In evaluating project performance it is necessary to be able to predict the equilibrium dry beach width. If the native sand and the nourishment sand are nearly the same grain size, it is reasonable to assume that the equilibrium profile form will be the same as that of the native beach before nourishment but is simply displaced seaward, and the equilibrium beach width can be calculated using simple equations. However, sand finer or coarser than the native sand will have equilibrium beach profiles that are of flatter or steeper slopes than the native sand, respectively. In such cases, methods are available for approximating the equilibrium dry beach width (see Appendix C). Calculation of the equilibrium beach width requires estimation of the depth to which the profile will equilibrate; this depth is usually estimated on the basis of the statistical wave height and period characteristics.

Alongshore Spreading

The rate of alongshore spreading of the placed sand is a dominant engineering measure of the success of a project and is fundamental to determining success relative to economic measures as well. If, for example, one-half the placed sand were transported from the region within 2 years and a substantially more frequent renourishment cycle than anticipated was required, the project could probably not be considered successful. However, if this process were to take a decade or more, equaling or exceeding the planned renourishment cycle, the project would likely be judged favorably.

Both simple and detailed methods for predicting the rate of alongshore spreading depend primarily on wave height, background erosion rate, and sediment grain size. For projects constructed in the vicinity of engineered structures, a littoral barrier, or a sink, such as an inlet, wave direction also is important. Because nourishment projects are constructed along an eroding coast, in addition to the spreading caused by the project planform anomaly, it is assumed that the beach will continue to erode at the same rate as before the nourishment. However, if the nourishment sand is of different size than the native sand, adjustment to the background erosion rate may be appropriate and needs to be considered. Sand transported in an alongshore direction from a nourishment project on a long, straight beach will also provide benefits to the beaches adjacent to the project.

DIVERSITY OF SETTINGS FOR BEACH NOURISHMENT

Beach nourishment projects are undertaken over a wide range of shoreline conditions. As noted, an eroding shoreline can result from jetty or groin construction, natural causes, or development too near the shoreline. Figure 4-3 presents four relevant situations of interest. Figure 4-3a depicts the simplest case of nourishment on a long straight shoreline. Here it is somewhat surprising that, when the nourishment sand is equal in size and shape to the native sand, the performance depends only weakly on wave direction. Therefore, at the preliminary design stage, it is usually not necessary to consider wave direction. Also relevant to design for this situation is the fact that there exists a *single* wave height that will cause the same average spreading losses as the actual wave climate. This fact facilitates calculations at the preliminary design stage.

For the case shown in Figure 4-3b, in which the nourishment area is downdrift of a complete or partial littoral barrier, approximate methods are less effective and wave direction is important in addition to wave height. Further, the sequences in which wave events occur influence the planform at any particular time. In this case, the capability to predict performance using simple methods is reduced and may be further limited by the available knowledge of wave conditions, particularly wave direction. Figure 4-4 presents an example of shoreline change associated with the Delray Beach, Florida, nourishment project. Figure 4-5 presents an example of computer-modeled planform evolution for an initially rectangular planform and a uniform background erosion rate of 0.6 m/year.

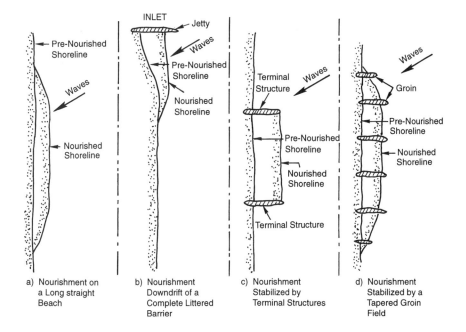

FIGURE 4-3   Planviews of various scenarios of nourishment placement and stabilization.

USE OF STRUCTURES AND OTHER SHORE PROTECTION DEVICES IN CONJUNCTION WITH BEACH NOURISHMENT

The use of traditional shore protection structures and nontraditional[1] shore protection devices (including structures) is controversial, both within and outside the coastal engineering profession. From an engineering perspective, structures can sometimes benefit beach nourishment projects. Nontraditional devices are more problematic because there is little definitive information on their performance capabilities as well as a history of innovative devices that have failed to live up to their claimed potential.

Use of Hard Structures with Beach Nourishment

In some cases, particularly when the project is relatively short or significantly affected by inlets, it may be desirable to limit alongshore losses by con-

---

[1]Nontraditional structures may be described as shore protection structures of an experimental nature whose performances cannot at this time be predicted to a reasonable degree (see further discussion in the following section).

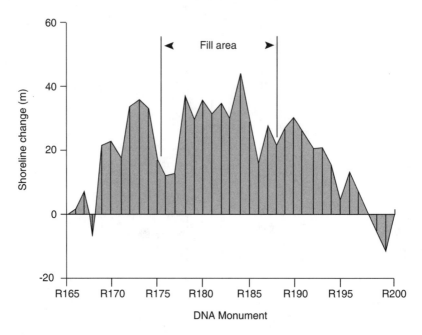

FIGURE 4-4   Shoreline change at Delray Beach nourishment project, 1974-1990, show-ing shoreline change outside the project area; nourishments involved 2.78 million m³ of material.

structing terminal structures, as shown in Figure 4-3c. This approach must be employed with knowledge of the potential adverse effects on the adjacent shore-lines, especially if the net alongshore sediment transport is substantial. Terminal structures are especially appropriate at project ends where potential damage to the adjacent shorelines is small to nil (e.g., at a so-called littoral sink, such as at an inlet or submarine canyon). If structures are used on the downdrift end of a project on a long shoreline, it may be appropriate to place sand downdrift of the structure in anticipation of adverse effects of the structure and to develop a monitoring plan that responds to structure-related erosion. One possibility is to use an *adjustable* structure to regulate sand transport from the nourished beach without significant impacts to adjacent beaches. An example is a groin con-structed from "H" piles with panels that can be added or removed (Dean, 1975). Prediction of project performance in the presence of terminal structures requires knowledge of both wave height and wave direction, and capabilities are limited for both the preliminary and detailed methods (see Appendix C for further discus-sion).

A different use of structures is their placement in the interior of a nourish-ment project, such as the groins shown in Figure 4-3d. The same general precau-

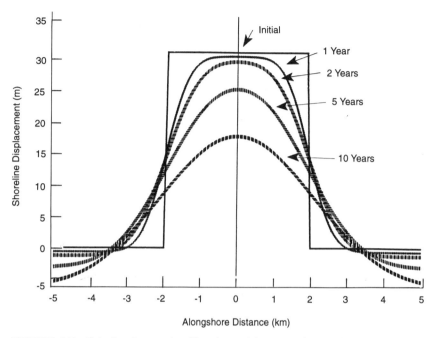

FIGURE 4-5   Calculated example of beach nourishment project evolution.

tions apply as for terminal structures. Although the intent of the groins is to increase the longevity of the project, if the project is in an area of strong unidirectional alongshore sediment transport, updrift accretion and downdrift erosion often result. One approach is to taper the groin field toward the project ends in order to make the planform less abrupt and thereby induce the ambient sand transport to move around the groin ends, minimizing any adverse impacts. In addition, nourishment material can be placed on the downdrift side of the project in anticipation of any erosional effects. Predicting the detailed effects on adjacent beaches when structures are employed is relatively unproven, and it is generally necessary to develop and carry out monitoring to identify adverse effects and establish a contingency plan to mitigate such effects when they occur. Nourishment on a beach with a seawall results in downdrift migration of the placed material (see Appendix C).

Use of Nontraditional Shore Protection Devices

Nontraditional shore protection devices have been offered commercially as countermeasures for shore erosion problems. Such devices have often been installed without the benefit of objective laboratory or field evaluations, although there are notable exceptions. In general, nontraditional devices, often of proprietary design, have taken the form of fences, walls, mazes, or flexible elements and have been designed to interfere with wave-driven motions and to "trap" in shallow water sand that otherwise would not be available to the littoral system. In other cases, prefabricated structures have been designed to interact with incident waves in an attempt to trap or retard the alongshore movement of sand. However, no device, conventional or unconventional, can create sand in the surf zone. Any accumulations must necessarily be at the expense of an adjacent section of the shore. This effect sets structures and other devices apart from beach nourishment, which is the only demonstrated technology that addresses the basic problem in coastal erosion—a shortage of sand.

Some of the nontraditional devices involve large concrete structures placed near the shore. They may or may not be beneficial. If they are not, any unfavorable conditions that develop could be difficult and expensive to correct, including the necessity of removing devices that do not perform well or become hazards to beach users. Further, in the committee's view, some nontraditional devices have been oversold and, with respect to their performance, have shown no lasting capability for shore protection.

Specific research would be needed to determine the performance capabilities of such devices and their suitability for use in conjunction with beach nourishment. Evaluation of any beach protection system is expensive because of the large size of any meaningful experiment, and it is time-consuming because of concerns for testing under a full set of climate conditions; however, a uniform and effective methodology could be developed. A performance demonstration specification is needed for evaluating the effectiveness of nontraditional shore protection and beach stabilization and restoration devices. The results of such a program would be expected to provide a more complete basis for the probable performance before any interested agency or private buyer commits to their use.

With respect to a testing methodology, wave tank experiments could be conducted for preliminary evaluation of nontraditional structural alternatives. These experiments appear to have been done only to a limited extent, but they would be a wise investment before commitment is made to field trials. Ultimately, performance monitoring of sufficient duration would need to be conducted to ensure that actual performance over the long term is not masked by positive or negative performance in the near term. Such monitoring would need to be in terms of years because of seasonal and annual variations in environmental conditions. For a fully valid performance assessment, field testing would need to be conducted of the technology in the absence of beach nourishment, with beach nourishment, and with beach nourishment only at comparable sites to establish actual capabilities.

LIMITATIONS OF EXISTING MODELS AND METHODS

The models and methods discussed in this report are state of the art. Nevertheless, there are uncertainties and limitations associated with their use that need to be understood in order to assess the confidence to be placed in the resulting predictions. Some of the published criticism of the models relates to the lack of effective monitoring and analysis of beach nourishment projects.

The concept of an equilibrium beach profile is based on measurements of many profiles in the field and laboratory, but it applies only to profiles of sandy beaches. Pilkey et al. (1993) criticized the engineering application of equilibrium profiles owing to concerns that include the complexities of natural profiles, such as the presence of mud, or rock outcrops, or a bar feature. In addition, the profile may not approach equilibrium after placement owing to gradients in alongshore sediment transport. An equilibrium profile represents an approximate profile of the average of many profiles composed of the sediment considered. This fact and the utility of an equilibrium beach profile methodology are of great importance to designers.

The depth of closure is a useful engineering approximation for establishing the offshore depth that delimits, for practical purposes, the movement of bed materials. When applied to beach nourishment projects in which the initial profile is usually placed steeper than equilibrium, the depth of closure is an imperfect approximation of the level and frequency of active profile adjustment in nature. Measurements have shown that sand does move beyond this depth. Nevertheless, the depth of closure provides a reasonable boundary condition when the equilibrium dry beach width associated with the addition of a certain quantity of sand of a particular grain size is developed.

Sediment size of nourishment material can affect the performance of a project in at least two ways. First, use of material of smaller sizes results in flatter slopes and a smaller additional equilibrium beach width (for the same amounts of fill material) than when the native and nourishment sediments are compatible. Second, there is some evidence (Dean et al., 1982; del Valle et al., 1993) that finer sediments are more easily transportable in the alongshore direction and thus will result in a shorter project life than would occur using coarser sediment. Quantification of the nourishment sediment size characteristics and assessment of their effects on project performance can be accounted for only in an approximate manner. The uncertainties increase with differences between the native and nourishment sediment sizes.

Application of alongshore and cross-shore sediment transport models to represent project evolution requires quantification of substantial physical characteristics, including waves, sediments, and boundary conditions. In addition, the application of numerical models may require a calibration phase involving the use of approximate data. In those applications involving structures, the interaction with ambient flows is poorly understood. Most numerical models that predict planform evolution are the so-called one-line models in which the assumption is made that the profile moves landward or seaward without a change of form. As a result, the effects of profile steepening and flattening on the updrift and downdrift sides of a structure can be represented only approximately. In the application of some numerical models, the model designers recommend adjustment in the calibration phase of the coefficients to replicate the background erosion rate. For some other numerical models, the background erosion rate is interpreted directly as alongshore background transport, thus ensuring that the model will predict the background erosion rate in the absence of the project.

In view of the limitations in using the various models and methods, it is necessary and appropriate for designers of beach nourishment projects to consider carefully the applicability of the methodology to the particular natural system that is assessed. All relevant sources of design information and procedures need to be considered and used when economically justified. Sources of design information and procedures can include transfer of information from projects that are in the same general area as the area under consideration. If the magnitude of the project justifies application of the more complete, complex, and costly design procedures, it is still appropriate to apply the more simple and direct methods, including the completely empirical method described by Verhagen (1992). If significant differences exist in the major performance measures, as determined by the models, it is important to identify the causes of the differences for the purpose of ensuring that the final design is based on the most credible of the available information and procedures. Some level of sensitivity study is appropriate to evaluate the effects of various data and model uncertainties on the important performance parameters. As with all evolving design fields, beach nourishment requires the designer to be cognizant of the uncertainties, to use all available design tools, and to be able to recognize and respond to results that may be contrary to intuition or that were obtained from other methods.

PREDICTION

This section presents estimates of the predictability of beach nourishment projects under various degrees of complexity. Estimated performance predictability presented in Figure 4-6 is based to a considerable extent on the committee's judgment and experience.

The demonstrated ability to predict the performance of beach nourishment projects is best for the most simple situation, that is, for a project constructed on a long, straight shoreline without the complications of inlets or engineered structures. In addition, predictability is better for the overall performance of the project, such as an average shoreline change as contrasted to the detailed performance or the shoreline change at a particular location.

There are three types of conditions that can result in differences between the measured (or actual) and predicted performances of beach nourishment projects:

Performance Predictability

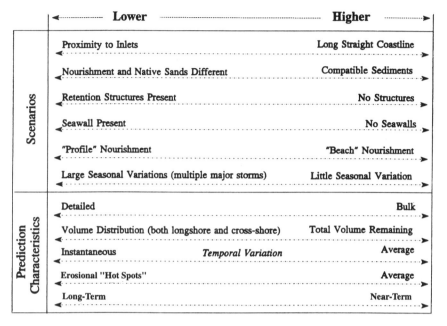

	Lower ⟵	Higher ⟶
Scenarios	Proximity to Inlets ⟵	Long Straight Coastline ⟶
	Nourishment and Native Sands Different ⟵	Compatible Sediments ⟶
	Retention Structures Present ⟵	No Structures ⟶
	Seawall Present ⟵	No Seawalls ⟶
	"Profile" Nourishment ⟵	"Beach" Nourishment ⟶
	Large Seasonal Variations (multiple major storms) ⟵	Little Seasonal Variation ⟶
Prediction Characteristics	Detailed ⟵	Bulk ⟶
	Volume Distribution (both longshore and cross-shore) ⟵	Total Volume Remaining ⟶
	Instantaneous *Temporal Variation* ⟵	Average ⟶
	Erosional "Hot Spots" ⟵	Average ⟶
	Long-Term ⟵	Near-Term ⟶

FIGURE 4-6 Estimated ability to predict performance relative to various factors that can affect beach nourishment projects.

- inadequate knowledge of coastal processes,
- wave conditions that differ from those considered in the design, and
- differences between the designed and constructed projects.

Table 4-1 presents the committee's estimates of prediction errors caused by inadequate knowledge.

Both preliminary and detailed prediction methods exist for beach nourishment design. The paragraphs below describe the general characteristics of these two levels and some of the more basic results.

Preliminary Design

At the preliminary level, two primary questions are addressed: How wide will the nourished beach be after equilibration, and how long will the sand last after placement? As noted, profile equilibration generally occurs within a few years, and for preliminary design it is usually assumed to occur instantly. Approximate methods exist to address this question for nourishment material that is

TABLE 4-1   Estimated Prediction Capabilities

Scenario	Variable Being Predicted	Percentage Error in Prediction
Long straight beach, compatible sand	Volume losses from project area	± 25
	Shoreline changes owing to profile equilibration	± 25
	Shoreline changes owing to volumetric losses	± 25
	Shoreline changes owing to combined profile equilibration and volumetric losses	± 35
Nourishment near an inlet (first kilometer)	Volume losses from project area	± 50
	Shoreline changes owing to profile equilibration	± 25
	Shoreline changes owing to volumetric losses	± 50
	Shoreline changes owing to combined profile equilibration and volumetric losses	± 60

compatible with, finer, or coarser than the native beach material; these methods are presented in Appendix C. Methods developed by Pelnard-Considére (1956) can be employed to address the question of volumetric longevity due to alongshore spreading, especially for such cases as nourishment on a long, straight beach. These methods are available in the form of equations or graphs. A detailed summary is presented in Appendix C. One finding from Pelnard-Considére (1956) for the case of a long straight beach is that the volumetric longevity of material placed in a project is proportional to the square of the project length and inversely proportional to the wave height to the 2.5 power. For preliminary design, estimates of wave height are required, and if the setting involves alongshore sediment transport and structures such as groins or jetties, estimates of wave direction also are required. Usually, at the preliminary level, it is assumed that after equilibration the nourished berm height will be the same as the native berm height, and attention is not directed to other profile characteristics (e.g., dune design).

Detailed Design

At the detailed design level, for some applications it may be important to consider detailed design of the dune cross-section to obtain certain flood protection benefits. In addition, the most detailed wave data can be employed in complex numerical models. The numerical models in general consider the alongshore and cross-shore sediment transport components separately. The cross-shore models are employed to evaluate the effects of severe storms on the design cross-section, whereas the alongshore transport models are used to address the volumetric distribution of material remaining at various times in the future. In the cross-shore application, considerable attention may be directed to the effectiveness of placing sand in particular candidate geometries to provide flood protection benefits. At this design level, it is possible to investigate in greater detail the stabilizing benefits of structures and the effects of particular hypothesized storm events in the vicinity of structures. In general, the detailed models provide greater flexibility to evaluate and compare the relative merits of particular alternative designs.

SAND SOURCES—A CONSIDERATION IN PROJECT DESIGN

Over the past three decades, the materials for practically all large beach nourishment projects have been obtained from offshore deposits. A few medium-sized projects have been constructed by hauling the material from land borrow sites to the nourishment areas using large trucks or by moving sand from an onshore source via conveyer belts. It is essential that material obtained from the sea be located a sufficient distance offshore that the sand placed in conjunction with the nourishment will not be carried back into the borrow areas. In most cases, borrow areas need to be a minimum of 2 km from the shoreline, well seaward of the depth of closure.

The most important borrow material characteristic is the sediment grain size. Borrow material grain size matching the native material is considered synonymous with quality. A candidate borrow area may be considered unacceptable if the silt and clay fraction exceeds a certain percentage. This percentage needs to be related to the natural turbidity in the nourishment area. Fine material also adversely affects project performance. Early projects constructed without regard for grain size performed relatively poorly, and recent developments indicate that nourishment sand that is only slightly smaller than native sand can result in significantly narrower equilibrated dry beach widths compared to sand the same size as (or larger than) native sand. To identify potential borrow sources and to evaluate the material quality, a sand survey must be carried out that usually includes collecting geophysical profiles, surface samples, and cores. This report assumes that all sand sources are sufficiently free of contaminants to meet federal, state, and local requirements. Therefore, contaminated sediments are not otherwise considered in these discussions.

Sediment Sources and Construction of Projects

The selection of a source of suitable material for a particular project depends on the design needs but also on environmental factors and on the cost of transport of the material from the borrow area to the placement site. These factors and their long-term implications need to be considered with respect to beach nourishment programs and conveyed to all participants and parties of interest. The actual construction of a beach nourishment project normally involves (1) the search for a source of sediment that meets, as nearly as possible, the criteria specified in design documents; (2) the removal and transfer of the material to the nourishment site; and (3) its placement on the beach as prescribed by the design. These three components of a beach nourishment project are fundamental to its performance and often determine the cost and feasibility of a project.

The search for viable sediment sources occurs early in the planning of a project because it can affect the design by determining the mode of delivery of the sediment and its placement on the beach; it also effectively defines the grain sizes of the fill. All these construction aspects are also important to the economic analyses and the environmental factors that must be determined early in the project. For these reasons, it is essential that project decision makers and designers have a basic understanding of sediment sources, transfer, and placement. The search for suitable material generally involves locating a deposit of sand and gravel of sufficient volume and grain size that could serve as a suitable source. Potentially, beach-quality sand and gravel can be obtained from inland, inlet, or offshore sources. Nonindigenous sediments imported from other areas or countries and artificial materials are also potential sources. The general attributes of each of these potential sources are summarized in Table 4-2 and are described in greater detail in Appendix F.

Locating and Assessing Offshore Sand Deposits

The completion of a detailed geotechnical investigation is important in the search for offshore sediment sources on the continental shelf (Prins, 1980). The investigation generally begins with high-resolution seismic reflection profiling that employs equipment towed behind a survey vessel (Williams, 1982). The record is derived from reflected sound from the bottom and subbottom layers of sand or other sediments and with confirming observations from sediment cores taken from the area. The seismic data are used to map the stratigraphy and identify ancient fluvial and tidal inlet channels. Surveys may also include the use of side-scan sonar, which focuses a broad acoustic beam across a swath of seabed to define the small-scale shoals, bedforms, and variations in seabed texture. Records from the side-scan sonar can be used to produce photo-like images of the seabed (Williams, 1982). Seismic reflection and side-scan observations are sometimes augmented by diver observations, particularly to define the limits of potentially useful sediments. Such tools are important to determine the areal extent of sediment that potentially could be used in a project and also to locate any reefs or areas of hard bottom that are environmentally sensitive (e.g., Beachler and Higgins, 1992).

TABLE 4-2   Potential Sources of Beach Nourishment Sediment

Offshore source	The most difficult operational conditions because of exposure to open sea. Increasingly difficult to obtain permits because of concern for impacts on hard bottom and migratory species. Must consider the effects of altering depth on wave energy at the shoreline. May be combined with a navigation project.
Inlet source	Sand between jetties in a stabilized inlet. Often associated with dredging of navigational channels and the ebb- or flood-tide deltas of both natural and jettied inlets.
Accretional beach source	Generally not suitable to mine sand (1) from most of the stable shorelines or from any eroding shoreline, (2) where there are insufficient surveys to define volumes, or (3) where sediment size and type vary markedly in the cross-shore direction.
Upland source	Generally the easiest to obtain permits and assess impacts. Offers opportunities for mitigation. Both quantity and quality of economical deposits often limited. Adverse secondary impacts from mining and overland transport.
Riverine source	Has the potential for large quantities. Generally high quality. Transport distance a possible limiting factor. May interrupt a natural supply of sand to the coast.
Lagoon source	Typically difficult to obtain permits unless in conjunction with lagoon restoration or navigation projects because of regulations against loss of wetlands. Often low quality because of deposition of fine material. Convenient to barrier beaches and in protected waters for ease of construction. Flood-tide deltas the principal sources.
Artificial or nonindigenous material source	Seldom tested in the United States because of high transport and redistribution costs. Some laboratory experiments done on recycling broken glass. Aragonite from Bahamas a possible source.
Emergency source	Includes deposits around inlets and local sinks and sand from stable beaches with a sufficiently wide buffer. Generally used only in emergencies following storms, where a change in the shoreline planform is desired, or where, in the short term, is the only affordable option. May be combined with a navigation project. Not "true" source in that sand is not added to the system.

SAND BYPASSING AS A SOURCE

In some regions the need for beach nourishment has resulted from sand being trapped by the construction of breakwaters in the nearshore area to protect a harbor or by jetties built to fix the location of an entrance to an inland harbor. Where there is a net alongshore transport of sand in a dominant direction, sand can be trapped updrift of the structures, within the entrance and/or harbor, or in an ebb-tide shoal. This deprivation of sand to the downdrift beach will ultimately cause erosion of this beach. Sand trapped in an entrance channel or harbor may interfere with navigation and require removal. In some cases, harbors or entrances are designed to trap sand in a preferred location to minimize interference with navigation and facilitate its removal by dredging. Good engineering practice requires that this sand be deposited on the downdrift, or eroding, beach to maintain the littoral sand transport. This operation is referred to as bypassing and may be continuous or intermittent.

Availability of Suitable Sources

Reconnaissance studies have been completed by the U.S. Army Corps of Engineers (USACE) and the U.S. Geological Survey to assess the quantities of sand available on continental shelves that could be mined for various uses, including beach nourishment. The Inner Continental Shelf Sediment and Structure program of the Coastal Engineering Research Center included surveys from many areas along the U.S. seacoast and from the Great Lakes. Williams (1986) estimated sand and gravel resources within the U.S. exclusive economic zone (EEZ) at more than 1,200 billion m^3 in water not deeper than 60 m. Compared with the annual sand and gravel consumption in the United States, these estimated volumes might suggest that anticipated national needs can be satisfied for the foreseeable future. However, their use for beach nourishment may be prohibitive because many of the sand deposits are considerable distances from the shore and are at water depths at which sand mining may not be affordable. In addition, the thickness of some offshore deposits may not be sufficient for cost-effective use. Although large volumes of sand are present in the EEZ, economically located deposits of suitable quality and quantity to meet beach fill requirements are often limited.

The continuing use of beach nourishment in new areas as well as the maintenance of projects already in place will, in the future, place a burden on project planners to locate new and continuing sources of reasonably accessible borrow material for these projects.

Although the estimated reserves of sand suitable for nourishment programs are large, there have been local shortages, a situation that is likely to become more common in the future. For example, in Florida numerous projects have nearly depleted economically recoverable sand reserves in state waters. Increasingly, distant sources are being considered for use, including oolitic Aragonite sands found in the Bahama Islands (see Appendix F). The increasing shortages are particularly important to long-term nourishment programs that are expected to continue for 50 years or more. The shortages are likely to increase the costs of renourishment significantly because of the imposition of acquisition costs and increased transportation costs relative to local sources of beach-quality material.

The economic viability of projects using these sources will develop as more distant sources foster the construction and use of dredges capable of removing sediment from deep water, combined with the use of larger transport vessels and appropriate materials-handling schemes for the placement of this material. Areas such as the Pacific coast or regions where the use of offshore or navigational dredging sources may not yield sufficient amounts of sand in the long run will be the first to develop methods of recycling sand within segmented areas so as to use the littoral transport process as a relatively closed cycle process. Development, planning, and implementation of these processes remain a challenge; they may include artificial sand trap basins with continually operating pumping systems to relocate sand updrift; use of inlets as sand sources, with transport of material both updrift and downdrift via a dedicated hopper dredge to maintain a material balance; or implementation of construction methods that retard the transport process.

SAND TRANSFER EQUIPMENT AND METHODS

Generally, sand is excavated and transported from the borrow site to the beach by one or more of three types of equipment: cutter-suction dredge, trailing-suction hopper dredge, or a dedicated sand bypass system. However, the vast majority of beach projects have either used self-propelled hopper dredges with pump-out capability or pumped the borrow material directly to the beach fill site via pipelines with cutter-suction dredges. As noted previously, transport via trucks and placement directly onto the beach nourishment site have been used for some projects in which sand and gravel were obtained from upland sources.

At present, the major constraints on the transport and placement of material for beach nourishment from offshore borrow sites are weather-related delays owing to sea state and winds; restrictions on construction activity, methods, and timing relating to environmental concerns; equipment limitations for deepwater dredging; and distances over which sediment must be transported.

The construction of beach nourishment projects may involve the use of one or many possible combinations of equipment and techniques, depending on the site, the size of the job, environmental and other constraints, and the level of competition at bidding time. A more detailed discussion of the types of equipment, particularly dredging equipment, and their use in the mining, transfer, and placement of sand on beaches is contained in Appendix F. Herbich (1992) provides a detailed technical discussion of dredging engineering, including placement methods.

EROSIONAL HOT SPOTS

In the design phase it is assumed that the distribution of volumetric erosion along the project will conform to the detailed design calculations. However, in most projects, for reasons that are not obvious, there will be one or more areas that will erode more rapidly than their neighbors and more rapidly than predicted using accepted methodologies. These areas are called erosional hot spots. In some cases, they may occur at locations where a high rate of background erosion existed prior to the project. In other cases, the location may not correlate with preproject problem areas. Although the causes of hot spots in the latter case are not known, it has been hypothesized that they may be due to wave refraction and possibly wave focusing. Wave refraction could occur as a result of preproject bathymetry or bathymetry resulting from the geometry of the placed material. The composition of bottom material may also be a factor in that varying bottom conditions could affect the rate of movement and deposition. Regardless of the cause, erosional hot spots require renourishment earlier than the overall project, and because mobilization of the required dredging equipment is expensive, it is desirable to exercise measures to increase longevity in these areas. One approach during renourishment is to place a greater volume of sand in hot-spot areas, thereby extending the time before required subsequent renourishments.

FEDERAL DESIGN PROCEDURES

The USACE has developed guidelines and procedures to be used in the design of nourishment projects in which the federal government is a cost-sharing participant (see Appendix H). The implementation of these guidelines and procedures is evolving. Based on a general review of documentation for various beach nourishment projects by the committee, application of the best physics to project design has not been uniform among the USACE districts. Modern design profiles in the United States began with development of the "Caldwell Section" for emergency sand dune protection used after the great Ash Wednesday 1962 storm that struct the Mid-Atlantic coast (see Appendix H; Podufaly, 1962). The USACE standard design procedures have evolved since then, although the basic form of the Caldwell section is still reflected in design (Appendix H). Today, design procedures usually define a "design" cross-section and an "advanced-fill" cross-section, as shown in Figure 4-7.

The concept is that the design cross-section is the minimum cross-section that yields the expected benefits prior to *renourishment*. Advanced fill is the material placed seaward of the design cross-section to allow for erosion between nourishment events. Procedures are applied to attempt to optimize these two cross-sections. Ideally, these procedures would incorporate the concepts of profile equilibration and "spreading losses." However, in some recent designs the volumetric loss rates were based only on the historical erosion rates, a practice that fails to recognize that the "bulge" created by the nourishment can cause spreading losses that may be at least as great as the historical values. In addition, present federal guidelines for beach nourishment recommend the use of a "compatibility" factor to account for differences between the native and nourishment

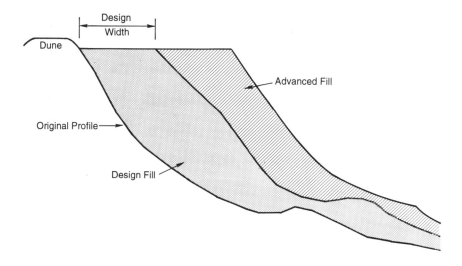

FIGURE 4-7   Schematic of design and advanced-fill nourishment profiles.

sediments and a "renourishment" factor to account for spreading losses. These two concepts were developed prior to recent developments in equilibrium beach profiles and in both preliminary and detailed methods for calculating spreading losses.

POSTCONSTRUCTION DESIGN REFINEMENT
AND CORRECTIVE ACTION

As discussed earlier, performance of a beach nourishment project, once constructed, often does not conform to predictions because of limitations in predictive models and supporting data or because the wave climate was different than assumed. Monitoring programs are needed to detect deviations from predicted performance that could compromise the design integrity of a new beach nourishment project unless they are corrected. Such programs need to be timely enough to support early detection of deviations in beach behavior from those predicted. Variations then need to be assessed for significance, and corrective action regimes need to be developed and implemented. Few monitoring programs identified during the committee's assessment were either timely enough or sufficiently developed to meet this objective.

Although experience has shown that erosion rates vary across a project, traditional construction practices with uniform levels of overfilling will result in the placement of too much material on slow erosion areas and the underfilling of erosional hot spots. Alternatively, placing fill where it is needed instead of overfilling slow erosion areas will usually conserve and reduce the overall amount of fill that is needed. Early detection and correction of erosional hot spots through the placement of additional advanced fill will also contribute substantially to maintaining the design integrity of the project. A well-founded project would provide for robust monitoring for the duration of the profile equilibration period (2 to 5 years) to enable early identification and implementation of design refinements and corrective measures.

SAND BYPASS SYSTEMS AND HYBRID SYSTEMS

Some regions need beach nourishment because of sand trapped by a harbor constructed by the installation of breakwaters in the nearshore area, or by jetties built to fix the location of a natural or constructed entrance into a coastal harbor or waterway system. A net alongshore transport of sand can cause:

- accreting sand updrift of structures,
- trapping of sand within the entrance or harbor,
- formation of an ebb-tide shoal seaward of the entrance, and
- erosion of the downdrift beach.

To maintain required navigation depths, sand must be dredged from the entrance channel and harbor or from a sand trap constructed contiguous to and updrift of them. In many cases, it is desirable that sand not accumulate updrift of the entrance structures. It may be appropriate to bypass the sand around the barrier to nourish downdrift beaches. Similarly, sand that accumulates in navigation channels as a result of harbor protection works could also be placed on downdrift beaches to help restore the sand budget of the littoral system. The importance of this fact relative to more traditional beach nourishment, in terms of quantities, is reflected in Tables 14 and 16 in *Shoreline Protection and Beach Nourishment Projects of the U.S. Army Corps of Engineers* (USACE, 1994).

Hybrid shore protection projects are combinations of beach nourishment and structures, such as detached breakwaters, groins, jetties, revetments, seawalls, and submerged sills. There is a considerable body of knowledge on the structural design of the components and some on their functional design. There are existing procedures for the functional design of detached breakwaters and fill, and for groins and fill but not for the other types of hybrid projects. Some details are given in Appendix D.

PROFESSIONAL ACCOUNTABILITY FOR DESIGN

A project must be both structurally and functionally sound in order to be successful. Therefore, it is imperative that the project designer be qualified to assess coastal processes affecting the site and design shore protection projects that are well correlated to these processes. Selecting a qualified engineer is somewhat difficult because, although coastal engineering is a demanding discipline requiring specific knowledge of coastal processes and the design of coastal works, it is not recognized as a separate engineering discipline by regulating bodies or certification entities. Possession of a professional engineer's license by itself does not mean that the holder has the necessary expertise to design coastal works, although possession of such a license generally helps to promote competent oversight and professional and official accountability. Because there is no formal licensing program for coastal engineers at the state level, federal agencies with coastal engineering interests could establish a federal certification program to encourage and enhance the professional development of federal employees involved in the planning, design, construction, and maintenance of coastal works. In view of the fact that coastal engineering expertise at the federal level resides primarily with the USACE, that agency is a logical choice to develop and implement a program designed to improve the professional credentials of federal practitioners.

REFERENCES

Beachler, K. E., and S. H. Higgins. 1992. Hollywood/Hallandale, building Florida's beaches in the 1990's. Shore and Beach 60(3):15-22.

Dean, R. G. 1975. Compatibility of borrow material for beach fills. Pp. 1319-1333 in Proceedings of the 14th Coastal Engineering Conference. New York: American Society of Civil Engineers.

Dean, R. G., E. P. Berek, C. G. Gable, and R. J. Seymour. 1982. Longshore transport determined by an efficiency trap. Pp. 954-968 in Proceedings of the 18th International Conference on Coastal Engineering. New York: American Society of Civil Engineers.

del Valle, R., R. Medina, and M. A. Losada. 1993. Dependence of coefficient K on grain size. Journal of the Waterway, Port, Coastal, and Ocean Engineering 1119(5):568-574.

Hallermeier, R. J. 1981. Seaward Limit of Significant Sand Transport by Waves: An Annual Zonation for Seasonal Profiles. Coastal Engineering Technical Aid No. CETA 81-2. Fort Belvoir, Va.: Coastal Engineering Research Center, U.S. Army Corps of Engineers.

Herbich, J. B. 1992. Handbook of Dredging Engineering. New York: McGraw-Hill.

Kraus, N. C. 1994. Importance of Beach Profile Surveying and Depth of Closure for Beach Nourishment Project Design. Presentation to the national meeting of the American Shore and Beach Preservation Association, October 6, 1994, Virginia Beach, Va.

Pelnard-Considére, R. 1956. Essai de Theorie de l'Evolution des Formes de Rivate en Plages de Sable et de Galets. 4th Journees de l'Hydraulique, Les Energies de la Mar, Question III, Rapport No. 1 (in French). Vicksburg, Miss.: U.S. Army Waterways Experiment Station, U.S. Army Corps of Engineers.

Pilkey, O. H., R. S. Young, S. R. Riggs, A. W. S. Smith, H. Wu, and W. D. Pilkey. 1993. The concept of shoreface profile of equilibrium: a critical review. Journal of Coastal Research 9(1):255-278.

Podufaly, E. T. 1962. Operation five-high. Shore and Beach 30(2):9-17.

Prins, D. A. 1980. Data collection methods for sand inventory-type surveys. Coastal Engineering Technical Aid 80-4. Fort Belvoir, Va.: Coastal Engineering Research Center, U.S. Army Corps of Engineers.

USACE. 1994. Shoreline Protection and Beach Nourishment Projects of the U.S. Army Corps of Engineers. IWR Report 94-PS-1. Fort Belvoir, Va.: Institute of Water Resources, Water Resources Support Center, U.S. Army Corps of Engineers.

Verhagen, H. J. 1992. Method for artificial beach nourishment. Pp. 2474-2485 in Proceedings of the 23rd International Conference on Coastal Engineering. New York: American Society of Civil Engineers.

Williams, S. J. 1982. Use of High-Resolution Seismic Reflection and Side-Scan Sonar Equipment for Offshore Surveys. Coastal Engineering Technical Aid 82-5. Fort Belvoir, Va.: Coastal Engineering Research Center, U.S. Army Corps of Engineers.

Williams, S. J. 1986. Sand and gravel deposits within the United States exclusive economic zone: resource assessment and uses. Pp. 377-386 in Proceedings of the 18th Offshore Technology Conference. Richardson, Tex.: Offshore Technology Conference.

5

Environmental Issues Associated with Beach Nourishment

This chapter addresses the major environmental issues associated with beach nourishment. It considers both beneficial and detrimental effects and notes where adequate research has not yet taken place. Suggestions for appropriate research are considered.

Beach nourishment operations can disrupt the existing biological communities in subaerial zones of beaches and in the borrow sites where dredging occurs. Effects have also been observed in the shallow subtidal habitats adjacent to some nourished beaches. Naqvi and Pullen (1982), W. G. Nelson (1985), Goldberg (1989), and Grober (1992) have reviewed studies of the ecological effects of beach nourishment. The effects can be quite varied, ranging from short- to long-term alterations and including both detrimental and beneficial effects. Several reviewers have also noted that there has been little standardization in the design of environmental monitoring studies and that most of the studies conducted to date have been limited in duration or scope. As a result, many of the environmental concerns regarding beach nourishment remain unresolved. Technical and scientific knowledge is incomplete, especially with respect to the indirect effects on biota that use the habitats affected by nourishment operations.

SUBAERIAL BEACH HABITATS

The subaerial beach can be divided into two major zones. The uppermost zone is the supralittoral (dry) portion of the beach that lies landward of mean high water and may extend into the primary dune system. On eroded beaches requiring replenishment, the upper extent of this zone may terminate at a seawall, rock revetment, or other hard structure associated with coastal development. The intertidal zone, located between mean high water and mean low water, forms the second distinct zone of the subaerial beach. The width and characteristics of this zone can vary considerably, depending on tidal range, sediment size, and wave energy.

Because one of the primary purposes of beach nourishment is to restore eroded portions of the subaerial beach, most of the fill material is placed in the supralittoral and intertidal zones. However, burial of shallow subaqueous habitats also occurs as the beach is widened. This mimics naturally occurring rapid burial events associated with berm or beach cusp formation except that it occurs on broader spatial scales and may involve greater changes in sediment loads. Physical changes to the beach environment vary during and after nourishment, depending on the source and type of sand used. Most projects attempt to use sandy material that is comparable in composition and grain size to the existing beach. Sand sources with a high silt/clay content are generally avoided, although some nourishment projects have used material with a relatively high percentage of these fine-grained materials (e.g., Reilly and Bellis, 1978). In addition to its not being particularly suitable as beach fill material, dredging sand deposits with a high percentage of fines can have adverse effects on existing biota in adjacent habitats as a result of increased turbidity and sedimentation. Several studies have shown that even when beach-compatible materials are used, the nourished beach may be physically altered compared to nonnourished beaches with respect to sand compaction, shear resistance, moisture content, grain size and shape, and other factors (Nelson and Dickerson, 1988; Ackerman et al., 1991, 1992; Grober, 1992). The slope of the beach in the intertidal zone is also generally steeper after nourishment until the beach reaches a more stable profile, and there is often a distinct scarp that forms in this zone as the beach fill adjusts. The height of this scarp can vary from a few centimeters to more than a meter (Nelson et al., 1987; Reilly, 1979). However, it should be noted that scarps also occur on beaches that have not been nourished.

The obvious benefits of a nourishment project include improved protection of coastal properties from wave damage and improvement of the beach for recreational activities. Beach nourishment projects are generally not done to protect undeveloped upland habitats or to restore the beach for indigenous biota or biota that use the beach for foraging or nesting, although this benefit has been cited occasionally.

Potential negative consequences of beach nourishment include:

- disturbance of the indigenous biota inhabiting the subaerial habitats, which may in turn affect the foraging patterns of the species that feed on those organisms and
- disruption to species that use subaerial beach habitats or adjacent areas for nesting, nursing, and breeding.

The ecological consequences of beach nourishment on subaerial habitats have not been well studied, even though several hundred nourishment operations have been completed along the coastline of the United States alone.

The indigenous fauna of a sandy beach are primarily burrowing species that are well adapted to this constantly changing and relatively stressful environment. In the upper beach zone, dominant fauna generally include talitrid and haustoriid amphipod species and crabs of the genus *Ocypode* (ghost crabs) in more southern latitudes (Dahl, 1952; Trevallion et al., 1970; Shelton and Robertson, 1981; Williams, 1984). Macrofauna typically found in the intertidal zone include haustoriid amphipods, polychaetes, isopods, mollusks, and some larger crustacean species such as mole crabs (*Emerita* spp.) and burrowing shrimp (*Callianassa* spp.) in the lower intertidal and swash zones (Dexter, 1972; Croker et al., 1975; Shelton and Robertson, 1981; Knott et al., 1983; Williams, 1984). Both the abundance and diversity of these organisms are higher in the lower intertidal zone and can vary seasonally, especially in more temperate latitudes. W. G. Nelson (1985) provides an excellent review of the distribution and life history patterns of dominant beach fauna typically found along the U.S. Atlantic and Gulf coasts. Parr et al. (1978) describe similar patterns for a beach on the Pacific coast.

When a beach is nourished, large volumes of sand are placed within the supralittoral and intertidal zones. The amount of sand overburden varies across the width of the beach, but the greatest volume of material is generally placed along the upper extent of the beach where biological diversity is lowest. Sand flowing onto the lower portions of the beach during the nourishment operation can increase the beach height in the intertidal zone from several centimeters to more than a meter. Organisms living in the sands of the nourished beach will be smothered unless they are able to leave the area or burrow up through the sand overburden.

Among the infaunal organisms typically found on a sandy beach, only the larger, more mobile organisms such as the ghost crab are likely to be able to avoid smothering by leaving the area. Reilly and Bellis (1978) observed a decrease in the density of ghost crabs following a nourishment project at Bogue Beach, North Carolina, and suggested that the crabs may have moved away from the nourished area in response to the physical disruption or loss of suitable food resources. Their study did not identify the period required for the ghost crab populations to recover, and other researchers have not attempted to monitor these decapod populations.

Only two documented projects have examined the burrowing abilities of intertidal and/or subtidal sand-dwelling species following burial by sand overburdens (Maurer et al., 1978, 1981a, b, 1982, 1986; W. G. Nelson, 1985). Maurer and his colleagues examined seven species commonly found in nearshore subtidal environments and found that some of the organisms were able to burrow up through sand overburdens of up to 40 cm, although survival depended on sediment composition and temperature. W. G. Nelson (1985) also noted that the three species tested could deal with instantaneous burial at depths of up to 10 cm, although some mortality occurred, depending on grain-size characteristics. No studies have been published on the effects of burying sand-dwelling benthos with sediment overburdens of a meter or more, which may occur during nourishment. Lynch (1994) evaluated this issue for several infaunal species typically found on southeastern beaches and found that many of the species can migrate through large overburdens of sediment in the range of 0.6 to 1 m.

The temporary loss of infaunal communities through sand burial is expected and largely unavoidable during beach nourishment operations. The more important issue is the recovery rate of these communities following completion of the project. Only a few studies have evaluated the changes occurring among infaunal assemblages of subaerial beach habitats following nourishment. Table 5-2 lists the studies considered in this review. Most of them have documented only temporary alterations in the abundance, diversity, and species composition of the intertidal fauna following nourishment, ranging in duration from a few weeks to a few months. However, sampling efforts for many of these studies were limited with respect to the number of samples collected at a given site or the duration and frequency of sampling. The studies have also been limited to areas south of 36° N latitude on both coasts. Thus, although past monitoring projects indicate that infaunal communities in intertidal portions of the beach recover fairly rapidly, additional studies are warranted to evaluate recovery rates more fully in regions where extensive intertidal habitats exist and where studies either have not been conducted or the data are too limited to assess recovery rates adequately.

The indirect effects of temporary losses or alterations in the benthos on the foraging activities of marine and avian predators should also be considered in these studies. Loss of preferred food resources for marine predators may be less critical in the intertidal zone than in subtidal habitats, but many shore bird species actively feed in the intertidal zone and may be adversely affected by nourishment operations. To date, no studies have been published on the effects of beach nourishment on shore bird foraging patterns.

The effects of beach nourishment on the nesting success of threatened or endangered sea turtle species is another major concern related to beach nourishment projects completed in southern regions of the United States. The threatened loggerhead turtle (*Caretta caretta*) is commonly found nesting on southern beaches, and leatherback (*Dermochelys imbricata*) and green (*Chelonia mydas*) turtles are known to nest in this region as well. The turtle nesting season generally extends from the spring through late summer, although there is some variability in the initiation and completion of nesting activities, depending on location within the region (Dodd, 1988). Sea turtles emerge from the ocean at night, lay their eggs in a nest cavity in the supralittoral zone, and return to the ocean. Nourished beaches can restore or provide suitable nesting habitat for sea turtles, resulting in an increased number of nests on several beaches where nest densities have been

TABLE 5-1   Beach Nourishment and Beach Disposal Projects Considered
Beneficial to Biota Using the Beach or Adjacent Upland Areas

Location	Resource Benefited	Reference
Bird Key, SC	Brown pelicans and other shore birds (protection of nesting habitat from erosion)	Unpublished data, P. Wilkinson, South Carolina Wildlife and Marine Resources Department
Boca Raton, FL	Threatened or endangered plant species (protection from loss through erosion)	Spadoni (1993)
Miami Beach, FL	Loggerhead turtles (improvement of turtle nesting habitat and/or nesting sources)	LeBuff and Haverfield (1990), Flynn (1992), Spadoni and Cummings (1992); and Witham (1990)
Jupiter Island, FL		
Captiva Island, FL		
South Seas Plantation, FL		
Pompano Beach/		
Lauderdale-by-the-Sea, FL		
Boca Raton, FL, and		
John V. Lloyd Beach, FL		
Cape Cod, MA	Piping plovers (increase in available nesting habitat)	Melvin et al. (1992)

monitored (see Table 5-1). However, some physical aspects of the nourished
beach can influence the viability of turtle nests and nesting activities, and propos-
als to conduct nourishment projects during the turtle nesting season have generated considerable debate, particularly in Florida.

There are several known effects that active nourishment operations can have
on sea turtles during the nesting season. Pipelines placed on the beach can create
a barrier that prevents females from reaching suitable nesting sites. Artificial
lights, noise, and the increase in human activities during these projects may also
deter nesting females. Many of these problems can be minimized through light-
ing restrictions and by limits on bulldozer activity during the night. If a nest
relocation project is needed, concerns have been raised that the movement of
eggs may result in decreased hatching success, altered sex ratios, decreased
hatchling fitness, and interference with imprinting mechanisms. The success of
nest relocation programs has been monitored on several beaches in Florida
(Spadoni and Cummings, 1992; Higgins, 1993). The results indicate that hatching success of relocated nests is not significantly different on nourished versus
nonnourished beaches. However, more work is needed to resolve all the issues
associated with these programs. Concerns related to active beach nourishment
operations are obviously less important on beaches that have eroded to a point at
which successful turtle nesting is not possible or does not normally occur. In
other situations, natural resource agencies at both the state and federal levels may
deny a permit request for beach nourishment or place special permit conditions
on the project to minimize adverse effects on sea turtles.

Even after the nourishment operation has been completed, physical characteristics of the beach may affect turtle nesting success. As noted previously, nourished beaches often form scarps in the intertidal zone that can result in an increased number of false crawls. Alterations in the compaction, density, shear resistance, color, moisture content, and gas exchange of the beach sands can also influence the incubating environment of a nest, in turn affecting hatching success and hatchling sex ratios (Nelson and Dickerson, 1988; D. A. Nelson, 1991; Ackerman, 1991; Ackerman et al., 1991, 1992). Some of the physical changes that adversely affect nesting success can be dealt with as part of the construction plan. For example, the negative effects of sand compaction and scarp formation can be reduced or eliminated through mechanical tilling and grading of the beach. Other factors that may affect the suitability of the beach as an incubating environment may be more difficult to resolve, but it should be noted that several monitoring programs have documented no significant difference in hatching and emergence success of turtles on nourished versus nonnourished beaches (Raymond, 1984; Nelson et al., 1987; LeBuff and Haverfield, 1990; Steinitz, 1990; Ryder, 1992). One study (Broadwell, 1991) even documented greater hatching emergence success and hatchling weights for a nourished beach in Boca Raton compared to an adjacent natural beach. The results of these studies suggest that nourished beaches can provide a suitable habitat for turtle nesting, but more research is needed to resolve all the problems of this complex issue.

Concerns have also been raised regarding the effects of beach nourishment on threatened or endangered bird and plant species. For example, the piping plover (*Charadrius melodus*) is listed as an endangered (Great Lakes watershed only) and threatened species by the U.S. Fish and Wildlife Service (USFWS) (1993). This species nests on beaches above the high tide line during the spring and summer. Melvin et al. (1991) noted that beach nourishment can improve the quality and availability of plover habitat by creating substrate that is higher, wider, and less vegetated compared to an eroded beach. However, they noted that nourishment may adversely affect breeding plovers if the dredged material is not a suitable nesting substrate or if deposition of the material occurs at a time and place that disturb nesting plovers. The U.S. Fish and Wildlife Service recently placed the seabeach amaranth (*Amaranthus pumilus*) on its list of threatened plant species. Beach nourishment projects completed where this species is present will need to incorporate measures to protect these plants from adverse effects related to construction activities, but the USFWS does note that nourishment can have a positive impact on this species (Federal Register, 1993).

SUBTIDAL BEACH HABITATS

Bottom habitats in the nearshore surf zone immediately adjacent to a beach often support a diverse array of biota that may be directly or indirectly affected by beach nourishment operations. These biota include benthic invertebrate assemblages inhabiting the sandy substrata, epifaunal invertebrate and macrophyte assemblages that form reef communities on hard substrata, and the fish and motile crustacean assemblages that reside in or forage on these habitats.

Infaunal macroinvertebrate communities typically found in the nearshore surf zone and deeper subtidal sand-bottom habitats include polychaetes, amphipods, isopods, decapods, polychaetes, mollusks, echinoderms, and a variety of other taxa (Marsh et al., 1980; Knott et al., 1983; Gorzelany and Nelson, 1987; Rackocinski et al., 1991, 1992; Van Dolah et al., 1992; Deis et al., 1992). Many of the dominant infaunal species found in the surf zone are the same as those inhabiting the lower intertidal zone, but the diversity and abundance of these fauna are generally much higher in the subtidal zone. Many other epibenthic invertebrate and finfish species are found in the nearshore sand-bottom habitat, and in some areas, these resources are commercially important. For example, the nearshore zone along the southeastern and Gulf coast states supports large populations of penaeid shrimp species, which represent a major part of the commercial fisheries harvest for those states. Hard-bottom reef habitats are most commonly found along the Florida coastline (W. G. Nelson, 1989, 1990; Goldberg, 1989), although extensive nearshore reefs have been documented in South Carolina (Van Dolah and Knott, 1984). The dominant sessile biota in these habitats include sponges, octocorals, hard corals, hydrozoans, bryozoans, ascideans, and attached macroalgae. These taxa, in turn, support a diverse assemblage of motile epibenthic invertebrate and finfish species, including many that are commercially important. In general, the diversity of species found in reef habitats is much greater than that observed on sand-bottom habitats (Knott et al., 1983; Jaap, 1984; W.G. Nelson, 1985; Coastal Planning and Engineering, 1992).

Beach nourishment may affect adjacent sand-bottom and hard-bottom habitats, both physically and biologically. Physical alterations may include:

- burial of bottom habitats in the surf zone as the beach is widened;
- increased sedimentation in areas seaward of the surf zone as the fill material redistributes to a more stable profile;
- changes in the nearshore bathymetry and associated changes in wave action; and
- elevated turbidity levels, particularly in the vicinity of the pipeline effluent.

The movement of sediments away from the nourished beach can have both beneficial and detrimental effects. Down-current drift of coarser sediments may benefit beaches adjacent to the nourishment project by providing additional sand material. However, this drift may accelerate the filling of navigation channels in down-current areas, which could increase the frequency of dredging required to maintain the channel. Increased sedimentation in areas seaward of the surf zone may also occur as the fill material redistributes to a more stable profile. In most situations the accumulation of sandy material in the nearshore zone may be gradual and will not result in a major change in sediment composition. However, when there is a relatively high percentage of silts and clays in the fill material, the composition of sediments may be temporarily altered in the nearshore zone. Few studies document the alongshore movements of sand beyond the limits of most nourishment projects.

Biological effects resulting from physical alterations in the nearshore zone are not well documented. Motile invertebrates and fishes typically found in this zone should be able to avoid most of the direct effects of beach nourishment, although larval forms found in the surf zone could be adversely affected by high turbidity levels if they occur. Two surveys of fish populations conducted in Florida before and after beach nourishment showed no evidence of adverse effects to the composition and abundance of the fishes sampled (Holland et al., 1980; Nelson and Collins, 1987). Quantitative assessments of the effects of beach nourishment on crustacean populations, such as penaeid shrimps, have not been conducted, but these species are often found in turbid waters.

The extent and biological effects of turbidity plumes resulting from beach nourishment operations are not well understood. The state of Florida currently restricts the levels of turbidity that can occur outside a predetermined mixing zone to 29 NTUs (nephelometric turbidity units) above corresponding background samples, but this limit is not based on any published studies that would provide a clear biological rationale (Goldberg, 1989). Within the mixing zone, which has specified dimensions, turbidity is not limited. Other states generally do not have restrictions on the turbidity levels resulting from pipeline effluents, which can be high in the immediate vicinity of the outfall. For example, Van Dolah et al. (1992) conducted a limited survey of turbidity levels near the pipeline outfall of a nourishment operation at Hilton Head Island, South Carolina, and observed turbidities that were approximately 50 to 150 NTUs above background levels in an area extending approximately 200 m from the outfall. These background levels were determined under calm conditions and do not represent the maximum naturally occurring turbidity levels, which can be very high during major storms or other disturbances.

Biological resources that may be most adversely affected by elevated turbidities include many of the sessile species typically found in hard-bottom reef habitats or seagrass beds. High turbidities and silt loads can smother these organisms, inhibit filter-feeding processes, or significantly decrease photosynthetic activity, potentially resulting in long-term damage to these resources (Courtenay et al., 1974, 1980; Goldberg, 1989). Even where turbidity levels are low, nearshore reef habitats that lie within the depth of closure may be destroyed by sand burial resulting from the redistribution of beach fill material. Considerably more data are needed to evaluate the sensitivity of nearshore reef biota to high turbidity levels and changes in sediment overburdens.

The direct effects of beach nourishment operations on nearshore soft bottom communities have been evaluated by a few investigators. Table 5-2 lists the studies considered in this review. In general, these studies documented only limited or short-term alterations in the abundance, diversity, and species composition of nearshore infaunal communities sampled off new beaches. However, several of these studies had inadequate sampling designs that may have precluded detection of significant alterations in the population or community parameters measured (W. G. Nelson, 1991, 1993). Thus, although it appears that detrimental effects to the nearshore soft-bottom communities adjacent to a nourished beach may be limited, additional studies are warranted, particularly in areas where these resources have not been monitored. In addition to evaluating changes in the general community parameters and species composition of the benthic and demersal resources in these habitats, efforts should be directed toward obtaining a better understanding of functional changes in the trophic contribution of benthic assemblages to the fish and crustacean species that rely on the benthos as a major food resource.

BORROW SOURCE AREAS

There are many environmental issues related to the sites used for the source of sand material for beach nourishment projects. Potential source areas include sand deposits in upland areas; deposits in estuarine, lagoonal, or inlet systems behind the front beach; sandy shoals in channels that may be dredged for navigational purposes; and sand deposits in nearshore areas within the operational depths of dredging.

Mining sand deposits from upland areas can reduce project costs if an adequate source of sand near the projects can be transported by truck (Kana, 1990), and assessment of the impacts resulting from the mining operation is much simpler. However, upland areas with sufficient sand resources are often not near the beach nourishment site, and the quality of the fill material may be unsuitable for placement on the beach. Nourishing the beach by a trucking operation also can have substantial secondary impacts resulting from transporting the sand, such as damage to road systems and disruption of traffic and beach recreation.

Dredging sands from inshore estuarine or inlet deposits may represent another relatively low cost method of obtaining fill material, but permits to dredge these areas are often difficult to acquire because estuarine habitats serve as important nursery areas for many marine species. The quality of sand deposits in these areas is also often lower owing to an increased percentage of fines that are commonly present. When suitable sediments are available, inshore areas offer the opportunity to conduct dredging operations in relatively protected waters. This situation can reduce downtime owing to bad weather, particularly if dredging must be done during the winter months. Dredging in inland waters and inlets may also serve a dual purpose if it is tied to the maintenance of navigational channels.

Sand deposits located in nearshore ocean habitats are the most common

TABLE 5-2 Biological Monitoring Studies that Examined Intertidal and Nearshore Subtidal Beach Habitats Following Beach Nourishment Projects

Location	Nourishment Period	Type of Monitoring Conducted	Postnourishment Survey Period (years)	Reference
Lido Key, FL	1970	Subtidal: fishes	1	Holland et al. (1980)
Pompano Beach/ Lauderdale-by-the-Sea, FL	1970-72	Subtidal: hard-bottom reef biota, fishes (qualitative only)	2	Courtenay et al. (1972, 1974)
Hallandale Beach, FL	1971	Intertidal, subtidal: macroinfauna	7*	Marsh et al. (1980)
Cape Hatteras, NC	1973	Intertidal: macroinfauna	< 0.1	Hayden and Dolan (1974)
Panama City Beach, FL	1976	Swash zone, subtidal: macroinfauna	1-4	Culter and Mahadevan (1982), Saloman et al. (1982)
Imperial Beach, CA	1977	Intertidal, subtidal: macroinfauna	0.5	Parr et al. (1978)
Ft. Macon Beach, NC	1977-78	Intertidal: macroinfauna, microalgae	0.25	Reilly and Bellis (1978)
Delray Beach, FL	1978	Subtidal: hard-bottom reef biota	5	Arthur V. Strock and Assoc. (1983)
Melbourne Beach, FL	1980-81	Intertidal, subtidal: macroinfauna	1	Gorzelany and Nelson (1987)
Pompano Beach/ Lauderdale-by-the-Sea, FL	1983	Intertidal, subtidal: macroinfauna, hard-bottom reef biota	< 0.1	Continental Shelf Assoc. and Tropical Ecosystems, Inc. (1984)
Delray Beach, FL	1984	Intertidal, subtidal: macroinfauna, hard-bottom reef biota	1	Coastal Planning and Engineering (1987), Goldberg (1985)
Myrtle Beach, SC	1986-87	Intertidal, subtidal: macroinfauna	3	Baca and Lankford (1988)
Key Biscayne, FL	1987	Subtidal: submerged aquatic vegetation	1	Flynn et al. (1991)

Location	Year	Biota		Reference
Boca Raton, FL	1988	Subtidal: hard-bottom reef biota, macroinfauna	3	Coastal Planning and Engineering (1992)
Captiva Island, FL	1988-89	Subtidal: macroinfauna2		Continental Shelf Assoc. (1992); Deis et al. (1992)
Upham Park Beach, FL	1991	Subtidal: macroinfauna1		Bell (1992)
Hallendale Beach, FL	1991	Subtidal: hard-bottom reef biota, macroinfauna1		Fisher et al. (1992)
Hilton Head Island, SC1990		Intertidal, subtidal: macroinfauna	1	Van Dolah et al. (1992)
Folly Beach, SC	1993	Intertidal, subtidal: macroinfauna	1	Van Dolah et al. (1994)
		Subtidal: fish and invertebrates, plankton	1	

*Only one sampling period 7 years after project construction.

source of beach fill material. Possible sources include low-tide bars or accreting beaches, ebb-tide deltas around inlets, and offshore sand deposits. Offshore deposits provide as much as 95 percent of the sand for beach nourishment projects at this time. Sediment composition in these areas is often nearly compatible with the beach to be nourished, but costs may be greater if the borrow site is not located near the project area or if downtime is increased owing to sea conditions in which dredging operations are unworkable.

The long-term physical alterations resulting from the dredging of sand borrow sites in estuarine and marine habitats have not been well documented. The borrow areas are often surveyed immediately after dredging to obtain estimates of the volume of material removed, but subsequent monitoring of bottom bathymetry and sediment composition have been examined in only a few studies (see Table 5-3). The majority of those studies have shown decreases in the mean grain size, including, in some cases, increases in the percentage of silts and clays in the borrow sites following dredging. Data on the refilling rates of borrow pits are especially lacking, but both published and unpublished observations suggest that many borrow areas used in past nourishment projects had not filled in or were filling at a slow rate when they were reexamined (Watts, 1963). This point has significant environmental implications because long-term renourishment programs may require the use of several borrow areas that will be altered both physically and biologically for extended periods.

The physical effects of inshore and offshore borrow areas on surrounding habitats generally have not been evaluated. In estuarine areas, large borrow sites may affect tidal prisms, current flow, and bottom bathymetry in areas surrounding the site. In nearshore and offshore areas, creation of a borrow pit may affect the stability of ebb-tide shoals or reduce sediment transport to areas down-current of the borrow site. Wave energy and the stability of the beach may also be affected if the borrow site lies within the depth of closure.

The primary biological effect of dredging borrow sites is the removal of benthic assemblages inhabiting the surficial sediments. This change may indirectly affect other species that use the benthos as a major food source. Dredging activities can also increase turbidity in the vicinity of the borrow area, both during dredging and afterwards if the site accumulates silts and clays (Naqvi and Pullen, 1982; Goldberg, 1989; Grober, 1992). Deep holes may also result in altered water-quality conditions, such as decreased dissolved oxygen levels or increased hydrogen sulfide levels (Murawski, 1969; Saloman, 1974). This problem may be more likely to occur in protected waters that do not have good circulation. Further, dredging operations have been known to damage reef habitats in areas adjacent to the borrow area when buffer areas have been inadequate (Grober, 1992). This latter problem is avoidable, however, by requiring adequate buffer zones and using accurate positioning systems.

Recovery of the benthic communities in borrow sites following the dredging operation has been studied in a few areas (see Table 5-3 for a list of studies

8

TABLE 5-3 Physical and Biological Monitoring Studies that Examined Borrow Areas Used for Beach Nourishment Projects

Location	Dredging Period	Type of Monitoring Conducted	Postdredging Survey Period (years)	Reference
Harrison County, MS	1951	Physical: filling rate, sediment type	7	Watts (1963)
Revere Beach, MA	1954	Physical: filling rate, sediment type	8	Watts (1963)
Prospect Beach, MA	1957	Physical: filling rate, sediment type	3	Watts (1963)
Hillsboro Beach, FL	1971	Physical: filling rate, sediment type; Biological: macroinfauna	(?)	Turbeville and Marsh (1982); Wilber and Stern (1992)
Panama City, FL	1976	Physical: sediment type; Biological: macroinfauna	1-4	Saloman et al. (1982); Culter and Mahadevan (1982)
Delray Beach, FL	1978	Physical: sediment type; Biological: macroinfauna	1	Bowen and Marsh (1988); Wilber and Stern (1992)
Delray Beach, FL	1984	Physical: sediment type; Biological: macroinfauna, adjacent reef biota	1	Coastal Planning and Engineering (1987)
Ft. Pierce Inlet, FL	1980	Physical: sediment type; Biological: macroinfauna	1	Johnson and Nelson (1985)
Lauderdale-by-the-Sea, FL	1983	Biological: macrofauna	1	Continental Shelf Assoc. and Tropical Pompano Beach Ecosystems (1984); Wilber and Stern (1992)
Boca Raton, SC	1988	Physical: sediment type; Biological: macroinfauna	3	Coastal Planning and Engineering (1992)
Captiva Beach, FL	1988-89	Physical: sediment type; Biological: macroinfauna	2	Continental Shelf Associates (1992); Deis et al. (1992)
Hilton Head Island, SC	1990	Physical: sediment type; Biological: macroinfauna	1-2	Van Dolah et al. (1992, 1993)
Buckroe Beach, VA	1990	Physical: filling rate, sediment type; Biological: macroinfauna	2.5	Hobbs (1993); Schaffner and Hobbs (1992)
Folly Beach, SC	1993	Physical: sediment type; Biological: macroinfauna	1	Van Dolah et al. (1994)

considered in this review). Results from these studies indicate that recovery periods have been quite variable, ranging in duration from a few months to several years. The abundance and diversity of benthic fauna within the borrow sites often returned to levels comparable to prenourishment or reference conditions within a relatively short time (less than 1 year). However, several studies documented changes in the species composition of the benthos that lasted much longer, particularly in areas where bottom sediment composition was altered (Johnson and Nelson, 1985; Bowen and Marsh, 1988; Van Dolah et al., 1992, 1993; Wilber and Stern, 1992). The consequences of these long-term alterations are not well understood, especially with respect to how changes in species composition affect the functional structure and trophic contribution of these communities to marine predators that rely on the benthos as a primary food source. In some cases, long-term changes in the bottom habitat may alter the bottom communities or bottom habitats in a way that is perceived to be an improvement over the preexisting condition. For example, dredging down to hard substrata may result in increased biological diversity through the creation of reef habitat.

Based on the limited number of studies that have been conducted in borrow areas to date, there appears to be considerable variability in the physical and ecological responses that have occurred after completion of a project. More monitoring should be conducted to resolve whether these areas return to the physical and biological conditions that existed before dredging and, if so, how long it takes. This monitoring is particularly needed in regions where there has been little, if any, physical or biological monitoring of borrow areas used for beach nourishment projects. Until there is a better understanding of the ecological consequences of these projects, the most prudent action would be to design projects so that alterations in the physical conditions and biological resources of a borrow site are minimized or are short term relative to the planned frequency of renourishment.

RESTORATION OF ABANDONED PROJECTS

In Chapter 2, in the discussion of economic issues, it was clearly stated that beach renourishment may not continue to be a viable alternative indefinitely. That is, even for those programs that are presently viable, future conditions may change such that they are abandoned. Abandoning a beach nourishment project has certain predictable results. In the case of projects utilizing hard structures, as described in Chapter 4, those structures may be required to be removed upon abandonment of the project. However, there are other, perhaps more significant, consequences from other structures such as homes and streets. Although these are not strictly a part of the beach protection process, the environmental impacts of allowing these structures to remain in the face of an eroding shoreline are such that the problem needs to be firmly addressed in state and local coastal plans. In particular, the restoration of dunes and dune plants in any area that was previously developed and now has become part of the active beach because of abandonment strategies now becomes a critical requirement. It appears that federal funding would not be available to assist in this operation under present regulations, so state and local agencies must plan for adequate resources to accomplish these objectives. Studies of the restoration of aquatic ecosystems (NRC, 1992) and on restoring marine habitat (NRC, 1994) provide guidance for these activities.

REFERENCES

Ackerman, R. A. 1991. Physical factors affecting the water exchange of buried eggs. Pp. 193-211 in C. Deeming, and M. Gerguson, eds., Egg Incubation—Its Effect on Embryonic Development in Birds and Reptiles. Cambridge, England: Cambridge University Press.

Ackerman, R. A., T. Rimkus, and R. Horton. 1991. The Hydric Structure and Climate of Natural and Renourished Sea Turtle Nesting Beaches Along the Atlantic Coast of Florida. Unpublished report prepared by Iowa State University for Florida Department of Natural Resources, Tallahassee.

Ackerman, R. A., T. Rimkus, and R. Horton. 1992. Hydric and Thermal Characteristics of Natural and Renourished Sea Turtle Nesting Beaches Along the Atlantic Coast of Florida. Unpublished report prepared by Iowa State University for Florida Department of Natural Resources, Tallahassee.

Baca, B. J., and T. E. Lankford. 1988. Myrtle Beach nourishment project. Biological monitoring report Years 1, 2, 3 submitted to City of Myrtle Beach by Coastal Science and Engineering, Inc. CSE87-88 R-11. 46 p.

Bell, S. S. 1992. Upham Park beach nourishment project. The effect of sedimentation on macroinfauna, one year post-nourishment studies. Report submitted to Pinellas County Coastal Management Division, Clearwater, Fla. 27 pp.

Bowen, P. R., and G. A. Marsh. 1988. Benthic Faunal Colonization of an Offshore Borrow Pit in Southeastern Florida. Miscellaneous Paper D-88-5. Vicksburg, Miss.: U.S. Army Engineer Waterways Experiment Station, U.S. Army Corps of Engineers.

Broadwell, A. L. 1991. Effects of Beach Renourishment on the Survival of Loggerhead Sea Turtles. Unpublished master's thesis, Florida Atlantic University.

Coastal Planning and Engineering, Inc. 1987. Environmental monitoring report for the 1984 Delray Beach Maintenance Nourishment Project. Boca Raton, Fla. 25 pp.

Coastal Planning and Engineering, Inc. 1992. Boca Raton Beach Restoration Project: Three Year Post-Construction, Vol. I. Environmental monitoring report prepared for the city of Boca Raton, Fla.

Continental Shelf Associates, Inc. 1992. Boca Raton beach restoration project. Three year post-construction. Vol. I. Environmental monitoring report prepared for the City of Boca Raton, Fla.

Continental Shelf Associates, Inc. (Jupiter/Tequesta, Fla.) and Tropical Ecosystems, Inc. (West Palm Beach, Fla.). 1984. Biological analysis of macroepibiotal and macroinfaunal assemblages following beach nourishment in North Broward County, Florida. Study prepared for the Broward County Environmental Quality Control Board. 30 pp.

Courtenay, W. R., Jr., D. J. Herrema, M. J. Thompson, W. P. Azzinaro, and J. Van Montfrons. 1972. Ecological monitoring of two beach nourishment projects in Broward County, Florida. Shore and Beach 40:9-13.

Courtenay, W. R., Jr., D. J. Herrema, M. J. Thompson, W. D. Azzinaro, and J. van Montfrans. 1974. Ecological Monitoring of Beach Erosion Control Project, Broward County, Florida and Adjacent Areas. Technical Memorandum No. 41. Washington, D.C.: Coastal Engineering Research Center, U.S. Army Corps of Engineers.

Courtenay, W. R., Jr., B. C. Hartig, and G. R. Loisel. 1980. Ecological Evaluation of a Beach Nourishment Project at Hallandale (Broward County), Florida: Evaluation of Fish Populations Adjacent to Borrow Areas of Beach Nourishment Project, Hallandale (Broward County), Florida, Vol. I. Miscellaneous Report 80-1(I). Fort Belvoir, Va.: Coastal Engineering Research Center, U.S. Army Corps of Engineers.

Croker, R. A., R. P. Hager, and K. J. Scott. 1975. Macroinfauna of northern New England marine sand, Vol. II. Amphipod-dominated communities. Canadian Journal of Zoology 53:42–51.

Culter, J. K., and S. Mahadevan. 1982. Long-term effects of beach nourishment on the benthic fauna of Panama City Beach, Florida. U.S. Army Corps of Engineers, Coastal Engineering Research Center, Misc. Rept. No. 82-2.

Dahl, E. 1952. Some aspects of the ecology and zonation of the fauna on sandy beaches. Oikos 4:1-27.

Deis, D. R., K. W. Spring, and A. D. Hart. 1992. Captiva Beach restoration project—biological monitoring program. Pp. 227-241 in New Directions in Beach Management: Proceedings of the 5th Annual National Conference on Beach Preservation Technology. Tallahassee, Fla.: Florida Shore and Beach Preservation Association.

Dexter, D. M. 1972. Comparison of the community structure in a Pacific and Atlantic Panamanian sandy beach. Bulletin Marine Science 22:449-462.

Dodd, C. K., Jr. 1988. Synopsis of the Biological Data on the Loggerhead Sea Turtle, *Caretta caretta* (Linnaeus, 1758). Biological Report 88(14), FAO Synopsis NMFS-149. Washington, D.C.: U.S. Fish and Wildlife Service.

Federal Register. 1993. Endangered and threatened wildlife and plants; *Amaranthus pumilus* (Seabeach Amaranth) determined to be threatened. 50 CFR Part 17, Vol. 58. No. 65.

Fisher, L. E., R. E. Dodge, C. G. Messing, W. M. Goldberg, and S. Hess. 1992. The first renourishment at Hollywood and Hallandale (Florida) beaches: Monitoring of sediment fallout, coral communities and macroinfauna: preliminary results. Pp. 209-227 in S. Tait, ed., New Directions in Beach Management. Proceedings of the 5th Annual National Conference on Beach Preservation Technology. Florida Shore and Beach Preservation Association.

Flynn, B. 1992. Beach nourishment, sea turtle nesting, and nest relocation in Dade County, Florida. Proceedings of the 1992 National Conference on Beach Preservation Technology. St. Petersburg, Fla.

Flynn, B. S., S. M. Blair, and S. M. Markley. 1991. Environmental monitoring of the Key Biscayne beach restoration project. Pp. 234-247 in S. Tait, ed., Preserving and Enhancing Our Beach Environment. Proceedings of the 1991 National Conference on Beach Preservation Technology. Florida Shore and Beach Preservation Association.

Goldberg, W. M. 1985. Long term effects of beach restoration in Broward County, Florida. A three year overview. Unpublished report to Broward County Environmental Quality Control Board and Erosion Prevention District. 51 pp.

Goldberg, W. M. 1989. Biological effects of beach nourishment in south Florida: the good, the bad and the ugly. In: Proceedings of Beach Preservation Technology 1988. Tallahassee: Florida Shore and Beach Preservation Association.

Gorzelany, F. J., and W. G. Nelson. 1987. The effects of beach replenishment on the benthos of a subtropical Florida beach. Marine Environmental Research 21:75-94.

Grober, L. E. 1992. The Ecological Effects of Beach Replenishment. Unpublished master's thesis, Duke University School of the Environment.

Hayden, B., and R. Dolan. 1974. Impact of beach nourishment on distribution of *Emerita talpoida*, the common mole crab. J. Waterways, Harbors and Coastal Engineering Division. American Society of Civil Engineers 100:123-132.

Higgins, S. 1993. Long-term benefits of turtle nest relocation and protection programs at Broward County and Jupiter Island, Florida. In: Sixth Annual National Conference on Beach Preservation Technology. Tallahassee: Florida Shore and Beach Preservation Association.

Hobbs, C. H., III. 1993. Sand mining in lower Chesapeake Bay: A progress report. Marine Georesources and Geotechnology 11: 347-352.

Holland, H. T., J. R. Chambers, and R. R. Backman. 1980. Effects of Dredging and Filling for Beach Erosion Control on Fishes in the Vicinity of Lido Key, Florida. Unpublished report. Jacksonville, Fla.: Jacksonville District, U.S. Army Corps of Engineers.

Jaap, W. C. 1984. The Ecology of the South Florida Coral Reefs: A Community Profile. Report No. EWS/OBS-82/08. Washington, D.C.: U.S. Fish and Wildlife Service.

Johnson, R. O., and W. G. Nelson. 1985. Biological effects of dredging in an offshore borrow area. Florida Scientist 48:166-188.

Kana, T. W. 1990. Conserving South Carolina Beaches Through the 1990s: A Case for Beach Nourishment. Report prepared for South Carolina Coastal Council, Charleston, S. C.

Knott, D. M., D. R. Calder, and R. F. Van Dolah. 1983. Macrobenthos of sandy beach and nearshore environments at Murrell's Inlet, South Carolina, USA, estuarine coast. Shelf Scientist 16:573-590.

LeBuff, C. R., Jr., and E. M. Haverfield. 1990. Nesting success of the loggerhead turtle (*Caretta caretta*) on Captiva Island, Florida, a nourished beach. Unpublished data. Sanibel Island, Fla.: Caretta Research.

Lynch, A. E. 1994. Macrofaunal recolonization of Folly Beach, South Carolina, After Beach Nourishment. Unpublished master's thesis, University of Charleston, Charleston, S. C.

Marsh, G. A., P. R. Bowen, D. R. Deis, D. B. Turbeville, and W. R. Courtenay, Jr. 1980. Ecological Evaluation of a Beach Nourishment Project at Hallandale (Broward County), Florida. Vol. II. Evaluation of Benthic Communities Adjacent to a Restored Beach, Hallandale (Broward County), Florida. Miscellaneous Report 80-1(II). Fort Belvoir, Va.: Coastal Engineering Research Center, U.S. Army Corps of Engineers.

Maurer, D., R. Keck, J. C. Tinsman, W. A. Leathem, C. A. Wethe, M. Huntzinger, C. Lord, and T. M. Church. 1978. Vertical Migration of Benthos in Simulated Dredged Material Overburdens. Vol. I: Marine Benthos. DMRP Technical Report D-78-35. Report prepared by University of Delaware, College of Marine Studies. Vicksburg, Miss.: U.S. Army Engineer Waterways Experiment Station, U.S. Army Corps of Engineers.

Maurer, D., R. Keck, J. C. Tinsman, and W. A. Leathem. 1981a. Vertical migration and mortality of benthos in dredged material. I. Mollusca-Mar. Environmental Research 4:299-319.

Maurer, D., R. Keck, J. C. Tinsman, and W. A. Leathem. 1981b. Vertical migration and mortality of benthos in dredged material. II. Crustacea-Mar. Environmental Research 5:301-317.

Maurer, D., R. Keck, J. C. Tinsman, and W. A. Leathem. 1982. Vertical migration and mortality of benthos in dredged material. III. Crustacea-Mar. Environmental Research 6:49-68.

Maurer, D., R. T. Keck, H. C. Tinsman, W. A. Leathem, C. Wethe, C. Lord, and T. M. Church. 1986. Vertical migration and mortality of marine benthos in dredged material; a synthesis. International Revue Hydrobiology 71:49-63.

Melvin, S. M., C. R. Griffin, and L. H. MacIvor. 1991. Recovery strategies for piping plovers in managed coastal landscapes. Coastal Management 19:21-34.

Murawski, W. S. 1969. A Study of Submerged Dredge Holes in New Jersey Estuaries with Respect to Their Fitness as Finfish Habitat. Miscellaneous Report No. 2M. Division of Fish and Game, New Jersey Department of Conservation and Economic Development.

Naqvi, S., and E. Pullen. 1982. Effects of Beach Nourishment and Borrowing on Marine Organisms. Miscellaneous Report No. 82-14. Fort Belvoir, Va.: Coastal Engineering Research Center, U.S. Army Corps of Engineers.

Nelson, D. A. 1991. Issues associated with beach nourishment and sea turtle nesting. Pp. 277-294 in Preserving and Enhancing Our Beach Environment: Proceedings of the 4th Annual National Beach Preservation Technology Conference. Tallahassee: Florida Shore and Beach Preservation Association.

Nelson, D. A., and D. Dickerson. 1988. Hardness of Nourished and Natural Sea Turtle Nesting Beaches on the East Coast of Florida. Unpublished report. Vicksburg, Miss.: U.S. Army Engineer Waterways Experiment Station, U.S. Army Corps of Engineers.

Nelson, D. A., K. A. Mauck, and J. Fletemeyer. 1987. Physical Effects of Beach Nourishment on Sea Turtle Nesting, Delray Beach, Florida. Technical Report No. TR-87-15. Vicksburg, Miss.: U.S. Army Engineer Waterways Experiment Station, U.S. Army Corps of Engineers.

Nelson, W. G. 1985. Physical and Biological Guidelines for Beach Restoration Projects. Part I. Biological Guidelines. Report No. 76. Florida Sea Grant College, Gainesville.

Nelson, W. G. 1989. An overview of the effects of beach nourishment on the sand beach fauna. Pp. 295-309 in Proceedings of the 1988 National Conference on Beach Preservation Technology. Tallahassee: Florida Shore and Beach Preservation Association.

Nelson, W. G. 1990. Beach nourishment and hard-bottom habitats: the case for caution. Pp. 109-116 in Proceedings of the 1989 National Conference on Beach Preservation Technology. Tallahassee: Florida Shore and Beach Preservation Association.

Nelson, W. G. 1991. Methods of biological monitoring of beach restoration projects: problems and solutions in the real world. Pp. 263-276 in Preserving and Enhancing Our Beach Environment: Proceedings of the 1991 National Conference on Beach Preservation Technology. Tallahassee: Florida Shore and Beach Preservation Association.

Nelson, W. G. 1993. Beach restoration in the southeastern US: environmental effects and biological monitoring. Ocean and Coastal Management 19:157-182.

Nelson, W. G., and G. W. Collins. 1987. Effects of Beach Nourishment on the Benthic Macrofauna and Fishes of the Nearshore Zone of Sebastian Inlet State Recreation Area. Unpublished report to Jacksonville District, U.S. Army Corps of Engineers from the Department of Oceanology and Ocean Engineering, Florida Institute of Technology.

NRC. 1992. Restoration of Aquatic Ecosystems: Science, Technology, and Public Policy. Water Science Board, Commission on Geosciences, Environment, and Resources. Washington, D.C.: National Academy Press.

NRC. 1994. Restoring and Protecting Marine Habitat. Marine Board, Commission on Engineering and Technical Systems. Washington, D.C.: National Academy Press.

Paar, T., D. Diener, and S. Lacy. 1978. Effects of Beach Replenishment on the Nearshore Sand Fauna at Imperial Beach, California. Miscellaneous Report 78-4. Fort Belvoir, Va.: Coastal Engineering Research Center, U.S. Army Corps of Engineers.

Rackocinski, C., S. E. LeCroy, J. A. McLelland, and R. W. Heard. 1991. Responses by Macroinvertebrate Communities to Beach Nourishment at Perdido Key, Florida: Initial Faunal Impact. Semiannual Report No. GCRL 03:06-30-91 prepared by Gulf Coast Research Laboratory. Ocean Springs, Miss.: National Park Service.

Rackocinski, C., S. E. LeCroy, J. A. McLelland, and R. Heard. 1992. Responses by Macroinvertebrate Communities to Beach Renourishment at Perdido Key, Florida: monitoring phase. Semiannual Report No. GCRL 05:06-30-92 prepared by Gulf Coast Research Laboratory. Ocean Springs, Miss.: National Park Service.

Raymond, P. W. 1984. The Effects of Beach Restoration on Marine Turtles Nesting in South Broward County, Florida. Unpublished master's thesis, University of Central Florida, Orlando.

Reilly, F., Jr. 1979. A Study of the Ecological Impact of Beach Nourishment with Dredged Materials on the Intertidal Zone. Unpublished master's thesis, East Carolina University.

Reilly, F., Jr., and V. Bellis. 1978. A Study of the Ecological Impact of Beach Nourishment with Dredged Material on the Intertidal Zone. Technical Report No. 4. Institute for Coastal and Marine Resources, East Carolina University.

Ryder, C. E. 1992. The effect of beach renourishment at Sebastian Inlet State Recreation Area. Unpublished master's thesis, Virginia Polytechnic Institute, Blacksburg.

Saloman, C., S. Naughton, and J. Taylor. 1982. Benthic Community Response to Dredging Borrow Pits, Panama City Beach, Florida. Miscellaneous Report No. 82-3. Fort Belvoir, Va.: Coastal Engineering Research Center, U.S. Army Corps of Engineers.

Schaffner, L. C., and C. H. Hobbs, III. 1992. Effects of sand-mining on benthic communities and resource value: Thimble Shoal, lower Chesapeake Bay. Technical report from the Virginia Institute of Marine Science, Gloucester Point, Va. under contract with the Virginia Department of Conservation and Recreation via the Joint Commonwealth Programs Addressing Shore Erosion in Virginia.

Shelton, C. R., and P. B. Robertson. 1981. Community structure of intertidal macrofauna on two surf-exposed Texas sandy beaches. Bulletin of Marine Sciences 31:833-842.

Spadoni, R. H. 1993. Environmental impacts of beach erosion. Presentation made at the Florida Shore and Beach Preservation Association Technical Conference on the "State of the Art in Beach Nourishment," St. Petersburg, Fla., February 10, 1993.

Spadoni, R. H., and S. L. Cummings. 1992. A common sense approach to the protection of marine turtles. New Directions in Beach Management: Proceedings of the 5th Annual National Conference on Beach Preservation Technology. Tallahassee: Florida Shore and Beach Preservation Association.

Steinitz, J. 1990. Reproductive Success of Sea Turtles on Jupiter Island, Florida, 1990. Unpublished report prepared for town of Jupiter Island.

Strock, A. V., and Associates, Inc. 1983. Five year environmental follow-up reef survey for the 1978 Delray Beach maintenance nourishment project. Report submitted to the City of Delray Beach, Florida. 23 p.

Trevallion, A., A. D. Ansell, P. Sivadas, and B. Narayanan. 1970. A preliminary account of two sand beaches in southwest India. Marine Biology 6:268-279.

Turbeville, D. B., and G. A. Marsh. 1982. Benthic fauna of an offshore borrow area in Broward County, Florida. U.S. Army Corps of Engineers Coastal Engineering Research Center. Misc. report 82-1. pp. 1-43.

USFWS. 1993. Endangered and Threatened Wildlife and Plants. Notice 50 CFR 17.11 and 17.12, August 23. Washington, D.C.: U.S. Fish and Wildlife Service.

Van Dolah, R. F., and D. M. Knott. 1984. A Biological Assessment of Beach and Nearshore Areas Along the South Carolina Grand Strand. Final report. Agreement No. 14-16-004-84-924. Prepared for the U.S. Department of the Interior. Charleston, S. C.: U.S. Fish and Wildlife Service.

Van Dolah, R. F., P. H. Wendt, R. M. Martore, M. V. Levisen, and W. A. Roumillat. 1992. A Physical and Biological Monitoring Study of the Hilton Head Beach Nourishment Project. Unpublished report prepared by South Carolina Wildlife and Marine Resources Department for Town of Hilton Head Island, S. C.

Van Dolah, R. F., R. M. Martore, and M. V. Levisen. 1993. Physical and Biological Monitoring Study of the Hilton Head Beach Nourishment Project. Supplemental report prepared by the South Carolina Marine Resources Research Institute for the town of Hilton Head Island, S. C.

Van Dolah, R. F., R. M. Martore, A. E. Lynch, M. V. Levisen, P. H. Wendt, D. J. Whitaker, and W. D. Anderson. 1994. Environmental Evaluation of the Folly Beach Nourishment Project. Final report, Charleston District, U.S. Army Corps of Engineers, and the Marine Resources Division, South Carolina Department of Natural Resources.

Watts, G. M. 1963. Behavior of offshore borrow zones in beach fill operations. Pp. 17-24 in International Association for Hydraulic Research (IAHR) Tenth Congress, Vol. 1. London: IAHR.

Wilber, P., and M. Stern. 1992. A re-examination of infaunal studies that accompany beach nourish-
    ment projects. Pp. 242-257 in New Directions in Beach Management: Proceedings of the 5th
    Annual National Conference on Beach Preservation Technology. Tallahassee: Florida Shore
    and Beach Preservation Association.
Williams, S.J., S. Penland, and A.H. Sallenger Jr., eds. 1992. Louisiana barrier island erosion study.
    Atlas of Shoreline Changes in Louisiana from 1853 to 1989. USGS Misc. Inv. Series. No. I-
    2150-A. 107 pp.
Williams, A. B. 1984. Shrimps, lobsters, and crabs of the Atlantic coast of the eastern United States,
    Maine to Florida. Washington, D.C.: Smithsonian Institution Press.
Witham, R. 1990. A case report on beach erosion, beach nourishment, and sea turtle nesting. Pp.
    157-160 in Proceedings of the 10th Annual Workshop on Sea Turtle Biology and Conservation.
    NOAA Technical Memorandum NMFS-SEFC-278. Washington, D.C.: National Oceanic and
    Atmospheric Administration.

6

Monitoring

Time-series data can help establish the need for, and evaluate the performance of, beach nourishment programs and projects. This chapter discusses the need for physical, environmental, and economic time-series data and issues surrounding the evaluation of beach nourishment project performance.

OVERVIEW

Monitoring is the systematic collection of physical, environmental, or economic time-series data or a combination of these data on a beach nourishment project in order to make decisions regarding the need for or operation of the project or to evaluate the project's performance. Beach nourishment projects are continually responding to storms and seasonal changes in the physical and biological environments. Thus, their dimensions and the level of protection they provide usually decrease with time. The level of protection at any given time may also vary along the beach in a given project.

These data are needed to address the management questions listed in Box 6-1. Data acquisition programs must be designed with a clear definition of what data are needed and how the data will eventually be used. The objectives must be clearly defined at the outset, and the monitoring program must be designed to meet those objectives. Too often, data are collected without consideration for their analysis or how they will be used to make decisions. As a result, data collected at considerable expense may never be fully analyzed or, if analyzed, will not provide the answers needed (NRC, 1990). Obviously, appropriate mea-

---

BOX 6-1
Management Questions Requiring an
Effective Monitoring Regime

- Is this beach nourishment project needed and justified?
- Can a viable beach nourishment project be constructed and maintained at the project site?
- Is the project providing satisfactory remediation or control of chronic beach erosion?
- Are upland areas being protected from waves and coastal flooding?
- Is the project replacing lost recreational beaches?
- Are new beaches and/or dunes being formed?
- Do economic benefits exceed project construction, operation, and maintenance costs?
- Have unacceptable environmental impacts occurred?
- How can these adverse impacts be avoided in the future?
- When is renourishment necessary?
- Should future renourishment procedures be modified?
- When should alternate borrow sources be sought?
- When should structures be included as part of a project to increase the time between periodic renourishments?
- When should existing structures be modified to reduce adverse effects on project beaches and adjacent beaches?
- When should the permeability of terminal structures be decreased to hold more sand within a project area?

---

surements must be made at a suitable frequency to permit decision makers to use the information in renourishment activities.

Types of Monitoring

The physical processes monitored are usually those that move sand within and away from the project area—the fate of the sand—and those that cause elevated water levels. Often, many physical monitoring programs address only the beach's response to sand-moving forces and do not include important forces such as waves and currents.

Environmental monitoring is undertaken to document a project's effects on the biota of the nourishment project. It involves collecting data on the impacts that projects have on the flora and fauna in a project area and in adjacent areas. Biological data are obtained to determine whether any short- or long-term changes have occurred to the biota. Data need to be obtained on the beach where sand is placed and in any offshore borrow areas. Preconstruction data on species diversity, species composition, and numbers are compared with data taken during the life of the nourishment project. For example, the monitoring of turtle nesting areas during the nesting season may be conducted to ensure protection of nesting sites. These efforts must be carefully designed to eliminate seasonal effects that may bias conclusions.

Economic monitoring is undertaken to evaluate the economic impacts of a project and to determine whether predicted economic benefits were actually realized, whether other unanticipated benefits resulted, whether projected construction costs were correct, and whether hidden costs were incurred. It involves determining whether a project's economic justification was valid.

Purposes of Monitoring

Monitoring is undertaken for various purposes. *Operational monitoring* may simply involve periodic inspections to determine the need for remedial action. Such remedial actions might include renourishment, structure repairs, and other maintenance. Operational monitoring includes both pre- and poststorm monitoring and the assessment of project performance. *Performance monitoring* is undertaken to develop information and procedures for design verification and to document lessons learned that may be applied in the design of future projects.

Phases of Monitoring

Monitoring phases coincide with project phases: preconstruction monitoring, construction monitoring, and postconstruction monitoring.

Preconstruction monitoring involves collection of data on the physical and biological environments that describe regional and site-specific processes. It includes collecting data helpful for design as well as baseline biological data. Physical data are needed on waves, currents, water levels, beach composition and profiles, and meteorological conditions. Baseline biological data include information on habitat type and physical conditions, species composition and abundance, and distribution patterns.

Preconstruction economic data are also important and may be collected as part of the cost-benefit analysis for the project. Specifically, surveys of beach users (including information that would support both travel cost and contingent valuation analyses) are important. In addition, preconstruction assessments of the market value of commercial and residential real estate in the area would contribute to a hedonic analysis of the effects of beach nourishment on property values.

Construction monitoring involves collecting data on how much sand was actually placed and where, on short-term effects construction may have caused, and on the materials that were actually used (e.g., the size of the sand placed on the beach). Monitoring may include the effects of construction-induced turbidity on the biota as well as recreational values lost during construction if construction takes place during the recreational season.

Postconstruction monitoring involves systematic collection of data after construction is complete to study the project's performance. Is it functioning as intended? What, if any, are its adverse effects? What are its short- and long-term biological impacts? What economic benefits did it actually provide? What monetary costs were actually incurred, and what additional costs were imposed on the area when it was time to renourish?

Scale and Duration of Monitoring Programs

The scale of monitoring is generally related to the scale of the project itself. Smaller projects may require only simple inexpensive measurements that provide the information needed to make operational decisions. However, for small projects with a potential for significant impacts, more extensive monitoring, commensurate with the project's potential for physical and biological enhancements, damage and economic loss, may be needed. For larger-scale projects, a more comprehensive monitoring program is warranted.

Monitoring needs to be undertaken in order to apply the findings to the design of subsequent nourishment efforts. For example, if a borrow site experiences long-term adverse impacts, a different borrow site or configuration must be selected. If beach fauna show only limited impacts during nourishment, monitoring of these impacts may not be necessary in subsequent renourishments or for similar nourishment projects. The analysis of data from an effective monitoring program would provide feedback to the design process. Monitoring the post-construction economic impact of beach nourishment projects has not been widespread. There have been few follow-up analyses of projects to determine whether projected benefits were actually realized, whether secondary benefits occurred, or if unanticipated costs could be attributed to the project (Stronge, 1992a, 1994).

Monitoring programs need to be evaluated periodically and adjusted to meet the needs of a project. As experience is gained with a project, some measurements may be phased out or the frequency with which they are taken reduced. For example, the infilling of a borrow area may show significant changes only following major storms; consequently, surveys need to be conducted only after such storms. Similarly, after a period of years, seasonal variations in a beach's profiles may be known, so frequent beach surveys become unnecessary.

PHYSICAL MONITORING

Monitoring the physical processes associated with a beach nourishment project needs to be done within the framework of a sediment budget for the project area and, when relevant, adjacent areas. A sediment budget requires that all sand sources and sinks be identified and quantified for a defined sediment budget area. The gains and losses are balanced against the changes in sand volume in the area. Sand sources include rivers, local bluff erosion, and alongshore transport from adjacent areas. Sinks include ebb- and flood-tide shoals, wind transport of sand to back bay areas, losses to submarine canyons, and sand carried out of the area by alongshore transport.

Monitoring data collected to quantify the physical processes that comprise sources, sinks, and sand volume changes in a project area can include:

- the previous history of the coastal site,
- beach profiles,
- waves,
- currents,
- water levels,
- structures,
- sediment characteristics, and
- photographic documentation.

Previous History of Site

The history of a coastal site can provide important information on how a beach nourishment project may perform. Historical data may include anecdotal information in addition to well-documented information on the physical environment and on the performance of earlier coastal projects. Information may include:

- historical erosion rates from aerial photographs or shoreline-change maps;
- relative changes/trends in sea level;
- astronomical tides;
- local anthropogenic impacts, such as past nourishments;
- documented information on historical storms and wave climate; and
- assessment of the geological setting (i.e., the type of underlying geology that may influence coastal processes and the sediment budget).

Beach Profiles

Changes in the volume of sand in a beach nourishment project along with the width of the subaerial beach can be documented by periodic beach profile surveys. Factors to be considered in establishing a beach profile survey program include:

- profile line spacing,
- profile length (from dune line to depth of closure),
- survey frequency, and
- surveying procedures.

Knowledge of the profile line spacing and length permits the accurate definition of sand volumes in a project area and in adjacent areas that might receive sand from the project. To accomplish this, profile lines must extend seaward to the profile closure depth. Survey frequency varies over the life of a project. Initially, surveys need to be conducted often enough to quantify seasonal changes. For example, quarterly surveys may be needed because of profile adjustments following construction, but subsequent project performance may permit less frequent surveys. Because substantial changes can occur as a result of major storms, it is prudent to conduct pre- and poststorm surveys in order to quantify the effects of individual storms. Various surveying procedures can be used. Onshore surveys can be conducted with standard level-rod surveying procedures. Offshore surveys extending to wading or swimming depths can also use standard level-rod procedures. However, surveys in deep water (soundings) require special equipment and procedures such as echo sounders or survey sleds. When two different survey procedures are employed onshore and offshore (often on different days), the two surveys must be overlapped and spliced in the surf zone—a region where elevation changes are significant and rapid. A survey sled avoids this problem because it allows a single survey procedure to be used across the profile from deep water to shore (Grosskopf and Kraus, 1994).

Waves

Waves produce the most important forces that move sand in the coastal zone. Alongshore sand transport is caused by the suspension of sand by breaking waves and its movement by wave-induced alongshore currents. Waves also produce an increase in water level, termed *setup*. Wave and water-level data provide a quantitative measure of storms affecting a project site and can be used to assess project performance in response to differences in storm wave height, period, direction, and duration and storm surge. Historical wave information, including wave height, period, and direction, are available for U.S. shorelines in the form of wave hindcasts developed for a 20-year period by the U.S. Army Corps of Engineers (USACE). These are valuable for the design of beach nourishment projects but are generally not useful for evaluating the performance of a specific project. For this latter purpose, wave measurements are necessary. There are numerous types of wave gauges that can provide wave height and period data. They include surface-piercing gauges, pressure gauges, accelerometer buoys, and inverted echo sounders. Measurements of wave direction, necessary to determine alongshore sediment transport rates, require directional buoys in deep water, multiple gauge arrays, or pressure-gauge slope arrays in shallow water. Visual observations of nearshore wave conditions can also provide data, but they are generally inaccurate and are not collected during severe storm periods when observers cannot visit the beach. Waves also provide the loading on any structures that might be associated with beach nourishment projects.

Currents

Currents are typically not measured directly as part of beach nourishment project monitoring; alongshore currents are usually calculated from measured or hindcast wave conditions. Some wave gauges rely on current measurements to determine wave duration. However, data on currents associated with tidal inlets may be important in understanding the performance of some beach nourishment projects. Speed and direction can be measured by deploying current meters or by tracking floating drogues or dye. Current meters can provide data recorded at selected points over a long period—several tidal cycles or longer; drogues and dye provide data for very short time intervals and reaches. Storm-driven currents are also difficult to measure unless incorporated into the regular gauging program.

Water Levels

Elevated water levels during storms cause flooding and allow waves to act higher up on the beach profile, where they cause erosion and damage to upland development. Water levels are routinely measured by the National Oceanic and Atmospheric Administration's National Ocean Survey at tide gauges located along U.S. coastlines (NOAA, 1993). These gauges record water levels that include the astronomical tides, and when the predicted astronomical tide is subtracted from the gauge record, they yield data on the meteorologically caused water levels (storm surges). In most cases, these data will be available at nearby gauges for beach nourishment projects in the United States; however, there may be special cases where data are needed nearer the project. In these cases, a local tide gauge could be installed.

Structures

If coastal structures such as seawalls, bulkheads, groins, nearshore breakwaters, and jetties are present, monitoring of their effects on waves and currents, their permeability to sand, and, ultimately, their effect on the stability of the beach nourishment project is needed.

Sediment Characteristics

Sediment characteristics of interest include mineralogy, specific gravity, mean grain size, grain-size distribution, grain shape, and settling velocity (Smith, 1992). Most important are the mean grain size, size distribution, and settling velocity. Sediment data are needed for the native beach sand, the intended borrow sand, and the sand actually placed on the beach. Spatial variations in sediment characteristics may also play a role with changes in mean grain size across the profile and along the beach. Ultimately, settling velocity determines the important hydraulic characteristics of the sediment and the nearshore beach slope and equilibrium profile shape.

Photographic Documentation

Photography provides a relatively inexpensive method of obtaining data on the performance of beach nourishment projects. Controlled vertical aerial photographs can document upland conditions, shoreline location, and beach topography at a specific point in time. They can also be used to document storm effects. Strategically positioned ground-level photographs taken from the same location over time can provide a ready indication of the success or failure of a project. In addition, videotape can supplement still photography in documenting beach conditions. Videos taken from a small airplane or helicopter can provide an inexpensive way to document beach conditions over large reaches of shoreline before and after storms.

BIOLOGICAL MONITORING

There are several major objectives that need to be incorporated into any biological impact assessment of a beach nourishment project. They are to:

- determine the existing biological resources that may be altered by the project and provide recommendations that will avoid long-term negative consequences to those resources,
- characterize the preconstruction temporal and spatial variability in the biological resources present within and near the project area, and
- evaluate the postnourishment recovery of biological resources that may be impacted by the project.

Many previous monitoring studies of beach nourishment projects have failed to adequately incorporate one or more of these objectives. Although the specific design of a monitoring program may vary considerably, depending on the size and location of the project, some general guidelines can be stated.

Before any nourishment project is conducted, it is essential to obtain adequate baseline data on carefully selected, significant flora and fauna in an area and to document natural spatial and seasonal variabilities in their numbers, species composition, and diversity. These data can then be compared with postnourishment monitoring to evaluate the extent and duration of changes that occur, both on the beach and in the borrow area. A complete monitoring program would provide adequate data to ensure that biological impacts are only short term relative to the interval between renourishment projects. If long-term impacts are experienced, other approaches to the project must be considered.

The scope of the preliminary biological surveys required within and adjacent to a project depends largely on the quantity and quality of historical data available for the area, but, as a minimum, a comprehensive assessment would include the following:

- surveys to locate and quantify ecologically sensitive habitats, such as nearshore reefs, hard-bottom habitat, and nesting habitats that should not be disturbed by construction activities, including information on the seasonal use of the project area by threatened or endangered species or important fishery resources, and
- surveys of other biota, such as benthic infauna, that will be affected by disturbances from dredging and nourishment activities within and adjacent to the project area.

Methods for surveying sensitive-bottom habitats vary, depending on water clarity and the size of the project. In areas where waters are clear and shallow, aerial surveys supported by diver or underwater television observations may be sufficient to map reef habitats. When water clarity or depths preclude visual mapping methods, side-scan sonar, underwater television or photography, and subbottom profiling systems may be used. A combination of two or more of these systems is often preferable because each has its limitations in detecting or mapping bottom types, particularly in areas where there is no bottom relief. The size of the survey area and the spacing of transects in the area will depend on the equipment used, but all bottom habitats in the area potentially affected by the project need to be mapped fully.

Data on fishery resources in the project area or on use of the area by threatened or endangered species are often available through monitoring programs conducted by state and federal natural resource agencies. However, some preliminary reconnaissance may be necessary when such data are not available.

Quantitative sampling of other biological resources, such as the benthic macrofaunal communities, is also usually warranted because these assemblages are the principal macrofaunal component inhabiting beach sands and borrow areas, and they form an important component of the nearshore food web. Preliminary sampling of these assemblages needs to be conducted, when feasible, to select the appropriate sample size and sampling design to be used in pre- and postnourishment monitoring studies. It is not necessary to include biota that cannot be adequately quantified or that are not good indicators of the local environmental quality in any subsequent monitoring program. Similarly, emphasis is appropriately placed on monitoring only those resources and habitats of greatest concern because there is rarely enough funding to adequately monitor all aspects of the affected ecosystem. For example, if the areal extent of the intertidal zone is limited owing to low tidal amplitude, monitoring of intertidal communities may represent a lower priority compared to monitoring the borrow area, where longer-term effects have been noted, or the nearshore zone in areas where there are sensitive habitats that may be disturbed.

The extent, duration, and frequency of pre- and postconstruction monitoring will largely depend on the size of the project, the habitats to be affected, and the projected frequency of renourishment. Determining the sampling precision for the biological monitoring effort merits specific consideration. Elliot (1979), Green (1979), and Nelson (1991, 1993) provide more comprehensive information on recommended sampling designs, sample size, and sampling frequency and on statistical constraints that merit consideration in developing a biological monitoring program. Sampling precision is especially important because many previous studies involved the collection of only a few replicate samples per site. The low number of replicates used was probably not sufficient to detect statistically even major changes in the biological parameters being monitored. In addition, many studies have focused more on characterizing community structure such as faunal abundance, biomass, and measures of species diversity than on identifying and assessing trends and changes in the faunal communities with respect to trophic structure and function.

There is a large variability in the physical characteristics and biological resources of beach and nearshore habitats along the coastline of the United States. The conditions that exist at a beach nourishment site need to be considered in forming the specific sampling approaches that are incorporated into a biological monitoring program. Based on the limited data available from previous monitoring efforts, several key questions need to be addressed in developing the biological study design:

- What is the duration of disturbance to the biological resources of concern, and is it compatible with the anticipated frequency of redisturbance resulting from subsequent renourishment operations?
- Are biological resources adjacent to the project area affected by construction activities or subsequent movement of sediments from the project area?
- Do turbidity levels associated with nourishment operations exceed levels known to be harmful to the indigenous biota of concern, or, if that is not known, do the levels exceed those naturally observed over various seasons at the site of concern?

Monitoring programs that are designed to address these questions adequately and that are relevant to the area where a project is planned will greatly improve our understanding of the biological consequences of beach nourishment activities.

ECONOMIC MONITORING

A well-designed economic monitoring program would attempt to answer the following questions:

- How large are the realized recreational benefits, and do they approximate those predicted for the project?
- What are the effects of the project on property values, and to what extent are these effects linked with storm damage reduction, enhanced aesthetics, and recreational amenities?
- What were the construction and other related costs, and were they well approximated by the cost estimates?
- Are there other significant but perhaps unanticipated costs and/or benefits accruing from the project?
- From the locality's standpoint, did the project stimulate growth, and, if so, what desirable or undesirable effects did the growth have on the community?
- Did the project encourage construction that places more property at risk from storm destruction?
- What was the actual distribution of the costs and benefits of the project— that is, who benefited and who paid?

Although the USACE is charged with conducting preconstruction cost-benefit analyses, there have been few follow-up analyses of projects to determine whether projected benefits were actually realized, whether secondary benefits occurred, or whether unanticipated costs could be attributed to the project (Haveman, 1979; Stronge, 1992b, 1994). Without such follow-up studies, it is difficult to determine whether USACE methodologies for assessing recreational and storm damage reduction benefits are sufficiently accurate for beach nourishment analysis, and it is impossible to determine whether its cost-benefit analyses incorporate all significant categories of costs and benefits that usually accrue from these projects. Although full-scale follow-up analyses may not be warranted for all projects, postconstruction analysis of a sampling of projects is necessary to answer these questions.

As discussed in Chapter 2, none of these categories of costs and benefits is easy to estimate. Analysis of recreational benefits is in some ways the easiest because this methodology is the most well developed. The purpose of the recreational monitoring component would be to quantify the actual recreational benefits accruing specifically to the beach nourishment activity and whether the benefits were well approximated by the preconstruction analysis. This analysis requires valuing the change in use directly associated with the change in the quality/size of the beach brought about by the nourishment.

Ideally, both before and after the nourishment activity, surveys based on random samples of the area's population need to be taken in conjunction with onsite surveys of beach users. The surveys would provide both information on participation rates for beach use that are unavailable from onsite surveys and a means of extrapolating survey sample to total beach use. However, onsite surveys are still useful because they provide a means of oversampling users, thus ensuring adequate coverage of this group. Both types of surveys would need to collect information on the total number of beach trips to different beaches in the area on a seasonal basis as well as the location of household residence, travel costs, and household socioeconomic variables.

Given access to respondents, contingent valuation questions might also be included in the survey. Such questions are a useful way to elicit information on how individuals value quality aspects of the beach and the surrounding area that may have changed owing to the nourishment activity. As explained in Appendix E, contingent valuation questions ask people how much they would be willing to pay (in increased entrance fees, parking fees, or some other payment vehicle) for a change in quality characteristics of the beach. A pertinent experiment would be to ask such a question before construction, describing the expected outcome of the nourishment activity, and then to ask a similar postconstruction question when individuals can witness the results of the nourishment project directly.

It is, of course, difficult even after construction to assess the accuracy of estimated storm damage reduction benefits. The reason is that storm events are random, and estimates must be based on expectations. However, it is possible to attempt to assess the effects of a nourishment project on property values by collecting property value data before and after the project and completing a hedonic analysis. A hedonic analysis attempts to explain property values as specific functions of characteristics of the property (see Appendix E for further discussion of hedonic analysis). Data on important property characteristics are required, including distance to, view of, and accessibility of the beach. The intent would be to see how changes in the quality of the beach affect property values, controlling for all other features of the properties.

There are several difficulties with hedonic analyses of this sort, however, not the least of which is timing; the added value of a beach nourishment project will begin being capitalized into property values as soon as a potential project is announced. Nonetheless, it would be useful to design a hedonic study that attempts to reveal the marginal value associated with beach nourishment, although it may require incorporating a lagged response in the model. It would also be useful if the hedonic analysis could be designed to separate the storm damage reduction benefits from the aesthetic and recreational benefits of the nourishment; however, the high correlation between these two characteristics may preclude doing so.

Beach nourishment projects can potentially have additional effects on an area although few, if any, studies have attempted to even list them. Projects may stimulate new construction and/or commercial development, for example. Such activity may have positive or negative net benefits for the community depending on the nature and size of the development and the type of community. A postconstruction survey of these effects would be useful, including an assessment of their fiscal impacts (increases in the tax base and employment versus increased costs of infrastructure and services). If a nourishment project stimulates construction that increases the risk to property of storm damage, then this increase needs to be accounted for. Further, it would be especially useful to survey the population to determine the community effects of the beach nourishment project.

Because there is increasing debate over the share of beach nourishment costs incurred by federal and local partners, an analysis of the recipients of the costs and benefits would be useful. First, of course, the construction and related costs of the project need to be tallied, compared to original cost estimates, and attributed to the sponsoring parties. They would then be compared with the incidence of the benefits. If properly done, such an analysis will provide accurate information as to who benefits from the project. One caveat is necessary here. If the project was made necessary by actions elsewhere (e.g., USACE dredging), these negative externalities must be taken into account. For example, some of the nourishment operations may have been dredged-material disposal operations in which sand was deposited on the beach only because doing so was the cheapest disposal option. Alternatively, the need for a particular project may be due to interruption of the natural sand flow by a navigational project. Information on the distribution of costs and benefits from beach nourishment projects of different types would help inform the cost-sharing policy makers in the future.

REFERENCES

Elliot, J. M. 1979. Some Methods for the Statistical Analysis of Samples of Benthic Invertebrates. Freshwater Biological Association, Scientific Publication No. 25. Kendal, U.K.: Titus Wilson & Son, Ltd.

Green, R. H. 1979. Sampling Design and Statistical Methods for Environmental Biologists. New York: John Wiley & Sons.

Grosskopf, W. G., and N. C. Kraus. 1994. Guidelines for surveying beach nourishment projects. Shore and Beach 62(2):9-16.

Haveman, R. H. 1979. The Economic Performance of Public Investments. Baltimore: Johns Hopkins University Press.

Nelson, W. G. 1991. Methods of biological monitoring of beach restoration projects: problems and solutions in the real world. Pp. 263-276 in Preserving and Enhancing Our Beach Environment: Proceedings of the 1991 National Conference on Beach Preservation Technology. Tallahassee: Florida Shore and Beach Preservation Association.

Nelson, W. G. 1993. Beach restoration in the southeastern US: environmental effects and biological monitoring. Ocean and Coastal Management 19:157-182.

NOAA. 1993. Tide Tables for the East Coast of North and South America. Washington, D.C.: National Ocean Survey, National Oceanic and Atmospheric Administration.

NRC. 1990. Managing Troubled Waters. Marine Board, Commission on Engineering and Technical Systems. Washington, D.C.: National Academy Press.

Smith, A. W. S. 1992. Description of beach sands. Shore and Beach 60(3):23-30.

Stronge, W. B. 1992a. Impact of Captiva's Beaches on Property Values and Taxes. Paper prepared for the Captiva Erosion Prevention District by Regional Research Associates, Inc., Boca Raton, Fla., December.

Stronge, W. B. 1992b. The economic impact of the Marco Island beach restoration: a preliminary analysis. In: New Directions in Beach Management, Proceedings of the 5th Annual National Conference on Beach Preservation Technology. Tallahassee: Florida Shore and Beach Preservation Association.

Stronge, W. B. 1994. Beaches, tourism and economic development. Shore and Beach 62(2):6-8.

7

Conclusions and Recommendations

GENERAL FINDINGS

Beach nourishment projects can be used effectively to provide a broader beach, which affords protection from storm and flooding damage within human time scales (decades, not centuries) when:

- projects are carried out on sites at which the erosion processes are understood,
- uncertainties in design and prediction are accounted for realistically, and
- state-of-the-art engineering standards of planning and design are used.

Well-designed, -constructed, and -maintained projects provide the storm damage reduction and erosion protection for which they are intended. Beach nourishment may not be technically or economically justified for some sites, particularly those with high rates of natural erosion.

RECOMMENDATION: Federal, state, and local authorities with responsibility for coastal protection should view beach nourishment as a viable alternative for providing shore protection and for restoring lost recreational beach assets.

The planning and execution of successful beach nourishment projects can best be accomplished through a broadly based coalition of disciplines and interests that brings together all the scientific, engineering, economic, and governance knowledge and experience available. Narrowly developed projects have resulted in technical, environmental, or economic deficiencies. All project planning should recognize the need for maintenance.

RECOMMENDATION: **Federal, state, and local agencies involved with beach nourishment projects should require multidisciplinary project planning, design, monitoring, and evaluation. The methodology employed should:**

- **establish the goals and expectations of the project and its continuation as a long-term program;**
- **establish clear and quantifiable measures of success;**
- **establish and maintain an effective monitoring program that supports the management, design, and execution of subsequent nourishment cycles;**
- **develop and maintain a public awareness program; and**
- **account for the uncertainties implicit in shore protection measures through the implementation of contingency planning and the identification of future sources of both renourishment material and project funding.**

SPECIFIC FINDINGS

Design

The design of a successful beach nourishment project depends on an understanding of the underlying causes of erosion at the site and a capacity to model or evaluate quantitatively the coastal processes, such as wave climate variations and the cross-shore and alongshore transport rates of sediments. Deficiencies exist in our understanding of many of these processes and adversely affect our ability to predict the evolution and fate of nourishment fill; even when the basic processes are understood, large uncertainties can remain in numerical evaluations. Further, there are significant differences among coasts' geological settings, geomorphologies, sand sources and sinks, sediment characteristics, and physical forces, such as waves, tides, currents, and winds. The great diversity of conditions and the mix of coastal processes result in major regional differences that make it neither practicable nor desirable to establish a national standard design for beach nourishment projects. Each must be designed to satisfy the conditions at its location.

Nourished beaches usually experience significant spatial alongshore variations that range from high rates of erosion to accretion. When locations erode faster than anticipated (erosional hot spots), reserve protection capacity may be lost and the design compromised along a portion of the beach. The renourished beach will require more sand than the net background erosion from the project because erosional hot spots require overfill. In addition, accretional areas store advanced fill, and the accretion should not be deducted from the estimated erosion. Designers underestimate renourishment needs when they base their estimates solely on net erosion projections. A potential savings can be realized when the initial renourishment interval is shortened and less advanced fill is placed in the first renourishment in order that fine tuning of the project to address erosional hot spots can be implemented at an early stage.

> **RECOMMENDATION:**   The design methodology for beach nourishment projects should include the following:
>
> - **design profiles based on natural profiles at the site suitably adjusted for nourishment grain size rather than straight line segments or other unrealistic approximations;**
> - **spreading losses owing to the nourishment project accounted for explicitly in the design;**
> - **volumes adjusted to account for rock outcrops and seawalls in order to provide sufficient volume to nourish the entire profile from the berm or dune to the seaward limit of the active profile and avoid underestimating fill requirements;**
> - **sediment performance characteristics included in the analysis of sediment considered for use as beach nourishment material, with specific attention to the equilibrium shape of the profile, the transportability of the sediment alongshore, and the erodibility of the material during a storm; these factors used at first in conjunction with overfill and renourishment factors and later as a substitute for these factors as more experience is gained;**
> - **the possibility of erosional hot spots recognized in the design;**
> - **analytical and numerical models used to estimate end losses that will be caused by spreading of the fill material to adjacent beaches;**
> - **the first renourishment time interval shortened to allow for uncertainties in alongshore erosion rates, thus enabling correction of erosional hot spots before the design is compromised and avoiding overbuilding of accretional areas; and**
> - **safety factors developed to account for variability and uncertainty and applied appropriately to both design volumes and advanced-fill volumes.**

Although technologically outdated, the *Shore Protection Manual* published by the U.S. Army Corps of Engineers (USACE) in 1984 is the de facto standard for coastal engineering throughout most of the world. Strong legal constraints and liability considerations reinforce its continued use in the United States by engineers in private practice, even though it is no longer the design standard used by the USACE.

> **RECOMMENDATION: The U.S. Army Corps of Engineers should publish detailed and comprehensive state-of-the-art engineering guidance on the design of beach nourishment projects, either as part of the planned Coastal Engineering Manual or in a separate document.**

Differences exist in the planning and design methodologies used by the USACE field offices. Some of these differences relate to regional differences in the beaches that have been designed (South Atlantic barrier islands versus West coast bluff-backed beaches). Design approaches must therefore vary to account for regional differences. However, other differences in designs are a result of the methodologies selected, some of which do not employ state-of-the-art practices realistically. This situation results in uneven effectiveness in project design and contributes to less than optimum solutions.

> **RECOMMENDATION: The U.S. Army Corps of Engineers should develop and implement a consistent methodology for beach nourishment design while retaining sufficient flexibility to accommodate regional variations in physical conditions.**

Structural Alternatives

Fixed Structures

Fixed (hard) structures, when appropriately designed and placed at suitable locations, can improve the performance of some beach nourishment projects. These structures may be perpendicular to the shore, to reduce end losses (e.g., jetties and groins); offshore and shore parallel, to reduce local wave intensity (e.g., detached breakwaters); and onshore and shore parallel (e.g., seawalls), to provide a reserve capability to prevent flooding and wave attack where dunes cannot or do not exist, especially in areas like the Pacific coast, where storm surges are small and to reduce wind-blown losses to the land. Broad prohibitions on the use of fixed structures in conjunction with beach nourishment projects can contribute to suboptimal project performance where fixed structures can provide secondary storm damage reduction or are needed to anchor the ends of projects.

> **RECOMMENDATION: Agencies should modify their prescriptive laws, regulations, and management plans for the coast to allow the use of fixed structures in conjunction with beach nourishment projects where project performance can be significantly improved, out-of-project negative effects are acceptably small or are mitigated as necessary, and beach access or use is not impaired. The costs of**

the structures should not exceed the savings achieved by increasing the level of protection or the times between successive renourishments. Environmental impacts should also be considered.

Structures do not increase the volume of sand in the littoral system; they simply rearrange and control the movement of the sand that is placed or is already there. Failure to provide fill along with the structures often results in erosion of the beach system at another location. Even when a groin field is filled to its holding capacity, localized erosion effects may nevertheless occur. These effects need to be addressed more effectively and accommodated in project design and construction.

RECOMMENDATION: Each fixed structure that is used in conjunction with a beach nourishment project should be filled to the upper limit of its holding capacity if it would otherwise accumulate sand. Where uncertainties exist, fill should exceed the calculated upper limit of the holding capacity of the structure. If a beach nourishment project is not maintained, adverse effects of any structure should be mitigated or the structure should be removed.

Nontraditional Shore Protection Devices

The techniques used in conventional shore protection have had the benefit of decades of field performance and the development of demonstrated design models to predict that performance. This experience has clearly shown that there are no cheap and easy solutions to the difficult and expensive process of protecting the shore while maintaining its environmental assets. The use of nontraditional shore protection devices needs to be approached carefully because of uncertainties about their performance and beneficial value relative to traditional technology, for which performance capabilities are established.

The Committee on Beach Nourishment and Protection is concerned that some nontraditional devices that involve large structures placed near the shore may cause unfavorable conditions that will be difficult and expensive to correct. At the same time, the committee believes that technical innovation should be encouraged and that entrepreneurs should have access to the marketplace in this field. Evaluation of any beach protection system is expensive because of the size of any meaningful experiment and is time consuming because of concerns for testing under a full set of climate conditions. It is prudent to consider as experimental new approaches that purport to be low-cost solutions until their performance has been adequately demonstrated. Further, unconventional approaches that do not involve addition of sand to the littoral system from outside sources and that involve the trapping or rearrangement of sand must be recognized as providing local improvement only at the expense of neighboring areas that lose this material. A uniform and effective methodology consisting of a performance-based specification is needed for evaluating the effectiveness of nontraditional shore protection and beach stabilization and restoration devices so that any interested agency or private buyer can be more fully informed before committing to their use.

RECOMMENDATION: **The performance of nontraditional shore protection and beach stabilization and restoration devices should be successfully demonstrated under a performance-based specification before these devices are used in lieu of conventional shore protection and beach stabilization and restoration alternatives, including beach nourishment. A performance-based specification should be developed by the U.S. Army Corps of Engineers for nontraditional devices to guide their application in projects in which there is federal involvement. This specification or a similar procedure developed objectively by qualified coastal engineers acting in a third-party role should be used to guide the application of nontraditional devices in nonfederal projects.**

Adequate studies and engineering analyses of borrow sites are critical to the success of a nourishment effort. In particular, the impacts of creating a local depression in the sea bottom on offshore sand movement from the nourished beach need to be assessed in order to determine the effects on the littoral system and any mitigation measures that need to be implemented. It is necessary to avoid dredging within the depth of active sediment transport and minimize wave modifications that would adversely affect the nourishment project.

RECOMMENDATION: **Sponsors of beach nourishment projects should use a methodology for selecting borrow sites that assesses:**

- **the required quality and quantity of sand,**
- **the effect of borrow sites on adjacent beaches when these sites are located within the closure depth of the beach profile or are part of a shoal that normally feeds the downdrift beach, and**
- **the need for, and negative and positive effects of, bypassing sand.**

If sand must be taken from borrow sites located within closure depths, it should be done as a planned sand bypass operation that is designed specifically to mitigate the effects of a feature or structure that interrupts the littoral movement of sand.

Relevance of Sea-Level Rise

Relative sea-level changes are occurring along most U.S. coasts. The effects of sea-level rise are particularly important along the Atlantic and Gulf coasts with low-lying topography. Erosion or beach recession, which is the result of current relative sea-level rise, is incorporated into the background erosion rate. The overall effect of a gradual relative sea-level rise at the present rate will not be detectable in the rate of beach loss. If the relative sea-level rise accelerates, the beach loss also will accelerate. Because beach nourishment programs consist of a series of projects, and because reevaluation of erosion rates is included in the design of projects, no additional considerations are necessary to account for erosion that is induced by relative sea-level rise.

Sea-level change, however, is just one of many factors impacting beach behavior. Its magnitude and relative importance are difficult to ascertain because changes are masked by more dramatic near-term fluctuations caused by other physical forces. Relative sea-level rise will probably remain a minor factor affecting replenished beach durability during the next several decades.

Major Management Issues

Public Involvement

Before a beach nourishment project begins, there is a compelling need to inform the public about:

- the anticipated time frame of the program (e.g., a 20-, 30-, or 50-year program);
- the nourishment intervals and especially the beach state or condition (e.g., width of dry beach) that will trigger renourishment;
- the timing and extent of the expected profile adjustment and its impact on beach widths;
- the possible impacts of major storms on beach character and on projected costs, sand volumes, and the timing between renourishment projects;
- the potential occurrence of erosional hot spots and the requirements for corrective action; and
- the adjustment from the temporarily wider and steeper construction profile to the expected equilibrium profile.

Inadequacies in public involvement and information programs have exacerbated public controversy over beach nourishment. Measures to inform the interested and affected publics about beach nourishment projects have been inadequate with respect to design expectations for beach behavior and costs, uncertainties in the design process, prediction of project performance, future environmental conditions, and replenishment cycles. The promulgation of information essential to public support of programs described in technical and design manuals is not an effective substitute for well-designed and -executed public involvement and information programs.

After a beach fill has been completed, there is a continuing need to regularly update the public on its progress, including reports on the sand volumes and beach widths remaining, the nature and extent of erosional hot spots, the condition of the storm berm, and the implications of this information.

RECOMMENDATION: Sponsors of beach nourishment programs should establish public information and involvement programs as an integral component of each beach nourishment project, beginning with the design phase and continuing through the maintenance stage.

Commitments for Long-Term Project Maintenance

The long-term financial commitment required to maintain a beach replenishment program effectively is generally recognized by communities involved in these projects but is not always incorporated into the planning process. The 50-year life cycle for a typical USACE beach nourishment program is rarely, if ever, paralleled by similar long-term planning by the public and local project sponsors. In particular, an existing beach nourishment program may not be backed by dedicated sand resources for the projected life of the program or for supplemental renourishments that may be necessitated by severe storms or other factors. It is inaccurate to characterize planned beach nourishments as a bona fide program unless long-term planning and commitments to maintain a program are in place.

RECOMMENDATION: Given the long-term sand commitments necessary to ensure sufficient sand for the planned life cycle of a nourishment program, federal and state agencies should investigate mechanisms that would help sponsors identify and, where feasible, contract for or secure mineral rights to sources for long-term sand commitments. These mechanisms may include the use of unconventional sources for later cycles of nourishment so long as the projected costs are reflected in the cost-benefit analyses.

Sand deposits that are located in state waters and that are free to publicly funded within-state beach nourishment projects are often not sufficient in quality or quantity to sustain beach nourishment over a program's life. Sand sources under federal jurisdiction on the continental shelf and administered by the Minerals Management Service of the U.S. Department of the Interior will become increasingly important for the continued maintenance of some beach nourishment programs. Existing mechanisms for allocating these mineral resources through competitive bidding, and by negotiated agreement between the USACE and the Minerals Management Service for projects involving federal cost sharing, do not incorporate provisions for contracting forward for sand resources. Procedures for allocating sand resources to accommodate long-term needs merit further investigation.

RECOMMENDATION: When future renourishment sand sources cannot be identified with certainty, each construction project should independently meet the tests for economical viability.

Emergency Maintenance and Contingency Plans

The need for rapid emergency restoration of a beach or dune system can be created by severe storms that exceed design criteria. When emergency restoration is warranted, procedural delays caused by locating appropriate sources, obtaining permits, and contracting for construction can further jeopardize endangered buildings and infrastructure. Contingency plans and arrangements are needed to facilitate the timely implementation of emergency restorations.

RECOMMENDATION: Program sponsors should develop contingency plans for emergency repair of beach and dune systems necessitated by severe storm damage as part of the beach nourishment program at each site. Emergency-use borrow sites should be identified as a minimum and the necessary permits obtained and held in reserve when possible. Sponsors should investigate the feasibility of and plan appropriately for expedited procurement procedures to identify and secure dredging services from U.S. contractors.

Project Scope

Beach nourishment programs are often undertaken without due consideration for their relationship to and impact on other portions of the littoral cell that often cross political boundaries. Most programs encompass only a portion of an area that can be considered a littoral geographic region or littoral cell. However, actions in one area of a littoral cell have generally affected other areas in the cell and, in some cases, areas in adjacent littoral cells. The length of a project has typically been prescribed as the minimum design needed to protect an arbitrarily specified shoreline sector without regard for uncertainties. The program scope has not been adequately recognized by policies governing USACE beach nourishment project planning, design, and approval. It is recognized that tough, less-than-ideal choices must be made during the evolution of a project because of jurisdictional, budgetary, and time constraints.

RECOMMENDATION: Beach nourishment programs should be planned as part of an overall regional beach management plan. All involved participants should take action to ensure that the process used for planning, design, and approval of beach nourishment programs achieves this objective.

It is common for economic analyses to show that a broad range of potential projects produces positive and comparable cost-benefit ratios, but the single project beach width that provides maximum net benefits is selected as the federal National Economic Development (NED) plan. Because of uncertainties in both the design and the physical processes, selection of a plan larger than the NED plan would provide a safety margin against uncertainty and variability. In many cases, the larger project selection would not significantly change the cost-benefit ratio but would significantly increase the margin of safety for reducing storm damage.

RECOMMENDATION: **The federal government should modify its policies to allow for the selection of a project larger than the National Economic Development plan as long as it provides a positive cost-benefit ratio and is within the financial capability of the local sponsor. A sensitivity analysis should be performed for each prospective and existing program for which one has not been done in order to identify the scope of a more inclusive program that would reduce the risks of excessive damage. The sensitivity analysis should be applied to both the advanced-fill and design beach components.**

Measures of Success

There is no single measure of success for beach nourishment programs because programs usually serve a variety of objectives. Therefore, various measures of success need to be defined for beach nourishment programs. A program may or may not be successful in meeting all objectives underlying its establishment. Some of the performance measures may occur in the near term, such as a program's response to physical forces. Other objectives may occur over a much longer term—for example, the realization of related shore community economic development goals and reduction of shoreline retreat. Effective program performance from an engineering perspective may or may not change the economic conditions that motivated local support for a beach nourishment program because socioeconomic conditions can change over the life of a program.

The fundamental measure of success is the life span of the beach fill and how nearly actual performance conforms to predicted performance.

Success in enhancing recreation can be related to the width of the dry beach, whereas success in shore protection is better evaluated in terms of the total sand volume (subaerial and subaqueous) remaining in the program area and the protection it provides during storms. Two simple measures of a successful beach nourishment program are the dry beach width and the volume per unit length of shoreline remaining in the program area during its design life. Two more complex measures are the assessment of property damage avoided and the remaining level of protection.

RECOMMENDATION: Sponsors of beach nourishment programs should quantify and report on four measures of performance of beach nourishment projects. The measures are:

- **dry beach width,**
- **total sand volume remaining,**
- **poststorm damage assessments, and**
- **residual protection capability.**

The federal process for renourishing a beach from the reconnaissance study through the first nourishment typically takes 10 to 15 years. On authorized projects that require only preconstruction engineering, design, and real estate (or right-of-way) acquisition, the process takes 5 to 6 years. These long planning times burden the local sponsor with years of uncertainty about storm damage. Some of the delays are caused by the rigid and sequential federal process, which includes detailed agency reviews and waiting times for next-phase funding. Other delays are caused by slippage in USACE planning schedules. To speed the planning process, the federal approval process can be streamlined and delays minimized through contracting technical services. The Water Resources Development Act of 1992 enabled local governments to undertake the planning process for authorized projects to reduce schedule slippage. That authority has not been exercised because local governments are required to finance the federal share of project costs until after project construction and acceptance by the USACE.

RECOMMENDATION: The federal government should reduce the time now needed to process a beach nourishment project. The following steps should be taken:

- **revise the federal approval process to streamline approvals and funding time frames,**
- **increase the level of contracting for technical services by consultants to the USACE, and**
- **modify the laws and regulations to make federal funding for locally constructed federal projects available upon approval of preconstruction engineering and design by the Assistant Secretary of the Army for Civil Works.**

Environmental and Monitoring Issues

Most beach nourishment programs are inadequately monitored following construction. Monitoring of the physical environment and the performance of the fill material is often too limited in scope and duration to quantify project performance adequately. Comprehensive assessments of the effects on biological resources have been limited, especially at sand borrow sites. Resources associated with beach habitats are affected both positively and negatively, with negative effects generally of short duration relative to the expected renourishment interval. Alterations to biological resources in the sand borrow areas are generally of longer duration, and the consequences of those changes have not been well defined.

RECOMMENDATION: Sponsors of all beach nourishment projects and programs should establish adequate monitoring programs to evaluate changes in the physical and environmental conditions. The scope of the monitoring program should be appropriate to the scale of the nourishment program, and the monitoring design should recognize how the data will be used to make project-related decisions. Monitoring data should be analyzed in a timely manner and used to make management and operational decisions regarding continuation of the beach nourishment project or program.

RECOMMENDATION: Project sponsors should plan beach restoration programs so as to avoid significant long-term degradation of the biological resources that are affected, either directly or indirectly by construction activities. Emphasis should be on monitoring resources and habitats of greatest concern, including the borrow areas. The appropriateness of the dredging equipment to be used and the manner in which dredged materials will be discharged should also be considered. Where feasible, construction projects should incorporate design features that would enhance biological resources of concern.

Costs and Benefits

Assessing and Allocating Costs and Benefits

Beach nourishment programs result in economic benefits in a variety of forms and to a variety of recipients. Cost-share ratios arbitrarily mandated by Congress do not necessarily reflect the actual distribution of benefits; nor do these ratios take into account the impact of navigation projects on nearby and downdrift shores.

RECOMMENDATION: The full range of benefits that accrue from a beach nourishment program should be assessed and quantified. Cost sharing should more accurately reflect the spread of benefits that stem from a project.

RECOMMENDATION: The federal government should bear an appropriate share of beach nourishment project costs when it can be clearly established that federal navigation projects have exacerbated the erosion problems on adjacent or downdrift shores, even when these projects were not the only or even the primary cause.

Cost-benefit Analysis

Although the theory and methodology for conceptualizing and measuring costs and benefits are well developed, the valuation of beach nourishment programs does not take full advantage of these capabilities. As a result, social costs and benefits are not always fully represented in the analysis used to determine whether a program should be undertaken or in the choice among alternative project designs and implementation strategies.

The procedures for calculating costs and benefits are overly restrictive, allowing only storm damage reduction and limited recreational benefits. There is a wide range of potential costs and benefits that are not currently counted, such as the full complement of recreation benefits and the beneficial effects to adjacent beaches outside a project's domain.

RECOMMENDATION: The U.S. Army Corps of Engineers should modify the rules governing both its cost-benefit analysis and its choices among alternative project design and implementation strategies so that the true social costs and benefits provided to the entire coastal region are captured. In particular, the policy should recognize the storm damage reduction and recreational values to the total area affected and account for the benefits of sand transport to adjacent areas.

Because only limited postconstruction assessment of beach nourishment programs has taken place, there is little information about the types of costs and benefits (beyond storm damage reduction and recreation) that might accrue from these projects and might be sufficiently significant to warrant measurement.

RECOMMENDATION: The U.S. Army Corps of Engineers should conduct postconstruction economic evaluations to identify and measure the wide range of costs and benefits that actually result from beach nourishment programs. A particular focus of this effort should be reassessment of the categories of costs and benefits that should be included in future cost-benefit analysis procedures.

The procedures used for calculating the benefits that are allowed under current cost-benefit guidelines do not uniformly reflect state-of-the-art methodology. This point applies to assessing recreational benefits and may apply to other areas as well.

RECOMMENDATION: To improve the basis for policy analysis and decision making, the U.S. Army Corps of Engineers should become aware of and employ the methodological progress that has been made in economic valuation, especially in measuring nonmarket benefits such as recreation. The guidelines for measuring benefits should be updated and applied consistently throughout all U.S. Army Corps of Engineers divisions and districts.

RECOMMENDATION: The U.S. Army Corps of Engineers should improve the basis for economic valuation of beach nourishment projects by:

- reassessing the categories of costs and benefits included in evaluating a project,
- incorporating uncertainties in assessing uncertain costs and benefits both with and without the project,
- investigating behavioral responses stimulated by beach nourishment projects; and their policy ramifications, and
- coupling projects with local growth and land-use plans to increase the net benefits of projects and designing financing schemes that provide efficient incentives.

Coordination of Navigation and Shore Protection Projects

The USACE constructs and maintains both navigation and beach nourishment projects. The implementation of one type of project can have significant impacts on the other; yet the costs and benefits of the two types of activities have not been considered jointly insofar as the committee can determine.

Construction and maintenance of navigation projects that result in the trapping of sand from adjacent beaches often cause erosion of those beaches. Although the USACE has authority to address cause and effect on specific projects, current practice does not encourage coordination and correlation of the effects of navigation projects with the erosion mitigation and nourishment needs of nearby beaches. The occasional placement of beach-quality sand obtained from navigation projects on eroding beaches is more a matter of economic convenience as a least-cost disposal option rather than a planned action to minimize disruption of the littoral system. The many instances in which dredged beach-quality sand has been disposed of offshore rather than on adjacent beaches does not recognize the economic value of the sand. The cost of offshore disposal is greater than estimated in the past when only the direct cost of offshore disposal was considered.

RECOMMENDATION: Beach-quality sand dredged from federal navigation projects should be used for beach nourishment projects where the benefits to the latter exceed the extra direct costs to the navigation projects. Implementing such an approach requires that a navigation project be "charged" the cost of any sand budget deficit that it might impose on the adjacent shoreline.

RECOMMENDATION: The U.S. Army Corps of Engineers should modify its policies to require both consideration of the economic value of the sand and the placement of beach-quality sand dredged from federal navigation projects in the littoral system from which it was removed. The U.S. Army Corps of Engineers should coordinate and correlate the construction and maintenance of coastal navigation projects with erosion mitigation along adjacent beaches.

RECOMMENDATION: The U.S. Army Corps of Engineers should revise its procedures for cost-benefit analysis of navigation and beach nourishment projects in which there is federal involvement to require calculation of both the benefits provided and the costs that one type of project imposes on another.

Flood Protection

Role of Beach Nourishment

A beach nourishment program located seaward of upland buildings or infrastructure provides storm damage reduction relative to the level of protection that would exist if there were no program. Adequate methods exist for approximating the damage reduction owing to a beach nourishment program; however, there is significant uncertainty about the frequency of storm conditions that could compromise project performance. Nevertheless, the increase in the level of protection provided by beach nourishment projects and programs supports a finding of reduction in flooding risk, which would merit a reduction in insurance premiums.

RECOMMENDATION: The Federal Emergency Management Agency should weigh the effect of an adequately designed, constructed, and maintained beach nourishment program on flooding risk and hence on flood insurance premiums.

Qualification of Engineered Beaches for Disaster Assistance

Under the disaster assistance program administered by the Federal Emergency Management Agency, the definition of an engineered beach that is used to qualify for payment of sand losses from a beach nourishment program does not provide sufficient specific criteria to define the engineering adequacy of proposed programs.

RECOMMENDATION: The Federal Emergency Management Agency should revise its definition of and requirements for an engineered beach to consist of technical criteria, monitoring requirements, and measures to promote accountability for program performance.

- The technical basis for certification should be the establishment of a design level of storm and flood protection, including the level of protection provided by the design beach and the advanced-fill section seaward of the design portion. The Federal Emergency Management Agency should establish a standard risk factor and then contract for engineering studies to establish return periods or other appropriate design standards that will result in the establishment of standard risk for each of the major coastal regions. Designs for beaches intended to qualify for engineered beach status should meet the joint storm and flood levels appropriate to these return periods or design standards.

- An assessment of the capacity of a beach to protect against storms should be updated through periodic surveys conducted at least annually to document the evolution of the beach and to determine any change in storm and flood damage reduction potential.

- Identification of sources of emergency nourishment material should be made well before the need arises.

There are two mechanisms for the Federal Emergency Management Agency to participate in emergency actions following a severe storm. If there is a disaster declaration by the President, public assistance funds may be used to support the costs of replacing sand lost to an engineered beach. Second, mitigation funds may be used to restore beach and dune dimensions as soon as possible to protect against subsequent storm damage. At present, these are the only standing emergency assistance programs available at the federal level for shore protection and are relied on by coastal communities following damaging storms.

RECOMMENDATION: Beach and dune dimensions lost as the result of a severe storm should be restored as quickly as possible to protect against subsequent storm damage. The Federal Emergency Management Agency should continue to provide support for these essential activities.

Shore Construction Standards

Although nourishment offers effective reduction of storm damages to onshore construction, the level of protection afforded by the fill is subject to rapid reduction during a major storm and will diminish through time if the beach is not maintained by subsequent renourishment. It is not advisable to reduce or eliminate construction or location standards based on prefill hazard assessments or dune protection setback requirements because of (1) uncertainties about continuing financial means and political will to maintain a beach nourishment program in the absence of a requirement to do so and (2) uncertainties about sediment availability in the absence of dedicated sediment resources.

> **RECOMMENDATION:**   **In recognition of uncertainties in the prediction of coastal processes, cognizant government authorities should establish and maintain construction and location requirements to set construction back from the storm hazard regardless of whether a beach nourishment project is in place.**

> **RECOMMENDATION:**   **In recognition of uncertainties in the prediction of coastal processes, the Federal Emergency Management Agency should establish and maintain construction standards for buildings or lots within the benefit area of a beach nourishment program and should prepare Flood Insurance Rate maps as if a beach nourishment project were not in place.**

Research Needs to Support Design and Prediction Capabilities

There is a need for research to better understand the physical, economic, and biological processes associated with beach nourishment programs and to minimize uncertainties. Research is needed on a regional basis to accommodate regional differences in these processes. In particular, a more complete understanding is needed in the following areas to improve the design of beach nourishment programs:

- the natural variability of beach profiles and how they respond to changing wave and current conditions and sediment textures;
- the significance of profile closure depths beyond which the profiles appear to show minimal responses to changing wave conditions, particularly the degree to which sediment exchange occurs between the beach and offshore out to these closure depths and how these depths can be predicted as a function of sediment and wave conditions;
- the choice of grain size and other characteristics of the nourishment material for best retention on the beach and how that choice affects the dynamics of the beach profiles and alongshore spreading of the nourishment sediment;
- the further development of cross-shore sediment transport models related to profile changes; and

- the causes of erosional hot spots occurring on natural beaches and within beach nourishment programs.

RECOMMENDATION: An intensive study for a few large-scale beach nourishment programs should be undertaken by a third-party group of investigators under federal sponsorship. The objective of the study should be to test the validity of current predictive methods and design assumptions and improve prediction and design methodologies further. The study should include postconstruction assessment of the costs and economic benefits of the programs and the overall effects on economic development.

Directional Wave Data

On a major project, especially at a site with complex bathymetry, directional wave data are essential to verify the design methodology and to improve performance in future beach nourishment. These data are needed to establish the coastal wave climate for the program. Collateral uses of the data should be considered when justifying the cost of measuring waves.

RECOMMENDATION: The U.S. Army Corps of Engineers should require the collection, analysis, and dissemination of directional wave data as part of major beach nourishment programs in which there is a federal cost share.

Erosion Data

There is a need for a uniform, national, reliable data base on historical erosion rates. Erosion rate data based on historical charts collected by the National Oceanic and Atmospheric Administration and profile data collected by the USACE and some local agencies are uneven and of varying usefulness.

RECOMMENDATION: The U.S. Army Corps of Engineers, the National Oceanic and Atmospheric Administration, and the U.S. Geological Survey should undertake a cooperative program to establish standardized decadal rates of erosion or accretion for all U.S. shorelines subject to significant change over this time scale. The detailed data base used in these assessments should be readily available to coastal engineers and scientists.

APPENDIXES

A

Biographical Sketches

RICHARD J. SEYMOUR is director of the Offshore Technology Research Center and professor of civil engineering at Texas A&M University, where he also holds the Wofford Cain Chair in Ocean Engineering. Concurrently, he is director of the Ocean Engineering Research Group at Scripps Institution of Oceanography. Prior to moving to Texas in 1991, he held positions as a research engineer at the University of California at San Diego, as executive director of the Foundation for Ocean Research, and as a staff oceanographer for the state of California, among others. He also served as program manager of the National Sea Grant Program's Nearshore Sediment Transport Study. His career of over 40 years has been focused on the fields of ocean technology, wave mechanics, wave climatology, and nearshore processes, including sediment transport, cross-shore transport, and shoreline erosion. His professional activities have included service on the National Research Council's Marine Board as a board member and chair of the Committee on Information for Port and Harbor Operations; on the American Society of Civil Engineers Ocean Energy, Waterway, Port, Coastal & Ocean Division; and as a member of the Shoreline Erosion Task Force of the San Diego Association of Governments. He has also served as associate editor of the *Ocean Engineering Journal*; on the editorial board of the *Journal of Estuarine, Coast, and Shelf Sciences*; and as editor of a special edition of *Shore and Beach*, the journal of the American Shore and Beach Preservation Association. Dr. Seymour is a graduate of the U.S. Naval Academy (B.S.) and the Scripps Institution of Oceanography, University of California at San Diego (Ph.D.).

NANCY E. BOCKSTAEL is a resource economist and professor in the

Department of Agricultural and Resource Economics at the University of Maryland. Her scholarly pursuits include economic assessments and benefits of natural resources and relationships between recreational benefits and the valuation of natural resources and environmental quality. Her many publication credits include economic modeling of marine recreational resources, such as fisheries and boating. She has served as vice president of the Association of Environmental and Resource Economics and as associate editor of the *Journal of Environmental Economics and Management*. She also served as an adviser to a number of state, federal, and foreign government environmental panels and commissions, including the National Oceanic and Atmospheric Administration, the U.S. Environmental Protection Agency, the National Science Foundation, and the Ocean Studies Board of the National Research Council. Dr. Bockstael holds a B.A. in economics from Connecticut College, an M.S. in economics from Brown University, and a Ph.D. in resource economics from the University of Rhode Island.

THOMAS J. CAMPBELL is president of Coastal Planning and Engineering, Inc., and a registered engineer in Florida, Virginia, and New York. He has served as chief engineer for the design and construction of eight major beach replenishment projects in Florida. His 20-plus years of experience include the design and supervision of projects related to environmental assessment and monitoring, erosion assessments, beach and coastal structures, beach and hydrographic surveys, and storm damage evaluation. He has also testified as an expert witness in court cases and administrative hearings involving beach and coastal issues. Mr. Campbell is the recipient of an award for outstanding contributions to coastal engineering in Florida from the Florida Shore and Beach Preservation Association. He holds a B.E. degree in civil and structural engineering and an M.E. in ocean and coastal engineering.

ROBERT G. DEAN is a graduate research professor in the Coastal and Ocean Engineering Department of the University of Florida in Gainesville, a position he has held since 1982. Prior to joining the faculty at Florida, he held faculty positions at the University of Delaware (Department of Civil Engineering and College of Marine Studies), the University of Washington, and the Massachusetts Institute of Technology. He has also served as a consultant on coastal and ocean engineering to various firms and government agencies, including the Coastal Engineering Research Board of the U.S. Army Corps of Engineers and the Division of Beaches and Shores of the Florida Department of Natural Resources. He has been a member of the National Research Council's Marine Board and chair of the Committee on Engineering Implications of Sea-Level Rise. Dr. Dean's expertise is in wave mechanics and coastal engineering problems. He is the author of many publications on wave theory, beach erosion problems, tidal inlets, and coastal structures. He has coauthored a book on water wave mechanics. Dr. Dean is a member of numerous professional societies, including the

American Society of Civil Engineers, the American Association for the Advancment of Science, and the American Geophysical Union. He also received the John G. Moffatt-Frank E. Nichol Harbor and International Coastal Engineering Award of the ASCE. Dr. Dean received a B.S. degree from the University of California at Berkeley, an M.S. from the Agricultural and Mechanical College of Texas, and an Sc.D. in civil engineering from the Massachusetts Institute of Technology. Dr. Dean is a member of the National Academy of Engineering.

PAUL D. KOMAR is a professor of oceanography at Oregon State University, where he has been on the faculty since 1970, achieving the rank of professor in 1978. Dr. Komar's area of research specialty is the generation of nearshore currents on beaches and the resulting transport of sediments, coastal erosion processes and problems, grain and sediment transport under waves, turbidity currents and deep-sea fan sedimentation, and other topics. Prior to joining the faculty at Oregon State, he was a NATO fellow at the Wallingford Hydraulics Research Station in England and St. Andrews University in Scotland. He has also been a United Nation's lecturer on coastal processes in Poona, India. He is a member of several professional organizations, including the American Geophysical Union and the Geological Society of America, and has been associate editor of several professional journals, including *Marine Geology* and *Sedimentology.* He has over 100 technical publications to his credit and is the author of two books: *Beach Processes and Sedimentation* and *Handbook of Coastal Processes and Erosion.* Dr. Komar holds a B.A. and M.S. in mathematics and an M.S. in geology from the University of Michigan. He received a Ph.D. in oceanography from the University of California at San Diego.

ORRIN H. PILKEY is James B. Duke Professor of Geology at Duke University, founder and director of the Duke University Program for the Study of Developed Shorelines, and a nationally known expert on beach processes. He has served on numerous boards and expert panels and testified before congressional committees during deliberations on a barrier islands bill. He is author or coauthor of well over 100 articles and 20 books and coproduced a one-hour PBS documentary titled "The Beaches Are Moving." Dr. Pilkey's myriad professional activities include membership in the Geological Society of America, the International Association of Sedimentologists, Sigma Xi, and the North Carolina Academy of Sciences (serving as president). He is also a fellow of the American Association for the Advancement of Science. Dr. Pilkey was educated at Washington State University (B.S., geology), Montana State University (M.S., geology), and Florida State University (Ph.D., geology).

ANTHONY P. PRATT is environmental program manager for the Delaware Department of Natural Resources and Environmental Control, Division of Soil and Water Conservation. He oversees numerous programs related to beach construction, dune building and maintenance, and the National Flood Insurance Community Assistance Program, among others. His public service career with the state has also included managing the Delaware Coastal Management Program, a $1.4 million program that provides oversight to coastal projects in the areas of wetlands, beaches, storm hazard reduction, land use, and public access. He has served as chairman of the Ad Hoc Committee on Beach Management/Sea-Level Rise for Delaware's Environmental Legacy and as lead staff member for the Beaches 2000 Planning Group. He also currently is a member of global change committees for the state of Delaware, the National Governor's Association, and the Council of State Governments. Mr. Pratt received his B.S. degree from Hampshire College.

MARTIN R. SNOW is vice president and division manager of the South Atlantic Division of the Great Lakes Dredge and Dock Company. His many years of engineering experience have given him an understanding of dredging technology and procedures, which are important in determining how engineering elements can affect shorelines and the environment. He has been involved in numerous major projects to deepen harbors, maintain channels, and replenish beaches all along the U.S. East coast and in Saudi Arabia. He has worked on beach nourishment projects for Rockaway Beach, New York, and Miami and Hollywood, Florida. Mr. Snow is a graduate of the Missouri School of Mines and Metallurgy, with a B.S. in civil engineering.

ROBERT F. VAN DOLAH is assistant director and senior marine scientist of the Marine Resources Research Institute of the South Carolina Wildlife and Marine Resources Department and holds adjunct faculty positions at three universities. His research specialties are in the fields of population and community ecology, particularly the effects of environmental perturbations in marine and estuarine systems. Among the research projects he has conducted are the impacts of jetty construction on beach and nearshore infauna and the effects of nourishment projects on beach communities. He has over 50 publications to his credit in these and related areas. Dr. Van Dolah holds a B.S. degree in biology from Marietta College and an M.S. and Ph.D. in zoology from the University of Maryland.

J. RICHARD WEGGEL is professor of civil engineering at Drexel University in Philadelphia and former chief of the Coastal Structures and Evaluation Branch of the Engineering Development Division, U.S. Army Corps of Engineers' Coastal Engineering Research Center (CERC). Early in his tenure at the CERC, Dr. Weggel was involved in developing design criteria and served as technical editor for the *Shore Protection Manual*, the Corps' internationally recognized coastal design manual. He was also involved in many of the Corps' studies of sand movement around coastal structures and sediment budgets. Concurrently, he taught graduate courses at George Washington University in sediment transport, coastal processes, and structures. His teaching and research areas at Drexel include hydraulics, hydrology, and coastal and port engineering. He has served on the ASCE research and executive committees of the Waterway, Port, Coastal & Ocean Division of the American Society of Civil Engineers and the Board of Directors of the American Shore and Beach Preservation Association and is a member of the Permanent International Association of Navigation Congresses, as well as many other professional association activities. Dr. Weggel has authored or coauthored over 50 technical publications in the areas of coastal and beach processes, protection, and structures, including articles on beach nourishment and protection strategies. He received his B.S. in civil engineering from the Drexel Institute of Technology and his M.S. and Ph.D. degrees in civil engineering from the University of Illinois at Urbana-Champaign.

ROBERT L. WIEGEL is professor emeritus of civil engineering at the University of California at Berkeley, where he began his academic career in 1946 as a research engineer following service in the U.S. Army Ordnance Corps. His research interests encompass nearly all areas of coastal engineering and include beach erosion control and harbor arrangements, such as breakwaters and entrances. In addition to writing more than 145 publications, 95 technical reports, and the book *Oceanographical Engineering*, he is the editor of the books *Coastal Engineering Instruments* and *Earthquake Engineering* and has been the editor of *Shore and Beach* since 1988. Mr. Wiegel's professional activities include numerous prestigious appointments to state, national, and international panels. Among others, he has served as commissioner of the California Advisory Commission on Marine and Coastal Resources; as a member of the Steering Committee of the National Academy of Sciences and the National Academy of Engineering International Decade of Ocean Exploration and the National Science Foundation advisory panel for that program; as a member of the U.S. Army Corps of Engineers' Coastal Engineering Research Board; on the National Research Council's Marine Board and its Committee on the Engineering Implications of Changes in Relative Mean Sea Level; on the Advisory Council of the Permanent Secretariat of the International Conferences on Coastal and Port Engineering in Developing Countries; as a U.S. State Department observer to UNESCO's Intergovernmental Oceanographic Commission; and as special advisor to Egypt and a United Nation's Development Program on the Coastal Protection Plan for the Nile Delta. In addition to being a member of the National Academy of Engineering, Dr. Wiegel is an honorary member and fellow of the American Society of Civil Engineers (and former chairman of its Coastal Engineering Research Council) and a fellow of the American Association for the Advancement of Science. He received B.S. and M.S. degrees, both in mechanical engineering, from the University of California at Berkeley.

B

Papers Prepared for this Study*

Churchill, K., and W. Young. 1994. Results of Inquiry on State of Practice of Beach Nourishment and Protection. Unpublished background paper prepared for Committee on Beach Nourishment and Protection, Marine Board, National Research Council, Washington, D.C.

Jarrett, J. T. 1994. Design Storms. Unpublished background paper prepared for the Committee on Beach Nourishment and Protection, Marine Board, National Research Council, Washington, D.C.

Schmidt, D. V. 1994. U.S. Army Corps of Engineers Beach Fill Design Practices. Unpublished background paper prepared for the Committee on Beach Nourishment and Protection, Marine Board, National Research Council, Washington, D.C.

Stronge, W. B. 1994. Economic Issues in Beach Nourishment: Practical Considerations. Unpublished background paper prepared for the Committee on Beach Nourishment and Protection, Marine Board, National Research Council, Washington, D.C.

Weggel, J. R. 1994. Case Study: Ocean City, Maryland. Unpublished background paper prepared for the Committee on Beach Nourishment and Protection, Marine Board, National Research Council, Washington, D.C.

Wiegel, R. L. 1992. Case Histories. Unpublished background paper prepared for the Committee on Beach Nourishment and Protection, Marine Board, National Research Council, Washington, D.C.

---

*Copies of these papers are available upon request from the Marine Board, 2101 Constitution Avenue, Washington, D.C. 20418.

APPENDIX

C
Prediction of
Beach Nourishment Performance

INTRODUCTION

Beach nourishment is the placement of relatively large quantities of good-quality material on a beach to advance the shoreline seaward and to provide an elevation to adequately protect the upland area. Usually, beach nourishment is carried out in areas where the shore protection beach, the recreational beach, or both are inadequate to fulfill the intended function or functions. Beach width and elevation inadequacies can occur because the shoreline is retreating or by imprudent location of upland construction. Erosion can be either natural or human induced. In the latter instance, it is important to attempt to remove or reduce the cause of erosion whenever possible.

Beach nourishment material is usually placed on a steeper-than-equilibrium slope; it also represents a planform perturbation. These disequilibriums in both the planform and profile induce sediment flows that, over time, will reduce the disequilibrium, thereby approaching the equilibrium state. Retention structures can be employed to increase the longevity of the project, but in many situations they can also increase erosion on adjacent shorelines. Performance can be predicted with simple, relatively rapid, inexpensive methods and also through the use of numerical models. The time scales associated with project equilibration are of considerable design interest and are critical to the economic viability of a project. Figure C-1 illustrates the complicated three-dimensional sediment transport patterns associated with various phases of project evolution.

Although beach nourishment projects have been carried out actively for several decades, there is still not an adequate methodology to predict their de-

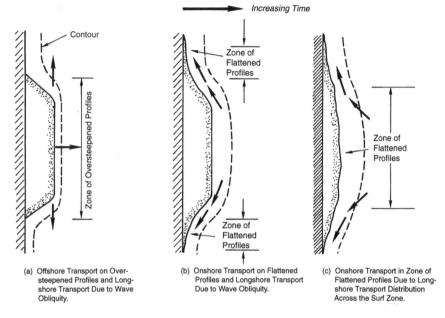

(a) Offshore Transport on Over-
    steepened Profiles and Long-
    shore Transport Due to Wave
    Obliquity.

(b) Onshore Transport on Flattened
    Profiles and Longshore Transport
    Due to Wave Obliquity.

(c) Onshore Transport in Zone of
    Flattened Profiles Due to Long-
    shore Transport Distribution
    Across the Surf Zone.

FIGURE C-1   Three Phases of observed sediment transport in the vicinity of nourished projects. Note: cross-contour transport due to profile disequilibrium (from Dean et al., 1993).

tailed performance. This is due in part to the complicated alongshore and cross-shore transport processes, the near uniqueness of every setting for such projects, and the generally inadequate monitoring of both the forces on and responses of past projects to provide a basis for assessment of available methodologies and guidance for their improvement.

This appendix reviews simple analytical and numerical procedures available for prediction of beach nourishment project performance, introduces some less-well-known behavioral characteristics affecting performance, and provides estimates of predictability under various nourishment scenarios.

METHODS FOR PREDICTING
BEACH NOURISHMENT PROJECT EVOLUTION

Simple Analytical Procedures

The simple analytical prediction procedures are best suited for the less complex geometries and for preliminary design in the early phase and scoping of the volumes, costs, and renourishment intervals. More complex geometries, including the effects of structures, require the use of numerical models and are discussed later.

Evolution of a beach nourishment project is a result of both cross-shore and alongshore sediment transport. For the simple case of a long nourishment project on a long straight beach, the time scales for cross-shore and planform equilibration are disparate. The cross-shore and alongshore time scales are on the order of 2 to 3 years and decades, respectively. This discussion will assume that the profile adjustment occurs instantaneously. For this adjustment, predicting the equilibrium width of dry beach is the principal focus. For the alongshore equilibration, the focus is on the time scales and evolutionary behavior. The disparity of time scales is fortunate because current knowledge of alongshore sediment transport has been developed over a period of 4 or 5 decades. The knowledge of alongshore sediment transport is much more advanced than for cross-shore transport, which has been studied actively for only about a decade.

Equilibrium Dry Beach Width

In cases in which the nourishment material is similar to the native beach material, the additional dry beach width after equilibration, Δy_o, can be shown to be approximately

$$\Delta y_o = \frac{V}{h_* + B} \tag{C-1}$$

in which V is the volume of fill added per unit beach length and $h_* + B$ represents the dimension of the active vertical profile, where h_* is the depth of active motion (depth of closure) dependent on the upper ranges of wave height experienced, as given by Hallermeier (1978) and Birkemeier (1985), and B is usually selected as the height of the active natural berm but may exceed this elevation for flood control purposes.

Dean (1991) has shown that for the general case in which the native and fill materials differ the additional dry beach width can differ substantially from that given by Equation (C-1). In this case, the best approach is to use the equilibrium beach profile concept, in which the simplest profile form is

$$h = Ay^{2/3} \tag{C-2}$$

where h is the depth at a distance y from the shoreline.

Equation (C-2) represents the ideal profile that occurs naturally and cannot represent bar features or effects of rock outcrops, hard bottoms, or coral reefs. Use of these idealized assumptions in applying Equation (C-2) has been criticized by Pilkey et al. (1993). Equilibrium beach profile forms other than Equation (C-2) have been proposed by Bodge (1992), Komar and McDougal (1993); and

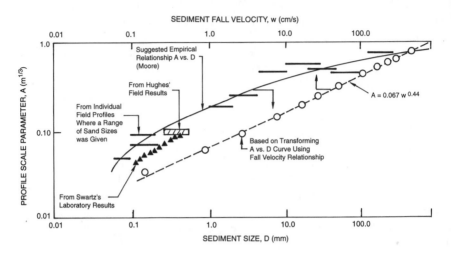

FIGURE C-2   Variation of sediment-scale parameter, A, with sediment size and fall velocity (from Dean, 1987).

Inman et al. (1993), however, these authors provide no guidance for applying these forms in cases where only the grain size is known.

In order to apply Equation (C-2) to beach nourishment, a relationship is needed between the sediment-scale parameter, A, and the grain size, D, or equivalent sediment fall velocity, w. Such a relationship, originally developed by Moore (1982) and modified by Dean (1987), is shown in Figure C-2. In applying Equation (C-2) the parameters for the native and fill materials will be indicated by subscripts N and F, respectively. In general, three types of nourished profiles can occur, depending primarily on the relative A parameters and the amounts of fill placed. These types, intersecting, nonintersecting, and submerged, are illustrated in Figure C-3.

It can be shown that the nondimensional dry beach width, $\Delta y_0/W_*$, is a function of the three nondimensional variables:

$$\frac{\Delta y_0}{W_*} = \left[\frac{V}{BW_*}, \frac{A_F}{A_N}, \frac{h_*}{B} \right] = \left[V', A', \frac{h_*}{B} \right] \tag{C-3}$$

where V is the volume added per unit beach length and B is the berm height. W_* is the width of the active profile (to h_*) on the *native* profile, that is, from Equation (C-2):

$$W_* = \left(\frac{h_*}{A_N} \right)^{3/2} \tag{C-4}$$

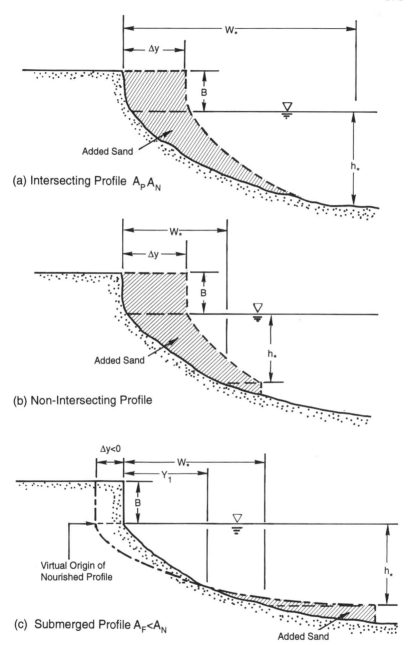

(a) Intersecting Profile $A_P A_N$

(b) Non-Intersecting Profile

(c) Submerged Profile $A_F < A_N$

FIGURE C-3   Three generic types of nourished profiles (from Dean, 1991).

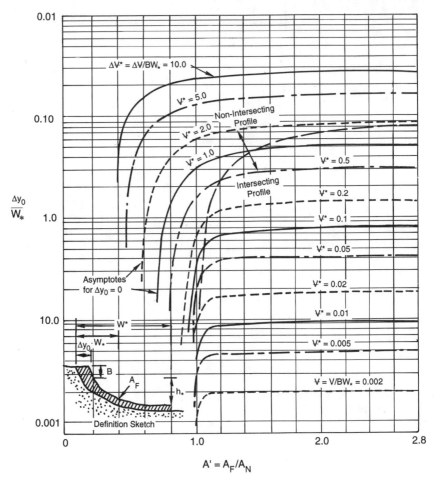

FIGURE C-4   Variation of nondimensional shoreline advancement, $\Delta y_0/W_*$, with A' and results shown for $h_*/B = 2.0$ (from Dean, 1991).

Figures C-4 and C-5 present graphical solutions to Equation (C-3) for values of h_*/B of 2 and 4, respectively.

Planform Evolution

Planform evolution is influenced by the general morphology of the system to be nourished; the simplest case is a long straight beach. The planform of the nourishment can influence the performance; however, the initial discussions here will address the case of an initially rectangular planform for which analytical solutions exist.

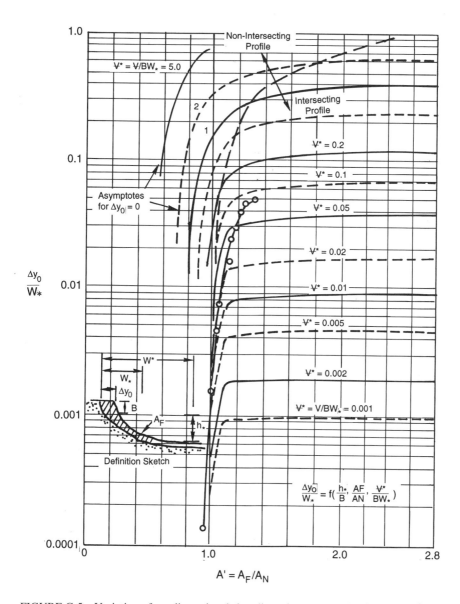

FIGURE C-5   Variation of nondimensional shoreline advancement, $\Delta y_0/W_*$, with A' and results shown for $h_*/B = 4.0$ (from Dean, 1991).

Pelnard-Considére (1956) combined the linearized equation of sediment transport and the equation of continuity, considering the profiles to be displaced without change of form, to yield

$$\frac{\partial y}{\partial t} = G \frac{\partial^2 y}{\partial x^2} \tag{C-5}$$

in which G is the so-called alongshore diffusivity and can be expressed in terms of breaking or deepwater wave conditions, respectively, as

$$G = \frac{K h_b^{2.5} \sqrt{g/\kappa}}{8(s-1)(1-p)(h_* + B)} \quad \text{(for breaking conditions)} \tag{C-6}$$

$$G = \frac{K H_o^{2.4} C_{G_o}^{1.2} g^{0.4}}{8(s-1)(1-p) C_* \kappa^{0.4}(h_* + B)} \quad \text{(for deepwater conditions)} \tag{C-7}$$

in which K is a sediment transport factor usually taken as 0.77 but is probably a function of sediment grain size or other characteristics, H is the wave height, and κ is the ratio of breaking wave height to local water depth (usually taken as 0.78). C_G is the wave group velocity, C_* is celerity at the depth of closure, s is the ratio of the specific gravity of the sediment to that of the water in which it is immersed (≈ 2.65), p is the porosity (≈ 0.35), and g is the acceleration of gravity. The subscripts b and o denote breaking and deepwater wave conditions, respectively.

Project Longevity for Simplest Case

It can be shown that in the absence of background erosion the fraction of material remaining, M, in the region where fill is placed depends only on the parameter $\sqrt{Gt}/\ell$, in which ℓ is the length of the initially rectangular project and t is time (see Figure C-6). For values of M between 0.5 and unity, it can be shown that within a 15 percent error band in M an approximate expression for the relationship in Figure C-6 is

$$M = 1 - \frac{2}{\sqrt{\pi}} \frac{\sqrt{Gt}}{\ell} \tag{C-8}$$

A useful result developed from Equation C-8 is the time ($t_{50\%}$) for 50 percent of the placed volume to be transported from the original project limits:

$$t_{50\%} = K' \frac{\ell^2}{H_b^{5/2}} \tag{C-9}$$

in which $t_{50\%}$ is expressed in years, and $K' = 0.172$ years $\text{m}^{5/2}$/square kilometer for ℓ in kilometers and H_b in meters.

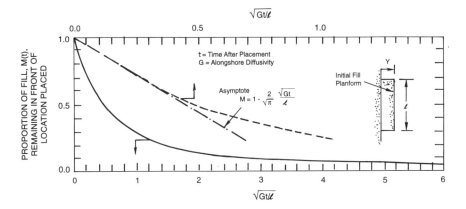

FIGURE C-6   Proportion of material remaining, M, in region placed as a function of the parameter.

Fill Performance with a Uniform Background Recession Rate, E

For the case in which a uniform background shoreline recession rate, E, is present, it can be shown that for values of

$$\frac{\sqrt{Gt}}{\ell} < 0.5$$

the time required for a fraction $(1-M)$ of the material placed to be removed from the project area (or equivalently for a fraction M of the material placed to remain in the project area) is

$$t_M = \frac{-b + \sqrt{b^2 - 4ac}}{2a} \tag{C-10}$$

in which

$$a = (E/\Delta y_o)^2,$$

$$b = \frac{2E(M-1)}{\Delta y_o} - \frac{4}{\pi}\frac{G}{\ell^2}$$

and

$$c = (1 - M)^2$$

in which Δy_o is the initial dry beach width, as defined earlier.

Effect of Wave Refraction Around the Project

It can be shown, consistent with intuition, that waves refract, wrapping around the nourishment planform and thereby tending to prolong its life. Equation (C-6), applied in conjunction with Figure C-6, does not include the refraction effects, but they can be approximated simply by multiplying the G value in Equation (C-6) by the fraction C_b/C_*, in which C is the wave celerity and the subscripts b and * denote values at breaking and depth of closure h_*, respectively. Since this ratio is generally less than unity, the effect is a greater project longevity with reduced G values. In some applications in Florida the effect of this correction results in a $t_{50\%}$ that is 40 percent greater than without this factor.

Residual Bathymetry

In contrast to the usual assumption that the entire placed beach profile moves without change of form during evolution of the project planform, in some cases the beach nourishment may extend to greater depths than will be mobilized, at least during the first few years following nourishment. If the initial placement is irregular, this can affect the quasi-equilibrium planform. In an idealized fashion the upper portions of the placed profile are "planed off" by the alongshore transport, leaving the placed material below this level of activity as "residual bathymetry." Although this residual bathymetry is not active in the transport processes, it does influence the wave transformation, in particular wave refraction. The effect of the wave refraction is to cause the quasi-equilibrium planform to remain irregular rather than to be straight, as would be the case if the entire placed planform moved in response to gradients in the alongshore sediment transport. The equilibrium shoreline planform will be a somewhat damped form of the offshore residual bathymetry. Denoting the celerity of the waves at the outer depth of the placed bathymetry as C_1 and that at the depth of limiting motion, h_2, as C_2 ($C_1 > C_2$), it can be shown that the project-related transport, Q_P, is

$$Q_P = \frac{KE_oC_{G_o}\cos(\beta_o - \alpha_o)C_b}{\rho g(s-1)(1-p)C_2}\left[\left(\frac{C_2}{C_1}-1\right)\Delta\beta_1 + \Delta\beta_2\right] \qquad \text{(C-11)}$$

in which the β variables represent the azimuths of the outward normals of the various contours as depicted by their subscripts, and the $\Delta\beta_n$ are defined by $\Delta\beta_n = \beta_n - \beta_o$. ρ is the mass density of the water, and α is the azimuth from which the wave is propagating in deep water.

This result can be interpreted intuitively as the onshore contours "mimicking" those offshore. This phenomenon, as represented by Equation (C-11), may explain why some beach nourishment projects experience erosional hot spots at which the beach erodes faster than the average for the project. Other possible causes of some erosional hot spots are a break in the offshore bar and wave refraction over an offshore mound, which allow wave energy to impact the shoreline. Returning to the case in which the erosional hot spots are explained by Equation (C-11), if for some unintended reason the placed material along the shoreline is not distributed uniformly and if the sediment at the deeper portions of the profile does not move at the same rate as that at the upper elevations, Equation (C-11) may provide an explanation of the cause of erosional hot spots. Regardless of their cause, Equation (C-11) may provide a basis for remedying such effects. For example, if the natural contours seaward of the placed material are such that they cause localized erosion, it may be possible (although not practical in all cases) to place material seaward of the active zone in a planform to refract the waves in a manner that balances the tendency for localized erosion. Equation (C-11) can be used to find the shoreline of approximate planform equilibrium. This occurs, of course, for $Q_P = 0$ and yields

$$\Delta\beta_2 = \Delta\beta_1 \left[1 - \left(\frac{C_2}{C_1} \right) \right]$$

$$(C\text{-}12)$$

from which it can be seen that if there is no residual bathymetry ($C_2 = C_1$) the equilibrium shoreline orientation, β_2 is equal to β_0. As an example, if the planform relief in the offshore residual contours were 50 m and the celerity ratio $C_2/C_1 = 0.5$, the planform relief of the shoreline would be 25 m.

Numerical Models for Predicting Beach Nourishment Performance

Computer Models of Alongshore Shoreline Evolution

An important tool in the design and implementation of many beach nourishment projects is the application of computer models that simulate the processes of alongshore sediment transport and the resulting evolution of the shoreline planform. Such models incorporate equations that relate sediment movements to the nearshore waves and currents. They also include a continuity equation that in essence keeps track of the total volume of beach sediment as it is redistributed alongshore and permits computations of the resulting patterns of shoreline recession or advance. Such numerical simulation models have proved to be useful tools in a number of applications, including analyses of the impacts from construction of jetties and breakwaters on the shoreline configuration and predicting the patterns of shoreline change. Only in recent years have they been applied to beach nourishment projects. However, the use of numerical models has become a standard tool in the design of beach nourishment projects involving the U.S. Army Corps of Engineers (USACE), although the application of this tool varies between USACE districts.

The general approach to computer models of shoreline change involves the conceptual division of the shoreline into a large number of individual cells or compartments. Equations relating the alongshore sediment transport rate to the wave parameters—that is, to wave heights or energies—and to velocities of alongshore currents are employed to calculate the shift of sand from one cell to the next. The continuity equation, based on the conservation of sediment, makes sure that none is unaccountably created or destroyed. But more importantly, it can convert volumes of sand entering or exiting a particular cell into the resulting shoreline changes, whether these changes are net advances or recessions. In general, sand enters a particular cell from one direction and exits in the same direction, so it is the net volume of these transfers that ultimately governs whether there is recession or advance of the shoreline as represented by that cell. Such an analysis involves many computations of sand exchanges between cells and the resulting net volumes of sand in the many cells, and such a computationally intensive analysis requires the use of a computer. Furthermore, the model is run through time so as to simulate the shoreline evolution spanning months to decades. In some cases, the models must be run on large powerful computers if an extended stretch of shoreline is being analyzed for predicted shoreline changes spanning many years. Reduced versions of such model analyses are also available for desktop computer applications.

Early examples of computer models of shoreline change that have a range of applications are provided by Price et al. (1973), Komar (1973, 1977), and Perlin and Dean (1979). These early studies established the validity of computer models and demonstrated their reliability in a number of applications. The study by Price et al., an analysis of the impoundment of sand by groins, is especially noteworthy in that it provided the first comparison between the results from a computer model and a physical model undertaken in a laboratory wave basin.

The most recent advances in numerical models used to simulate shoreline changes have been incorporated into GENESIS, an acronym for generalized model for simulating shoreline change. GENESIS was developed by the USACE. Details of the technical development of GENESIS are given in a report by Hanson and Kraus (1989), and a report by Gravens et al. (1991) serves as a workbook and user's manual. One of the chief contributions of the GENESIS model is that it provides a flexible basis for analyses that can be applied to an arbitrary prototype situation—a basis that calculates wave transformations as they shoal and undergo refraction and diffraction, calculates the patterns of alongshore sediment transport, and then determines the resulting shoreline changes. One of the principal modifications of the GENESIS model from earlier models is in the calculation of alongshore sediment transport rates, an approach that includes the transport caused by waves breaking obliquely to the shoreline and alongshore variations in wave breaker heights. This modification enhances the capability of GENESIS to simulate shoreline changes in proximity to structures such as jetties and groins, where local sheltering from offshore waves is a factor. The importance of this inclusion in numerical shoreline models was first demonstrated by Kraus and Harikai (1983) in their analyses of Oarai Beach, Japan, where wave diffraction at a long breakwater is a dominant process, and subsequently in some of the applications of GENESIS that also include shoreline structures.

Hanson et al. (1988) applied GENESIS to a simulation of the shoreline development on Homer Spit, Alaska, and the erosion downdrift from a seawall on Sandy Hook, New Jersey. The most complex analysis, examined in great detail by Hanson and Kraus (1991a), was of shoreline changes at Lakeview Park, in Lorain, Ohio, on Lake Erie. This analysis simulated the shoreline changes observed following the construction of three detached breakwaters in the offshore and two bounding groins and the addition of sand to create a new beach. The simulation involved analysis of wave diffraction through the gaps between the breakwaters and of the resulting readjustment of the shoreline from its original smooth curvature after sand emplacement. Cusps or salients developed in the sheltered region behind each breakwater, with intervening bays opposite the gaps between the breakwaters. The agreement between the measured shoreline and that computed by GENESIS was excellent. However, the result represents a calibration of the model that included some adjustment of empirical coefficients to optimize the fit. After the model had been calibrated and tested versus observed shoreline changes, Hanson and Kraus (1991a) explored alternative project designs for maintaining the beach fill. This included analyses of the beach retention for various lengths of the bounding groins and for the absence of any groins. Such analyses demonstrate the usefulness of numerical shoreline models in general and GENESIS specifically, as many alternative designs can be examined at minimal expense. Hanson and Kraus (1991b) compared GENESIS predictions to the results obtained in physical models, again for a series of detached breakwaters such as those at Lakeview Park but also for the impoundment of sand in a series of groins built across the beach. In all cases, the numerical models closely reproduced the shoreline changes that occurred in the physical models.

GENESIS includes analyses of wave refraction in the offshore. Therefore, its use can incorporate design and implementation aspects involving predictions of potential impacts that result, for example, from changes in offshore water depths that are produced by dredging in the source area for sand for nourishment. These potential impacts are illustrated by the earlier study of Motyka and Willis (1975), which also developed shoreline simulation models coupled with wave refraction/diffraction analyses. The necessity for computing wave refraction patterns considerably increases the complexity of the model in that it requires an offshore array to account for the bottom topography as well as to define the shoreline position, with the possibility of both evolving through time. The problem analyzed by Motyka and Willis involved an examination of whether dredging of sediment from the continental shelf could alter the wave refraction to a sufficient degree that it induces shoreline erosion.

One example of the model calculations of Motyka and Willis (1975) is the consideration of the effects of dredging a 4-m-deep hole in water that is 7 m deep and 500 m offshore. The model used realistic profiles of the beach and offshore and had a dredged hole inserted. The root-mean-square wave height was 0.4 m, and periods of 5 and 8 seconds were used. Wave directions were selected so as to yield a net alongshore sediment transport of 30,000 m³/year. The results demonstrate that the dredged hole would cause recession of the shoreline in its lee and an advance to either side. The pattern is asymmetrical owing to the superimposed alongshore sediment transport that results from an overall oblique wave approach. The shoreline alterations are greater with the 8-second waves than with the 5-second waves because the longer-period waves undergo more refraction. The models predict major erosion that results from offshore dredging—a shoreline retreat of 20 to 35 m that exists over a kilometer of shoreline length. Another example of shoreline recession induced by offshore dredging for a beach nourishment project can be seen at Grand Isle, Louisiana (Combe and Soileau, 1987). The dredging there occurred over a wide area about 500 m offshore and lowered the bottom by 3 to 6 m. The resulting development of an erosional embayment between accretional cusps is very similar to that obtained in the numerical models of Motyka and Willis (1975). Although Combe and Soileau confirmed that the impact at Grand Isle was due to the effects of the dredged hole on wave refraction, detailed numerical analyses were not undertaken.

In a somewhat comparable fashion, offshore shoals can focus the wave energy on specific stretches of shoreline through their effects on the patterns of wave refraction over the shallower water. In some instances, this process may account for erosional hot spots in nourishment projects. The process has been suggested as a cause of the erosional hot spots that have occurred at Ocean City, Maryland. Analyses using shoreline models such as GENESIS that include wave refraction have the potential for predicting locations of erosional hot spots and could be used to analyze whether the focus of erosion might be eliminated by dredging the offshore shoals to some determined water depth.

Shoreline models such as GENESIS have been discussed here as an aspect of the design of beach nourishment projects and have been used to predict the shoreline evolution of the sand fill. They can be equally useful during the monitoring phase of a project because the models unite measurements of beach profiles that can be used to determine the actual resulting patterns of shoreline recession and advance. This is illustrated by Work (1993), who analyzed monitoring data for the nourishment project at Perdido Key, Florida. The continued use of numerical shoreline models in the monitoring phase of this project has provided an additional basis for improvements in the models themselves and a greater confidence in future projects, especially at this site.

One advantage of computer models is that they allow determination of the effects of particular placement configurations and wave variability. For example, Hanson and Kraus (1993) have investigated the effectiveness of transitioning the ends of a project to reduce total costs, including that of renourishment. The numerical methods could use actual wave data or a simulation of serial wave data rather than an equivalent wave height, period, and direction, or a combination of the three. At present, the prediction of shoreline position by numerical models in some applications may be limited by the accuracy of available wave information.

There are at least two options to account for the background erosion rates with numerical models. In applying GENESIS the model should be calibrated with historical shoreline changes, so that it can faithfully represent the causes of the background erosion. A second procedure, recommended by Dean and Yoo (1992), is that the empirical background erosion be represented as background sediment transport and be superimposed on the transport induced by the nourishment project. In the absence of nourishment, this method ensures that the background erosion will be reproduced exactly.

The numerical models of shoreline evolution are based on the same equations as the analytical method described earlier, except that one of the equations is linearized in the analytical method. Generally, if the two methods are applied to the same initial planform and wave conditions, the results are essentially the same. The numerical models also share many of the uncertainties in applications with the analytical models discussed earlier. Model predictions are limited by the ability to predict alongshore sediment transport rates. Any uncertainties in the transport calculations carry over into the model predictions of the shoreline evolution. The dependence of the alongshore transport on sediment grain sizes is not well established. This especially affects the ability to model the evolution of a beach fill where the nourishment material does not fully match the grain-size distribution of the native beach sand. Although full three-dimensional models that account simultaneously for cross-shore and alongshore sediment transport are available, the commonly applied models such as GENESIS deal only with alongshore evolution of the shoreline, and separate models, such as SBEACH, analyze the cross-shore sediment transport. The models sometimes need recalibration for the specific site of the application or verification during the monitoring phase of a nourishment program because of uncertainties in the transport calculations and because of simplified assumptions that are used in developing the shoreline evolution models.

Profile Evolution

Numerical models are also available to represent profile evolution and can, in principle, be used to simulate the equilibration of a placed profile or the profile response during a storm. The structure of these models is similar to that described for planform evolution—that is, there is a dynamic or transport equation that prescribes the sediment flow across the profile and a continuity equation that conducts the bookkeeping of differences between sediment flows in and out of a computational cell and equates those differences to changes in profile elevation. These computational models have been employed and verified to a limited degree in the equilibration phase of a fill; however, only limited efforts have been devoted to the recovery phase following storms.

The earliest profile evolution models include those of Edelman (1972), who assumed that the profile maintained the same shape as the original while it is translated and that the profile equilibration processes kept pace with the rising sea level. Swart (1974) developed a complex computational model based on a series of laboratory tests. Moore (1982), Kriebel (1982), and Kriebel and Dean (1985) have described a profile response model based on a transport that is proportional to the difference between the actual and equilibrium wave energy dissipation per unit of water volume. Limited evaluations of prototype and laboratory data provide support for this transport relationship. Kriebel et al. (1991) and Kriebel and Dean (1993) have described an analytical method, based on observations from numerical models, in which the profile tends to approach the equilibrium in an exponential manner for a constant water level. Kriebel (1990) has described modifications to his model that allow the effects of seawalls and overwash to be represented. The Kriebel and Dean (1985) model (EDUNE) was used to some extent in the design of the Ocean City, Maryland, beach nourishment project, although its use was limited because it was not calibrated or verified for erosion events at Ocean City. The numerical modeling system and storm erosion models were used to evaluate and compare the relative effectiveness of each plan rather than to determine the dimensions of the alternative proposed plans.

The profile evolution model employed by the USACE is called SBEACH (Larson and Kraus, 1989a, 1991) and uses a modified form of the transport equation described earlier. This model is well documented and is in the public domain. It differs from the others described earlier in that it can predict the formation of bars in the eroding profile. The model has been calibrated and verified for both laboratory and prototype profiles. Larson and Kraus (1989b, 1990) have compared SBEACH predictions with results from a test using a large wave tank and field data from Duck, North Carolina. The model was also used to analyze the design of the Ocean City nourishment project after the storm of January 4, 1992. It was tested both with and without overwash, a feature that was added to the model to attempt to represent the processes contributing to profile changes during the storm (Kraus and Wise, 1993; Wise and Kraus, 1993). SBEACH allows the effects of seawalls to be represented. With respect to SBEACH simulations for the Ocean City project, the model calibration parameter was 20 percent below that determined in an earlier publication treating a lesser storm on a smaller fill section at the same site. For Ocean City, Maryland, Hansen and Byrnes (1991) quote an SBEACH transport coefficient of 1.0×10^{-6} m^4/N, Kraus and Wise (1993) quote $1.5 \times 10^{-6} m^4/N$, and Wise and Kraus (1993) quote $1.2 \times 10^{-6} m^4/N$. The SBEACH simulations were not correlated with the original application of the Kriebel-Dean model. The present version of SBEACH (Version 3.0) contains additional improvements not found in the versions used in either of the previous studies mentioned.

NOURISHMENT IN THE PRESENCE OF STRUCTURES

Coastal structures can be used to increase the longevity of beach nourishment projects. Structures for this purpose include groins, terminal structures, and submerged or emergent offshore breakwaters. In addition, some projects will be carried out in areas where seawalls are present. Due to the complexity of the interaction of sediment transport processes with coastal structures, prediction of the performance of beach nourishment projects in the presence of coastal structures will usually require the use of numerical models. Knowledge of the interaction of coastal structures with beach systems is on the edge of the state of the art.

Retention Structures

The "spreading out" losses due to alongshore sediment transport can be reduced by placing retention structures near or at the ends of a project. These structures, also frequently referred to as "terminal structures," increase the longevity of the project by reducing transport from the project to adjacent areas. In considering the use of such structures, careful consideration must be given to the possibility and degree to which they might affect the shorelines adjacent to the project. The potential for impact is much greater in those cases where a substantial alongshore sediment transport exists. To partially alleviate the early impacts of transport interruption, a surcharge of sand can be placed on the downdrift side of the downdrift retention structure.

Seawalls

A *limiting* effect of mismatch of the native and nourishment materials occurs when nourishment is placed in front of a shoreline that is backed by seawalls and has alongshore transport potential but little sediment-to-transport potential. In this case, it can be shown that the planform evolution is markedly different from nourishment on a beach of compatible sand. The behavior of the beach planform has been modeled in GENESIS since its inception and is documented in both the technical reference and specialized publications (Hanson and Kraus, 1991a,b; Gravens et al., 1991). Dean and Yoo (1994) have shown theoretically, numerically, and experimentally that the planform evolution is critically dependent on the transport characteristics near a project's end, in particular for those portions of the project where the "active" profile does not extend up to the free surface. The general differences include a downdrift migration of the planform centroid, with initially increasing and later decreasing speed, and a spreading of the planform, which can be significantly less or greater than would occur on a beach with compatible sand. The behavior of the beach planform in front of seawalls was previously incorporated into GENESIS (Hanson and Kraus, 1985, 1989).

Figure C-7 presents an example of a calculated planform and volumetric evolution for the case of nourishment in front of a seawall and under the action of oblique waves. The upper panel shows the shoreline displacement and the lower panel the volumetric distributions. The "threshold volume" is that associated with an incipient dry beach; that is, sufficient sand is present to just fill the profile to the water line at the seawall. The planform migrational tendency shown in the

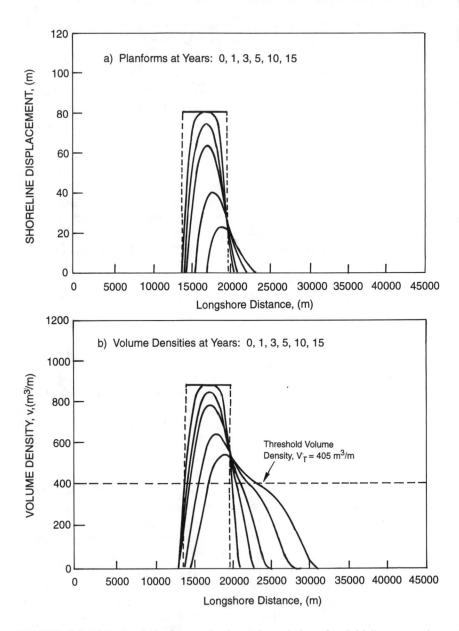

FIGURE C-7   Calculated planform and volumetric evolution of an initially rectangular beach nourishment project fronting a seawall. Deepwater waves at 10° to shore normal (from Dean and Yoo, 1994).

TABLE C-1   Beach Nourishment Invariants

Description of Invariant	Conditions
Initially symmetric planforms remain nearly symmetric even under oblique wave attack (Note: this implies that wave direction is relatively unimportant)	Nourishment on a long, straight beach with compatible sediment
Planform evolution at any time is independent of the sequencing of the previous waves causing the evolution	Same as above
Good-quality sand remains in the active beach profile	Good-quality sand has the same general size characteristics as that originally present on the beach

figure can be interpreted as due to the oblique waves "cannibalizing" the sand on the updrift end of the project and depositing it on the downdrift end. In the case of nourishment on a shoreline of compatible sand, owing to the small aspect ratio of the project, the transport patterns can be linearized approximately as the superimposition of alongshore transport on an unperturbed shoreline and normally incident waves acting on the nourishment project. This is the reason that nourishment on a beach of compatible sand will result in little downdrift migration or planform asymmetry. In those cases in which nourishment occurs in front of a seawall, there is a much greater need to establish the directional characteristics of the waves than for nourishment on a beach of compatible sand.

INVARIANTS

Although there are uncertainties associated with the design of beach nourishment projects, there are also some invariants or performance characteristics that are insensitive to some physical processes. Three relevant design invariants are characterized in Table C-1.

REFERENCES

Birkemeier, W. A. 1985. Field data on seaward limit of profile change. Journal of the Waterway, Port, Coastal, and Ocean Engineering 3(3):598-602.
Bodge, K. R. 1992. Representing equilibrium beach profiles with an exponential expression. Journal of Coastal Research 8(1):47-55.

Combe, A. J., and C. W. Soileau. 1987. Behavior of man-made beach and dune, Grand Isle, Louisiana. Pp. 1232-1242 in Proceedings of Coastal Sediments '87, Specialty Conference on Advances in Understanding of Coastal Sediment Processes, Vol. 2. New York: American Society of Civil Engineers.

Dean, R. G. 1987. Coastal sediment processes: toward engineering solutions. Pp. 1-24 in Proceedings of Coastal Sediments '87, Specialty Conference on Advances in Understanding of Coastal Sediment Processes, Vol. 1. New York: American Society of Civil Engineers.

Dean, R. G. 1991. Equilibrium beach profiles: characteristics and applications. Journal of Coastal Research 7(1):53-84.

Dean, R. G., and C-H. Yoo. 1992. Beach nourishment performance predictions. Journal of the Waterway, Port, Coastal and Ocean Engineering 118(6):557-586.

Dean, R. G., and C-H. Yoo. 1994. Beach nourishment in the presence of seawalls. Journal of the Waterway, Port, Coastal, and Ocean Engineering 120(3):302-316.

Dean, R. G., T. R. Healy, and A. Dommerholt. 1993. A "blind-folded" test of equilibrium beach profile concepts with New Zealand data. Marine Geology 109:253-266.

Edelman, T. 1972. Dune erosion during storm conditions. Pp. 1305-1311 in Proceedings of the 13th Coastal Engineering Conference. New York: American Society of Civil Engineers.

Gravens, M. B., N. C. Kraus and H. Hanson. 1991. GENESIS: generalized model for simulating shoreline change. In: Report 2: Workbook and System User's Manual. Technical Report CERC-89-19. Vicksburg, Miss.: Coastal Engineering Research Center, U.S. Army Engineer Waterways Experiment Station, U.S. Army Corps of Engineers.

Hallermeier, R. J. 1978. Uses for a calculated limit depth to beach erosion. Pp. 1493-1512 in Proceedings of the 16th International Conference on Coastal Engineering. New York: American Society of Civil Engineers.

Hanson, M. E., and M. R. Byrnes. 1991. Development of optimum beach fill design cross-section. Pp. 2067-2080 in Proceedings of Coastal Sediments '91. New York: American Society of Civil Engineers.

Hanson, M. E., and N. C. Kraus. 1985. Seawall constraint in the shoreline numerical model. Journal of Waterways, Ports, Coastal and Ocean Engineering 111(6):1079-1083.

Hanson, H., and N. C. Kraus. 1989. GENESIS: generalized model for simulating shoreline change. In Report 1: Reference Manual and Users Guide. Technical Report No. CERC-89-19. Vicksburg, Miss.: Coastal Engineering Research Center, U.S. Army Engineer Waterways Experiment Station, U.S. Army Corps of Engineers.

Hanson, H., and N. C. Kraus. 1991a. Numerical simulation of shoreline change at Lorain, Ohio. Journal of Waterway, Port, Coastal and Ocean Engineering 117:1-18.

Hanson, H., and N. C. Kraus. 1991b. Comparison of shoreline change obtained with physical and numerical models. Pp. 1785-1799 in Proceedings of Coastal Sediments '91. New York: American Society of Civil Engineers.

Hanson, H., and N. C. Kraus. 1993. Optimization of beach fill transitions. Pp. 103-117 in D. K. Stauble and N. C. Kraus, eds., Volume on Beach Nourishment Engineering and Management Considerations, Proceedings of Coastal Zone '93. New York: American Society of Civil Engineers.

Hanson, H., M. B. Gravens, and N. C. Kraus. 1988. Prototype applications of a generalized shoreline change numerical model. Pp. 1265-1279 in Proceedings of the 21st Coastal Engineering Conference. New York: American Society of Civil Engineers.

Inman, D. L., M. H. S. Elwany, and S. A. Jenkins. 1993. Shorerise and bar-berm profiles on ocean beaches. Journal of Geophysical Research 98(C10)18, 181-18, 199.

Komar, P. D. 1973. Computer models of delta growth due to sediment input from rivers and longshore transport. Geological Society of America Bulletin 84:2217-2226.

Komar, P. D. 1977. Modeling of sand transport on beaches and the resulting shoreline evolution. Pp. 499-513 in E. Goldberg et al., eds., The Sea, vol. 6. New York: John Wiley & Sons.

Komar, P. D., and W. G. McDougal. 1993. The analysis of exponential beach profiles. Journal of Coastal Research 10(1):59-69.

Kraus, N. C., and S. Harikai. 1983. Numerical model of the shoreline at Oarai Beach: Coastal Engineering 7:1-28.

Kraus, N. C., and R. A. Wise. 1993. Simulation of January 4, 1992 storm erosion at Ocean City, Maryland. Shore and Beach 61(1):34-41.

Kriebel, D. L. 1982. Beach and Dune Response to Hurricanes. Master's thesis, University of Delaware, Newark.

Kriebel, D. L. 1990. Advances in numerical modeling of dune erosion. Pp. 2304-2317 in 22nd International Conference on Coastal Engineering. New York: American Society of Civil Engineers.

Kriebel, D. L., and R. G. Dean. 1985. Numerical simulation of time-dependent beach and dune erosion. Coastal Engineering 9:221-245.

Kriebel, D. L., and R. G. Dean. 1993. Convolution method for time-dependent beach profile response. Journal of Waterway, Port, Ocean and Coastal Engineering 119(2):204-227.

Kriebel, D. L., N. C. Kraus, and M. Larson. 1991. Engineering methods for predicting beach profile response. Pp. 557-571 in Proceedings of Coastal Sediments '91. New York: American Society of Civil Engineers.

Larson, M. 1988. Quantification of beach profile change. Report No. 1008. Department of Water Resources and Engineering, University of Lund, Lund, Sweden.

Larson, M., and N. C. Kraus. 1989a. Prediction of beach fill response to varying waves and water level. Pp. 607-621 in Proceedings of Coastal Zone '89. New York: American Society of Civil Engineers.

Larson, M., and N. C. Kraus. 1989b. SBEACH: Numerical Model for Simulating Storm-Induced Beach Change. Report 1: Empirical Foundation and Model Development. Technical Report No. CERC-89-9. Vicksburg, Miss.: Coastal Engineering Research Center, U.S. Army Engineer Waterways Experiment Station, U.S. Army Corps of Engineers.

Larson, M., and N. C. Kraus. 1990. SBEACH: Numerical Model for Simulating Storm-Induced Beach Change. Report 2, Numerical Foundation and Model Tests. Technical Report CERC-89-9. Vicksburg, Miss.: Coastal Engineering Research Center, U. S. Army Engineer Waterways Experiment Station, U.S. Army Corps of Engineers.

Larson, M., and N. C. Kraus. 1991. Mathematical modeling of the fate of beach fill. Coastal Engineering 16:83-114.

Larson, M., N. C. Kraus, and M. R. Byrnes. 1990. SBEACH: Numerical Model for Simulating Storm-Induced Beach Change. Report 2: Numerical Formulation and Model Tests. Technical Report CERC-89-9. Vicksburg, Miss.: Coastal Engineering Research Center, U.S. Army Engineer Waterways Experiment Station, U.S. Army Corps of Engineers.

Moore, B. D. 1982. Beach Profile Evolution in Response to Changes in Water Level and Wave Height. Unpublished master's thesis, Department of Civil Engineering, University of Delaware.

Motyka, J. M., and D. H. Willis. 1975. The effect of refraction over dredged holes. Pp. 615-625 in Proceedings of the 14th Conference on Coastal Engineering. New York: American Society of Civil Engineers.

Pelnard-Considére, R. 1956. Essai de Theorie de l'Evolution des Formes de Rivate en Plages de Sable et de Galets. 4th Journees de l'Hydraulique, Les Energies de la Mer, Question III, Rapport No. 1 (in French). Vicksburg, Miss.: U.S. Army Engineer Waterways Experiment Station, U.S. Army Corps of Engineers.

Perlin, M., and R. G. Dean. 1979. Prediction of beach planforms with littoral controls. Pp. 1818-1838 in Proceedings of the 16th Coastal Engineering Conference. New York: American Society of Civil Engineers.

Pilkey, O. H., R. S. Young, S. R. Riggs, A. W. S. Smith, H. Wu, and W. D. Pilkey. 1993. The concept of shoreface profile equilibrium: a critical review. Journal of Coastal Research 9(1):255-278.

Price, W. A., K. W. Tomlinson, and D. H. Willis. 1973. Predicting changes in the plan shape of beaches. Pp. 1321-1329 in Proceedings of the 13th Conference on Coastal Engineering. New York: American Society of Civil Engineers.

Swart, D. H. 1974. Offshore Sediment Transport and Equilibrium Beach Profiles. Publication No. 131. Delft, The Netherlands: Delft Hydraulics Laboratory.

Wise, R. A., and N. C. Kraus. 1993. Simulation of beach fill response to multiple storms, Ocean City Maryland. Pp. 133-147 in Proceedings of Coastal Zone '93. New York: American Society of Civil Engineers.

Work, P. A. 1993. Monitoring the evolution of a beach nourishment project. Pp. 57-70 in D. K. Stauble and N. C. Kraus, eds., Proceedings of Beach Nourishment Engineering and Management Considerations. New York: American Society of Civil Engineers.

APPENDIX

D

Design of Beach Nourishment Projects

INTRODUCTION

A beach that is under consideration for nourishment typically will have eroded over an extended period, so that its storm protection and recreational potential have been substantially reduced. The objectives of beach nourishment are to improve shore protection and recreational opportunities. The design process for beach nourishment projects determines the quantity, configuration, and distribution of the sediment to be placed along a specific section of coast in order to restore natural storm protection, recreational area, or both. The design objective is to identify a unique project that best addresses and accommodates site conditions, erosion rates, wave climate, available sand, costs, funding sources, and environmental considerations. The design must consider long-term erosion and storm impacts to assess the appropriate nourishment quantity, quality, and placement along the shore. As a rule of thumb, the nourished beach can be expected to erode at least as fast as the prenourished shoreline. Therefore, an allowance for continued erosion of beach fill is also part of the design assessment. Further, the combination of higher tides and waves during storm conditions can erode the upper beach and directly impact upland areas, causing damage and failure of structures. Thus, reducing the vulnerability of coastal structures to storm damage is also an important design consideration.

Each nourishment project has unique environmental and economic conditions that affect the design process. The beach nourishment project ought to be of sufficient size to provide a financially feasible level of protection to the upland structures. Impacts to sensitive nearshore or offshore environments should be minimized to the extent possible. The following defines the beach nourishment formulation processes.

Design is the process of solving problems or achieving a desired objective or objectives by:

- proposing one or more alternative solutions;
- evaluating those solutions in view of physical, economic, environmental, and other constraints;
- adopting or adapting elements of the best alternatives; and
- formulating the solution that best meets the desired objective or objectives.

Good design is an iterative process that requires attention to details. Beach nourishment design involves selecting the project's length, beach profile cross-section, dune height, use of structures for erosion control, sediment characteristics, and borrow source.

Analysis is an important tool by which various designs or elements of a design can be objectively evaluated. For beach nourishment, analysis brings knowledge of coastal processes to bear on the evaluation of alternative designs. Analytical and numerical models of alongshore sand transport and cross-shore transport are examples of coastal process models that are important in beach nourishment project analysis.

Judgment is also needed in evaluating candidate designs or elements of a design because coastal processes are complex (NRC, 1987, 1989, 1990, 1992) and design methodologies are constantly evolving. Judgment, however, is not totally objective because it depends on a designer's experience. Different designers may interpret objectives and constraints differently. Therefore, no two designers approach a problem in exactly the same way and, in general, will not arrive at identical designs. There are always trade-offs, and judgment is the factor that selects from among those trade-offs where no quantitative analytic procedures or criteria exist. Because judgment is not objective, *design review* is an important element of the process. Design review brings the experience and judgment of a number of designers to bear on a problem. The criterion for evaluating a design is how well it achieves the desired objectives within the given constraints. For beach nourishment, project objectives usually include protecting backbeach areas from waves and flooding damage and providing a beach for recreational purposes. Where sea turtles nest on coastal beaches, replacing seawalls with nourished beaches can reestablish nesting habitat.

Public participation is important throughout the design process for any public works project such as beach nourishment, initially to ensure that objectives and constraints are clearly defined and later to ensure that the original objectives are still valid and have been met within the given constraints.

DESIGN HISTORY

The design process has evolved over time from the first project design on Coney Island in 1922 (Farley, 1923; Davison et al., 1992; Dornhelm, 1995) to the latest computer-aided designs of nourishment at Ocean City, Maryland (Hanson and Byrnes, 1991), and the third periodic nourishment at Delray Beach, Florida (Coastal Planning and Engineering, 1992a). Since the early 1950s, the scientific basis for beach nourishment project design has increased significantly. Although some of the early projects used finer bay and lagoon sediments, which performed poorly, later projects used coarser offshore sand with more favorable results (Davison et al., 1992).

The evolution of the design process at Wrightsville Beach, North Carolina, demonstrates the changing nature of the design process. The early design cross-section placed sand primarily on the nearshore profile without consideration for building the offshore portion of the profile. The dry beach quickly adjusted to flatter natural slopes when sand moved offshore. The later renourishment designs for Wrightsville Beach provided enough fill for the entire active profile; the offshore movement of sand was properly anticipated.

Hall (1952) documents 72 beach nourishment projects constructed in the United States between 1922 and 1950. Most were in New York, New Jersey, and Southern California. He also discusses design parameters and needs for further development of established source requirements and the quality of borrow materials.

Krumbein (1957) published the first papers that dealt with grain size as a design factor for nourished beaches. Later work by Krumbein and James (1965), James (1974, 1975), and Dean (1974) further developed the concepts of native beach sand as a hydraulically stable population from which performance of a borrow material with dissimilar grain sizes can be compared. The work of James (1974, 1975) has been incorporated into the standard practices of the U.S. Army Corps of Engineers (USACE, 1984). These practices are based on (1) the overfill factor, R_A, which predicts how much fill will remain after sorting by hydrodynamic processes, and (2) the renourishment factor, R_J, which predicts how much nourishment will be necessary when compared with the performance of native sand (Davison et al., 1992).

Early nourishment projects did not consider the offshore profile properly, often using unrealistic slopes, which subsequently caused an excessive loss of subaerial (dry) beach (Vallianos, 1974; Jarrett 1987; Hanson and Lillycrop, 1988; Davison et al., 1992). Hallermeier (1981a, b) developed zonations of the active profile based on wave parameters. Two limiting depths were defined. One of them, d_L, is the maximum water depth for sand erosion and seaward transport by an extreme yearly wave condition and corresponds to the seaward limit of appreciable seasonal profile change. The second is the maximum water depth for sand motion (on a flat bed) by median wave conditions and corresponds to the seaward limit of the constructed wave profile. Hallermeier suggested that d_L be used as the basis of beach nourishment design; later analysis showed field observations supporting this recommendation (Houston, 1991a; Hands, 1991). Birkemeier (1985) refined the seaward limit of profile change. His results were based on more accurate surveys at Duck, North Carolina.

Dean (1983, 1991) proposed the use of equilibrium profile concepts for beach nourishment design. He suggested that the shape of the offshore profile can be approximated by a shape described as follows:

$$h(y) = Ay^{0.67} \tag{D-1}$$

where $h(y)$ is the depth at distance (y) and A is a scale factor related to grain size. The use of the Dean and Hallermeier/Birkemeier concepts provides a direct method for estimating nourishment quantities for various wave and sand source conditions. These concepts are generally accepted in the industry but are not widely used by designers, because overfill and renourishment factors are used to determine fill compatibility. Since profile shape change and winnowing occur on nourished beaches, both measures need to be considered in a design when the borrow sand is finer than the native beach sand. When an unconsolidated beach is nourished for the first time, sand will move offshore in sufficient quantities to flatten the offshore profile. Significantly less sand will move offshore in subsequent nourishments, because the slope of the beach will have already been moderated by the first nourishment.

The response of the native and natural beach to higher sea levels was first addressed quantitatively by Bruun (1962). He suggested a balance of onshore erosion with offshore deposition in response to a change in sea level. Storm recession methods were proposed by Edelman (1972) using an approach similar to that of Bruun and applying these principles to storm surge. Edelman's method was used in a number of federal beach nourishment designs in the 1970s and 1980s (Strock and Associates, 1981, 1984). His method tended to overpredict storm recession, because the technique assumed the profiles would reach full equilibrium with the peak storm surge without consideration of the duration of the storm.

Swart (1974) proposed methods to evaluate erosion induced by storms based on evaluation of coastal erosion problems on the Danish North Sea. Kriebel (1982) developed a time-dependent dune recession model based on the equilibrium profile and a uniform dissipation of wave energy per unit volume in the surf zone. This method was further developed and described by Kriebel and Dean (1985). In the Kriebel-Dean method, storm duration, waves, and storm surge were combined for the first time to analyze the profile response in storms. More recently, this model has been refined (EDUNE) by Kriebel (1990) to account for the existence of coastal structures and overtopping of the profile by wave runup.

From 1988 through 1990, Larson (1988) and then Larson and Kraus (1989b) developed the SBEACH (Storm-Induced Beach Change) model for predicting beach and dune erosion. This model allows for offshore bar formation during storms. It was recently refined (Wise and Kraus, 1993) to include the effects of seawalls, runup, and overwash quantities of sand that are pushed over the dune. The EDUNE and SBEACH models are the two numerical dune recession models in use today by U.S. beach designers. An analytical model for storm recession was first developed by Kriebel et al. (1991) and refined by Kriebel and Dean (1993).

The erosion rate of the nourished beach has been estimated by beach designers primarily by using historical erosion rates. Fill is added to the design quantity in sufficient volume to account for beach losses between nourishments. This additional quantity is called *advanced fill*. Most federal designs prior to 1983 estimated advanced-fill requirements based on the rate of erosion of the native beach and grain-size considerations only. The USACE issued a technical note on beach fill transitions (USACE, 1982a) that suggested the inclusion of "end losses" in advanced-fill quantities.

Pelnard-Considére (1956) developed an analytical one-line (i.e., the shoreline) model to predict spreading losses of nourished sand to adjacent beaches. Bakker (1968) developed a two-line analytical model to predict alongshore and cross-shore changes. Perlin and Dean (1979) developed an *N* line analytical model that enabled prediction of the evolution of multiple contours along a project's beach. As noted in Appendix C, Price et al. (1973) and Komar (1973, 1977) demonstrated a range of computer-based numerical models for shore processes. Price et al. (1973) correlated computer-based models with the performance of sand in a groin field. These models were not commonly used for nourishment designs until the late 1970s and early 1980s.

Hanson and Kraus (1989) developed a one-line (i.e., the shoreline) numerical model that is referred to as GENESIS (Generalized Shoreline Simulation System). This model was applied by the Coastal Engineering Research Center (CERC) to the design of the Asbury Park to Sandy Hook, New Jersey, beach nourishment project in 1985. The GENESIS model was refined by CERC as a personal computer application and applied to a number of beach nourishment designs in the early 1990s (see Manatee County General Design Memorandum, USACE, 1991c).

Dean (1983) refined the work of Pelnard-Considére to further develop an analytical model for the prediction of performance of beach nourishment. It was applied to a number of beach nourishment projects in the late 1980s and early 1990s (Coastal Planning and Engineering, 1992a, b; USACE, 1989b) and has shown good correlation to monitored projects in Delray Beach, Florida (USACE, 1991c); see also Appendix C.

DESIGN METHODS

Fill placed on a nourished beach will erode over time, diminishing the protection afforded by the initial construction. Most nourishment projects are actually designed as a series of sequential fill placements over time to account for the long-term erosion process.

For design purposes, it is convenient to consider the fill placed on a beach as comprised of two components: the design cross-section, which achieves the project purpose (storm protection and recreational area), and an advanced-fill amount, which erodes between nourishment events (see Figure 4-7).

Federal design policy (USACE, 1991b) requires that the design cross-section be optimized to return maximum net benefits (benefits less costs). The advanced-fill quantities are designed to achieve the lowest annual cost for the renourishment program.

The construction volume contains both design and advanced-fill quantities. Construction templates reflect dune and berm elevations. However, the construction template incorporates a significantly wider berm and a steeper slope than the design and advanced-fill profile. The difference between the construction, design, and advanced-fill profile is necessary to accommodate the sand placement capability of the construction equipment that is expected to be available for the project. Within the first year or so after placement of beach fill, the construction profile will be reshaped by waves to an equilibrium profile, causing the berm to retreat to the design and advanced-fill profile (see Figure 4-7). For design purposes, the construction profile is treated as an anomalous temporary feature.

The Design Beach

It is standard practice to provide sufficient sand to nourish the entire profile, from the dune (where one exists) to the depth of significant sand movement, d_L. Estimates of fill are based on transferring the entire active profile seaward by the design amount (see Figure D-1). If the borrow sand matches the native sand and there are no rock outcrops, seawalls, or groins, the design profile at each cross-section should be a replica of the existing profile but shifted to a seaward location.

Enough sediment should be accounted for by the designer to nourish the entire profile (Bruun 1986; Hansen and Lillycrop, 1988). The total volume, V_T, is independent of profile shape, since the shape of the renourished profile will be parallel and similar to the existing natural profile. Using the limiting depth of profile change, d_L, the nourishment quantity can be directly estimated by

$$V_T = (B + d_L) L W \tag{D-2}$$

where B is the elevation of the berm as discussed in Appendix C, L is the length

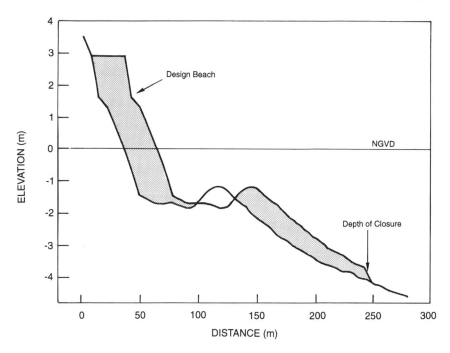

FIGURE D-1   Design cross-section transferred seaward.

of the nourishment project, and W is the desired amount of beach widening (Campbell et al., 1990). If rock outcrops or other nonerodible surfaces such as seawalls, revetments, or groins exist on the nearshore native beach, the existing profile shape will not be directly representative of the nourished profile. If a beach that is armored (such as with seawalls) has experienced erosion over an extended period, the nearshore bathymetry can become deeper and the profile will be steeper than the equilibrium natural profile. This condition would be expected to result in the need for a larger amount of fill during the initial nourishment. In such cases, the use of an equilibrium profile defined by the grain size of the borrow material or an adjacent natural beach profile can be used to approximate the nourished profile. Further, if seawalls, groins, or other structures or features have caused the profile to deviate significantly from the anticipated equilibrated profile after nourishment, then Equation (D-1) would be applied with appropriate modifications.

Figure D-2 shows the monitored profiles of a nourishment project in Captiva Island, Florida. The project was constructed in the winter of 1988-1989 with 0.56-mm sand; the sand was coarser than the native beach sand of 0.38 mm. The project has been monitored twice a year since nourishment. The profile shown in Figure D-2 is a typical profile 5 years after the construction of a project. The

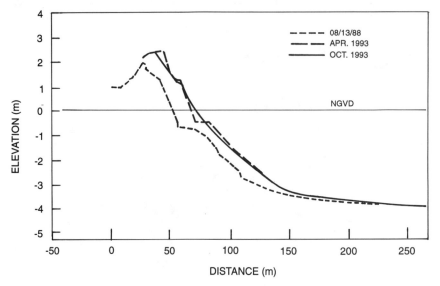

FIGURE D-2   Captiva Island beach nourishment monitoring cross-section.

nourished profile is similar to the native profile at a seaward location. Review of the profiles shows that they experienced little change beyond the 4-m depth contour.

It is common practice, however, to utilize uniform slopes for the design cross-section and to use this cross-section for the entire beach (see Figure D-3). When this is done, it can lead to an underestimate of the fill if the design cross-section intercepts the bottom above the depth of closure.

If rock, clay, or peat outcrops (or, in the special case of the Arctic, permafrost) exist, the shape of the native beach profile will be affected. In those cases, the nourished profile will take a different form than the native beach, and nourishment quantities cannot be estimated directly by shifting existing profiles seaward. Rock outcrops, offshore hard clay, and glacial till tend to flatten the native beach offshore profile and will perch the nourishment sand, requiring less sand to widen the beach a specific amount. Where rock exists, the best way to estimate design quantities is to use the equilibrium profile based on the grain size of the borrow materials and allow the profile to intercept the offshore areas above the depth of closure of the profile. Volumes of design fill can then be estimated by direct comparison between the nourished equilibrium and the native profiles.

It is a customary objective for nourishment designs in the United States to establish a uniform beach width along a project's length. The existence of seawalls can increase design beach requirements over estimates based on the seaward transfer of the profile. If a segment of the project shore has a seawall on or

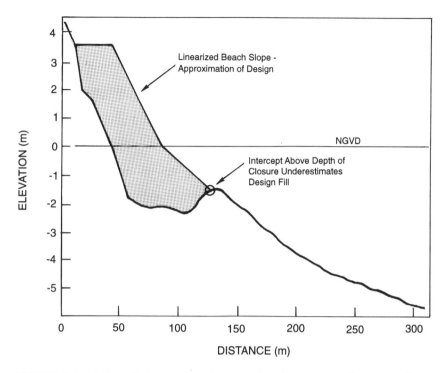

FIGURE D-3 A linear design cross-section sometimes intercepts sandbars, providing an underestimate of design fill.

near the water's edge, an amount of fill will be needed to bring the elevation of sand up to the proposed berm elevation in the area where seawalls exist. This can significantly increase the fill requirements where seawalls are in the water. Once these "seawall volumes" are established, nourishment fill estimates can be based on transfer of the entire profile. This is important because gross volume estimates are made in the preliminary phase of a project's design. The project's sponsors base their support and budgets on these early estimates. In the final design, template comparisons will include extra volumes to fill seawall areas. If the preliminary design volume is significantly deficient because the seawall volume was missing, the designer may encounter pressure to compromise the design in order to avoid project cost overruns. Figure D-4 shows the design cross-section of a nourishment project planned for Captiva Island, Florida. The shaded portion of the profile is that amount of sand needed to bring the beach level up to the proposed berm level before the beach berm is widened. Sand is needed along the *entire* profile—both subaerially and below the water. Once this amount of fill is accounted for, fill volumes can be estimated by shifting the profile seaward using

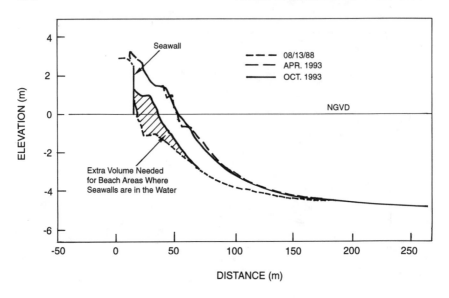

FIGURE D-4   Captiva Island beach nourishment monitoring cross-section at R-98.

Equation D-1. Because of the extra volume needed to build the berm in front of seawalls, the nourished shoreline will typically be shifted seaward in front of seawall areas as compared with nonseawall areas. This will cause alongshore gradients in littoral drift that need to be considered in advanced-fill designs. In USACE projects the target shoreline is designed to be fairly even. Any perturbation (such as a seaward-displaced shore to accommodate a seawall) will become an erosional hot spot. Surveyed profile variabilities are typically used to compute the quantities needed.

The alternative to providing seawall volumes is to allow for narrower berms in front of seawall areas. The storm protective value of the seawall reduces the need for storm protection provided directly by the berm, enabling the use of a narrower width than would otherwise be necessary to achieve the same level of storm protection. The use of a narrower berm reduces or mitigates the littoral drift gradients associated with overly wide sections of nourished beaches in front of seawalls.

The design beach is optimized by computing costs and benefits and determining the beach that would return the maximum net benefits (USACE, 1991b). Both storm damage reduction and recreational benefits are included in the analysis.

Storm damage benefits are based on the reduction in storm damage over the life of the project with the design beach in place. Because of the existence of the design beach, the upland properties will suffer less damage during each storm event. Damage estimates are based on inundation, wave attack, and erosion damages (USACE, 1991b).

Beach washout and profile response seaward of seawalls during a storm can be predicted using beach and dune recession models. Commonly used approaches include EDUNE by Kriebel (1986) and SBEACH (Larson and Kraus, 1990). These models predict the evolution of the profile toward the equilibrium storm profile. Both models are driven by the deviation between the actual and equilibrium wave energy dissipation per unit volume of water within the surf zone. The models assume that sand eroded from the upper beach deposits offshore, with no loss or gain of material to the profile.

Storm surge estimates to be used in recession models and for calculating runup are based on methods described in Chapter 3 of the *Shore Protection Manual* and other engineering manuals published by the USACE (1984, 1986, 1989a). Many beach designers use published storm-surge frequencies developed by the Federal Emergency Management Agency (FEMA) and the National Oceanic and Atmospheric Administration (NOAA). Storm hydrographs can be obtained from reports published by USACE, FEMA, and universities to generate storm recession probabilities that can be applied directly to damage functions and included in an economic model. Wave statistics can be obtained from wave gauge records, published summaries of observations, or wave hindcast estimates, such as the Wave Information Study (USACE, 1990, 1993).

It has been recognized that storm surge frequencies are not necessarily the same as damage frequencies (Kriebel and Dean, 1985; USACE, 1986, 1988). Beach and dune recession, for example, is dependent on storm duration and wave heights, as well as on storm surge. To address this problem, the USACE (1988) developed a storm simulation model for a project in Seabright, New Jersey, which develops a family of storm events similar to the historical record. In this way a series of storms was developed and used in the storm recession model to establish a series of storm recession events that could be independently ranked. Similarly, wave runup and flooding can be ranked from the 500-year event to the 10-year event. A more representative damage frequency curve can therefore be used to compute storm damage and protection values.

Natural and nourished beaches exhibit a variability in the level of storm recession measured along their length (USACE, 1991b). Some areas will show extensive washout, while others exhibit minor storm recession. Variability can be estimated by measuring poststorm beaches in the project area and establishing the levels of variability to be applied to the model. For example, if it is determined that beach recession varies by a factor of two, beach recession will vary from zero to twice the average that is represented by the computed value.

As mentioned previously, the design beach is optimized by maximizing total net benefits, including storm protection and recreation. Recreational benefits are generated when a nourishment project rebuilds or maintains a public beach area. It is important for designers to recognize the basis for this economic benefit. If a public beach erodes away, recreation on it is eliminated; therefore, a benefit is derived from building and maintaining a beach. More people will visit a nourished beach over the project's life, generating a net benefit to the nourishment project. Beach visits saved or increased by beach nourishment represent an economic benefit.

Using standard economic principles, the annual costs and benefits of a project are compared to establish the design beach. The design beach is that added width of beach that returns maximum net benefits.

Advanced-Fill Design

Both the quantity and distribution of advanced fill—the erodible portion of the profile before nourishment becomes necessary—can be determined by analyzing the historical erosion and shoreline changes of a beach and estimating how the project fill will affect coastal processes. Procedures used include the historical shoreline change method (USACE, 1991b) or analytical (Campbell et al., 1990) or numerical methods (Hanson and Kraus, 1989). The historical shoreline method assumes that the nourished beach will erode at the same rate as the prenourished beach. This method is commonly used by beach designers (based on survey results) but can yield a significant underestimate of nourishment requirements, as discussed below.

Most long-term erosion of a nourished beach is caused by increasing gradients of littoral drift along the project's length. The two major littoral drift gradients affecting the nourished beach are the preexisting littoral drift gradients that were responsible for the background or historical erosion of the prenourished beach and those gradients associated with the anomaly in the shoreline created by the project fill that cause end losses and spreading of the fill. All of these littoral drift gradients combine on the nourished beach to cause a progressive loss of fill from the beach nourishment project. Exclusive consideration of the background erosion rate neglects the end (i.e., spreading) losses, causing an underestimate of nourishment needs and thus an overestimate of project life. Losses from the project area due to spreading will cause accretion of sand on adjacent beaches. Although this may be beneficial to the adjacent beaches, the spreading losses from the project must be included in the advanced-fill design in order to achieve performance objectives for the project area.

Delray Beach, Florida, is an example of a beach nourishment project where spreading losses represented the greatest component of the erosion rate on the nourished beach. The beach nourishment project was constructed in 1973 with 1.2 million m³ of sand from an offshore borrow source. Prior to the project, the beach was eroding at a rate of 15,000 m³/year. The beach has been monitored annually since 1973 with profiles from the dune to the 10-m depth contour. From 1973 through 1978, the beach eroded an average of 70,000 m³/year. The beach was renourished in 1978, 1984, and 1992. The erosion rate (the entire profile) was again about 70,000 m³/year from 1978 through 1984. Between 1984 and 1992, losses moderated and averaged 35,000 m³/year. Over half of the sand lost from Delray Beach can be accounted for as accretion on adjacent beaches in Highland Beach and Gulfstream (Beachler, 1993). This example demonstrates the importance of estimating spreading losses in the design of beach nourishment projects.

Along a project's length, gradients in littoral drift occur as a result of changes in the shoreline orientation or wave refraction and diffraction over discontinuous offshore contours (such as ebb shoals). This creates conditions of differential erosion and accretion along the project shore. The distribution of advanced-fill quantities ideally should be placed to anticipate these differences in expected erosion rates along the project. One such area mentioned earlier is the nourished beach in front of seawalls. A beach that is over-widened to provide a uniform berm in front of a seawall will erode faster as sand spreads to adjacent areas. Advanced-fill designs therefore need to recognize and accommodate these losses.

Analytical methods have been developed by Pelnard-Considére (1956) and refined by Dean and Yoo (1992) to estimate net erosion losses from a project fill. These methods can be used to estimate gross advanced-fill quantities and are good tools to help designers develop judgment about the level of losses to expect from a project over time. Analytical models can be used by designers during the preliminary design phase to establish early estimates of gross fill quantities (see Appendix C).

Numerical methods such as the GENESIS model (Hanson and Kraus, 1989) can estimate differential erosion patterns along a project's length to help design the distribution of advanced-fill placement. Calibrated numerical models predict both total erosion losses and differential erosion losses along a project. When numerical models are used for both purposes, however, analytical methods should be used in addition to the numerical models as a check on total erosion of the project fill.

Sand Compatibility

The grain-size distribution of the borrow material (nourishment sand) will affect how a beach erodes and how the nourished beach responds to storms. Nourished sand that is finer than the native material will form flatter slopes on the beach and underwater and provide a narrower dry subaerial beach. The most widely used methods are to compute the adjusted factor overfill, R_A, and renourishment factors, R_J (USACE, 1984).

The overfill method, R_A, estimates how much of the borrow sand matches the native beach sand distribution. This method assumes that the nourished beach sand will undergo sorting as a result of coastal processes and will in time approach the native grain-size distribution; the portion of the borrow sand not matching the native sand will be lost offshore. This method provides a multiplier for the amount of borrow material needed to produce the required comparable amount of native material (USACE, 1984).

The renourishment factor, R_J, addresses the higher alongshore transportability of the finer grain sizes in the borrow sands. R_J provides estimates of advanced-fill or renourishment needs.

There is some question about the continued use of grain-size comparison R_A and R_J as measures of beach performance (Bruun, 1990; Campbell et al., 1990; Pilkey and Clayton, 1987, 1988; Dixon and Pilkey, 1989, 1991; Leonard, 1988; Leonard et al., 1989, 1990a, b). A more appropriate design approach would be comparisons of native and borrow sands based on the evolving concepts of the equilibrium profile (Dean, 1983, 1991), alongshore transport dependency by grain size (Dean and Grant, 1989; USACE, 1984), and the storm recession performance of a beach with various grain sizes (Larson and Kraus, 1989a). This design approach has been suggested by Campbell et al. (1990).

Because finer beaches take flatter slopes than coarser beaches, they would require more fill to provide the same amount of beach widening. Estimates of these quantities can be made using the mean grain size of the borrow and native materials and the equilibrium profile concepts shown in the section on "Prediction" in Appendix C. If the material used to nourish a beach is finer than the native material, extra fill will be needed to flatten the slopes of the nourished beach. This extra fill is required only for the first nourishment; renourishment quantities would require no additional materials because slopes would already be adjusted by the first nourishment. Very fine portions of the fill such as silt and clay will be lost offshore during nourishments and renourishments. Most of the loss of fine material occurs during construction. It is therefore not customary to count these losses in the pay quantities.

For the same wave climate, the rate of alongshore transport is dependent on the grain size of the sediments (Walton, 1985; Dean, 1987; Kamphuis, 1990, 1991; Kamphuis et al., 1986; del Valle et al., 1993). Although field measurements of this dependency in the sand-size range of sediments are limited and of questionable validity (Komar, 1988), estimates have been made by Dean (1989) and USACE (1984) of the variation of alongshore transport with grain size. Further evidence and quantification of the dependence of transport on sand grain size have been shown by the USACE (1985). The transport rate variance with grain size can be applied through analytical and numerical models to predict the erosion rates of dissimilar borrow sands. Long-term erosion and, therefore, renourish-ment quantities for finer sands would be greater than for coarser sands and can be estimated by this procedure. Although it is widely recognized that grain size affects transport rates, there are few empirical data on these effects. Therefore, transport rates must be estimated, and the accuracy of these estimates is uncertain. Research is needed to better define grain size and transport rate relationships.

For the same wave climate, finer sands are more prone than coarser sands are to erosion during storms with a storm surge of more than a 6-hour duration. This can be considered in the analysis of a design beach for storm protection. Generally with a significant storm surge and storm duration, more fine sand will be required to protect upland property against undermining than would be required if coarser sand were used. Coastal models such as SBEACH and EDUNE take grain size into account.

Finer sands are not always more prone to erosion during storms than coarser sands. The selection of a fine sand lessens the slope of the beach, which causes waves to break farther offshore, especially when there is a limited storm surge. If this occurs, wave energy is dissipated over a wider surf zone. Beaches consisting of coarser sand have steeper slopes and narrower surf zones. As a result, wave energy is more concentrated and therefore more directly impacts the shore. When affected by the same wave conditions without storm surge, the profiles of coarse-sand beaches undergo larger and more rapid changes during storms of limited duration and surge than profiles consisting of fine-sand beaches and show greater responses to individual storms (Shih and Komar, 1994). Therefore, the selection of coarser sand for a nourishment project may increase the dynamic behavior of beach profiles, leading to greater erosion during storms of limited duration with small storm surges.

By considering the above described performance characteristics of sand, assessment of alternative borrow areas can be made. This analysis can complement or substitute for the overfill and renourishment factor approaches previously mentioned. Before performance-based analysis can replace overfill methods, however, further research is needed to refine the dependency of sand transport on grain size.

Design and Construction Profiles

The *design profile* is the cross-section that the equilibrated beach is expected to take. On sandy beaches the best estimate of this profile is obtained by the seaward transfer of the existing beach by the amount of beach widening that is required (USACE, 1992b). Estimates should be modified if the borrow material is of a different grain size than the native material. For finer sands, these adjustments in volume should be based on the amount of fill needed to adjust the offshore slopes from the shoreline to the depth of closure.

Many designers specify linear design slopes as an approximation to the native beach and use this to estimate design volumes. This is a convenient and standard method to compute design volumes: superimposing a template over existing profiles and computing the resulting volumetric difference. However, if the design template intercepts a nearshore sand bar on the design beach profile, the designer will underestimate the design fill needs (see Figure D-3). For this reason, this method should be used with caution and judgment. It is suggested

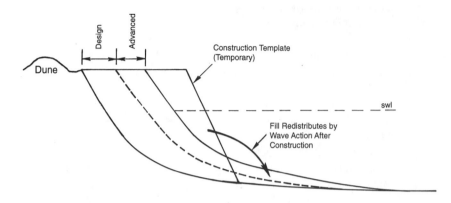

FIGURE D-5   The construction template.

that designers modify these procedures to better approximate equilibrated profiles using the methods described above.

The *construction profile* is the cross-section that the contractor is required to
achieve. The constructed beach contains both the design fill and the advanced-fill
quantities and is often steeper than the design cross-section because of construction limitations.

The construction cross-section is usually significantly wider than the design
profile because of the steeper slopes and because it contains the advanced fill
(Figure D-5). Wave action causes an adjustment of the construction cross-section
to a flatter equilibrium slope; this usually occurs within the first few months to a
year.

Since the adjusted equilibrium profile contains the design and advanced fill,
it is wider than the design profile during the renourishment interval. At the time
of renourishment, the design and equilibrium profile would (theoretically) be
equal.

PLACEMENT OF NOURISHED SEDIMENT
ON THE BEACH PROFILE

Various design schemes have been used for the placement of nourished
sediment on a beach. The approaches in common use are illustrated schematically in Figure D-6 and include (1) placing all of the sand as a dune behind the
active beach, (2) using the nourished sand to build a wider and higher berm above
the mean water level, (3) distributing the added sand over the entire beach profile,
or (4) placing the sand offshore to form an artificial bar. The selected design
depends in part on the location of the source material and the method of delivery
to the beach. If the borrow area is on land and the sand is transported by trucks to

A. Dune Nourishment

B. Nourishment of Subaerial Beach

C. Profile Nourishment

D. Bar Nourishment

FIGURE D-6   Nourishment profiles.

the beach, placement on the berm or in a dune is generally most economical. If the material comes from offshore dredging, it is usually more practical to place the sand on the beach and near the shore or to build an artificial bar.

After construction, sand is redistributed in the cross-shore direction to form a more natural profile, governed by the sediment size of the fill and the prevailing wave conditions. This is illustrated schematically in Figure D-7 for nourishment placed on a beach as a "construction profile" to form a wide elevated berm

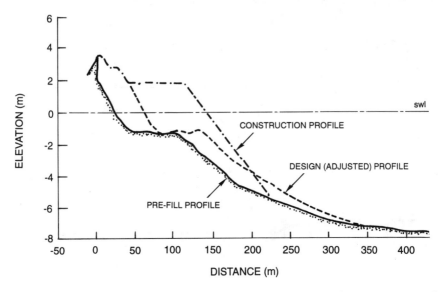

FIGURE D-7   Sand redistribution in the cross-shore direction to form a more natural profile.

(Houston, 1991a). This placement artificially steepens the beach and results in the offshore movement of sand as it is reworked by the waves and redistributed over the profile. The "equilibrium profile" of Figure D-7 is the profile predicted by the analysis as the equilibrium profile that will eventually be achieved by the nourished sand after its initial reworking. This adjustment, as noted earlier, usually requires a few months to several years. For this reshaping, the first year after placement may not be a sufficient interval if incident forces are unusually mild during the initial winter season. Figure D-8 provides an example of such profile changes derived from the monitoring program at Ocean City, Maryland (Houston, 1991a). The nourishment fill was in the form of a uniform sand slope over the prefill profile, confined to the berm and inner surf zone. After four months, the resulting profile (labeled "01/17/89" in Figure D-8B) shows the expected readjustment into a more natural profile, with sand having eroded from the nourishment wedge to form an alongshore trough and the eroded sand having moved offshore to form a bar. The profile of 04/20/89 in Figure D-8C shows the effect of the first major storm that enhanced the formation of the alongshore trough and bar, with significant erosion of the nourished sand placed on the subaerial part of the beach. That erosion of the berm did not represent a permanent loss of sand from the beach, however, as it was deposited on the offshore bar and therefore was still landward of the closure depth of profile changes. The profiles of Figure D-8C show the subsequent onshore return of much of that sand during the lower-energy conditions following the storm, with the width of the berm expanding.

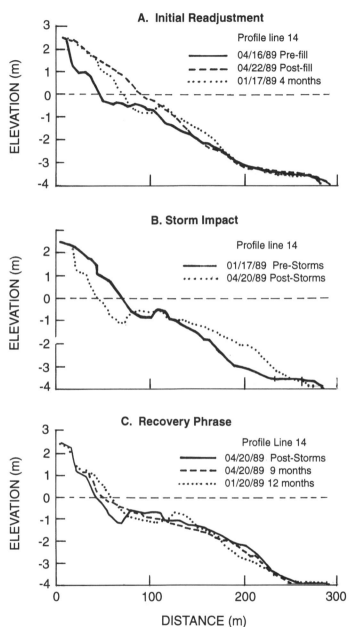

FIGURE D-8   Ocean City, Maryland, project profiles.

Larson and Kraus (1991) have similarly analyzed the readjustment of nourished profiles as they are first eroded by normal waves and subsequently attacked
by a hurricane or northeaster. They utilized the numerical model SBEACH to
evaluate the profile changes in response to "synthetic" storms and obtained results very similar to those seen in Figure D-8 for Ocean City.

With profile adjustments such as those illustrated in Figure D-8, the general
public may perceive the loss of nourished sand from the berm to the offshore as
a sign of failure of the project. There is a need for public education at the onset of
a project so that the public understands that some initial offshore sediment movement and erosion of the berm are expected and recognizes that, so long as the
sand remains in the littoral zone within the envelope of beach profile changes, the
sand has not actually been "lost." Although the profile adjustment will in most
cases result in shoreline recession, the material will still be present in the active
beach profile; much of it will be in the offshore bar and on the berm. Further, the
presence of sand in the offshore bar acts to break storm waves and to dissipate
their energy before they reach the shoreline; accordingly, the nourished sand
within the bar is still meeting the objective of protecting the coast from property
erosion.

When sand placed on a beach is finer than the native beach sand, the profile
adjustments will be greater, taking more sand from the subaerial beach to flatten
the offshore profile. If the designer has properly accounted for the difference in
grain size, the equilibrated beach will be of a width and height to provide the
desired level of storm protection. If the effects of grain size have not been properly considered, the adjusted profile may be narrower than desired.

Hansen and Byrnes (1991) have investigated the optimum nourishment cross-
section design for protection of the backshore against storm impacts. The beach
profile response was modeled by using SBEACH, and the analysis was based on
the nourishment project undertaken at Ocean City, Maryland, which involved the
initial placement of about 2 million m³ of sand on the beach in June 1988. Six
months after the project was completed, a northeaster hit the area, resulting in
erosion of the beach with significant profile changes. Approximately one-third of
the fill material was transported from the subaerial beach and deposited offshore
between the 3- and 5.5-m water depths, but the total quantity of sand was con-
served landward of the profile closure depth. Hansen and Byrnes (1991) used this
measured change to calibrate SBEACH and then used the calibrated model to
examine the responses of different beach fill designs (Figure D-6) that would
have occurred under that northeast storm, including both measured wave heights
and water levels in the model calculations. According to their analyses, all designs withstood the impact of one northeaster or hurricane. In simulations of
back-to-back northeasters, the design involving the placement of all nourishment
sand into a dune (Figure D-6A) provided the maximum protection of backshore
properties, with some dune remaining even after two major storms. In the case of
placing most of the nourished sand on the berm, SBEACH predicted that most of

the berm sand would have moved to the offshore bar. Therefore, excluding the desire to immediately have a wide berm for recreational purposes, the objective of providing backshore protection is best met by a profile design that places most of the nourished sand in dunes.

The use of large dunes (i.e., man-made dikes) as a coastal protection measure has long been recognized in the Netherlands (Watson and Finkl, 1990; Verhagen, 1990; Louisse and van der Meulen, 1991). The coastal dunes there are, for the most, part man-made and are designed to withstand the 1-in-10,000-years condition of wave intensity and storm surge. This extreme level of protection is justified because entire cities lie behind the coastal defenses, whose failure would have catastrophic consequences. However, such an extreme storm condition or level of protection may not be definable. Maintenance of these dunes in part involves nourishment, with some sand also placed on the fronting beach.

Bruun (1988, 1990) has been the primary proponent of nourishing the entire beach profile (Figure D-6C), which he terms "profile nourishment." The main advantage of this approach is that the sand is placed in approximately the same configuration as the existing profile, so that initial readjustments are, for the most part, avoided—in particular the rapid erosion of a nourished berm. This would avoid some problems with adverse perceptions by the general public but, according to the analyses of Hansen and Byrnes (1991), would provide less protection from flooding and erosion compared with placement of the entire volume of nourishment sand in the dune and berm (Larson and Kraus, 1994; Williams and Meisburger, 1987).

Beach nourishment has also involved the placement of dredged sand in the offshore (Figure D-6D; McLellan, 1990; McLellan and Kraus, 1991). Dredged material is deposited in shallow water, typically using split-hull barges, either as a mound or in the form of a long linear ridge that simulates a naturally occurring alongshore sand bar (the term "offshore berm" is generally used for the constructed bar but will not be used here because of potential confusion with the subaerial berm of the beach profile). It is expected that sand deposited in the offshore mound or bar will progressively move onto the beach, but even before that stage there may be benefits; the created bar could cause storm waves to break farther offshore, reducing the energy locally on the beach shoreward of the bar. This aspect of wave reduction has been shown in numerical models that calculate the theoretical wave attenuation owing to the presence of an offshore mound (Allison and Pollock, 1993) and also by field measurements of waves seaward and landward of a mound that is constructed from dredged sediments offshore from the entrance to Mobile Bay, Alabama (Burke and Williams, 1992).

Initially, there were disappointments in using offshore disposal to nourish adjacent beaches. For example, in 1935 the USACE built a sand bar at 6- to 7-m water depths off the updrift end of the eroding beach south of the breakwater at Santa Barbara, California. It was anticipated that this bar would supply sand to the eroding beaches. However, after 21 months of monitoring, there was no movement of the bar and no alleviation of the shore erosion (Hands and Allison, 1991). After several such disappointments, successes were finally reported at Durban, South Africa (Zwamborn et al., 1970), at Copacabana Beach in Brazil (Vera-Cruz, 1972), and in Denmark (Mikkelsin, 1977). These successes rekindled interest in beach nourishment by offshore disposal, and in recent years this approach has been used at a number of sites.

The question remains as to why in some instances sand from the offshore nourishment mound or bar moves onshore to the beach so that the project is successful, while in other instances the dumped sediment remains as a stable deposit and does not move shoreward and onto the beach. Hands and Allison (1991) have reviewed a number of projects in an attempt to answer this question. They compared the disposal depth with the closure depth of beach profile changes as predicted in the analyses of Hallermeier (1981b) and found that, if the disposal depth is less than the closure depth, the disposal sediment would be active and move quickly onto the subaerial beach. This activity of the nourishment mound or bar placed at a depth that is shallower than the closure depth is not surprising because this placement in effect immediately introduces the sand into the nearshore zone of active profile changes where the nourished material can be readily incorporated into the overall beach profile. More uncertain, Hands and Allison (1991) found that if the disposal sand is placed at water depths greater than Hallermeier's closure depth, in half the cases the material was still active and moved onto the beach, whereas in the remaining cases the disposal sediment was stable and did not nourish the shoreward beaches. They also compared "stable" versus "active" disposal mounds and bars with the local wave climate and met with reasonable success in characterizing the sediment movement on the basis of the annual distribution of near-bottom wave orbital velocities calculated from measured wave parameters. As expected, if the orbital velocities were sufficiently high due to combinations of large waves and shallow water depths, the disposal sands remained "active" and tended to move onshore. "Stable" mounds like the one placed offshore of Santa Barbara during the 1930s were explainable in terms of the low-wave orbital velocities experienced over the mound.

It can be expected that in the near future we will have a much better understanding of the movement of offshore disposal sediments and that there will be established criteria to predict their onshore movement, so that the sediment successfully nourishes adjacent beaches. Much of this understanding will be derived from projects where the disposal mounds or bars are carefully monitored. Recent examples of such monitoring programs are provided by Andrassy (1991) and Healy et al. (1991), respectively, for beaches near San Diego, California, and off Tauranga Harbor, New Zealand. Healy et al. (1991) found that dispersion of the mound was rapid in the first 2 years, with some sand moving onshore to nourish the beaches, but that it progressively slowed and became stable after 7 years as the depth over the mound increased and a lag of coarse-grained material restricted further sediment movement.

The Netherlands Method

Verhagen (1990) has described the beach nourishment design method employed in the Netherlands, which, rather than relying on numerical models, places substantial reliance on historical data and makes few design assumptions. The recommended procedure is described in five phases:

1. Perform coastal measurements (for at least 10 years).
2. Calculate the "loss of sand" in cubic meters/year per coastal section.
3. Add 40 percent loss.
4. Multiply this quantity with a convenient lifetime (e.g., 5 years).
5. Put this quantity somewhere on the beach between the low-water-minus-1-m line and the dune foot.

Verhagen addresses difficulties with this method, including approaches to use if detailed monitoring results are not available and the implicit assumption is that the beach will erode at the same rate as before nourishment. The explanation for the additional 40 percent volume is a recognition of end losses and the loss of finer particles during placement. According to Verhagen, the design basis for subsequent renourishments ought to be derived from the monitoring results of the earlier nourishments. Detailed placement on the profile is not a major concern because the waves will soon reshape the nourishment material. However, Verhagen indicates that the sand ought to be placed where placement is the least costly, as long as the site is within the nearshore zone of active wave breaking.

In comparison with the U.S. methods described earlier, the Netherlands method is similar in accounting for background erosion. The major difference is that in the U.S. method the "spreading out" or "end" losses and other uncertainties are accounted for by a calculation procedure rather than the empirical factor of 40 percent that is used in the Netherlands method.

The German Method

Dette et al. (1994) have described a method employed in Germany that represents the volumetric losses over time from a beach nourishment project using the assumption that the volume decays exponentially with time. Presumably, the decay constant must be based on experience or, after the first and subsequent nourishments, the monitoring results from the project. This representation, although approximate, allows analytical investigation of many design characteristics of interest. For example, it is possible to determine the total volumes required to maintain a beach at a minimum volume for various renourishment intervals. Also, it is shown that the minimum cumulative volume required to maintain the beach at a minimum width is accomplished by frequent additions of small volumes. However, the optimal nourishment frequencies must also consider the costs of mobilization and the fact that material lost through spreading flows to and benefits areas adjacent to the project.

EVALUATION OF THE STATE OF THE ART
OF DESIGN PRACTICE

The design of beach nourishment projects in the United States has evolved as knowledge of physical beach processes has increased. By necessity, designers use those tools that are available and that will enable them to bring a project to construction. Because of limited survey monitoring, the validity of design assumptions and procedures cannot always be verified before the design of a renourishment project. The variability of storm conditions further compounds the process of design and verification.

As a result of the above conditions, beach nourishment designers do not always consistently employ the latest design tools. This section identifies areas where improvements can be made to the design process to provide a more consistent and accurate beach nourishment design process.

Areas where improvements are needed and can be made include:

- design volume,
- design of advanced fill, and
- analysis of sand compatibility.

The *design volume* needs to be (consistently) based on shifting each natural beach profile seaward by the design width in lieu of a single straight-line design template. This would avoid underestimates of fill where the design template intercepts sand bars and would take into account the natural variabilities of profile shape along the project. Where seawalls, groins, rock outcrops, or other structures or natural features exist, the existing profiles can be steeper than adjacent natural beaches. In those cases, the design profile needs to be similar to the closest natural beach. An important design consideration is that profile steepening of the native beach can be very significant and may necessitate more than double the fill density requirements of adjacent natural beaches.

The design of *advanced fill* needs to accommodate the full range of conditions that will affect project performance. It is common for designers to specify a uniform advanced-fill amount for a project even though preproject erosion rates may have shown significant sporadic spatial variability. Advanced-fill quantities need to be proportioned along the project to anticipate expected erosion of each project segment. This is best accomplished by varying advanced-fill quantities consistent with preproject erosion rates and using the predictive tools that are available. These tools include use of analytical and numerical models and *not* just average background erosion rates. Although analytic and numerical shoreline models have been available since the early 1980s, their use has been limited.

Even when applied during project design, the results in some cases were not used to adjust advanced-fill quantities or distributions of that sand along projects. In most of the designs reviewed for this report, advanced-fill quantities were based primarily on average historical erosion rates distributed evenly along a project's length. An analytical model can be used during the preliminary design to establish gross fill quantities. A numerical model can be used in the final design of a beach to establish the proper distribution of advanced fill.

A performance-based procedure needs to be used in addition to R_A and R_J to analyze *sand compatibility*, providing, as a minimum, a second estimate of fill compatibility. This is necessary to reduce the margin of uncertainty. The performance-based analysis would include consideration of the equilibrium profile, the alongshore losses, and the storm performance of the borrow sands, thus establishing a basis for evaluating the economic acceptability of the material. Further field and laboratory tests are needed to define the dependence of littoral drift rates on grain size.

DESIGN FOR SEA-LEVEL RISE

Since background erosion rates are used to design beach nourishment projects, these designs include the effects of relative sea-level rise over the period of the shoreline change data (see NRC, 1987). If sea level rises at the same rate over the next 50 years, the nourishment design will include the effects of sea-level rise, as this effect is "built in" to the background erosion rates. If sea-level rise accelerates, additional sand will be needed in later renourishments. If the project is monitored effectively and the results are analyzed and applied, the effects of all physical factors on performance can be assessed and incorporated into renourishment designs.

At each renourishment, an economic reanalysis is undertaken to determine if the project is still cost effective. This analysis is based on the actual performance of the project, which includes the effects of sea-level rise. If sea-level rise accelerates, some projects may not be economically feasible in the future. However, because of the "noise" in the data on sea-level change, it may be several decades, at the earliest, before the role of any increases in sea-level rise can be determined.

SAND BYPASS SYSTEMS

In some regions the need for beach nourishment has resulted from sand being trapped by a harbor constructed (breakwaters) in the nearshore or by jetties built to fix the location of an entrance through a beach into an inland harbor. Where there is a net alongshore transport of sand, jetties and harbor construction can cause trapping of sand updrift of structures, within the entrance or harbor, and in an ebb-tidal shoal. It can also cause erosion of the downdrift beach. Sand must be dredged from the entrance channel and harbor, or from a sand trap constructed contiguous to and updrift of them, to maintain required navigation depths. In many cases, it is desirable that sand not accumulate updrift. It may be appropriate to bypass the sand around the barrier to nourish downdrift beaches. Similarly, sand that accumulates in navigation channels as a result of harbor protective works could also be placed on downdrift beaches to help restore the sand budget of the littoral system (Richardson, 1991).

The amount of sand to be bypassed is established by the natural coastal processes in the region. The quantity needed for downdrift beach nourishment may be greater than the amount trapped in the entrance and harbor, and bypassing only this amount may not be sufficient to adequately maintain the downdrift beaches. The system designed to bypass the sand depends upon:

- the quantity required to be bypassed, wave climate, and tidal characteristics;
- the size and layout of the entrance and the harbor;
- how often maintenance dredging is required;
- how often nourishment is needed; and
- the times of year that bypassing will be permitted (owing to environmental and multiple-use requirements).

The system that is optimum for maintenance dredging may not be optimum for beach nourishment (and vice versa), but the system chosen must be adequate for both functions. Owing to the complex relationships among wave dimensions and directional characteristics, water levels, and the transport and deposition of sand, a system that is optimum for normal use may be overwhelmed during some storms. The system used may have to be modified based on experience.

Several different systems have been designed and used that may be appropriate at a specific site:

- mobile dredges in the harbor/entrance (Santa Cruz, California);
- movable dredge in the lee of a detached breakwater forming the updrift sand trap (Channel Islands/Port Hueneme, California);
- floating dredge within an entrance using a weir jetty on the updrift side (Hillsboro Inlet, Florida; Boca Raton Inlet, Florida; Masonboro Inlet, North Carolina; Perdido Pass, Alabama);
- fixed pump with dredge mounted on a movable boom (Lake Worth Entrance, Florida; South Lake Worth Inlet, Florida);
- a series of fixed jet-pump/crater units mounted on a pier normal to the beach on the updrift side (Nerang River Entrance, Queensland, Australia); and
- jet pumps (eductor) mounted on a movable crane, with main water supply and booster pumps in a fixed building (Indian River Inlet, Delaware).

BOX D-1
Information Needed to Plan a Beach Nourishment Project
Based on Quantitative Data

1. A statement of the problem or problems.
2. Sand sources and sinks and sand characteristics in the littoral cell.
3. Number, type, location, and properties of coastal structures.
4. Background erosion and accretion rates and reasons for them.
5. Wave climate, including directions, measured or hindcast.
6. Tidal datums and calculations of flood/ebb-tidal sand transport characteristics.
7. Calculations and observations of alongshore transport of sand.
8. Cross-shore movement of sand by waves and tides.
9. Estimates of sand transport into the entrance/harbor, ebb- tide shoal, and external sand trap if one is part of the project.
10. Sand budget based on calculations and observations of accretion at nearby structures, such as groins and jetties.
11. Storm surge climate.
12. Calculation of wave/water level/sand movement during severe storms for evaluation of safety of system components.
13. Identification and mapping of habitats.
14. Effects of system on biological communities.
15. Effect of pumping and deposition of sand on biological communities, on other uses, and on public safety.
16. Calculation of downdrift changes with time of several scenarios of sand budget and placement schedules.

These and other installations and their operational performance are described in the USACE's engineering and design manual *Sand Bypassing System Selection* (1991a), which provides guidance for the design and evaluation of sand bypassing systems.

A coastal processes study for a project is very important (USACE, 1991b). Also essential are sufficient reliable data (see, for example, Herron and Harris, 1966). The information shown in Box D-1 is based on quantitative data needed to plan a project.

After the above information has been obtained or estimated, a system can be designed. Some details on layouts, pumps, and other mechanical components are available in the USACE design manual.

MEASURING SUCCESS

Much of the debate over the performance of beach nourishment projects stems from the fact that projects are often criticized on the basis of publicly stated positions and expectations that may not coincide with those of the design engineers. Nevertheless, opponents of beach nourishment projects have identified issues that need to be addressed during design, including the amount of dry beach added and the expected life of a project. Resolving these issues during design would further minimize uncertainties in prediction and would provide a more complete basis for assessing project performance.

Success needs to be measured through comparisons of performance against design parameters, as determined through adequate monitoring with design predictions. These include shoreline and berm positions, total volume, and the response of the beach to a storm.

The first measure of success should be the longevity of the fill volumes—that is, the evolution of the fill from the construction volumes (design and ad-

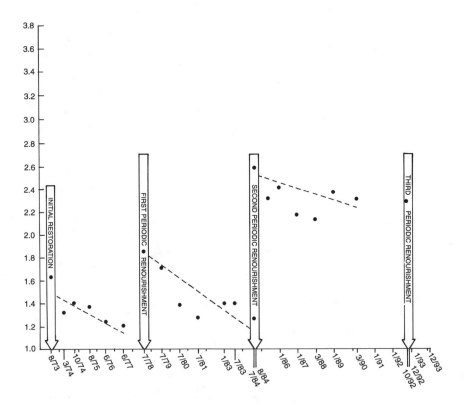

FIGURE D-9   Nourishment fill performance at Delray Beach, Florida.

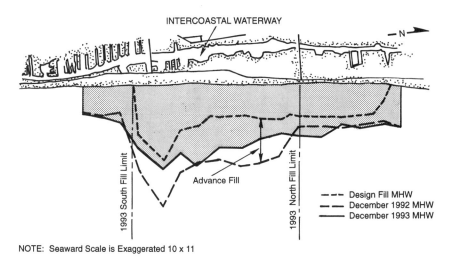

FIGURE D-10   Schematic of Delray Beach mean high water versus design.

vanced-fill) to the design volume over the renourishment interval. Figure D-9 shows the volumetric change of the Delray Beach project with time, which can be used to analyze the erosion rate for the beach and predict the time for periodic nourishment. For example, Figure D-10 from Delray Beach, Florida, and Figure D-11 from Captiva Island, Florida, show the mean high-water and berm crest locations versus the design beach standards. Figure D-10 shows that the beach exceeded the design standard mean-high water location as of 1993. Figure D-11 shows that the design berm crest has eroded, indicating the need for renourishment.

HYBRID PROJECTS

Hybrid projects are combinations of beach nourishment and structures, such as detached breakwaters, groins, jetties, revetments, seawalls, and submerged sills. There is a considerable body of knowledge on the structural design of the components and some information on their functional design. Procedures exist for the functional design of detached breakwaters and fill, and for groins and fill, but not for the other types of hybrid projects.

Some examples of projects are given here to illustrate what can be done. Also given is information on their functional performance (nontraditional shore protection devices are discussed in Chapter 4). Studying these examples and others should help planners and designers decide whether to use a hybrid project at a specific site, rather than just beach nourishment. One type of hybrid project, a perched beach, which consists of a fill and an underwater sill to hold most of the

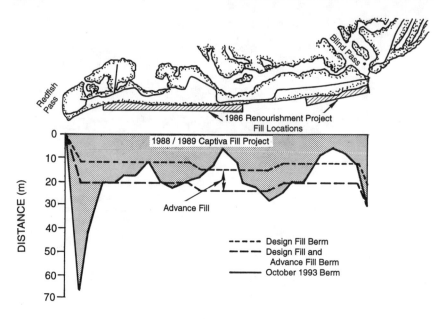

FIGURE D-11   Captiva Island project showing designed versus actual berm locations in
October 1993.

sand from moving offshore seaward of the sill, has been used only twice in the
United States, although its possible use has been discussed a number of times.
Such projects have been used in a few other countries, and examples are given in
this appendix.

Detached Breakwaters

Although hundreds of detached breakwaters, usually shore parallel, have
been constructed worldwide to hold sand on beaches using the tombolo effect
(Silvester and Hsu, 1993; Wiegel, 1988), only 21 major projects (235 segments)
have been built in the United States (Chasten et al., 1994). Many of the projects
have functioned well (Hanson and Kraus, 1991). However, breakwaters sometimes cause downdrift erosion if there is a net alongshore littoral transport in the
region. In some circumstances they may fill too much, causing other problems
(Wiegel, 1987). There are a large number of papers on the theory and design
(both functional and structural) of detached breakwaters and their effects on
beaches (see, for example Dally and Pope, 1986; Rosati, 1990).

The detached breakwater and beach fill at Redington Shores on the Gulf of
Mexico coast of Florida was constructed in late 1985 and early 1986 (Terry and
Howard, 1986). The northern 80 m of the rubblemound structure is parallel to the

Pinellas County Park seawall and about 100 m seaward of it, with a 30-m-long 45 degree (seaward) dogleg at the southern end. The breakwater was constructed in 3 m of water, and the crest elevation was originally at +0.5 m above mean low water. About 23,000 m³ of sand was placed along 300 m of shore in front of the seawall. A tombolo formed in the lee of the breakwater, extending out to 35 m from the seawall by April 1, 1986 (Terry and Howard, 1986). By October 1987 it had nearly reached the breakwater. Between April 1986 and February 1988, 44,000 m³ of sand had accumulated in the survey area, including the 23,000 m³ of initial fill (USACE, 1992a). In August 1988, 38 armor stones were removed from the breakwater to lower the crest elevation to 0.1 m above mean low water so that more wave energy would overtop it, and 290,000 m³ of fill was placed for the authorized Pinellas County project, a portion of which was placed at the site (USACE, 1992a). Monitoring data on the project are available in a paper by Davis (1991). When the committee members visited the project on February 8, 1993, the sand beach was out to the edge of the breakwater at low tide. For the safety of beach and water users, a series of poles and a line with floats had been installed just landward of the structure, together with a warning sign.

Lakeview Park, Ohio, is located on Lake Erie about 40 km west of Cleveland. The coast in this region consists of glacial till bluffs about 6 m high, which were eroding (recession rates of 0.6 to 1 m/year) and would continue to do so unless protected artificially (Pope and Rowan, 1983). The project, completed in October 1977, has three detached rubblemound breakwaters, each 75 m long, roughly parallel to shore, and separated by 50-m gaps (Hanson and Kraus, 1991). They are located in water depths ranging from 3 to 4 m, depending on the lake level, with the west end of the west breakwater 135 m offshore and the east end of the east breakwater 150 m offshore. A groin was constructed at each end of the fill, about a half a kilometer apart. About 85,000 m³ of sand (0.5 mm median diameter) was placed to form an artificial beach about 60 m wide. The berm elevation was +2 m low water datum (LWD), and the sand was placed with a 1 on 5 slope into the water (Walker et al., 1980). Backpassing of sand is performed at yearly intervals by the city of Lorain, Ohio, using either dump trucks or pumps (Bender, 1992). About 3,000 m³ is backpassed each time from the east (downdrift end) to the west (updrift end).

Groins

Groins can be beneficial, they can serve no useful purpose, or they can be harmful, depending on local conditions. As is well known to coastal engineers and scientists, groins do not create sand; they only affect its disposition. They serve no useful purpose unless there is alongshore transport of sand at the site. When used, it must be understood by all concerned that a long-term maintenance program is required. There is extensive technical literature on groins, some of which includes information on their use with sand fill. An annotated bibliography

has been prepared by Balsillie and Bruno (1972). Some details on design procedures, including sand fill, are given in the *Shore Protection Manual* (USACE,
1984) and by Kraus et al. (1994).

There are instances where groins have been installed as part of a project plan
but without the sand fill being implemented. A well-known example of an incomplete project is at Westhampton Beach, on the Atlantic shore of Long Island, New
York (Kraus et al., 1994). Fifteen quarry-stone groins were built in two incre-
ments, eleven from 1965 to 1966 and four from 1969 to 1970 (interestingly, they
have required no maintenance). They are about 400 m apart and 146-m long
along a 5,600-m section of shore. The original plan included an extension west-
ward to Moriches Inlet with six more groins, but a 4,000-m gap exists between
the last groin and the inlet owing to the objection of the Cupsoque County park
management to placing groins on the park in this section of the beach (O'Brien,
1988). Beach nourishment and dune construction were part of the plan, but the
sand fill in the 10 compartments between the first 11 groins was not made owing
to local economic problems. Dune and beach fill was placed in the four westerly
compartments when the additional groins were built (Nersesian et al., 1992). The
first 10 compartments have filled naturally (substantially, including the formation of dunes); this has deprived downdrift beaches of sand, and major erosion
has occurred. The net alongshore sand transport is from east to west, so this has
adversely affected the county park beach between the westernmost groin and the
inlet. The shore, dune, and buildings fronted by the 15 groins have had a high
level of protection from a number of storms, some very severe (including the
Halloween 1991 storm and the December 10-12, 1992 northeaster; Nersesian et
al., 1992). This section of the barrier island had a history of breakthroughs and
inlet creation prior to construction of the project (Figure D-12).

There are six groins along the beach at Atlantic City, New Jersey, and a
modified jetty at its north end. These were planned as a part of the beach nourishment project (Weggel and Sorenson, 1991). As Weggel and Sorenson state:

> Historically, shore stabilization structures have contributed to the relative
> stability of Atlantic City's beaches. Prior to the construction of inlet and beach
> stabilization structures, Atlantic City's inlet and ocean shorelines experienced
> large-scale, erratic fluctuations as the inlet migrated. Compared with the pre-
> stabilization fluctuations, current shoreline changes are small. Inlet stabiliza-
> tion, initially by bulkheading and groins and subsequently by construction of
> the Oriental Avenue and Brigantine jetties, is perhaps the most significant ele-
> ment contributing to beach stability in Atlantic City.
>
> The groin and jetty modifications undertaken by the State of New Jersey in
> 1984 appear to have improved the performance of the 1986 fill when compared
> with earlier fills. Raising the crest elevation of the jetty has retained fill and
> prevented its return to the inlet by overtopping and by deflation. Extending the
> Illinois Avenue groin appears to have resulted in a beach that is about 100 feet
> wider near Profile 5 at Indiana Avenue. Similar, though less dramatic improve-
> ments occurred in the vicinity of the other improved/repaired structures.

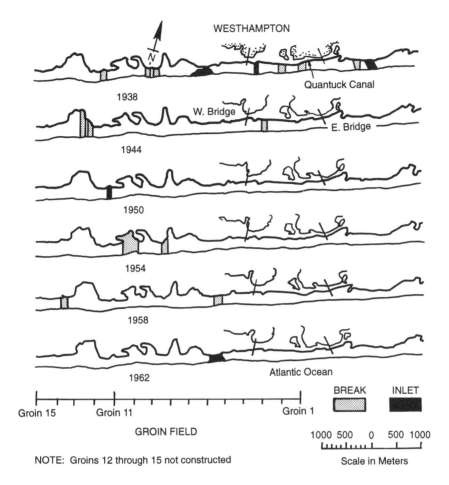

FIGURE D-12   Historic barrier island breaching and inlet creation near Westhampton, Long Island, New York.

From 1963 to 1967, the city of Deerfield Beach, Florida, built a series of relatively short, low-profile groins with rock mounds at their seaward edge. Although these groins are short, they have effectively trapped sand in the alongshore drift without significant downdrift impacts.

Sand-Tight Jetties

The concept of using long shore-normal structures to create compartments (relatively short "littoral cells," or "pocket beaches") has been considered a number of times. Under what conditions they might be successful and how to ensure they will function as planned are not clear.

Nearly all projects that are combinations of sand-tight jetties and beach nourishment exist because of jetties already in place for navigation purposes. The jetties, and the entrances they fix, may well be the cause of the erosion downdrift, which is why beach nourishment is needed at the site. There is some evidence that a sand-tight jetty (or long groin) can help establish a compartment for the sand fill (Egense and Sonu, 1987). It may be necessary to design, construct, and operate a sand bypass system as a part of the project.

There are three sand-tight jetties in the Dade County, Florida, project (Wiegel, 1992a). One, the north jetty at Government Cut (the entrance to the port of Miami), is at the south boundary of the sand fill. The other two are the jetties at Bakers Haulover Inlet, located 15 km north of the cut, about two-thirds of the distance to the Dade County–Broward County line. The north jetty of the cut was originally not sand tight but was made fairly so during its 1986 rehabilitation. The south jetty of the Bakers Haulover Inlet has its outer 91 m curved southwardly to deflect alongshore currents to the south and encourage a gyre to dissipate these currents and minimize sand loss (von Oesen, 1973). It was completed in July 1974. The north jetty of the inlet was rehabilitated in 1986, making it sand tight, raising its crest elevation, extending its length to 130 m, and constructing a 30-m-long "dogleg" toward its north end. The dogleg was used as a result of a hydraulic model study by the University of Florida (1959). These sand-tight structures seem to have served their secondary purpose of compartmentalizing the beach.

Doheny Beach State Park, California, is a sand fill between the east breakwater of Dana Point Harbor and the north jetty (called a groin locally, the purpose of which is to train the river flow to the ocean when floods cut a breach through the beach). The harbor and beach are located at the updrift end of the oceanside littoral cell. The rubblemound jetty is sand tight because its center is constructed of concrete sheet piles. The sand fill was placed in 1964, and the original jetty was constructed at that time. A pocket beach was formed that is still in place and heavily used. It is about 425 m long, and 72,000 m^3 of sand fill was placed (Price, 1966). Prior to the fill the surface was basically rock and cobbles, although a sand beach forms whenever the winter runoffs of the creek are heavy. Rock and cobbles can be seen at the present time seaward of the beach at low tide (Wiegel, 1993b). Probably owing to this and the wave climate at the site, little sand is transported through or around the east breakwater and lost into the harbor.

Revetments, Seawalls, and Bulkheads

There are a number of examples where revetments, seawalls, and bulkheads have been constructed for protection of buildings, walkways, streets, and utilities prior to the use of beach nourishment and then left in place after a fill has been made. Locations where this approach has been used include Miami Beach and

Redington Shores, Florida. If the structures are well designed, well built, and well maintained, they can provide a backup to the major protection provided by the sand fill. This is important because of the episodic nature of coastal forces (such as waves, storm surges, currents) and an inability to predict future episodes reliably from data obtained from short-term studies.

Galveston, Texas, presents a different category. Grade raising, seawalls, and embankments provide the primary protection of the city from hurricane storm surges and waves (Wiegel, 1991). The purpose of a new beach nourishment project is to provide a recreational beach.

There are a few cases where a revetment, seawall, or bulkhead has been designed and constructed as an integral part of a project. The beach nourishment and storm protection project on Fenwick Island at Ocean City, Maryland, nearly 11 km long, was completed in 1991 with about 5 million m^3 of sand placed. A 1.3-km-long seawall was built along its southern end to protect the boardwalk. The project was constructed in two separate phases. The sand (0.30 to 0.35 mm median diameter) was obtained from two offshore borrow areas, pumped to shore, placed subaerially, and redistributed by use of bulldozers. The state of Maryland placed a recreational beach fill of 2 million m^3 of sand between 3rd Street and the Maryland-Delaware border. This was intended to widen the beach (above mean high water) by about 18 m. Two years after the placement, the severely eroded area between 74th Street and 86th Street was found to be significantly narrower than 18 m. This was probably due to preproject profile steepening, which would have required more volume to provide 18 m of widening. Then, during 1990-1991, the USACE placed 4 million m^3 of sand. This was for storm protection and included a sand dune between 27th Street and the border with Delaware, and a concrete-capped, steel-sheetpile bulkhead along the seaward edge of the boardwalk from 3rd Street to 27th Street, with a berm in front of both.

The second project described herein is at Bate Bay, New South Wales, Australia, 25 km south of Sydney Heads. It is a crescent-shaped bay with a 5.5-km shoreline. It is being described here for four reasons. One is that it is a hybrid project, with a 340-m-long seawall constructed along part of the project (Prince Street) with a walkway along its crest (Hirst and Foster, 1987). The second is that about 10 metric tons of dyed sand was placed in the surf zone at the updrift end of the bay and tracked for several months. The third is that the sand sink is wind-blown sand, transported inland into dune fields (much of the sand in the central portion of the back-dune region has been mined over the past 40 years for construction and foundry uses). The fourth is that a new equilibrium seems to have been developed, reducing substantially the loss of sand inland owing to the reformation of dunes, vegetation, and the resulting moderation of wind action and sand washouts (Gordon, 1994). There was severe erosion and changes in beach orientation in the Sydney region that took 3 to 5 years to recover, with foredunes taking about 6 years. There has not been as severe a sequence of events since

(Gordon, 1994). Much of the erosion of Bate Bay beaches occurred during a series of severe storms in May and June 1974 (Gordon, 1992).

Using calculations of estimated littoral drift (net transport from south to north in most of the bay) and sand blown inland into dune fields, profile measurements, aerial photographs, wave data, and sand tracer studies, it was concluded that Bate Bay was a closed system, with the loss of sand (the sink) being inland along the center portion of the bay at an average rate of about 46,000 m³/year. This was because the foredunes had degraded substantially, with washouts (troughs) and blowouts (Gordon, 1994). A mathematical model was developed and applied similar to the GENESIS model developed later at CERC (Gordon, 1994). The gross alongshore transport in the southern third of the bay was estimated to be 700,000 m³/year with a net of 41,000 m³/year (only about 6 percent of the gross) toward the north. Along the central third of the shore, the estimate of gross transport rate was 165,000 m³/year with a net of 21,000 m³/year toward the north. Along the northern third of the shore, the estimate was 86,000 m³/year with a net of only 1,200 m³/year toward the south. The net transports are all small differences of relatively large estimated quantities of gross transport.

The management plan adopted was to establish a well-vegetated foredune along much of the bay and:

> . . . rather than mechanically forcing a new shoreline alignment on the embayment, the technique used involved: the establishment of some initial dunes on the existing alignment; feeding of the surf zone with nourishment sand; allow[ing] the natural processes to distribute the material throughout the embayment and also allow[ing] these processes to adjust foreshore/dune alignment and the offshore seabed.

After this was done, the back dunes in the center of the embayment would be stabilized.

Remedial work was taken along the center reach of the foredunes, installing sand-catching fences, beach access tracks, infilling blowouts and washthroughs, and planting dune-stabilizing vegetation. Then in 1977 and 1978 about 80,000 m³ of sand was hauled by trucks from the inland portion of the dunes to the south end of the bay (at South Cronulla) and spread by bulldozer. After the 1978 swimming season, another 47,000 m³ of sand were transported and placed, for a total of 127,000 m³. In 1985, the 340-m-long seawall and walkway were constructed. The project has been monitored since completion and found to be effective (Gordon, 1992). The rebuilt dunes and vegetation have caused the sand to be deposited on the seaward face and become a part of the foredune system. This has also changed the local wind patterns in the beach and dune area, and there has been a progressive decrease in the amount of sand blown inland. The project has been subjected to a number of major storms since completion, although none as severe as the 1974 storm. South Cronulla Beach has been slowly eroding but after 15 years is still in usable condition, and no renourishment has been required. It has performed as expected (Gordon, 1994).

In the management plan it was recognized that if the beach were subjected to a series of storms similar to those of 1974, it would be expected that substantial erosion would occur and that it would be within the project fill but would require rebuilding of the foredunes and beaches (Gordon, 1994).

Submerged Sill (Perched Beach)

A beach nourishment and submerged sill (perched beach) project was constructed in Italy between mid-1989 and mid-1991 along 3 km of coast at Lido di Ostia, about 35 km from Rome, on the Tyrrhenian Sea. This is on the Tiber River Delta, which in recent decades has been eroding at a recession rate of about 1.7 m/year owing to a major reduction in sand transported to the coast by the river due to dams and the mining of building material from the river bed (Ferrante et al., 1992). The rubblemound submerged sill was constructed parallel to shore, about 150 m from it, in water about -4.0 to -5.0 m below mean sea level, apparently located where there was a natural sand bar. It has a 15-m-wide crest at -1.5 m below mean sea level, with a seaward slope of 1(V)ertical to 5(H)orizontal. The maximum weight of the stone is 1 metric ton, and there is a 5-m-wide rock toe protection in a 1-m-deep trench. The stone was placed on a geotextile base. For safety the location is marked with buoys. The fill was a double layer of quarry material, the thick lower layer a mixture of sandy gravel, poorly sorted (0.08 to 120 mm), with a 1-m-thick layer of sand (0.3 to .3 mm) placed on top. The berm crest was located at +1.0 m above mean sea level, and the seaward slope was about 2.5 percent. The new shoreline was about 60 m seaward of the then-existing location. About 1,360,000 m^3 of sand and selected sandy gravel were used for the beach, and about 300,000 m^3 of rock (basalt and limestone from different quarries) was used for the sill. The project has been monitored during the 3 years since completion and has performed reasonably well while subjected to a number of severe storms. The elevation of the berm increased to +1.5 to +2.0 m above mean sea level, and the submerged profile deepened. Minor scour occurred seaward of the barrier toe. No adverse effects were observed on adjacent beaches.

Subsequent to Ferrrante et al.'s 1992 paper, an additional kilometer of submerged sill was constructed in shallow water, closer to shore. This change in location was made based on observations of the performance of the first project. The new sill has performed in a more satisfactory manner, with sand moving in from the first beach fill, forming a wider beach along the section of coast in the lee of the new sill (Tomasicchio, 1994).

A 400-m-long artificial beach was constructed on the Mediterranean Sea coast at Monaco during 1965 to 1967. Three 80- to 100-m-long breakwaters were built with 80-m gaps between them, in water 6 to 10 m deep. Two were shore parallel and connected to it by groins made of concrete blocks. The third (west breakwater) was connected to the shore. A sill was constructed across each of the gaps, with tops at -2.5 m below datum and backfilled with quarry-run rock. The fill was 80,000 m^3 of local dolomite chippings that had a median diameter of 3 to 8 mm (gravel) (Tourman, 1968). The project has performed in a satisfactory manner, requiring only about 5,000 m^3 of replacement gravel during 23 years (Rouch and Bellessort, 1990).

RISK ASSESSMENT

The terms "risk assessment" and "risk analysis" are usually associated with the decision-making process for projects or practices where the potential for adverse environmental consequences or loss of life is high. In recent decades, risk assessment studies have dealt with the probability of occurrence of catastrophic events in the design of nuclear power plants, with public health issues such as the risk of smoking and exposure to carcinogens, and with studies of terrestrial and aquatic systems (Cohrssen and Covello, 1989). Good engineering design has always addressed the effects of unusual events on the performance and survival of engineering projects. This has been particularly true for civil engineering projects, where natural forces often present critical design conditions. Beach nourishment projects are no exception.

Calculating the risk that a specific project will be damaged or will cause damage can be difficult because establishing the level of acceptable risk involves socioeconomic trade-offs for which there are no simple formulas. Often, decisions involving risk are based on emotion or judgment more than on an actual quantification of the risk. Because beach nourishment projects often have relatively short renourishment cycles, the public may perceive them as failures and as economically risky when, in fact, they are economically justified.

For beach nourishment projects, there are two problems for which risks might be evaluated. These are (1) the risk that a project will bring about adverse biological effects at the beach or borrow site and (2) the risk that a project will not perform as anticipated. The following discussion deals only with this latter risk. Beach nourishment projects provide protection even when subjected to events that exceed their design level (see Appendix H). A project designed to protect against storm criteria with a 100-year recurrence interval will provide protection to some extent against storm criteria with a 200-year recurrence interval, although some damage will occur. Generally, there will be a low-level storm that will not cause any damage. However, a protected area may still sustain some damage during storms with a return period less than the storm criteria upon which the design was based. Even after a project has sustained some damage, most of the sand associated with the project usually remains immediately seaward of, or in close proximity to, the project area and continues to provide some level of protection.

The elements of risk analysis include:

- hazard identification—defining those hazards that could possibly result from a beach nourishment project and those to which a beach nourishment project might be subjected;
- risk assessment—a definition of the severity of the risk, the probability of an event's occurrence, and the consequences of that event's occurrence;
- significance of risk—how the designer, client, and public perceive the risk and how much risk is acceptable; and
- decisions—how the risk analysis will influence decision making in the design process, in scheduling and construction, and in the operation of a project.

In many cases, there is a paucity of data on which to base decisions that might minimize risk. Engineering always requires making decisions with incomplete data but strives to minimize the probability of failure or loss using the data that are available.

Risk Considerations in Beach Fill Design

The purposes of performing a risk analysis for a beach nourishment project include:

- identifying the physical and biological problems associated with beach nourishment,
- comparing technologies to determine their relative effectiveness in reducing the risk associated with beach nourishment projects, and
- setting management/operation priorities or selecting from among several actions.

The first step in risk assessment is to identify what events could possibly occur during a beach nourishment project's lifetime and then to quantify their severity and the consequences of their occurrence. Events can be classified as those that result in economic loss and those that are likely to result in loss of life. The latter are more critical but fortunately occur rarely in the case of failure of a beach nourishment project. Possible events include large waves, elevated water levels, and high alongshore transport rates. The likelihood that a given event will occur is generally expressed in terms of a probability distribution. For example, wave heights and other extreme events frequently follow an Extremal Type I (Gumbel) distribution or other typical distributions for extreme values (see Figure D-13).

There are various levels of sophistication by which risk can be incorporated into a beach nourishment project design:

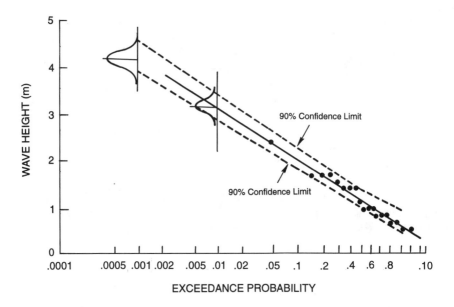

FIGURE D-13   Extremal Type I (Gumbel) distribution for annual maximum wave height statistics based on hindcast data for Atlantic City, N.J. (Jensen, 1983).

- Deterministic design uses a probabilistic description of the physical environment. This assumes a reasonable set of design conditions based on knowledge of the physical environment and tailors the design to that environment (e.g., design for the 100-year or 1,000-year storm).
- Probabilistic design considers the uncertainties in describing the physical environment. This approach develops the statistics of various events (e.g., high water levels, extreme wave heights, storm durations) and optimizes the design to minimize economic risk. The design wave height and water level that produce the maximum net benefits for the project are selected.
- Stochastic design or simulation includes procedures to generate one or more time series of data based on measurements of the physical environment at a project site. For example, an artificial wave environment having the same statistics of the real wave environment at a beach fill site may be generated synthetically. Based on knowledge of the physics of coastal processes important to the performance of beach nourishment projects, the synthetically generated data series is used to evaluate the response of the project for many possible, statistically similar scenarios. From the many simulations, the range of possible responses of the project to the environment is statistically defined. This constitutes an analysis of many simulations of a project's response to many statistically similar environments in order to define a range of possible outcomes.

As knowledge of coastal processes and the ability to describe them mathematically increases, design will rely more and more on computer simulations. Simulation as a design process requires:

- knowledge of, and the ability to quantitatively describe, the physical environment at a site and
- understanding of, and the ability to numerically model, the important coastal processes.

Risk Relative to Storm Intensities and Nourishment Intervals

For any beach nourishment design, there is a risk that storm intensities and durations will exceed those for which the project was designed. Assessment and quantification of this risk are important parts of the design analysis and the public information program. For beach restoration, there are basically two design elements for which risk needs to be considered separately. The first is the risk that the design cross-section that provides storm protection for upland properties could be impacted by a major storm. In that case, the larger storm could erode the entire profile, leaving upland structures vulnerable to undermining and wave impact. This is the risk that upland damage would exceed acceptable levels and that the project will require emergency repair. A safety factor that would increase the size of the selected design cross-section could be used to decrease the risk of emergency action.

The second risk concerns the renourishment interval. If weather conditions following a nourishment are generally stormier than average conditions or if portions of the project erode significantly faster than expected at hot spots, the time between renourishments may be shorter than the programmed postnourishment time period. It is also possible that the amount of offshore adjustment will exceed the design expectations, leaving a less-than-desired dry beach area—a common problem in the first nourishment that would also necessitate earlier renourishment. This constitutes a risk of having to nourish a beach earlier than programmed and, if significantly in advance of the planned renourishment, could strain a local sponsor's financial resources for cost sharing. A substantially shorter interval than programmed could also lead to a public perception that the project is not performing properly. Therefore, the implications of shorter nourishment intervals need to be properly estimated, incorporated into the economic analysis and local funding plan, and communicated to all concerned, including the public. In practice, because of limitations in a local sponsor's financial ability to support renourishment when first needed, the programmed time interval for renourishment is often followed despite increased vulnerability as the result of excessive erosion. When renourishment is not timely with respect to maintaining designed levels of protection, some of the shore protection benefits may not be realized if significant storms are experienced before renourishment actually occurs. It may be appropriate to increase advanced-fill quantities beyond those actually required in order to lower the risk of a shortened renourishment interval (or increased vulnerability to storms). A programmed shorter first renourishment interval would also help address the uncertainties of hot-spot erosion and offshore adjustment.

Sample Calculation of Probability for a Storm Return Period

The probability that an event with a given return period will be equaled or exceeded in a given period of time (usually the project's lifetime) can be estimated by the following equation:

$$R = 1 - \left(1 - \frac{1}{T}\right)^n \tag{D-3}$$

where R is the probability that an event equal to or greater than the design event will occur at least once in n years (risk), T is the return period of the design event in years (the reciprocal of the probability that the event will be equaled or exceeded in any one year), and n is the number of years. Consequently, if a nourishment project with a proposed lifetime of 10 years is designed for a 100-year storm, the risk of a 100-year storm occurring at least once in that 10-year period is:

$$R = 1 - \left(1 - \frac{1}{100}\right)^{10} = 0.096 \tag{D-4}$$

or about a 10 percent chance. The risk that a 10-year storm will occur at least once in a 10-year period is

$$R = 1 - \left(1 - \frac{1}{10}\right)^{10} = 0.651 \tag{D-5}$$

or a 65 percent chance. The risk equation is derived from the binomial probability distribution for 1 minus the probability that the event will not occur at all in n tries. This procedure assumes that the environment is known well enough that a statistical distribution can be developed for the event's occurrence.

The magnitude of the design event is generally found from a statistical analysis of measured data to give an estimate of the event's probability distribution. Figure D-13 shows a typical plot of wave height versus the estimated probability that the given wave height will be equaled or exceeded. In the figure the wave height that will be equaled or exceeded once in a 100-year period (the 100-year event or the event that has a probability of 0.01) is 4.6 m. Water-level data, alongshore sand transport data, and other parameters might also be analyzed in the same manner.

One complicating factor in this approach and in those discussed below is the question of how well the physical environment is known and how well it can be described. Probability distributions constructed for wave heights, periods, water levels, and so forth, are merely approximations of the true population. More sophisticated analyses can include the uncertainty in defining these distributions (USACE, 1992b, 1993).

Probabilistic Design

Another type of design is termed "probabilistic design." This approach evaluates the economics of building projects at various scales. As the scale of a project increases, the level of protection it provides and the economic benefits also increase, so that protection is provided against more severe conditions; however, the cost of providing this additional protection also increases. For a beach nourishment project, the project's scale might be indicated simply by the berm width or by the volume of sand per unit length of beach. Damages at various project scales are determined by using the probability that the design conditions will be exceeded. Figure D-14 shows the various economic elements of the probabilistic design procedure for a range of beach berm widths. For a narrow berm (or, alternatively, for a low volume of sand per unit length of beach), annual damages to the backbeach area will be high. As berm width increases, annual damages decrease, since the wider berm provides more protection. Also, as berm width increases the recreational area, benefits may increase. Project costs also increase with beach berm width, since more sand must be placed. The cost of replacing lost sand from the project to maintain a given level of protection initially increases for narrow berm widths but levels off for wider berms. The level of design selected is the berm width that minimizes the net annual cost or maximizes the net benefits. The damages decrease for larger berm widths, since the probability of occurrence of storms large enough to erode the beach gets smaller. It takes larger, less frequent storms to destroy a protective beach with a wider berm.

In the case of beach nourishment the analysis is further complicated by the fact that the berm width, and hence the level of protection, is a function of time. For example, during the second year following construction, the level of protection will generally be reduced because of any losses experienced by the project during the first year. During the third year, the protection will be further reduced; consequently, not only is the magnitude of a storm important but also when in the renourishment cycle it occurs. Figure D-15 shows how damages to backbeach areas might vary with berm width at the start of a storm and the wave conditions characterizing the storm. For increasingly wider berms, waves cause progres-

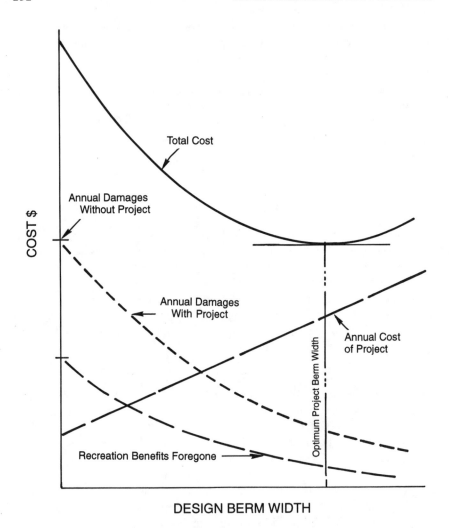

FIGURE D-14   Various economic elements of the probabilistic design procedure for a range of beach berm widths.

sively less damage. Application of this information requires that the berm width be known as a function of time. The berm width at any time depends on anteced-ent events and ideally should be defined statistically; however, an expression for average berm width as a function of time, if available, can be used. Figure D-16 presents the same information as Figure D-15 but in a different way. Here backbeach damage is plotted against wave height for various berm widths that could exist at various times during the renourishment cycle. For a given charac-

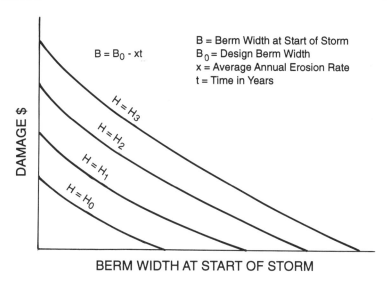

FIGURE D-15 Annual damages as a function of significant wave height and berm width at the start of a storm.

teristic wave height (or some other measure of storm intensity), there is a berm width that will completely protect the backbeach area. Waves larger than this zero-damage wave height will result in some damage. The risk of experiencing backbeach damage increases with time because of the beach erosion inherent in those areas where beach nourishment is needed.

It is important to recognize that damages do not depend simply on wave action but also on other factors such as water level and storm duration. There is currently no single simple parameter to describe the effect of storms on beach nourishment projects.

Risk Determination by Simulating the Performance of Beach Fills

Because of the stochastic nature of the coastal environment and the response of beach nourishment projects to that environment, the sequence in which events occur and the condition of the beach nourishment project at the times those events occur are important. Consequently, simulation of the performance of beach nourishment projects holds the promise of quantifying risks associated with such projects.

Simulating the performance of proposed beach fills requires that a long time series be generated of the physical events—storms, waves, and water levels—that could occur during the lifetime of a fill. The synthetically generated time series must have the same statistical characteristics as the real environment. The

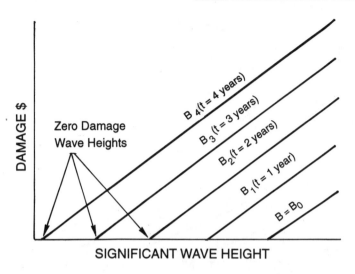

FIGURE D-16   Annual damages as a function of significant wave height and berm width. Berm width is a function of time since the last renourishment.

response of the beach fill to many possible enactments of that environment is determined and statistically summarized. Answers are sought to such questions as: How many times and how much damage will occur? How will the beach width vary with time? What range of beach widths might prevail 2, 3, or 4 years following nourishment? In effect, simulation will provide a range of possible outcomes or responses to building a beach fill at a given site.

Simulation requires extensive data on the physical environment at a site, specifically, information on waves (height, period, direction), water levels, storm durations, and their joint probability distributions. Simulation also requires that the important coastal processes involved be understood and amenable to quantitative description. Further confidence is required in the results of the simulations, and funds are available to run enough of them to obtain reliable statistics. Simulations using synthetic data have been used for decades in water resources engineering to optimize reservoir operating plans and to design reservoir systems (Fiering and Jackson, 1971). There have been few coastal engineering simulation applications, mainly because of the complexity of the processes involved and the paucity of good data on the physical environment. In recent years, however, progress has been made in the development of computer models of the relevant coastal processes, and several simulations have been made. Weggel et al. (1988) statistically described the alongshore sand transport environment from wave hindcasts and then used synthetically generated alongshore transport data to simulate the operation of a sand bypassing plant at Indian River Inlet, Delaware.

Strine and Dalrymple (1991) simulated the performance of a beach fill on the Delaware coast using synthetic wave data based on wave hindcasts.

One result of numerous simulations is statistical information on when renourishment will be necessary. The length of the renourishment cycle can be established in a statistical sense if a given berm width is to be maintained. In addition, input to a "project operating plan" can result from simulations. Simulations can provide information on what conditions in the project should trigger action. For example, when the shoreline recedes to a given width in a specified month, renourishment is needed to provide the desired level of protection.

BEACH NOURISHMENT AND THE BUDGET
OF LITTORAL SEDIMENTS

Beach nourishment can be viewed as a human intervention into the overall budget of littoral sediments, in many cases in response to adverse impacts on the natural system. The budget of sediments is simply an application of the principle of conservation of volume to the littoral sediments. The time rate of change of sand volume within the system is dependent upon the rate at which sand is brought into the system versus the rate at which sand leaves. The budget involves assessing the sedimentary contributions (credits) and losses (debits) and equating them to the net gain or loss (balance of sediments) in a given sedimentary compartment (Bowen and Inman, 1966; Komar, 1976). The balance of sediments between the losses and gains should be equal to the local beach erosion or accretion. Table D-1 summarizes the possible sources (gains) and sinks (losses) of sand for a littoral sedimentary budget. In general, alongshore movements of sand into a littoral compartment, river transport, and seacliff erosion provide the major credits; alongshore movements out of the compartment, offshore transport (especially through submarine canyons), and wind transport shoreward to form sand dunes are the major losses or debits. As listed in Table D-1, beach nourishment

TABLE D-1   Budget of Littoral Sediments

Credit	Debit	Balance
Alongshore transport into area	Alongshore transport out of area	Beach accretion or erosion
River transport	Wind transport out	
Sea-cliff erosion	Offshore transport	
Onshore transport	Deposition in submarine canyons	
Biogenous deposition	Solution and abrasion	
Hydrogenous deposition	Solution and abrasion	
Wind transport onto beach	Mining	
Beach nourishment		

SOURCE: After Bowen and Inman (1966).

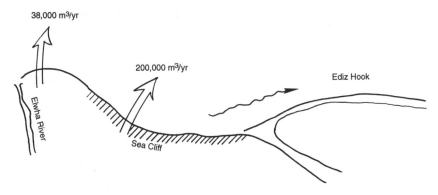

FIGURE D-17   Sand sources for Ediz Hook, Washington, spit (from Galster and Schwartz, 1990).

represents a credit, the volume of which is intended to shift the balance of the overall budget from erosion (a net deficit) to shoreline accretion (a positive balance).

The role of beach nourishment as a factor in the budget of sediments is illustrated by Ediz Hook on the Strait of Juan de Fuca coast of Washington (Figure D-17). The spit, composed mainly of gravels and cobbles derived from the Elwha River and cliff erosion into glacial outwash sediments, was formed by the eastward alongshore transport of those sediments (Galster and Schwartz, 1990). Erosion of Ediz Hook began early in the century as the river was dammed, cutting off its estimated supply of 38,000 m^3/year of sediment to the littoral zone, and then by the construction of a bulkhead along the eroding sea cliff, depriving its 200,000 m^3/year sediment contribution. Not unexpectedly, Ediz Hook began to erode, with the erosion being a maximum at its western end, while the terminal end of the spit continued to grow toward the east. The maintenance of Ediz Hook is important because it forms the natural protection of Port Angeles Harbor.

The response to the growing erosion problem was the construction of a revetment along the length of the spit, together with nourishment of the fronting beach (Galster and Schwartz, 1990). The initial nourishment involved placement of gravel and cobbles, derived from inland sources, along the length of the spit. It is apparent, however, that nourishment might be more effective if placed at the western end of the spit as a feeder beach, basically replacing the sediment that was formerly contributed by the natural sources. The situation at Ediz Hook provides an excellent example that beach nourishment often represents human intervention into the overall budget of littoral sediments. At Ediz Hook, the sediment budget was first affected by cutting off the two major sources, sediments derived from the Elwha River and from sea cliff erosion. Beach nourishment represents a further human manipulation of the budget in an attempt to restore those lost sources. This and other examples indicate the need for a broad analysis in developing a budget of sediments for the site. This is necessary in order to better understand the basic causes of the erosion and the reasons for needing a nourishment project.

VENEER BEACH FILLS

Veneer beach fills have been used in situations where beach-quality sand is not available in sufficient quantities to economically undertake a nourishment project. Veneer fills involve placing beach-quality sand over a relatively large volume of material that is generally unsatisfactory for beach nourishment. The unsatisfactory materials, which may either be too coarse or too fine, serve as an underlayer beneath the beach-quality sand. The usual reason for using a veneer fill is economic: the cost of providing a cross-section built totally of beach-quality sand is prohibitive.

Veneer fills are of two types:

- fills where the underlying materials are coarser than typical beach sands (e.g., boulders, coral, rocks) and
- fills where the underlying materials are finer than typical beach sands (e.g., silts or silty sands where the median grain size is much smaller than the native sand).

In the United States, veneer beach fills have been used in Corpus Christi, Texas; Key West, Florida; and Grand Isle, Louisiana. At Key West, the underlying material was a coral rock much coarser than typical beach sand. At Corpus Christi, the underlying material was silt or silty sand, much finer than typical beach sand. At Grand Isle, a core of compacted clay was included in the dune cross-section as a barrier to erosion if the sand veneer is eroded to expose the core.

A fundamental design problem associated with veneer fills is selecting a veneer that is sufficiently thick so as not to erode away and expose the core during storms or before scheduled replenishment. From a shore protection perspective, not making the veneer thick enough poses no particular problem if the underlying material is coarser than the sand veneer. Erosion of the veneer exposes the coarse underlayer, which is more resistant to erosion. However, the veneer might have to be replaced before recreational benefits can again be realized. Conversely, for the situation where finer underlying material is used, if the veneer erodes, the underlying fine material will be exposed to wave action to erode more quickly and reduce the level of protection afforded by the fill.

The design of veneer fills with fine underlying material requires knowledge of the seasonal and storm-induced profile changes along with knowledge of prevailing background erosion rates. The thickness of the veneer must be sufficient to provide an envelope to these profile variations and to the background

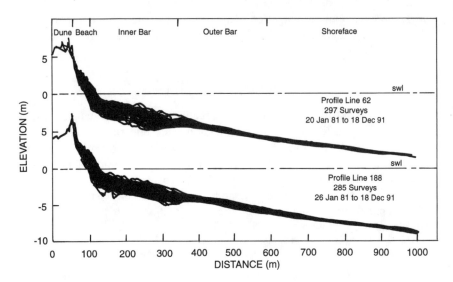

FIGURE D-18   Profile envelopes showing depth of profile changes (from Lee and Birkemeier, 1993).

erosion if the underlying fines are not to be exposed during storms or before
scheduled renourishment. Because of these constraints, veneer beach fills with
underlying fines are less likely to be used on beaches exposed to large waves or
beaches that experience a large tidal range. One procedure that can be used to
select a veneer thickness involves plotting many historical beach profiles for a
proposed fill site on a single axis system and constructing an envelope to the
profiles (see Figure D-18). This gives an indication of the required thickness of
the sand veneer on a beach profile involved in seasonal profile excursions. The
thickness found in this way provides a lower limit on the required veneer thickness. Similar plots for storm-induced profile changes, while often difficult to
obtain, are needed to determine the depth of profile changes that might occur
during storms. Selection of a design storm is thus also critical for a veneer's
design.

The selection of a veneer thickness for fills with coarse underlying materials
is less critical. The same procedure outlined above can be used to select the
thickness. In some sections of California the natural sand veneer over cobbles or
bedrock is removed after storms and during the winter but returns in calmer
weather.

Beach Veneer Experience

Corpus Christi, Texas

In 1978 a veneer beach fill was constructed at Corpus Christi Beach in Corpus Christi Bay, a sheltered area of relatively low wave action (Kieslich and Brunt, 1989). The tidal range at the site is less than 0.1 m. The project area had experienced erosion since the late 1800s. About 380,000 m^3 of a silty-sand material was dredged from Corpus Christi Bay and placed as an underlayer along the 2.3-km-long project area. Subsequently, 230,000 m^3 of coarse (median diameter, 0.4 mm) beach-sized material was trucked in and placed as a veneer. The 230,000 m^3 of veneer sand included 96,000 m^3 for 5 years of advanced nourishment to combat an estimated loss rate of 19,000 m^3/year (see Figure D-19). The thickness of the veneer varied from 0.5 m on the berm to about 1.0 m on the foreshore. The project was completed in March 1978 and has performed well. The loss rate actually experienced has only been about 13,000 m^3/year. The project was inundated during Hurricane Allen in 1980, which created an 2.4-m surge in Corpus Christi Bay near the beach. Consequently, the project was under about 1.5 m of water and so was cushioned from direct hurricane wave attack. The beach lost

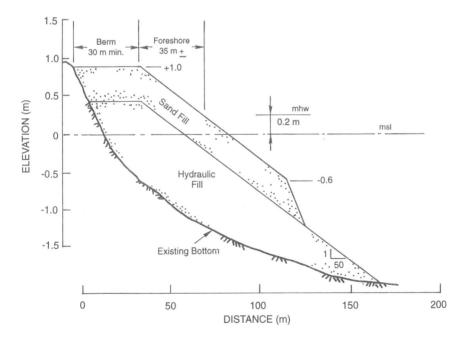

FIGURE D-19 Veneer beach fill cross-section, Corpus Christi Beach, Corpus Christi, Texas.

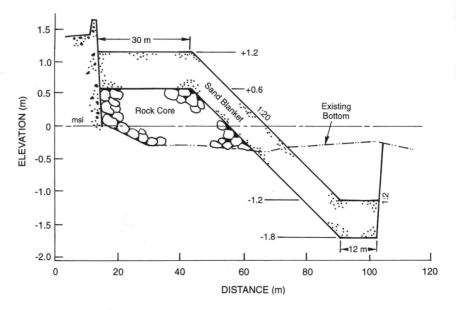

FIGURE D-20   Veneer beach fill cross-section, Key West, Florida.

about 6,000 m³ of sand as a result of Hurricane Allen. The north end of the project continued to experience erosion, as evidenced by the growth of a spit there. As a result of this erosion, a terminal groin was constructed in November 1985 to stabilize the north end of the fill.

Key West, Florida

A protective and recreational beach was constructed along the south shore of Key West by excavating a trench 2 m deep and 12 m wide in offshore relict coral and placing the rock material on the beach as an underlayer (USACE, 1957, 1982a). A veneer of calcareous sand was placed on top of the rock underlayer. The offshore trench was excavated, and the excavated material was used as the base for the beach fill. (See the project cross-section depicted in Figure D-20.) The project was authorized in 1960 and involved the improvement of 2,000 m of beach (termed "smothered beach") along the south shore of Key West along South Roosevelt Boulevard. The project area is exposed to ocean waves but is somewhat protected by a coral reef some 8 km offshore. The mean tidal range is 0.4 m and the spring range is 0.5 m. Approximately 64,000 m³ of rock was excavated and covered by a 0.6-m-thick blanket of beach sand obtained offshore by dredging a nearby navigation channel. Approximately 103,000 m³ of blanket material (veneer) was used. The native beach material, when present, had a median diameter ranging from 0.07 to 1.00 mm, with the finer materials coming from offshore. Veneer sand from two borrow area sources had sizes ranging from 0.24 to 1.00 mm. The bottom of the deepened offshore trench was also covered with a 0.6-m blanket of sand to an elevation of –0.6 m to serve as a bathing area. The slope of the trench on its seaward side is 1V (vertical) to 2H (horizontal). The elevation of the rock core beneath the berm is +0.6 m, while the sand blanket (veneer) is 0.6 m thick and extends up to an elevation of +1.2 m. The width of the berm is 30 m, and the beach slopes seaward at 1V to 20H to the bottom of the trench. The beach in the project area is backed by a concrete seawall with a crest elevation of +1.8 m. The bottom elevation seaward of the trench is only about –0.3 m, so the constructed trench actually serves as a bathing basin.

The project design anticipated a loss of about 15,000 m^3/year of veneer sand, of which approximately 7,500 m^3 was expected to be lost offshore to the trench while the other 7,500 m^3 would be lost by alongshore transport from the project area. Project operation called for retrieving 23,000 m^3 from the trench every 3 years and returning it to the beach. Every 6 years an additional 46,000 m^3 was to be obtained from other sources, presumably offshore, to restore the beach. The offshore sands have not been used to date because the erosion occurred more slowly than expected.

Grand Isle, Louisiana

Grand Isle is a low-lying Mississippi River delta margin barrier island approximately 12 km long, located 95 km south of New Orleans in Jefferson Parish (Combe and Soileau, 1987; Combe, 1993). Following Hurricanes Flossy (1956), Carla (1961), Betsy (1965), and Carmen (1974), all of which damaged Grand Isle, Congress authorized a beach nourishment and hurricane protection project. In 1983-1984 the USACE reconstructed the beach and dune using 1.8 million m^3 of sand dredged from two offshore borrow areas. The material dredged from the offshore borrow areas was stockpiled between the shore and a shore-parallel dike and allowed to drain. The fill contained significant amounts of silts and clays; consequently, the stockpiled material was reworked using bulldozers and draglines to speed up drying so that the material could be reshaped into the design cross-section. Winter storms during 1984-1985 resulted in the loss of 175,000 m^3 and led to the development of renourishment plans in 1985. However, Hurricane Danny struck in August 1985, Hurricane Elena in September 1985, and Hurricane Juan in October 1985, eroding 50,000, 30,000, and 280,000 m^3 of sand, respectively, from Grand Isle. Between January and July 1986, an additional 50,000 m^3 was lost. Hurricane Bonnie struck in September 1986 but caused little damage to the project; however, storms between July 1986 and February 1987 eroded an additional 95,000 m^3. Renourishment was delayed when a storm struck in March 1987. Bids had been received several days earlier for Phase I of the renourishment but were rejected due to the altered site conditions caused by the

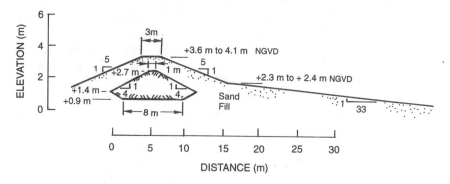

FIGURE D-21   Veneer beach fill cross-section, Grand Isle, Louisiana.

storm. Renourishment was finally begun in October 1987 and completed in March 1988. In Phase II of the renourishment project, completed in 1990, 1.1 million m³ was placed on the beach at a cost of $9 million, a clay core built of material excavated from the bay behind Grand Isle was added to the project's dune cross-section, and the dune elevation was raised (see the cross-section shown in Figure D-21). The compacted clay core is intended to contribute stability to the cross-section by reducing erosion once the core becomes exposed during a storm. The clay core is credited with preventing damage by Hurricane Andrew. Expenditures on Grand Isle to date have been $1.8 million for repairs and $9.0 million for the complete restoration, yielding a total of $10.8 million. Damages prevented by the project are estimated to be $12.5 million. Current plans are to restore the beach and dune and to investigate using nearshore breakwaters to stabilize a portion of the project.

Assessment of Veneer Fills

Experience suggests that veneer fills with finer underlying materials can work in some low-to-moderate wave environments and low tidal ranges (e.g., in sheltered waters such as Corpus Christi Bay). Their performance in areas exposed to large waves and large tidal ranges is less certain. Veneer fills with underlying coarse materials, such as the Key West project, might also work in areas that experience larger waves. There has not been enough experience with fills of this type to say with certainty that they will be successful. Certainly, for the case of coarser underlying materials, erosion rates should decrease if the core becomes exposed; however, recreational opportunities may be lost.

REFERENCES

Allison, M. C., and C. B. Pollock. 1993. Nearshore berms: an evaluation of prototype designs. Pp. 2838-2950 in Proceedings of Coastal Zone '93. New York: American Society of Civil Engineers.

Andrassy, C. J. 1991. Monitoring of a nearshore disposal mound at Silver Strand State Park. Pp. 1970-1984 in Proceedings of Coastal Sediments '91. New York: American Society of Civil Engineers.

Bakker, W. T. 1968. The dynamics of a coast with a groin system. Pp. 492-517 in Proceedings of 11th International Conference on Coastal Engineering. New York: American Society of Civil Engineers.

Balsillie, J. H., and R. O. Bruno. 1972. Groins: An Annotated Bibliography. Miscellaneous Paper No. 1-72. Washington, D.C.: Coastal Engineering Research Center, U.S. Army Corps of Engineers.

Beachler, K. E. 1993. The positive impacts to neighboring beaches from the Delray Beach nourishment program. Pp. 223-238 in Proceedings of the 6th Annual National Conference on Beach Preservation Technology. Tallahassee: Florida Shore and Beach Preservation Association.

Bender, T. 1992. Personal communication, U.S. Army Corps of Engineers, Buffalo District, with R. L. Wiegel.

Birkemeier, W. A. 1985. Field data on seaward limit of profile change. Journal of the Waterway, Port, Coastal, and Ocean Engineering 3(3):598-602.

Bowen, A. J., and D. L. Inman. 1966. Budget of Littoral Sands in the Vicinity of Point Arguello. California, Technical Memorandum No. 19. Washington, D.C.: Coastal Engineering Research Center, U.S. Army Waterways Experiment Station, U.S. Army Corps of Engineers.

Bruun, P. 1962. Sea level rise as a cause of erosion. Journal of the Waterways and Harbors Division 88:117-133.

Bruun, P. 1986. Sediment balances (land and sea) with special reference to Islandic South Coast from Torlakshofen to Dyrholarey. River nourishment of shores—practical analogies on artificial nourishment. Coastal Engineering 10:193-210.

Bruun, P. 1988. Profile nourishment: its background and economic advantages. Journal of Coastal Research 4:219-228.

Bruun, P. 1990. Beach nourishment—improved economy through better profiling and backpassing from offshore sources. Journal of Coastal Research 6:265-277.

Burke, C. E., and G. L. Williams. 1992. Nearshore Berms—Wave Breaking and Beach Building. In: Proceedings of Ports '92 Conference. New York: American Society of Civil Engineers.

Campbell, T. J., R. G. Dean, A. J. Mehta, and H. Wang, 1990. Short Course on Principles and Applications of Beach Nourishment. Organized by the Florida Shore and Beach Preservation Association and Coastal and Oceanographic Engineering Department, University of Florida.

Chasten, M. A., J. W. McCormick, and J. D. Rosati. 1994. Using detached breakwaters for shoreline and wetlands stabilization. Shore and Beach 62(2):17-22.

Coastal Planning and Engineering. 1992a. General Design Memorandum Addendum for Third Periodic Nourishment at Delray Beach with Environmental Assessment. Boca Raton, Fla.: Coastal Planning and Engineering.

Coastal Planning and Engineering. 1992b. Boca Raton Beach Restoration Project: Three Year Post-Construction, Vol. I. Environmental monitoring report prepared for the City of Boca Raton, Florida. Boca Raton, Fla.: Coastal Planning and Engineering.

Cohrssen, J. J., and V. T. Covello. 1989. Risk Analysis: A Guide to Principles and Methods for Analyzing Health and Environmental Risks. Washington, D.C.: U.S. Council on Environmental Quality.

Combe, A. J., III, 1993. Grand Isle, Louisiana, Hurricane Wave Damage Prevention and Beach

Erosion Control, Louisiana Shoreline Erosion: Emphasis on Grand Island. The Louisiana Governor's Office of Coastal Activities and the U.S. Minerals Management Service.

Combe, A. J., and C. W. Soileau. 1987. Behavior of man-made beach and dune, Grand Isle, Louisiana. Pp. 1232-1242 in Proceedings of Coastal Sediments '87, Specialty Conference on Advances in Understanding of Coastal Sediment Processes. New York: American Society of Civil Engineers.

Dally, W. R., and J. Pope. 1986. Detached Breakwaters for Shore Protection. U.S. Army Coastal Engineering Research Center, Technical Report CERC-86-1. Vicksburg, Miss.: Coastal Engineering Research Center, U.S. Army Waterways Experiment Station, U.S. Army Corps of Engineers.

Davis, R. A., Jr. 1991. Performance of a beach nourishment project based on detailed multi-year monitoring: Redington Shores, Florida. Pp. 2101-2115 in Coastal Sediments '91, Vol. 2. New York: American Society of Civil Engineers.

Davison, A. T., R. J. Nicholls, and S. P. Leatherman. 1992. Beach nourishment as a coastal management tool: an annotated bibliography on developments associated with the artificial nourishment of beaches. Journal of Coastal Research 8(4):984-1022.

Dean, R. G. 1974. Compatibility of borrow material for beach fills. Pp. 1319-1333 in Proceedings of the 14th Coastal Engineering Conference, New York: American Society of Civil Engineers.

Dean, R. G. 1983. Principles of beach nourishment. Pp. 217-232 in CRC Handbook of Coastal Processes and Erosion. Boca Raton, Fla..: CRC Press.

Dean, R. G. 1987. Coastal sediment processes: toward engineering solutions. Pp. 1-24 in Proceedings of Coastal Sediments '87, Specialty Conference on Advances in Understanding of Coastal Sediment Processes, Vol. 1. New York: American Society of Civil Engineers.

Dean, R. G. 1989. Pp. 313-336 in Measuring Longshore Transport with Traps in Nearshore Sediment Transport. R.J. Seymour, ed., New York: Plenum Press.

Dean, R. G. 1991. Equilibrium beach profiles: characteristics and applications. Journal of Coastal Research 7(1):53-84.

Dean, R. G., and J. Grant. 1989. Development of Methodology for Thirty-Year Shoreline Projection in the Vicinity of Beach Nourishment Projects. Prepared for Division of Beaches and Shore, Florida Department of Natural Resources, by the Florida Coastal and Oceanographic Engineering Department, University of Florida, Gainesville.

Dean, R. G., and C-H. Yoo. 1992. Beach nourishment performance predictions. Journal of Waterway, Port, Coastal and Ocean Engineering 118(6):567-586.

del Valle, R., R. Medina, and M. A. Losada. 1993. Dependence of coefficient K on grain size. Technical Note, Journal of Waterway, Port, Coastal and Ocean Engineering 119(5):567-574.

Dette, H., A. Fuhrboter, and A. J. Raudkiv. 1994. Interdependence of beach fill volumes and repetition intervals. Journal of Waterway, Port, Coastal and Ocean Engineering 120(6):580-593.

Dixon, K. L., and O. H. Pilkey. 1989. Beach replenishment on the U.S. coast of the Gulf of Mexico. Pp. 2007-2020 in Proceedings of Coastal Zone '89 Conference. New York: American Society of Civil Engineers.

Dixon, K.L., and O. H. Pilkey. 1991. Summary of beach replenishment on the U.S. Gulf of Mexico shoreline. Journal of Coastal Research 7:249-256.

Dornhelm, R. B. 1995. The Coney Island public beach and boardwalk improvement of 1923. Shore and Beach 63(1):7-11.

Edelman, T. 1972. Dune erosion during storm conditions. Pp. 1305-1311 in Proceedings of the 13th Coastal Engineering Conference. New York: American Society of Civil Engineers.

Egense, A. K., and C. J. Sonu. 1987. Assessment of Beach Nourishment Methodologies. Pp. 4421-4433 in Coastal Zone '87. New York: American Society of Civil Engineers.

Farley, P. P. 1923. Coney Island public beach and boardwalk improvements. Paper 136. The Municipal Engineers Journal 9(4).

Ferrante, A., L. Franco, and S. Boer 1992. Modelling and monitoring of a perched beach at Lido di

Ostia (Rome). Pp. 3305-3318 in Proceedings of the 23rd International Coastal Engineering Conference, Vol. 3. New York: American Society of Civil Engineers.

Fiering, M. B., and B. B. Jackson. 1971. Synthetic Streamflows. Water Resources Monograph 1. Washington, D.C.: American Geophysical Union.

Galster, R. W., and M. L. Schwartz. 1990. Ediz Hook—a case history of coastal erosion and rehabilitation. Artificial Beaches, Special Issue, Journal of Coastal Research 6:103-113.

Gordon, A. D. 1992. The restoration of Bate Bay, Australia—plugging the sink. Pp. 3319-3330 in Proceedings of the 23rd International Coastal Engineering Conference, Vol. 3. New York: American Society of Civil Engineers.

Gordon, A. D. 1994. Letter to R. L. Wiegel dated 28 March 1994, 11 pp.

Hall, J. V., Jr., 1952. Artificially constructed and nourished beaches in coastal engineering. Pp. 119-133 in Proceedings of the 3rd Coastal Engineering Conference. New York: American Society of Civil Engineers.

Hallermeier, R. J. 1981a. A profile zonation for seasonal sand beaches from wave climate. Coastal Engineering 4:253-277.

Hallermeier, R. J. 1981b. Seaward Limit of Significant Sand Transport by Waves: An Annual Zonation for Seasonal Profiles. Coastal Engineering Technical Aid No. CETA 81-2. Fort Belvoir, Va..: Coastal Engineering Research Center, U.S. Army Corps of Engineers.

Hands, E. B. 1991. Unprecedented migration of a submerged mound off the Alabama coast. In: Proceedings of the 12th Annual Conference of the Western Dredging Association and 24th Annual Texas A & M Dredging Seminar, Las Vegas.

Hands, E. B., and M. C. Allison. 1991. Mound migration in deeper water and methods of categorizing active and stable berms. Pp. 1985-1999 in Proceedings of Coastal Sediments '91. New York: American Society of Civil Engineers.

Hanson, M. E., and M. R. Byrnes. 1991. Development of optimum beach fill design cross-section. Pp. 2067-2080 in Proceedings of Coastal Sediments '91, New York: American Society of Civil Engineers.

Hanson, H., and N. C. Kraus. 1989. GENESIS: Generalized Model for Simulating Shoreline Change. Report 1: Reference Manual and Users Guide. Technical Report No. CERC-89-19. Vicksburg, Miss.: Coastal Engineering Research Center, U.S. Army Waterways Experiment Station, U.S. Army Corps of Engineers.

Hanson, H., and N. C. Kraus. 1991. Numerical simulation of shoreline change at Lorain, Ohio. Journal of Waterway, Port, Coastal and Ocean Engineering 117:1-18.

Hanson, M. E., and W. J. Lillycrop. 1988. Evaluation of closure depth and its role in estimating beach fill volumes. Pp. 107-114 in Proceedings of Beach Preservation Technology '88. Tallahassee: Florida Shore and Beach Preservation Association.

Healy, T., C. Harms, and W. de Lange. 1991. Dredge spoil and inner shelf investigations off Tauranga Harbour, Bay of Plenty, New Zealand. Pp. 2037-2051 in Proceedings of Coastal Sediment '91. New York: American Society of Civil Engineers.

Herron, W. J., and R. L. Harris. 1966. Littoral bypassing and beach restoration in the vicinity of Port Hueneme, California. Pp. 651-675 in Proceedings of the 10th Conference on Coastal Engineering. Vol 1. New York: American Society of Civil Engineers.

Hirst, E. H. W., and D. Foster. 1987. The design and construction of Prince Street seawall at Cronulla. Pp. 201-207 in Proceedings of the 8th Australian Conference on Coastal and Ocean Engineering. Launceston, Australia: Institution of Civil Engineers.

Houston, J. R. 1991a. Beachfill performance. Shore and Beach 59:15-24.

Houston, J. R. 1991b. Rejoinder to: Discussion of Pilkey and Leonard (1990) [Journal of Coastal Research, 6, 1023 et. seq.] and Houston (1990) [Journal of Coastal Research, 6, 1047 et. seq.]. Journal of Coastal Research 7:565-577.

James, W. R. 1974. Beach fill stability and borrow material texture. Pp. 1334-1349 in Proceedings of the 14th International Conference on Coastal Engineering. New York: American Society of Civil Engineers.

James, W. R. 1975. Techniques in Evaluating Suitability of Borrow Material for Beach Nourishment. Technical Manual No. 60. Ft. Belvoir, Va.: Coastal Engineering Research Center, U.S. Army Corps of Engineers.

Jarrett, J. T., 1987. Beach Nourishment—A Corps Perspective. Paper presented at the Coastal Engineering Research Board's 48th Meeting, Savannah, Georgia. Vicksburg, Miss.: Coastal Engineering Research Board, U.S. Army Corps of Engineers.

Jensen, R. E. 1983. Atlantic Coast Hindcast, Shallow Water Significant Wave Information. Wave Information Study Report No. 9. Vicksburg, Miss.: U.S. Army Waterways Experiment Station, U.S. Army Corps of Engineers.

Kamphuis, J. W., 1990. Littoral sediment transport rate. Pp. 2402-2415 in Proceedings of 22nd Coastal Engineering Conference. New York: American Society of Civil Engineers.

Kamphuis, J. W. 1991. Alongshore sediment transport rate. Journal of Waterways, Port, Coastal and Ocean Engineering 117(6):624-640.

Kamphuis, J. W., M. H. Davies, R. B. Nairn, and O. J. Sayao. 1986. Calculation of littoral sand transport rate. Coastal Engineering 10:1-21.

Kieslich, J. M., and D. H. Brunt III. 1989. Assessment of a two-layer beach fill at Corpus Christi Beach, Texas. Pp. 3975-3984 in Proceedings of the 6th Symposium on Coastal and Ocean Management, Coastal Zone '89. New York: American Society of Civil Engineers.

Komar, P. D. 1973. Computer models of delta growth due to sediment input from rivers and longshore transport. Geological Society of America Bulletin 84:2217-2226.

Komar, P. D. 1976. Beach Processes and Sedimentation. Englewood Cliffs, N.J.: Prentice-Hall.

Komar, P. D. 1977. Modeling of sand transport on beaches and the resulting shoreline evolution. Pp. 499-513 in E. Goldberg et al., eds., The Sea, Vol. 6.

Komar, P. D., 1988. Environmental controls on littoral sand transport. Pp. 1238-1252 in Proceedings of 21st Coastal Engineering Conference, Vol. 2. New York: American Society of Civil Engineers.

Kraus, N. C., H. Hanson, and S. Blomgren. 1994. Modern functional design of groins. In: Proceedings of the 24th Coastal Engineering Conference. New York: American Society of Civil Engineers.

Kriebel, D. 1982. Beach and Dune Response to Hurricanes. M.S. thesis, University of Delaware, Newark.

Kriebel, D. L. 1986. Verification study of a dune erosion model. Shore and Beach 54(3).

Kriebel, D. L. 1990. Advances in numerical modeling of dune erosion. Pp. 2304-2317 in Proceedings, 23rd International Conference on Coastal Engineering.

Kriebel, D. L., and R. G. Dean. 1985. Numerical simulation of time dependent beach and dune erosion. Coastal Engineering 9:221-245.

Kriebel, D. L., and R. G. Dean. 1993. Convolution method for time-dependent beach profile response. Journal of Waterways, Port, Coastal and Ocean Engineering 119(2):204-227.

Kriebel, D. L., N. C. Kraus, and M. Larson. 1991. Engineering methods for predicting beach profile response. Pp. 557-571 in Proceedings of Coastal Sediments '91. New York: American Society of Civil Engineers.

Krumbein, W. C. 1957. A Method for Specification of Sand for Beach Fills. Technical Memorandum No. 102. Washington, D.C.: Beach Erosion Board, U.S. Army Corps of Engineers.

Krumbein, W. C., and W. R. James. 1965. A Lognormal Size Distribution Model for Estimating Stability of Beach Fill Material. Technical Memorandum No. 16. Washington, D.C.: Coastal Engineering Research Center, U.S. Army Corps of Engineers.

Larson, M. 1988. Quantification of Beach Profile Change. Report No. 1008. Department of Water Resources and Engineering, University of Lund, Lund, Sweden.

Larson, M., and N. C. Kraus. 1989a. Prediction of beach fill response to varying waves and water level. Pp. 607-621 in Proceedings of Coastal Zone '89. New York: American Society of Civil Engineers.

Larson, M., and N. C. Kraus. 1989b. SBEACH: Numerical Model for Simulating Storm-Induced Beach Change. Report 1: Empirical Foundation and Model Development. Technical Report No. CERC-89-9. Vicksburg, Miss.: Coastal Engineering Research Center, U.S. Army Waterways Experiment Station, U.S. Army Corps of Engineers.

Larson, M., and N. C. Kraus. 1990. SBEACH: Numerical Model for Simulating Storm-Induced Beach Change. Report 2: Numerical Foundation and Model Tests. Technical Report CERC-89-9. Vicksburg, Mississippi: Coastal Engineering Research Center, U.S. Army Waterways Experiment Station, U.S. Army Corps of Engineers.

Larson, M., and N. C. Kraus. 1991. Mathematical modeling of the fate of beach fill. Coastal Engineering 16:83-114.

Larson, M., and N. C. Kraus. 1994. Temporal and spatial scales of beach profile change, Duck, North Carolina. Marine Geology 117:75-94.

Lee, G-H., and W. A. Birkemeier. 1993. Beach and nearshore survey data: 1985-1991 CERC field research facility. Technical Report CERC-93-3. Vicksburg, Miss.: Coastal Engineering Research Center, U.S. Army Waterways Experiment Station, U.S. Army Corps of Engineers.

Leonard, L. A. 1988. An Analysis of Replenished Beach Design on the U.S. East Coast. Unpublished M.S. thesis, Department of Geology, Duke University, Durham, N.C.

Leonard, L. A., T. D. Clayton, K. L. Dixon, and O. H. Pilkey. 1989. U.S. Beach replenishment experience: a comparison of beach replenishment on the U.S. Atlantic, Pacific, and Gulf of Mexico coasts. Pp. 1994-2006 in Proceedings of Coastal Zone '89. New York: American Society of Civil Engineers.

Leonard, L. A., K. L. Dixon, and O. H. Pilkey. 1990a. A comparison of beach replenishment on the U.S. Atlantic, Pacific, and Gulf coasts. Journal of Coastal Research, 6(Special Issue):127-140.

Leonard, L. A., T. D. Clayton, and O. H. Pilkey, 1990b. An analysis of replenished beach design parameters on U.S. East Coast Barrier Islands. Journal of Coastal Research 6(Special Issue):15-36.

Louisse, C. J., and F. van der Meulen. 1991. Future coastal defense in the Netherlands: strategies for protection and sustainable development. Journal of Coastal Research 7:1027-1041.

McLellan, T. N. 1990. Nearshore mound construction using dredged material. Journal of Coastal Research 7(Special Issue):99-107.

McLellan, T. N., and N. C. Kraus. 1991. Design guidance for nearshore berm construction. Pp. 2000-2011 in Proceedings of Coastal Sediments '91. New York: American Society of Civil Engineers.

Mikkelsin, S. C. 1977. The effects of groins on beach erosion and channel stability at the Limfjord Barriers, Denmark. Pp. 17-32 in Proceedings of Coastal Sediments '77. New York: American Society of Civil Engineers.

Nersesian, G. K., N. C. Kraus, and F. C. Carson. 1992. Functioning of groins at Westhampton Beach, Long Island, New York. Pp. 3357-3370 in Proceedings of the 23rd International Coastal Engineering Conference, Vol. 3. New York: American Society of Civil Engineers.

NRC. 1987. Responding to Changes in Sea Level: Engineering Implications. Marine Board, Commission on Engineering and Technical Systems. Washington, D.C.: National Academy Press.

NRC. 1989. Measuring and Understanding Coastal Processes for Engineering Purposes. Marine Board, Commission on Engineering and Technical Systems. Washington, D.C.: National Academy Press.

NRC. 1990. Managing Coastal Erosion. Water Science and Technology Board and Marine Board, Commission on Engineering and Technical Systems. Washington, D.C.: National Academy Press.

NRC. 1992. Coastal Meteorology: A Review of the State of the Science. Board on Atmospheric

Sciences and Climate, Commission on Geosciences, Environment, and Resources. Washington, D.C.: National Academy Press.

O'Brien, M. P., 1988. Letter to Professor Ben C. Gerwick, Jr., University of California, Berkeley (4 pp. plus four aerial photos concerning how a groin field functions, making the need for a sand fill part of the project).

Pelnard-Considére, R. 1956. Essai de Theorie de l'Evolution des Formes de Rivate en Plages de Sable et de Galets. 4th Journees de l'Hydraulique, Les Energies de la Mar, Question III, Rapport No. 1 (in French). Vicksburg, Miss.: U.S. Army Waterways Experiment Station, U.S. Army Corps of Engineers.

Perlin, M., and R. G. Dean.1979. Prediction of beach planforms with littoral controls. Pp. 1818-1838 in Proceedings of the 16th Coastal Engineering Conference. New York: American Society of Civil Engineers.

Pilkey, O. H., and T. D. Clayton. 1987. Beach replenishment: the national solution? Pp. 1408-1419 in Proceedings of Coastal Zone '87. New York: American Society of Civil Engineers.

Pilkey, O. H., and T. D. Clayton. 1988. Summary of beach replenishment experience on the U.S. coast barrier islands. Journal of Coastal Research 5:147-159.

Pope, J., and D. D. Rowen. 1983. Breakwaters for beach protection at Lorain, Ohio. Pp. 752-768 in Proceedings of Coastal Structures '83. New York: American Society of Civil Engineers.

Price, R. C. 1966. Statement of the California Department of Water Resources. Shore and Beach 34(1):22-32.

Price, W. A., K. W. Tomlinson, and D. H. Willis. 1973. Predicting changes in the plan shape of beaches. Pp. 1321-1329 in Proceedings of the 13th Conference on Coastal Engineering. New York: American Society of Civil Engineers.

Richardson, T. W. 1991. Sand bypassing. Pp. 809-828 in J. B. Herbich, (ed). Handbook of Coastal and Ocean Engineering, Vol. 2. Houston: Gulf Publishing Co.

Rosati, J. D. 1990. Functional Design of Breakwaters for Shore Protection; Empirical Methods. Technical Report CERC-90-15. Vicksburg, Miss.: Coastal Engineering Research Center, U.S. Army Waterway Experiment Station, U.S. Army Corps of Engineers.

Rouch, F., and B. Bellessort. 1990. Man-made beaches more than 20 years on. Pp. 2394-2401 in Proceedings of the 22nd Coastal Engineering Conference, Vol. 3. New York: American Society of Civil Engineers.

Shih, S. M., and P. D. Komar. 1994. Sediments, beach morphology and sea cliff erosion within an Oregon coast littoral cell. Journal of Coastal Research 10:144-157.

Silvester, R., and J. R. C. Hsu. 1993. Coastal Stabilization: Innovative Concepts. Englewood Cliffs, N.J.: Prentice-Hall.

Strine, M. A., Jr., and R. A. Dalrymple. 1991. A Probabilistic Prediction of Beach Nourishment Lifetimes. Research Report No. CACR-91-01. Newark: Center for Applied Coastal Research, Department of Civil Engineering, University of Delaware.

Strock, A. V., and Associates. 1981. Phase I General Design Memorandum, Segment II of Broward County, Hillsboro Inlet to Port Everglades, Beach Erosion Control and Storm Protection Study, November.

Strock, A. V., and Associates. 1984. General Design Memorandum, Second Periodic Nourishment Project. Delray Beach, Florida, January.

Swart, D. H. 1974. Offshore Sediment Transport and Equilibrium Beach Profiles. Publication No. 131. Delft, The Netherlands: Delft Hydraulics Laboratory.

Terry, J. B., and E. Howard. 1986. Redington shores beach access breakwater. Shore and Beach 54(4):7-9.

Tomasicchio, U. 1994. Personal communication with R. L. Wiegel.

Tourman, L. 1968. The creation of an artificial beach in Larvatto Bay-Monte Carlo, principality of Monaco. Pp. 558-569 in Proceedings of 11th Conference on Coastal Engineering. New York: American Society of Civil Engineers.

USACE. 1957. Beach Erosion Control Report on Cooperative Study of Key West, Florida. Jacksonville, Fla.: Jacksonville District, U.S. Army Corps of Engineers.

USACE. 1982a. Beach Fill Transitions. Coastal Engineering Technical Note CETN-II-6. Fort Belvoir, Va.: Coastal Engineering Research Center, U.S. Army Corps of Engineers.

USACE. 1982b. Feasibility Report and Environmental Assessment on Shore and Hurricane Wave Protection, Wrightsville Beach, N. C.: Wilmington, North Carolina: Wilmington District, U.S. Army Corps of Engineers.

USACE. 1982c. Final Feasibility Report and Environmental Impact Statement for Beach Erosion Control, Monroe County, Florida. Jacksonville, Fla.: Jacksonville District, U.S. Army Corps of Engineers.

USACE. 1984. Shore Protection Manual, 4th ed. two volumes. Coastal Engineering Research Center, U.S. Army Corps of Engineers Publication No. 008-002-00218-9. Washington, D.C.: U.S. Government Printing Office.

USACE. 1985. Sediment Size and Fall Velocity Effects on Longshore Sediment Transport. Coastal Engineering Technical Note CETN-II-11. Vicksburg, Miss.: Coastal Engineering Research Center, U.S. Army Waterways Experiment Station, U.S. Army Corps of Engineers.

USACE. 1986. Storm Surge Analysis. Engineer Manual No. EM 1110-2-1412. U.S. Army Corps of Engineers. Washington, D.C.: U.S. Government Printing Office.

USACE. 1988. Coastal Processes at Sea Bright to Ocean Township, New Jersey. Miscellaneous Paper CERC-88-12. Vicksburg, Miss.: Coastal Engineering Research Center, U.S. Army Waterways Experiment Station, U.S. Army Corps of Engineers.

USACE. 1989a. Water Level and Wave Heights for Coastal Engineering Design. Engineering Manual 1110-2-1414. Washington, D.C.: U.S. Government Printing Office.

USACE. 1989b. Wrightsville Beach, North Carolina, Renourishment Report and Supplement to the Environmental Assessment and Finding of No Significant Impact. Wilmington, N.C.: Wilmington District, U.S. Army Corps of Engineers.

USACE. 1990. Comparison of Atlantic Coast Wave Information Study Hindcasts with Field Research Facility Gauge Measurements. Technical Report CERC-90-17, Final Report. Vicksburg, Miss.: Coastal Engineering Research Center, U.S. Army Waterways Experiment Station, U.S. Army Corps of Engineers.

USACE. 1991a. Sand Bypassing System, Engineering and Design Manual. Engineering and Design Manual No. EM 1110-2-1616. Washington, D.C.: U.S. Army Corps of Engineers.

USACE. 1991b. National Economic Development Procedures Manual Coastal Storm Damage and Erosion. Institute of Water Resources Report No. 91-R-6. Fort Belvoir, Va.: Institute for Water Resources, Water Resources Support Center, U.S. Army Corps of Engineers.

USACE. 1991c. Manatee County, Florida, Shore Protection Project, General Design Memorandum, with Environmental Impact Statement. Revised September 1991. Jacksonville, Fla.: Jacksonville District, U.S. Army Corps of Engineers.

USACE. 1992a. Shoreline Response to Redington Shores, Florida, Breakwater. Coastal Engineering Technical Note CETB III-48. Vicksburg, Miss.: Coastal Engineering Research Center, U.S. Army Waterways Experiment Station, U.S. Army Corps of Engineers.

USACE. 1992b. Monitoring Coastal Projects. Engineer Regulation ER 1110-2-8151. Washington, D.C.: U.S. Army Corps of Engineers.

USACE. 1993. Reliability Assessment of Existing Levees for Benefit Determination, Engineering and Design, Engineer Technical Letter 1110-2-328. Washington, D.C.: U.S. Army Corps of Engineers.

University of Florida. 1959. Bakers Haulover Inlet Tidal Model Study on Beach Erosion and Navigation, Industrial Experiment Station.

Vallianos, L. 1974. Beach fill planning—Brunswick County. North Carolina. Pp. 1350-1369 in Proceedings of 14th Coastal Engineering Conference. New York: American Society of Civil Engineers.

Vera-Cruz, D. 1972. Artificial nourishment of Copacabana Beach. Pp. 1451-1463 in Proceedings of the 13th Coastal Engineering Conference. New York: American Society of Civil Engineers.

Verhagen, H. J. 1990. Coastal protection and dune management in the Netherlands. Journal of Coastal Research 6:169-179.

von Oesen, H. M. 1973. A beach restoration project: Bal Harbour Village, Florida. Shore and Beach 41(2):3-4.

Walker, J. R., D. Clark, and J. Pope 1980. A detached breakwater system for beach protection. Pp. 1968-1987 in Proceedings of 17th Coastal Engineering Conference, Vol. II. New York: American Society of Civil Engineers.

Walton, T. L. 1985. Sediment Size and Fall Velocity Effects on Longshore Sediment Transport. CETN II-11. Vicksburg, Miss.: Coastal Engineering Research Center, U.S. Army Engineer Waterways Experiment Station, U.S. Army Corps of Engineers.

Watson, I., and C. W. Finkl. 1990. State of the art in storm surge protection: The Netherlands delta project. Journal of Coastal Research 6:739-764.

Weggel, J. R., and R. M. Sorensen. 1991. Performance of the 1986 Atlantic City, New Jersey, beach nourishment project. Shore and Beach 59(3):29-36.

Weggel, J. R., S. L. Douglass, and J. E. Tunnell. 1988. Sand-bypassing simulation using synthetic longshore transport data. Journal of Waterway, Port, Coastal, and Ocean Engineering 114(2):146-160.

Wiegel, R. L. 1987. Trends in coastal erosion management. Shore and Beach 55(1):3-11.

Wiegel, R. L. 1988. Keynote address: some notes on beach nourishment, problems and advancement in beach nourishment. Pp. 1-18 in Proceedings of Beach Preservation Technology '88. Tallahassee: Florida Shore and Beach Preservation Association.

Wiegel, R. L. 1991. The coast-line, III, protection of Galveston, Texas, from overflow by gulf storms: grade-raising, seawall and embankment, American Shore and Beach Preservation Association Coastal Project Award for 1990. Shore and Beach 59(1):4-10.

Wiegel, R. L. 1992. Dade County, Florida, beach nourishment and hurricane surge protection. Shore and Beach 60(4):2-28.

Wiegel, R. L. 1993. Dana Point Harbor, California. Shore and Beach 61(3):37-55.

Williams, S. J., and E. P. Meisburger. 1987. Sand sources for the transgressive barrier coast of Long Island, N.Y.: evidence for landward transport of shelf sediments. Pp. 1517-1532 in N. C. Kraus, ed., Proceedings of Coastal Sediments '87. New York: American Society of Civil Engineers.

Wise, R. A., and N. C. Kraus. 1993. Simulation of beach fill response to multiple storms, Ocean City, Maryland. Pp. 133-147 in Proceedings of Coastal Zone '93. New York: American Society of Civil Engineers.

Zwamborn, J. A., G. A. W. Fromme, and J. B. Fitzpatrick. 1970. Underwater mound for protection of Durban's beaches. Pp. 975-994 in Proceedings of the 12th Coastal Engineering Conference. New York: American Society of Civil Engineers.

E

Economic Concepts and Issues: Social Costs and Benefits of Beach Nourishment Projects

INTRODUCTION

When assessing public projects, economists are likely to ask questions about their "economic efficiency" and "distributional" implications. The latter requires an assessment of who benefits from a given project and who pays (or is otherwise detrimentally affected). The former relates to the question of whether a particular beach nourishment project is an efficient use (i.e., the highest-valued use) of the scarce resources needed for the project. Determining efficient use involves measuring all of the social benefits from a project and comparing them with the social costs. The social costs are, strictly speaking, the benefits foregone—that is, a measure of the benefits that could have been produced for society by using these resources in a different way. Both of these questions are of considerable pragmatic importance for beach nourishment projects.

As with other publicly sponsored projects, beach nourishment undertaken by the U.S. Army Corps of Engineers (USACE) must undergo a cost-benefit analysis, although the currently mandated procedures for this analysis have not kept up with recent advances in the field and fall short of those adopted by other agencies, such as the U.S. Environmental Protection Agency (EPA) and the National Oceanic and Atmospheric Administration. As is commonly the case, recreational benefits from beach nourishment are allowed to be calculated by using either hypothetical (contingent) valuation or valuation using revealed preference (i.e., travel cost models). However, the USACE guidelines for contingent valuation surveys do not reflect appreciation for the effects of variability in format, payment mechanism, and other factors that are now widely recognized (see Mitchell

and Carson, 1989; Carson, 1991). The USACE guidelines do not advocate refer-
endum-type surveys or specify how to analyze this type of data using discrete-
choice models (see Freeman, 1993). Likewise, the procedures for deriving benefits from "travel cost"-type studies are not designed to take into account the
effect of substitutes or congestion (see Bockstael et al., 1991).

The distribution of the benefits of a project is also of considerable interest.
For one thing, the apparent distribution (as implied by the type of benefits generated) can have an effect on the cost-sharing formula applied. Perhaps more importantly, the relative incidence of costs and benefits can make a project more or
less politically acceptable and can influence the way the public views its success.
Finally, the rules used to determine who pays for the project can affect incentives
in both the private and the public sectors.

Many of the economic questions that arise with respect to beach nourishment
projects and their alternatives require for their resolution an assessment of their
social costs and benefits (Haveman, 1969). The evaluation must include the
present value of all costs and benefits during the effective life of the project,
whether or not privately appropriated through markets, in order for the evaluation
to be a true representation of the social costs and benefits associated with the
project. Factors that need to be counted include not only "direct" or intended
benefits but also externalities, whether positive or negative. The latter may involve "downstream" effects; effects on the ecology of the area, on local amenities, on local infrastructure burden; and other considerations. The theory and
methodology for conceptualizing and measuring these costs and benefits are well
developed, although the sparse economics work on beach nourishment has tended
to focus on a subset of these—the more obvious and the ones mandated by the
USACE guidelines.

Under some conditions, market prices are sufficient to provide good information about opportunity costs and benefits. More complicated methods must be
employed when market prices themselves are affected by the activity (e.g., more
beach nourishment activity might put upward pressure on the price of sand
sources). Goods and services, such as recreation, that are valued by society but
not bought and sold on markets are somewhat more difficult to value. Nevertheless, methods for doing so are well developed and have improved over the past
several decades. Finally, less easily defined goods, such as environmental and
community amenities, present the greatest (but not insurmountable) challenge to
economic valuation.

Assessing the true social costs and benefits of a project is important for a
number of reasons. Most obviously, such an assessment provides criteria for
deciding whether a project should be undertaken, for choosing among potential
projects, and for selecting the optimal project design. Equally important, a correct
assessment focuses attention on what could be considered long-term "side effects" of projects—providing incentives or disincentives for related activities,
increasing or decreasing society's liability in the long run, improving or degrad-

ing the quality of life in coastal communities, and so forth. Some of these have become extremely important *policy* issues: What types of incentives do these projects provide that affect community land-use planning and growth management? What effect do they have on long-term social liability (through the Federal Emergency Management Agency, for example)?

The realization of costs and benefits associated with a beach nourishment project is not independent of the financing of a project. Who pays for the project matters not only for the analysis of distributional implications but also because "pricing rules," especially if linked with access to benefits, will indirectly determine the nature of the output and the benefiting parties.

This appendix outlines the concepts of economic valuation (the definition and measurement of social costs and benefits) and discusses their application to beach nourishment. Beach nourishment projects present some difficult but not unique valuation problems. Attention is given not only to the types of immediate costs and benefits of projects but also to the longer-term incentives provided by such projects and to the effects on costs, benefits and incentives of pricing rules.

ECONOMIC VALUATION OR THE ANALYSIS OF SOCIAL COSTS AND BENEFITS

Cost-benefit analysis dates back to the 1930s in the United States, but the famous 1950 "Green Book" (prepared by the federal Inter-Agency River Basin Committee) was the first official publication to apply the language of conventional welfare economics to the analysis of federal projects and policies. By today's standards, the Green Book was technically simplistic, but it did encompass systematic, theoretically based definitions of costs and benefits; it made the important distinction between true "social benefits" and "economic impacts"; and it discussed the discount rate problem and the treatment of risk. The document also incorporated a recognition of costs and benefits associated with nonmarketed as well as marketed goods and services. Nonmarketed goods included tangible goods that were provided at no charge, such as outdoor recreational opportunities, as well as "intangibles" such as aesthetics, quality of life and health, and other environmental factors. These are all things for which people would be willing to pay but for which there are, for institutional or practical reasons, no markets in which people can express their preferences. Thus, the precedent for considering this array of costs and benefits is long standing.

The 1970s and 1980s brought important developments in both the theory and measurement of costs and benefits, as well as the adoption by several federal agencies of guidelines for using these developments to properly assess policies. Executive Order 12291, which required a regulatory impact analysis of any new regulation promulgated by a federal agency, was a stimulus for the latter. It was a particular stimulus for the development of methods for measuring nonmarket benefits by agencies such as the EPA, since the chief benefits of EPA regulations (health, recreation, and ecological goods) are not traded in markets. The federal valuation documents that emphasize nonmarket as well as market valuation are diverse and include EPA's *Guidelines for Regulatory Impact Analysis*, the U.S. Forest Service's Resource Planning Assessments, and the Electric Consumers Protection Act, as well as the Comprehensive Environmental Response, Compensation, and Liability Act of 1980 (also referred to as "CERCLA" and "Superfund") and regulations issued under the Oil Pollution Act of 1990 (P.L. 101-380) that detail how social damages are to be calculated for the purpose of establishing polluter liability in natural resource damage assessment litigation. The features of all these guidelines include a definition of the concepts of costs and benefits (as well as a distinction between these concepts and others often mistaken for "benefits"), a categorization of the types of costs and benefits that are to be considered, and recommended methods for measuring these social costs and benefits. Many of these guidelines draw on advances being made in applied welfare economics.

The concepts of costs and benefits—or, in the economist's jargon, the concept of "social value"—depend fundamentally on trade-offs. Given that society's resources are scarce, whenever we choose to do something, we forfeit the opportunity of doing something else. Implicit here is the notion that when we assess the costs and benefits of a public action we are doing so relative to other alternatives.

The value of a project equals society's willingness to pay for the increased quantity or quality of goods, services, and amenities provided by that project. These include not just the intended benefits but also the unintended spillover benefits (i.e., positive externalities) that might accrue. The present value of a project is the discounted stream of all future benefits provided by the project for however long the effects of the project last. This stream of future benefits is clearly an important issue in beach nourishment, as the time horizon over which benefits will accrue is especially uncertain. The costs of a project equal society's willingness to pay for what is given up as a consequence of the project. Again, these are not just the explicit costs associated with diverting scarce resources to the production of the project instead of something else. They also include implicit commitments of resources in the future and all the negative externalities that might result from the project over time.

A perusal of the above illustrates that the definition of "what counts" in this social (economic) accounting scheme of costs and benefits is well developed and accepted by federal agencies and courts of law. Sorting out the nature of the costs and benefits for any particular application requires, of course, understanding all the possible effects, side effects, and feedback effects on the natural and physical environmental systems and on human behavior (including, but not restricted to, the effects on markets). Measuring the actual magnitudes of the various costs and benefits requires a greater level of sophistication and is fraught with the kinds of empirical measurement problems that plague all sciences: errors in measurement, omitted variables, functional specification, noise in the system, and so forth.

Where markets exist, costs and benefits are measured as changes in consumer and producer surpluses in the relevant markets. Producer surplus is loosely equivalent to the common notion of profits and returns to factors of production, including labor, over and above what these factors would earn in their next-best alternative. Consumer surplus is the analog for consumers—their willingness to pay for the commodity they purchase over and above what they must pay on the market to obtain it. Just et al. (1982) provide an excellent text on the measurement of market welfare effects.

Sometimes the particular good, service, or amenity of interest is not actually marketed and therefore does not have attached to it a market price. Such goods are called nonmarket goods and are generally supplied publicly. Put another way, public actions affect the quantity and quality of these goods. Methods have been developed to obtain estimates of consumer surpluses associated with these nonmarket goods (see Freeman, 1979, and Braden and Kolstad, 1991). The most frequently cited methods are indirect ones such as travel cost (or, more broadly, recreational demand) models and hedonic models; and direct questioning methods, generally termed contingent valuation.

The contingent valuation method (CVM) avoids many of the problems inherent in valuing a nonmarketed commodity by asking individuals directly what they would be willing to pay for the commodity in different contexts. Reliable and valid CVM studies require considerable sophistication in survey design, sampling, and statistical analysis (see Mitchell and Carson, 1989; Carson, 1991). In theory, however, the approach can be used to estimate an individual's willingness to pay for almost any well-defined commodity, and it is this approach that could be used to value some of the less tangible costs and benefits of beach nourishment projects discussed in subsequent sections. A few studies have attempted to use contingent valuation techniques to measure recreational benefits associated with beach nourishment projects. Curtis and Shows (1984), Stronge (1991), Silberman and Klock (1988), and Bell (1986) have conducted contingent valuation studies of recreationists' willingness to pay for public beach use. Black et al. (1988) provide a well-developed discussion of recreational beach use but are forced to use secondary data to proxy benefits.

The travel cost method is applied chiefly to recreation and thus is particularly applicable to measuring the recreational benefits of beach nourishment projects for those individuals who travel some discernible distance to use the beach. This approach depends on applying conventional welfare economics methods to demand functions that are estimated by using the cost of accessing the recreational site as the "price" of the recreational trip. Modern applications include truncated and censored demand models and discrete-choice models of demand for recreation at multiple sites (see Smith, 1989, 1991; Bockstael et al., 1987a, 1991; Smith and Desvousges, 1986). Few, if any, travel cost models have been applied specifically to beach nourishment valuation problems, but the approach has been widely used to value beach recreational benefits in other contexts. Examples include Hanemann (1978), Feenberg and Mills (1980), Bockstael et al. (1987a, b, 1988), Caulkins et al. (1986), Bell and Leeworthy (1990); and Parsons and Kealy (1992).

The previous methods estimate annual or current-period benefits. The present discounted value of those benefits must be calculated from extrapolations of these measures into the future. In contrast, the hedonic approach measures the change in the capitalized value of property due to a change in its characteristics or surrounding amenities, where the capitalized value reflects the entire current and expected future values discounted to the present. The hedonic approach appears to be straightforward, but the conditions under which the analysis produces valid welfare measures are rather restrictive. Nonetheless, researchers use this method to approximate these values.

The hedonic method is most frequently applied to the housing market, where differences in property values are explained by differences in characteristics and amenities of the properties (see McConnell, 1987; Palmquist, 1991). As such, hedonic valuation is particularly well suited to valuing the net amenity and storm protection benefits of beach nourishment projects associated with local property, although appropriate data are often difficult to obtain before construction of a project. Curtis and Shows (1984), Stronge (1992), Black et al. (1988), Kerns et al. (1980), Kriesel (1989), and Edwards and Gable (1991) all attempt to assess the benefits of protection of private property by considering property values. Examples of hedonic models applied to related problems include Brown and Pollakowski (1977), Willman (1981), Edwards and Anderson (1984), and Parsons and Wu (1991).

The distinction between the concept of social (economic) value and that of economic impacts is worth mentioning here. Expenditures or revenues are economic impact measures. Economic *impacts* are often confused with economic *value*, but they are not necessarily related to people's preferences nor are they measures of what things are worth to people. Instead, economic impacts measure market activity: how much money changes hands. They do not take into account what is being given up or existing alternatives. Additionally, they never take into account anything that is not traded on the market.

A graphic example of why impacts are not measures of value can be seen by considering natural disasters. Most people would have considered society better off had Alaska's *Exxon Valdez* oil spill not occurred. Likewise, society would have been better off had the San Francisco earthquake, Hurricane Hugo, or the 1993 Mississippi flood not taken place. Each of these disasters generated enormous amounts of economic activity. A large amount of money changed hands. Yet no one would claim that society benefited.

BEACH NOURISHMENT COSTS AND BENEFITS

Beach nourishment projects, like other public investment projects, are public goods[1] in that their services can be consumed jointly. The public-good nature of a project suggests that even if it is worth doing from a social standpoint, it is unlikely to be in any one individual's (or firm's) interest to undertake the project privately because the costs will exceed the private gains to any one individual.

Since they are similar to other public investment projects, beach nourishment projects could be evaluated by using the same sorts of theory and methodology. Assessing the social value of a beach nourishment project is made more difficult, however, by the fact that the "commodity" provided by the project is multifaceted and difficult to define, and has an uncertain time horizon.

For a given beach nourishment project, the benefits may include any or all of the following:

- changes in property value resulting from changes in shoreline protection,
- changes in beach-user willingness to pay,
- changes in amenity value for local residents as a result of a change in beach quality,
- changes in commercial profits related to beach quality,
- "downstream" (i.e., out-of-project) benefits,
- ecological benefits, and
- positive effects on amenities and local quality of life.

Cost categories include:

- opportunity costs,
- negative downstream or ecological effects,
- negative effects on local amenities and quality of life,
- increased infrastructure burdens, and
- development-induced increases in risk.

Benefits Categories

Changes in Value Related to Changes in Storm Damage Reduction

The value of existing residential and commercial property may change in response to storm damage reduction and erosion control. If a project prevents or

---

[1]Strictly speaking, these are quasi-public goods. Public goods are goods that can be consumed jointly by many people without diminishing the utility anyone obtains from consumption and include the property of nonexcludability. A quasi-public good is one that can be consumed jointly but is subject to congestion at some level of use.

slows coastal erosion that would destroy existing residential property, benefits include the value of the property for the life of the project. If a project alters the probability distribution for storm damage to existing residential property, this needs to be captured as well. Benefits would be based on probabilistic assessments of damage together with information on repair and replacement costs. Under some circumstances, the change in the real estate value of the property will reflect this measure, but this change will not be observable a priori.

Consumer Surplus (or Willingness to Pay) by Recreationists Visiting the Beach

Even though beach visits are not generally directly purchased on a market, the consumption of beach visits generates surplus to consumers. The benefits from a project might be the total consumer surplus associated with beach use if the beach is threatened with destruction or the incremental consumer surplus associated with a change in the quality of the beach brought about by the project. (Substitutes, congestion, etc., must be taken into account.) The measure includes the present discounted value of future recreational values (i.e., consumer surplus, not expenditures) for the life of the project.

Changes in Amenity Values

Amenity values for local residents may change because of a change in the quality of the beach. This is often reflected in a change in real estate price for the life of the project. Private property owners can gain from an increase in shoreline and beach amenity value (i.e., from being near a more attractive shoreline or one that offers better recreational opportunities). To avoid double counting, the calculation of recreational values needs to include only those benefits associated with individuals that come from a distance at which property values are not affected by the beach amenity value.

Changes in Commercial Profits Related to Beach Quality

Profits to commercial establishments may change because of a change in the quality of the beach. If a new beach is provided or an existing one improved, surrounding businesses may benefit through greater profits. The proper measure is not revenues but net "producer surplus," which in this example is profits. (If measured as before-tax profit, local tax revenue need not be counted.)

Downstream Benefits

Benefits may ultimately accrue "downstream," that is, out of the project. If the sand eventually shifts to another location and provides benefits there, those benefits could be counted. They may, however, not start accruing for some time and must be discounted to the present. However, they start accruing "downstream" as soon as they start diminishing within the project area.

Ecological Benefits

Any ecological benefits that might arise from a project need to be considered and may include improved and increased nesting opportunities for endangered species.

Local Amenities and Quality of Life

Positive effects may occur with respect to local (public good) amenities and community quality of life. These may include the positive amenities associated with beach communities.

Costs Categories

Opportunity Costs

The opportunity costs of the labor, capital, energy, and materials used in the construction of a project are a reflection of what is given up elsewhere by using these resources in this employment. To the extent that any of these were previously unemployed, there is no opportunity cost to society. When the activity does not put upward pressure on the prices of inputs, accounting costs reflect social costs. The opportunity costs may exceed accounting costs when the level of activity is sufficient to bid up the prices of the above factors. These costs must include the present value of all renourishment activities required over the relevant time horizon. As renourishment needs are dictated by uncertain storm events, probability distributions on the events will be a necessary input into the valuation.

Negative Downstream or Ecological Effects

Any negative downstream or ecological effects that result from a project need to be considered. These would include valuing any loss of habitat, for example. Additionally, if the sand used for the project is removed from a site where it provides ecological or other benefits, those costs must be counted as well.

Negative Effects on Local Amenities and Quality of Life

Negative effects on local (public good) amenities and community quality of life might include changes in the character of a community resulting from increased development and congestion.

Increased Infrastructure Burdens

Beach nourishment projects may potentially increase the burden on local public infrastructure because of increased activity (commercial and recreational). Gains from changes in categories of benefits, in beach-user willingness to pay, increased amenity value for local residents owing to a change in beach quality, and increased commercial profits related to beach quality may be offset if increased commercial and recreational activity adds to the infrastructure costs of local communities by increasing the demand for roads, water, sewer, police, and other services.

Development-Induced Increases in Risk

Increased storm damage reduction and erosion control can potentially increase liability for society in the future because of development incentives created by a project that lead to increased inventories of properties at risk.

Analysis of Costs and Benefits Concepts

The preceding concepts do not necessarily align themselves with accounting concepts, and thinking in accounting terms can lead to serious errors. Some of the above concepts can be measured directly from observable market data, others by calculating producer and consumer surpluses from estimated supply and demand functions, and still others by using nonmarket methods of valuation.

In principle, the USACE's *National Economic Development Procedures Manual for Coastal Storm Damage and Erosion* (USACE, 1991) seems consistent with these valuation concepts. The manual draws on the most recent revision of the Water Resources Council's *Principles and Guidelines* (P&G; specifically, the 1983 revision of *Economic and Environmental Principles and Guidelines for Water and Related Land Resources Implementation Studies*), which sets out criteria by which federal water projects undertaken by the USACE, the Bureau of Reclamation, the Tennessee Valley Authority, and the Soil Conservation Service are to evaluate potential projects (WRC, 1983).

The USACE's (1991) procedures manual states that:

> . . . benefits are defined . . . as increases in the economic value of the goods and services that result directly from a project. . . . Because our concern is with the Federal interest, the NED [National Economic Development] analysis counts all benefits and all costs wherever they occur. Therefore, to the extent there are economic effects other than those specifically intended, they must be identified and taken into account. . . .Costs are the opportunity costs of diverting resources from another source to implement the project. Uncompensated economic losses from detrimental project effects are also economic costs.

What is missing from the procedures manual and is only implied in the P&G

is the underlying definition of economic value, and thus the spirit of modern cost-benefit analysis is lost. Instead, one finds mechanical prescriptions for calculating these measures that are overly restrictive relative to other federal guidelines.

The P&G distinguishes four types of accounts: National Economic Development (NED), Regional Economic Development (RED), Environmental Quality, and Other Social Effects. The NED account is restricted to the following goods and services: water supplies, agricultural products, flood protection, electricity generation, transportation, recreation, commercial fishing, and employment of otherwise unemployed or underemployed labor. In many of these categories, the methodological prescriptions appear to be out of date relative to the state of the art and to other agencies' guidelines, largely because the P&G has not been rewritten in a decade.[2]

Only the NED account is actually measured in comparable units, to be compared with direct construction costs of a project. The RED is appropriately omitted, since it reflects income and employment gains and losses to the region that would be canceled out at the national scale through redistribution (although it is interesting information for the assessment of distributional implications.) However, environmental quality effects, health effects, and other quality-of-life issues are segregated into accounts that are presented but never incorporated into the cost-benefit analysis. Other federal guidelines, notably those of the EPA, incorporate these effects. Methods for measuring society's willingness to pay for changes in these nonmarketed goods and services have been developed and continue to be improved. Failing to incorporate these effects biases the cost-benefit analysis. Neither the direction nor the magnitude of the bias can be predicted without further exploration. In some cases, a beach nourishment project that sustains a beach community will have positive amenity values. Little attention has been paid to these types of effects in beach nourishment analysis, so there is little prior information from which to extrapolate.

In practice, the USACE's evaluation of project costs and benefits is based on a comparison of the present value of the net benefits of a project to a "without"-project scenario. These net benefits are compared to construction costs. Guidelines for calculating storm damage and erosion benefits have received the most attention, chiefly from an engineering standpoint. The emphasis has been on calculating expected damages to private property and public infrastructure and the engineering costs of repair and replacement. Land values or capitalized net income measures are prescribed for erosion control benefit measurement.

In practice, the benefits that are emphasized include storm and erosion damage control. Recreational benefits are allowed but cannot exceed a given level (50

---

[2] As an example, the P&G seems to advocate *zonal* travel cost models, an approach that has been surpassed by more sophisticated models in the past decade.

percent) of the benefits of the project during formulation of that project. Prescribed methodologies for estimating recreational benefits include travel cost and contingent valuation. Costs and benefits associated with gains and losses of ecological, community, and other amenities; increased infrastructure burdens; and increased liability do not appear to be included in the evaluation guidelines.

SPECIAL FEATURES OF
THE BEACH NOURISHMENT PROBLEM

Beach nourishment projects provide two kinds of public goods—changes in local amenities and reductions in risk of property loss. Because projects are investment goods, the net social returns to projects accrue over time. The temporal nature of a project's impacts poses special problems for valuation, including extrapolating costs and benefits that would accrue in the future, accounting for behavioral responses resulting from the project, and evaluating the effects of uncertainty associated with random future events.

Costs and benefits accruing from a project in any period of time depend on the inventory of affected properties and the population of affected individuals. Although this is observable at the time of assessment, even in the simplest of cases it is unlikely to remain constant over the relevant time horizon of the project. An a priori evaluation will require forecasts of demographics, infrastructure, recreational activity, ecology, and other considerations over a long time horizon. The USACE's guidelines recognize the need for these forecasts.

The problem is complicated by the dynamic nature of human behavior. Beach nourishment projects, by providing access to new or different amenities, by changing the probability distribution for storm and erosion damage, and by potentially altering the liability for any damage, will cause behavioral responses that change demographics, recreational activity, infrastructure, property inventories, and so forth. To properly forecast the effects, over time, of a project, these behavioral adjustments *due to the project* must be taken into account.

A simple illustration can be found in the recreational benefits category. A beach nourishment project that increases the size of a beach would result in less congestion if the same number of people use the beach. But since demand for beach use is a function of congestion, demand will shift, leading more individuals to use the beach and more trips by those who previously used it. The new equilibrium is difficult to predict without empirical modeling but is unlikely to be characterized either by the same level of use or the same level of congestion as before the improvement. To assess the benefits of a project, the researcher needs to estimate both the change in demand for trips and the change in the value of trips as a result of the improvements in the quality of a trip (due to decreased congestion).

Potential behavioral responses of the private investment type have even more serious consequences. Consider a beach nourishment project that increases the amenity value of a given piece of privately owned property and reduces the risk of damage to or loss of the property from storms or erosion. As a result of the project, the land use of the property may change. The USACE guidelines recognize this and suggest that, in forecasting the "with-plan conditions," "any changes in population, land use, affluence, or intensity of use expected as a result of implementation of a plan" need to be included. In practice, however, these may be limited to gains from intensified or higher-valued uses of land owing to the reduction in risk. Thus, if a project provides risk reduction to private property, which subsequently stimulates private investment, the increase in net annualized income of the property (for example) may be counted as a benefit.

A private action of this sort may or may not be desirable from a social standpoint, and if the action is stimulated by public investment, the full social costs and benefits must be counted. For example, the locality's tax revenue gains from the higher-valued (private) use of the property must be weighed against increases in the burden on local public infrastructure (e.g., increased traffic or parking congestion, increased demands for sewer and water services and police). Additionally, the private investment may change the character of the community (for good or for bad) or may have further ecological ramifications, and these must be taken into account.

Estimating the behavioral responses to a project is difficult, but ignoring them can have serious policy implications. Where local land-use plans exist and are enforced, forecasts of "with"- and "without"- project scenarios will necessarily be more accurate. In any event, undertaking a beach nourishment project in conjunction with local land-use planning increase the chances of obtaining the maximum net social benefits from a project.

The nature of storm events produces great uncertainty about the relevant time horizon over which benefits will accrue—or, put another way, great uncertainty about the costs of ensuring a given level of benefits over a predetermined time horizon. The concept of the relevant time horizon of the project assessment is an important one for obvious reasons, but if the perceived time horizon of the private sector differs from the USACE plans, assessment can be greatly complicated. Private investment responses to projects will depend on what individuals believe the future risks to be and on the institutional structure for handling those risks. A beach nourishment project designed to provide some erosion or storm damage reduction over an average life of 10 years, for example, may be construed by individuals as a signal that the public sector intends to provide protection for the indefinite future. The nature of U.S. social institutions is such that the public frequently provides a safety net in the event of natural disasters. Because investment in private property has been treated as largely irreversible,[3] society incurs

---

[3] Programs administered by the Federal Emergency Management Agency may provide assistance for the acquisition, relocation, or demolition of private property exposed to erosion or other hazards.

an unknown (but potentially increasing) liability for an indefinite period of time into the future.

In the absence of controls, the behavioral response associated with perceived damage reduction of this sort is especially serious since it may raise the level of social liability. Beach nourishment projects may reduce the expected physical impacts of storms and erosion, but by stimulating private investment (and the accompanying public infrastructure), the economic damage associated with any given storm event might even increase. Society becomes liable to protect structures that would not have been built had the private investment decisions taken account of the true cost of insurance. This effect can be exacerbated when the presence of beach nourishment projects reduces the building code requirements along the shoreline.[4] The true costs of a project, then, must incorporate this increased liability in the future. Note that downstream benefits, otherwise a positive element in the cost-benefit calculus, may generate expectations and stimulate investment in locations where renourishment projects are not planned, potentially adding to long-term costs as well.

Problems are compounded by the uncertainty surrounding the incidence of storm events. The USACE's calculations of benefits from storm damage reduction appear to be based on expected values of damage reduction (i.e., means of probability distributions). This might be an appropriate procedure if the entire incidence of the uncertainty fell on the federal government.[5] However, to the extent that uncertain effects of projects accrue to individuals, expected values or certainty equivalence measures are inappropriate because individuals are generally believed to be risk averse. That is, given two uncertain situations with the same expected value, a risk-averse individual will prefer the situation with the smallest variance. Thus, two project designs that generate probability distributions of storm damage with equal means but differing higher moments would be valued differently. Additionally, alternative projects that are perceived to incorporate different levels of risk (i.e., different variances) will differentially stimulate private investment.

REFERENCES

Bell, F. W. 1986. Economic policy issues associated with beach renourishment. Policy Studies Review 6:374-381.

Bell, F. W., and V. R. Leeworthy. 1990. Recreational demand by tourists for saltwater beach days. Journal of Environmental Economics and Management 18:189-205.

---

[4]Additionally, "downstream" benefits from sand drift may be interpreted by property owners as long-term effects and provide false signals for development where no long-term commitment has been made.

[5] Whether federal government policies should be risk neutral is a debated issue.

Black, D. E., L. P. Donnelley, and R. F. Settle. 1988. An Economic Analysis of Beach Renourishment for the State of Delaware. Preliminary report. Dover: Delaware Department of Natural Resources and Environmental Control.

Bockstael, N. E., W. M. Hanemann, and I. E. Strand. 1987a. Measuring the Benefits of Water Quality Improvements Using Recreational Demand Models. Report prepared for the U.S. Environmental Protection Agency, Cooperative Agreement CR-811043-01-0. Washington, D.C.: EPA.

Bockstael, N. E., W. M. Hanemann, and C. L. Kling. 1987b. Modeling recreational demand in a multiple site framework. Water Resources Research 23:951-960.

Bockstael, N. E., K. E. McConnell, and I. E. Strand. 1988. Benefits from Improvements in Chesapeake Bay Water Quality. Report prepared for the U.S. Environmental Protection Agency, Cooperative Agreement CR-811043-01-0. Washington, D.C.: EPA.

Bockstael, N. E., K. E. McConnell, and I. E. Strand. 1991. Recreation. In: Measuring the Demand for Environmental Quality. J. B. Braden and C. D. Kolstad, eds., New York: North Holland.

Braden, J. B., and C. D. Kolstad, eds. 1991. Measuring the Demand for Environmental Quality. New York: North Holland.

Brown, G., and K. Pollakowski. 1977. Economic valuation of shoreline. Review of Economics and Statistics (August) 59(3):272-278.

Carson, R. 1991. Constructed markets. In: J. B. Braden and C. D. Kolstad, eds., Measuring the Demand for Environmental Quality. New York: North Holland.

Caulkins, P. P., R. C. Bishop, and N. W. Bouwes. 1986. The travel cost model for lake recreation: a comparison of two methods for incorporating site quality and substitution effects. American Journal of Agricultural Economics 68:291-297.

Curtis, T. D., and E. W. Shows. 1984. A Comparative Study of Social Economic Benefits of Artificial Beach Nourishment—Civil Works in Northeast Florida. Report for the Florida Division of Beaches and Shores by the University of South Florida.

Edwards, S. F., and G. D. Anderson. 1984. Land use conflicts in the coastal zone: an approach for the analysis of the opportunity costs of protecting coastal resources. Northeastern Journal of Agricultural Economics Management 13:73-81.

Edwards, S. F., and F. J. Gable. 1991. Estimating the value of beach recreation from property values: an exploration with comparisons to nourishment costs. Ocean and Shoreline Management 15:37-55.

Feenberg, D., and E. S. Mills. 1980. Measuring the Benefits of Water Pollution Abatement. New York: Academic Press.

Freeman, A. M. 1979. The Benefits of Environmental Improvement: Theory and Practice. Baltimore: Johns Hopkins Press.

Freeman, A. M. 1993. The Measurement of Environmental and Resource Values: Theory and Methods. Washington, D.C.: Resources for the Future.

Hanemann, W. M. 1978. A Methodological and Empirical Study of the Recreation Benefits from Water Quality Improvement. Ph.D. dissertation, Harvard University.

Haveman, R. H. 1969. The Analysis and Evaluation of Public Expenditures: An Overview. Washington, D.C.: U.S. Government Printing Office.

Inter-Agency River Basin Committee. 1950. Proposed Practices for Economic Analysis of River Basin Projects. Washington, D.C.: U.S. Government Printing Office.

Just, R. E., D. L. Hueth, and A. Schmitz. 1982. Applied Welfare Economics and Public Policy. Englewood Cliffs, N.J.: Prentice-Hall.

Kerns, W. R., R. J. Byrne, and C. H. Hobbs. 1980. An economic analysis strategy for management of shoreline erosion. Coastal Zone Management 8:165-184.

Kriesel, W. 1989. Coastal Erosion and the Residential Property Market. Fact Sheet 044, Ohio Sea Grant College Program, Ohio State University, Columbus.

McConnell, K. E. 1987. Congestion and willingness to pay: a study of beach use. Land Economics 53:185-195.

Mitchell, R. C., and R. T. Carson. 1989. Using Surveys to Value Public Goods: The Contingent Valuation Method. Washington, D.C.: Resources for the Future.

Palmquist, R. 1991. Hedonic methods. In: J. B. Braden and C. D. Kolstad, eds., Measuring the Demand for Environmental Quality. New York: North Holland.

Parsons, G. R., and M. J. Kealy. 1992. Randomly drawn opportunity sets in a random utility model of lake recreation. Land Economics 68:93-106.

Parsons, G. R., and C. Wu. 1991. The opportunity cost of coastal land-use controls: An empirical analysis. Land Economics 67(3):308-316.

Silberman, J., and M. Klock. 1988. The recreation benefits of beach nourishment. Ocean and Shoreline Management 2:73-90.

Smith, V. K. 1989. Taking stock of progress with travel cost recreation demand methods: theory and implementation. Marine Resource Economics 6:279-310.

Smith, V. K. 1991. Household production functions and environmental benefit estimation. In: J. B. Braden and C. D. Kolstad, eds., Measuring the Demand for Environmental Quality. New York: North Holland.

Smith, V. K., and W. H. Desvousges. 1986. Measuring Water Quality Benefits. Boston: Kluwer-Nijhoff.

Stronge, W. B. 1991. Recreational benefits of barrier island beaches: Anna Maria, Captiva, and Marco, A Comparative Analysis. In: Preserving and Enhancing Our Beach Environment, Proceedings of the 4th Annual National Conference on Beach Preservation Technology. Tallahassee: Florida Shore and Beach Preservation Association.

Stronge, W. B. 1992. Impact of Captiva's Beaches on Property Values and Taxes. Report prepared for Captiva Erosion Prevention District by Regional Research Associates, Inc., Boca Raton, Florida, December.

USACE. 1991. National Economic Development Procedures Manual for Coastal Storm Damage and Erosion. IWR Report No. 91-R-6. Fort Belvoir, Va.: Institute for Water Resources, Water Resources Support Center, U.S. Army Corps of Engineers.

Willman, E. A. 1981. Hedonic prices and beach recreational values. In: V. K. Smith, ed., Advances in Applied Microeconomics, Vol. I. Greenwich, Conn.: JAI Press.

WRC. 1983. Economic and Environmental Principles and Guidelines for Water and Related Land Resources Implementation Studies. U.S. Water Resources Council, Washington, D.C.: U.S. Government Printing Office.

F
Project Construction and Sediment Sources, Transfer, and Placement

The construction of a beach nourishment project normally involves the search for sources of sediment that meet the criteria specified by the design, the removal and transfer of material to the nourishment site, and finally its placement on the beach. These components of a project are fundamental to its performance and often determine its feasibility by controlling costs.

SEDIMENT SOURCES

The search for viable sediment sources occurs at an early stage in the planning because this controls, in part, project design and economics. Beach-quality sand and gravel can potentially be derived from a number of sources, which are summarized in this appendix in their order of importance as utilized in recent years in beach nourishment projects in the United States.

Offshore Sources

Over the past decade, the primary source of sand for beach nourishment has been "offshore" deposits on the continental shelf. One of the earliest beach nourishment projects using sand from offshore deposits was at Coney Island, New York, where over 1.3 million m^3 of sand dredged from the seabed not closer than 500 m from shore was placed on the beach during 1922-1923; (Farley, 1923, Domurat, 1987; Dornhelm, 1995).

Many of the offshore deposits are relict beach sand that was initially deposited in the littoral zone during the last 20,000 years when sea levels were lower than at present. This origin potentially makes the sand ideal for nourishment of the modern beach, although some fine-grained silts and clays may have been incorporated into the sand or may have partially covered desirable deposits. At the same time, the coastal processes that deposited these materials have shifted landward as sea level rose. Because the closure depth for measurable sand movement is well inshore of relict sand, offshore borrow sites tend to fill in with fine-grained material that is not suitable as beach fill. Therefore, it is unlikely that many deepwater borrow sites offshore will return to their predisturbed condition. Once the sand is used, other sources will have to be found (BEB, 1958; Gee, 1965; Watts, 1963).

Locating and Assessing Offshore Sand Deposits

The investigation generally begins with high-resolution seismic reflection profiling. The composition and thickness of the borrow sand are determined with a combination of grab samples of seafloor sediments and vibracore and jet-probe samples that can penetrate down into the sediment layers. Vibracore samples are relatively inexpensive to obtain and can recover the long and relatively undisturbed cores required to assess the compositions and grain sizes of the materials, as well as to establish the stratigraphy of the deposits (Meisburger and Williams, 1981). Cores as long as 6 m are routinely taken. Water jets are less expensive than cores, involving the water-jetted penetration of a pipe down through the sediment in order to determine the layering. An experienced operator can determine from the rate of penetration and "feel" of the probe whether it is passing through mud, clean sand, or sand containing some rock material. In general, jet probes are spaced between core borings in order to provide more documentation on sediment thicknesses, while reducing the cost that would result from utilizing vibracore samples for complete coverage.

Reconnaissance studies conducted to evaluate this resource and their overall findings are shown in Table 4-2.

Use of Offshore Sand Deposits for Beach Fill

Offshore sediments have been used as sand sources for many beach nourishment projects. In each case, the material was dredged from the seabed, transported to the beach, and either dumped or pumped into the littoral zone. Sand and shell material derived from the shallow-water continental shelf served as the source for the Dade County, Florida (Miami Beach) nourishment and hurricane surge protection project (Wiegel, 1992) constructed between 1976 and 1981. This is the largest-scale nourishment project undertaken in the United States and involved the dredging of some 13 million m^3 of sand in the offshore and its placement in the nearshore to produce a dry beach 55 m wide at an elevation of 3 m above mean low water (Egense and Sonu, 1987; Wiegel, 1992). The sand for the fill was obtained from offshore dredging. The borrow area consisted of trenches that ran parallel to the shoreline 1.8 to 3.7 km offshore at water depths between 12 and 18 m. The nourishment sand from this source generally had a high carbonate content, consisting of shell and coral fragments. The more recent nourishment project at Ocean City, Maryland, also derived its sand from an offshore source (Grosskopf and Stauble, 1993) from two borrow areas 4 to 5 km offshore, which yielded grain sizes of 0.30 to 0.35 mm.

Inlet Sources

Tidal inlets, especially those used for navigation, are an historic source of nourishment material. For example, sand for the 1986 nourishment of Atlantic City, New Jersey, was obtained from the large subaqueous shoal that develops in Absecon Inlet at the north end of the jetty (Weggel and Sorensen, 1991). Approximately 800,000 m^3 of sand was removed from the shoal by a hydraulic pipeline dredge and pumped directly to Atlantic City's beaches. In many cases, the sand dredged from inlets originally came from the beaches and accordingly should be returned rather than deposited offshore in deep water, where it may be permanently lost from the littoral zone. Dean (1987) documented that in the past 50 years more than 50 million m^3 of good quality sand has been dredged from Florida's east coast inlets and dumped offshore. The calculations indicate that this volume would have been sufficient to advance the shoreline by more than 7 m over the entire 600-km sandy shoreline of the east coast of Florida. Inlet sources are increasingly being considered for nourishment projects in other states. One potential problem is that inlet shoals may be the source of sand to downdrift beaches. For example, Ocean City, Maryland, has considered the removal of sand from the inlet's ebb-tide shoal, in effect returning the sand to the updrift side in front of Ocean City. But sand was obtained from offshore borrow areas because use of the ebb-tide shoal has been objected to because the shoal is the source of sand for the downdrift beach along Assateague Island, which has suffered extensive erosion since jetties were constructed at the Ocean City inlet.

Beach Sources

Littoral Drift

In some instances, accretional downdrift beaches have served as sources of sand for beach nourishment projects by "backpassing." An interesting example is the nourishment on Sandy Hook, New Jersey (Nordstrom et al., 1979). There is a significant northward alongshore transport of sediment along this spit. The construction of groins and other structures to the south has interrupted that transport and induced erosion, particularly at the South Recreational Beach. Sand eroded from South Recreational Beach moves north as littoral transport and has been deposited at the north end of the spit and within Sandy Hook Channel beyond the end of the spit. The beach nourishment project simply involves using the North Recreational Beach and channel as borrow areas and trucking the sand back to the South Recreational Beach, where it is recycled through the system. In another case, at Avalon, New Jersey, some of the sand eroded from the beach at the north end of town at Townsends Inlet that accretes on the beach at the south end of the town is excavated by construction equipment and transported back to the inlet area. The sand is placed back on the beach at the inlet to repeat the process.

Sand Bypassing

Bypassing of sand blocked by the construction of jetties or breakwaters is a special case of using an accretional beach as a sand source. There are a number of examples from Southern California (Wiegel, 1994) and from the Atlantic coast of the United States. The Santa Barbara breakwater was constructed on the California coast beginning in 1927–1928 as a detached structure but was later extended and connected to the shoreline to prevent harbor shoaling (Wiegel, 1959, 1964). It is estimated that the breakwater blocks some 200,000 m^3 of sand per year. A dredge operates from within the protection of the harbor, using the accreted sand spit from the updrift side to nourish the deprived beach on the downdrift side of the harbor. Sand bypassing systems are also in operation at South Lake Worth Inlet in Florida, at the Indian River Inlet on the Delaware coast (see Figure F-1), and at other locations on the Atlantic coast (USACE, 1991, 1994). Sand bypassing is discussed in more detail later in this appendix.

Inland Sources

Riverine Sources

In some instances, an inland source of sediment can be identified. This could involve the mining of sand and gravel from the active bed of a river or from deposits within the flood plain of a river. For example, the primary source of sand for the nourishment of Doheny Beach State Park in California has been from mining within Capistrano Creek (Herron, 1987). The potential impacts on the overall budget of sediments must be considered when drawing upon a river source; the operation could be self-defeating if the river is a natural contributor of sediments to the beach being nourished or it could induce erosion in another littoral compartment.

Dunes

Another potential inland source is dunes, particularly those found in the coastal zone. Dune sands, however, are typically finer grained than beach sands,

FIGURE F-1   Sand bypassing at Indian River Inlet, Delaware. Jet pump positioned by crane (from Wayne Young, Marine Board, National Research Council).

the smaller particles having been selectively removed by the winds from the beach and blown inland to form the dunes. This cycle would likely reoccur, potentially at an accelerated pace, if fine-grained sand were used as beach fill. Also, fine-grained sand is more susceptible to movement seaward than coarser-grained material. Use of dune sand for beach fill is generally not desirable because of the natural shore protection that dunes provide. Furthermore, dunes provide unique fragile habitats. In the case of barrier islands, dune systems are fundamental to the natural stability of the islands themselves. Thus, dune sand is not normally a primary source of beach fill material, although recoverable dune sand moved landward by overwash during major storms has sometimes been relocated back to beach areas to restore some measure of natural protection. Overwash deposits tend to be coarser than dune sand, since beach face sediment is carried inland and deposits on and/or mixes with dune sand.

Beach Ridge Deposits

Another inland source is sand from "beach" ridges, which are ancient deposits consisting of variable proportions of beach and dune sands. Beach ridge deposits are often weakly cemented but can be crushed in order to return them to their original sand sizes. When Capistrano Creek has been an insufficient source for fill in Doheny Beach State Park, sand has been derived from ancient beach deposits located on a nearby marine terrace (Herron, 1987). Glacial deposits composed of sand and gravel can also serve as ready sources in the northeastern and northwestern United States and in the Great Lakes region. As discussed previously, Ediz Hook, which projects into the Strait of Juan de Fuca at Port Angeles, Washington, has been nourished with gravel and cobbles derived from glacial outwash. This is the same type of sediment that was formerly delivered to the site by the Elwha River and alongshore transport and from sea cliff erosion before those sources were cut off by dam construction and the placement of a seawall (Galster and Schwartz, 1990).

Back Bay Sand Deposits

Historically, the most important source of nourishment sands in many areas has been from bays and lagoons, often as a byproduct of harbor dredging. Sand derived from bays and harbors has been particularly important in California, where the wide beaches observed today are largely the product of nourishment by sand dredged from harbors such as San Diego (Herron, 1987; Flick, 1993; Wiegel, 1994). During World War II, over 20 million m^3 of sand was pumped from San Diego Bay onto Silver Strand Beach and Imperial Beach. Prior to that nourishment, those beaches had been deficient in sand owing to construction of the Rodriguez Dam on the Tijuana River and were frequently overtopped by storm waves. Similarly, the entire Santa Monica Bay beach has been widened by 60 to 100 m by a series of replenishment measures (Herron, 1987; Leidersdorf et al., 1994). Activity of this type continues today. For example, the U.S. Army Corps of Engineers (USACE) places beach-quality material from ship channel maintenance on a river beach in Oregon on the lower Columbia River. Placement of sand from channel maintenance dredging has also been conducted by the USACE in Florida at the St. Johns River and Pensacola Bay entrance. Under existing federal policy for channel maintenance and shore protection, such placements are a matter of convenience to the federal government in order to reduce transportation costs for dredged material or as an alternative pending approval of cheaper disposal areas offshore. Alternatively, the local governmental entities can pay the additional cost for onshore placement.

Herron (1987), Flick (1993), and Wiegel (1994) provide quantitative comparisons of the volumes of sand supplied from nourishment projects to California beaches and the sand volumes derived from natural sources. In the 60 years prior to 1987, Herron estimates that within the 390 km of coast between Santa Barbara and the Mexican border some 70 million m^3 of nourishment sand has been the byproduct of projects in coastal areas, such as excavations for harbors, power plants, sewage treatment plants, and highways. During that same period, the natural supply from local rivers and alongshore transport from beaches north of Santa Barbara amounted to some 115 million m^3. About 70 million m^3 of this "natural" supply was bypassed, naturally or by human activity, around breakwaters and jetties on this stretch of Southern California coastline. Flick (1993) provides similar assessments for the individual littoral cells from Santa Barbara to the Mexican border, reconfirming the past importance of nourishment sands derived from land sources. Of concern is that the importance of this source has diminished over the years, in part due to the reduced dredging of rivers, lagoons, bays, and estuaries, which are now recognized as important and fragile environments. When those areas are dredged, however, they can be important sources of sand suitable for placement on beaches, and the sand should not be wastefully dumped offshore.

Nonindigenous and Artificial Sand Sources

Oolitic Sands

At times it is economical to utilize "exotic" sediments from more distant sources. Oolitic aragonite sands, for example, have been imported from the Bahamas for a nourishment project on Fisher Island, Florida, immediately south of Miami Beach (Bodge and Olsen, 1992). The potential use of oolitic sands for beach nourishment was initially explored in the 1960s, when laboratory wave-tank tests were undertaken to establish the properties of beaches composed of that sediment (Cunningham, 1966; Monroe, 1969). The project at Fisher Island represents its first full-scale use in the United States. This project was not large, however. It involved the barging of approximately 23,000 m^3 of fill from the Bahamas and its placement on the beach within compartments between six T-head groins built along the 620-m-long fill area. The median diameter of the oolitic sand is about 0.27 mm, which is estimated to be hydraulically equivalent (having the same fall velocity) to 0.36-mm quartz sand, as measured by sieving analyses (Bodge and Olsen, 1992). No adverse environmental impacts have resulted from this nourishment project using oolitic sand, and there has been no observed physical degradation of the aragonite grains owing to abrasion or dissolution.

The use of imported oolitic sands was also considered as an option in the nourishment project undertaken at Hollywood and Hallandale to the north of Miami (Beachler and Higgins, 1992), which was a substantially larger fill (790,000 m^3) than at Fisher Island. In this instance, the bids based on nearby sources of normal sand on the continental shelf were substantially lower than economically possible for the import of oolites from the Bahamas. This indicates that such imports will be limited to smaller projects and areas where the material has particularly desirable characteristics; in the Fisher Island project, the white oolitic sand was used to blend with the Mediterranean architecture of the development (Bodge and Olsen, 1992).

Crushed Rock

In a few instances, particularly for smaller projects, beaches have been constructed of gravel made by crushing coral or rock. Wiegel (1993) documented crushed rock material usage at the following beach nourishment projects:

- Smathers Beach, Key West, Florida;
- Larvotto Bay Beach, Monte Carlo, Monaco;
- "Marble Beach," Osaka Bay, Japan;
- Maumee Bay State Park, Lake Erie, Ohio: and
- Fort DeRussy, Waikiki Beach, Honolulu, Hawaii.

There is little published information on the performance of projects that used crushed rock material. By visual inspection, they generally appear to be performing as anticipated (Wiegel, 1993).

The Monte Carlo beach in Monaco was constructed during 1965-1967 using 80,000 m^3 of dolomite chippings, with a median diameter of 3-8 mm, from a local upland source (Tourman, 1968; Rouch and Bellessort, 1990). The 400-m-long beach was contained within a system of groins and breakwaters. The gravel-sized chippings soon became rounded by abrasion within the surf as had been predicted by tests using a Los Angeles "rattler," which is a large rotating drum similar to a rock tumbler, to simulate the process in the laboratory. The 800-m-long beach fill at Maumee Bay State Park, Ohio, was constructed along its western part with 115,000 m^3 of crushed Niagara limestone having a median diameter of 0.75 mm. After three and a half years, the beach has remained in good condition (Wiegel, 1993). These placements suggest that nonindigenous materials can be used successfully in lieu of native sediments for beach fill purposes.

TRANSPORT AND PLACEMENT

Bridging the gap between the investigation and analysis of potential borrow sites and the design parameters attendant to the configuration of a renourished beach requires a basic understanding of dredging equipment, processes, capabilities, and limitations. Furthermore, various choices and trade-offs with respect to increased protection, recreational benefits, and maintenance savings that affect the cost of construction are presented for decision making during the design process. The designer and project decision makers must decide whether the cost of construction should be increased in order to reduce the overall lifetime cost of the project.

Dredging Resources

Generally, sand borrow is excavated and transported from a borrow site to a beach by one or more of three types of equipment: cutter-suction dredge, trailing-suction hopper dredge, or dedicated sand bypass system. However, the vast majority of beach projects have been accomplished either by using self-propelled hopper dredges with pumpout capability or by pumping the borrow material directly to the beach fill site via pipelines from cutter-suction dredges. Transport via trucks and placement directly onto the beach fill site have been used in some projects in which sand and gravel were obtained from upland sources.

Transportation costs for a given material increase with distance. Although this is obvious whether a pipeline, hopper dredge, or truck is utilized, the effect on each varies and is not proportional to distance.

Selection of a borrow site inherently restricts the range of suitable equipment for a project. Varying resources among contractors establish degrees of cost advantage or disadvantage. The ability to work offshore or, to meet high production capabilities, ownership of certain equipment such as hopper dredges or certified dredges, and the financial resources to bond high-cost projects are all factors that tend to narrow the field of participants in large nourishment projects with offshore sources. Conversely, sources from inshore protected waters or closer borrow sites, including upland pits, allow a wider field of bidders.

Existing Fleet

At present, the U.S. marketplace for beach nourishment is served by the fleets of U.S. dredging companies utilizing equipment that is flexible and multipurpose over a large range of dredging requirements and materials to include navigation channel maintenance, land reclamation, and construction dredging, as well as beach replenishment. Utilization of the fleets in this manner, combined with a substantial overcapacity in the U.S. industry, results in extreme competition among the companies capable of nourishment projects, which in turn results in lower pricing to the marketplace.

Although few large cutter-suction dredges or hopper dredges have been constructed recently, the existing equipment is continually upgraded and is capable of meeting the requirements placed on it by the beach nourishment market at reasonable costs. As this market matures and greater offshore capabilities and higher productivity govern the pricing, the industry will respond with new vessels capable of earning favorable returns for their owners.

Equipment Types and Capabilities/Limitations

A cutter-suction dredge consists of one or more large pumps mounted on a barge with all the engines and drive mechanisms required to pump a slurry of sand and water to the beach through a pipeline without any double handling or intermediate processes. The material is excavated and introduced to the slurry by means of a cutterhead located on the end of an articulating ladder attached to the barge with a hinge mechanism. Figure F-2 shows schematically the layout of a

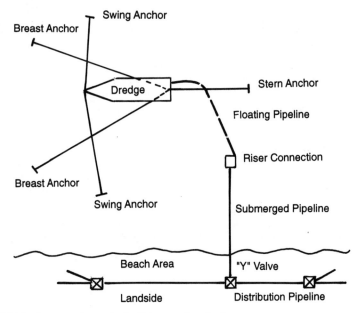

FIGURE F-2   Layout of a typical offshore cutter dredge.

typical offshore cutter dredge and its connected pipeline to the beach. The dredge is held in place on a system of cables, winches, and anchors. The stern of the dredge is moored in a single position with three anchors. On this pivot point the dredge and the submerged ladder swing through the width of a cut utilizing swing anchors set to each side. The dredge advances through the length of the cut by slacking the stern anchor and taking in on the two breast anchors after the material in each swing of the ladder is excavated.

Connected to the dredge is a floating section of pipeline consisting of either steel pipe sections mounted on flotation tanks or flexible hose segments with their own integral flotation collars. Extending from the floating pipeline is a section of pipe placed on the bottom and leading to the shore landing. It is connected to the floating section with a ball-joint connection on some type of barge or flotation arrangement. The purpose of the floating segment is to allow flexibility to the dredge in movement and to allow disconnection from the pipeline in cases where the dredge must be taken to safe harbor to escape bad weather conditions or for major repairs.

The shore landing is typically located in the center of a length of beach to be replenished so as to minimize the total pipeline length on which the dredge is pumping. At the landing, a Y valve is installed to allow the shore crew to choose the direction and segment of pipeline on which to pump. As the fill advances down the beach, the shore crew adds sections of shorepipe on whichever line is

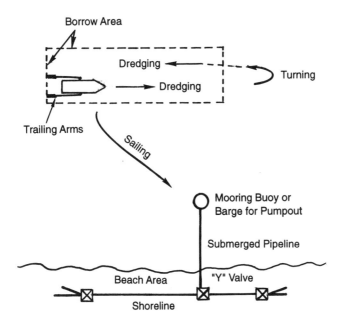

FIGURE F-3 Schematic of operation of a trailing-suction hopper dredge.

appropriate to control the distribution of the fill within the limits of the design template.

The operation of a trailing-suction hopper dredge is illustrated schematically in Figure F-3. This dredge differs from a cutter-suction dredge in that it is a free-traveling vessel that is either a ship or a tug-propelled barge that sails back and forth over the area of the borrow site and that trails one or two arms on which are mounted dragheads that loosen the sand and deliver it to the suction pipe, which then loads the slurry into the hopper of the vessel.

In order to deliver the sand to the beach, the hopper dredge must either (1) moor to a buoy or barge and pump the material through pipeline arrangements similar to that of a cutter-head dredge or (2) bottom dump the material directly in place through the use of doors in the bottom of the hull or via a split-hull arrangement where the ship divides itself into two halves hinged in the center on each end. Following are some characteristics of both types of dredges.

Hopper Dredges

U.S. vessels vary in size from about 700 to 12,000 m³ per load:

- loaded drafts range from 4 to 9 m;

- pumpout capabilities of from less than 1,000 Hp to over 12,000 Hp allow material to be delivered from the mooring area to up to 9,000 m away;
- the draghead process takes off thinner slices of material than the cutterhead and cannot effectively excavate very compact or cemented material;
- this operation generally leaves fewer potholes in a borrow site than a cutterhead; and
- sailing distances up to 10 km from the borrow to pumpout mooring are considered well within the efficient range for most sizes of U.S. vessels.

Cutter-Suction Dredges

Dredges of 20- to 36-in. pipeline diameter are typically used for beach replenishment. The larger sizes are used for longer-distance pumping and offshore work. These machines can typically pump the slurry efficiently up to 4,500 m or so without a booster pump and up to 10,000 m if a booster pump is used.

Offshore work typically requires U.S. Coast Guard certification of the vessel in addition to the assignment of a load line by the American Bureau of Shipping.

The cutterhead operation is most efficient in borrow excavation faces that are about 1.5 m. These dredges are usually more susceptible to adverse sea conditions than are hopper dredges. Cutter dredges can work in water depths of less than 5 m.

Continuous Pumping Process

The continuous pumping process is usually the more productive of the two types of dredges:

- trailing-suction hopper dredges are classified by their material transport volume and draft, and
- cutter-suction dredges are classified by the discharge diameter of their pumps and by the horsepower on their pump and cutter-head systems.

All U.S.-flag hopper dredges and some cutter-suction dredges are further classified by their qualifications under the Seagoing Barge Act (46 U.S.C. et seq.), which requires Coast Guard certification of the equipment for use in the oceans. Dredges utilized in more protected waters of rivers and bays or harbors may not meet these requirements. The difficulties of operating in the offshore environment led to many earlier projects using sand from protected bays and harbors or the intercoastal waterway.

Equipment Combinations

Typical beach nourishment projects in the United States are performed with the following equipment or combinations:

- a cutter-suction hydraulic dredge;
- a cutter-suction hydraulic dredge with booster pump;
- a self-propelled, trailing-suction hopper dredge with pumpout;
- a large-capacity dustpan dredge; or
- at least one major project with hopper dredges to continually feed a cutter-suction dredge rehandling the material on the way to the beach.

Both hopper dredges and cutter-suction dredges utilize large pumps to transport sand or gravel in a slurry through pipelines from the borrow source to the beach. The hopper dredges excavate the material from the borrow area, load the sand into their own hulls, and transport the material directly to near the placement site. At this location, the material is either pumped to its final template or dumped, by opening gates or trap doors in the hull or by using a hopper with a split-hull configuration that opens around pivot points. In the latter case, a cutter-suction dredge is used to excavate the material and pump it directly to the fill template through continuously connected pipelines.

The typical 30-in.-diameter cutter-suction dredge used on offshore projects in the United States has the capability to dredge from borrow sites in water depths ranging from 5 to 20 m. Hopper dredges are used in water depths of 7 to 15 m at full capacity. Smaller hoppers can operate in shoal water with 4 to 5 m of loaded draft. Large cutterheads and hopper dredges can readily be adapted to excavate in water depths of 25 to 30 m.

The distance to the beach is an important factor in the transport of dredged material by either pipeline or hopper dredges. Pipeline delivery systems or pumpout stations can be readily prepared to deliver material in pipeline lengths of up to 10 km with a single booster. Hopper dredges of the U.S.-flag fleet can economically deliver material to pumpout stations at sailing distances 8 to 12 km from the borrow site.

For hopper dredges, the sailing time between the borrow and placement areas is nonproductive and can significantly affect the amount of time required to move material and thus the duration and cost of placement operations. In the case of hopper dredges, the route is also important to the extent that distance is added if a transit directly to the placement site is not feasible, (e.g., to avoid shoal areas or reefs). For pipeline transport, there is an upper limit to the distance over which dredged material can be efficiently pumped and the rate at which it is delivered.

Choosing the Right Dredging Equipment

Decisions to utilize a certain type of equipment are made initially on comparison of the contractor's available equipment to the physical dimensions of the project. For example: Can the dredge excavate in the depths required by the borrow-pit dimensions? Can a hopper dredge operate close enough to the beach to pump out the material given its draft constraints? Can the power of the cutter-suction dredge pump the material directly from the borrow site to the beach? Will the dredge be able to pump efficiently in the winds and sea conditions to be expected for the project? Is a booster pump required? What production is required to meet the project schedule? Is the material cemented to any degree?

Once the contractor's equipment is checked for applicability to a certain project, the final choice of equipment or equipment combinations can vary widely based on the equipment's availability, cost structure, the mobilization costs of the equipment, historic productivity records on similar projects, and the risk to the plant offered by the physical conditions at the site. These factors vary widely with each contractor and often result in two contractors choosing what may seem to be completely opposite answers to the same question of which plant provides the lowest-cost construction.

An example of these choices is seen in the varying plants used on the recent major series of projects in Ocean City, Maryland. Two projects covering the same 13-km reach of beach fill showed a complete reversal of plant choices by two different contractors owing to equipment availability and borrow site location and type. An early state-funded project in the northerly sections used a hopper dredge to pump from the north borrow site and a large cutter-suction dredge and booster pump to nourish the southerly section. In the subsequent federal project the northerly sections were nourished with a large cutter-section dredge pumping directly to the beach, and the southerly segments were nourished by using two small hopper dredges moored to an anchored barge and then pumping to the beach. A second contractor bidding on the projects indicated that three large hopper dredges would be used.

The direct pumping with a large floating booster pump would be more cost effective and of shorter duration if the weather were good. On the other hand, the multiple hopper-dredge scenario would be less profitable should the weather be calm but more likely to finish the project within the allotted time frame and less susceptible to the impact of bad weather.

Occasionally, there may be unusual requirements on a project that require specialized equipment, construction techniques, or materials. One such project involved phases III, IV, and V of the Miami Beach restoration. The products of the borrow areas, which were located between ancient reefs offshore, consisted of large shell and coral fragments and large pieces of cemented sand and shell, as well as the major sand component. This material was undesirable from an aesthetic viewpoint and made walking on the beach very uncomfortable; thus, it was designated as unsuitable fill in the contract. So as not to lose the material as a borrow source, on phases III and IV the contractor chose to pump the material, large fragments and all, to a surge bin on the beach and then screen the oversized material, crush it to sand size, and repump it into the fill location. Later contracts were completed utilizing a large hopper dredge, screening the oversized material on board, and disposing of it into a designated offshore site when sufficient quantity had been collected.

Trade-offs in Design and Construction

At present, the major constraints to transport and placement of material for beach nourishment from offshore borrow sites are those of weather-related delays caused by sea state and winds, restrictions on construction activity or methods relating to environmental concerns, equipment limitations for deepwater dredging, and distances over which sediment must be transported.

Effects of Sediment Character on Construction

Material type, grain size, and composition have a large effect on the cost of the dredging process. All the hydraulic transport processes used by the pumps on the dredges are largely a function of grain size. The density of the slurry pumped and the economically feasible length of pipeline for either direct pumping or pumpout of a hopper dredge are dependent on the grain size of the material, as indicated in Figure F-4. The degree of cementation of the sands is also an important factor in the excavation process. Fine-grained sands that are slightly cemented will greatly affect the ability of a hopper dredge to load material and of a cutter dredge to extract material without having to make several nonproductive sets or moves per hour following the sand face. Conversely, freely running sands that will flow to the suction mouth or draghead without much movement on the dredge's part will greatly increase the efficiency of the dredge's production.

Deposits in the borrow site that are primarily fine grained or that contain inclusions of silt or soft clay layers will result in difficulty in the placement process on the beach end of the construction. The slopes will generally be flatter than for coarser-grained material, and intermittent pumping of the silty or clayey material will wash out or flatten the slopes of material already in place. Control of these types of deposits in the borrow site is extremely difficult because their location and thickness often vary by more than the 0.6 m or so of vertical tolerance applicable to the dredging process.

The quality of available material in the borrow source is specified by the design parameters for the project. The contractor typically adopts a rather narrow viewpoint on this issue. The contractor's job is to accept the designated borrow site limits, excavate the available material, and place it within the design template on the beach. Unless otherwise indicated, special processes, such as screening or separation of oversized material or washing of fines, are not considered part of this process. The designer must therefore be certain that the designated borrow site contains material that meets the type and size parameters desired. Dealing with excess fine-grained material causes the most problems, at the borrow site and on the beach, both in retaining material within the template and in controlling turbidity. Finer material is also easier to pump for a given distance than larger-sized sediments and will usually be selected by the contractor if available.

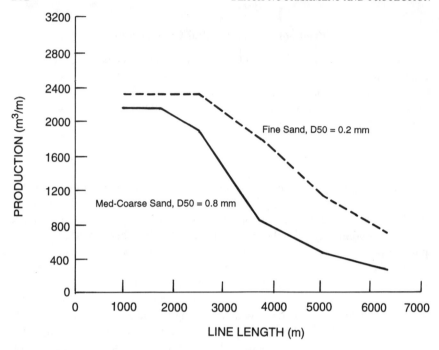

FIGURE F-4   Effect of grain size on production.

Implications of Borrow Site Configurations and Location

The general configuration of a borrow site has some impact on the efficiency of the dredging process. The manner in which a hopper dredge transits over the area from which it borrows the material dictates that shoal depths of the borrow site are limited to approximately 0.6 to 1 m below the loaded draft of the equipment being utilized. The shoal depths also apply to the sailing route chosen between the borrow site and the bottom placement or pumpout site. This equipment also favors borrow sites that allow the longest possible trail lengths without turning, since no dredging is accomplished during turning. Because sailing time between the borrow site and the pumpout site is also nonproductive, borrow sites closer to the beach are favored. Design profiles that allow hopper dredges to bottom-dump material directly into the profile will also increase the efficiency of the hopper dredge's operation.

For a cutter-suction dredge, the distance to the beach is critical in relation to pumping distance. Also important to the operating characteristics of this type of dredge is the amount of available material face or the depth of material from the original bottom to the dredged depth. As the dredge swings from side to side and steps ahead to access the material, the less forward movement necessary, the more productive the cycle will be. This would indicate that the borrow site needs to be sufficiently wide to accommodate the ideal swinging width of the dredge and needs to have as large an excavation depth as possible.

The material must be available in sufficient quantity to supply the project after taking into account excess material placed beyond design templates, loss of finer-grained material placed under water, erosion of the beach during construction, and rejection of material because of sand quality or environmental restraints. In a recent project in Manatee County, Florida, the principal sand source was initially identified as 18 million m^3 but was reduced to 3 million m^3 after analysis of limiting factors.

In addition to the transport distance discussed above, the project length and its relation to the borrow sources often are factors in the cost of a project. Unimpeded access to the fill point from the borrow site will result in the lowest costs. Shoal waters that interrupt the line from borrow site to placement artificially extend the transportation distance, as do other natural or man-made structures that require rerouting of pipelines or transiting barges around an obstacle.

Depth Constraints and Accessibility

In marine borrow sites the navigational depths of the site and surrounding area are critically limiting to certain types or classes of dredging vessel. In addition to hull clearance (loaded draft clearance for hoppers and scows), some operational depth for maneuvering or operation of attendant plant is required. Very shallow borrow sites are restrictive to cutter- suction and hopper dredges, while very deep ones may exceed excavation depth limits and pump constraints. Pipeline operations in deep areas are more difficult than those in shallower waters.

Implications of Distant and Deepwater Sources

In the future, near-term localized borrow shortages or environmental concerns may necessitate transportation of sand from sources far from the site of a constructed beach. In order to conserve transportation costs, this would necessitate the use of larger transport vessels and alternative methods of sand delivery to the beach from those presently in use. Vessels suited for this type of operation are generally not available in the U.S.-flag dredging fleet. Furthermore, the capability for deepwater mining of sand is constrained to depths of about 60 m by the limits of existing dredging technology and to depths of 30 m for the U.S.-flag dredging fleet. The increased costs of such operations might make nontraditional sources of material for fill, such as artificial sand, financially attractive or perhaps stimulate development of improved resource recovery technology. The development of deepwater mining technology and equipment, like the development of offshore oil production, will be a slow process that requires a profitable marketplace for its product.

Other Design Impacts on Construction Costs

In any fill placement process involving slurry transport, the ability to advance the pipeline along the project length without interrupting the production of the dredge is critical to the efficiency of the operation. High-productivity equipment is required for long transport distances or the ability to work offshore. If the fill quantities are limited (in terms of volume per unit length of beach), the dredging must be halted frequently to move the distribution pipeline or must be used at less than its minimum continuous production. This will result in a premium unit price being paid without the full benefit of the equipment's capability.

To avoid expensive special equipment or productivity delays, the berm width must provide an allowable working platform for the pipelines above the level of the wave runup at high water.

Most design procedures recognize the inability of present dredging contractors to grade or place material to close tolerances under water or within the wave-action zone without special equipment or procedures. These procedures limit well-defined templates to the dry beach and usually mandate volumetric requirements and tolerances below the surf area in anticipation of natural shaping of the material through wave forces. Any requirement for design slopes that is contrary to natural processes, such as a steep slope requirement for fine material, will result in extra cost to the project without extra benefit.

Projects that include an artificial dune should allow for shaping of the dune as a parallel effort to berm and slope construction. Insufficient berm width, unrealistic dune slopes, or a constricted construction area will result in inefficient and costly overfilling or production interruptions.

Structures such as pedestrian and vehicular crossovers, seawalls, drainage outfalls, or sand-retaining fencing, as well as various dune grasses or plantings designed to stabilize the sand, add materials procurement time to a project that normally contains no scheduling for anything other than equipment time. These interfaces with the dredging schedule should be given considerable thought in planning.

Local and Seasonal Weather Conditions

Also of great effect on the dredging process are the weather conditions that may be encountered. For dredging sites in rivers or bays that are relatively protected, the weather will have little effect except for cessations caused by short squalls or shutdowns caused by major hurricane events or flooding. The offshore borrow sites, however, will be subject to periods of reduced productivity as well as complete stoppages because of the effects of sea state and wind.

Possible multiple interim local remobilizations because of the effects of major storms or hurricanes exacerbate the difficulties of accurate cost estimation. Unpredictable storms may cause 2 to 10 days of unproductive time when the payroll and other costs remain in place and no revenue is being generated. Additionally, the potential for damage to equipment, injury to the contractor's personnel, and third-party liability is great. These storms may also destroy work already in place, which may or may not be accepted depending on the contractual arrangements.

Borrow Site Considerations

Typical designs for borrow site use establish limits to excavation both horizontally and vertically. The dimensions are set to include sufficient borrow material for all facets of the project but to horizontally exclude proximate hard structure, reefs, historical areas, nesting or spawning sites, and commercial- or recreational-use areas. Vertical dimensions exclude pockets or layers of unsuitable material, as well as design dimensions, to eliminate holes that may trap fine-grained sediments or cause variations in wave energy at the shoreline. Design parameters for anchoring systems and turbidity generation must be considered in sites with closely adjacent sensitive areas. Limitations on equipment types or processes, such as on hopper dredging during turtle migrations, have an extreme impact on the cost of some projects.

Construction Site Requirements

Another area in which the designer must sometimes balance requirements of the project is in the fill itself. Typically, a construction contract has a requirement for the placement of material to a specific construction slope with a tolerance either above and below the construction template or only above the template. During construction, the actual slope is influenced by the material being pumped, the rate of pumping, the degree of effort used by the contractor to control the flow of material, and the effects of the surf conditions at the time. In some regions the need for beach nourishment has resulted from sand being trapped by a harbor being constructed (breakwaters) in the nearshore or by jetties built to fix the location of an entrance through a beach into a inland harbor. Net alongshore transport of sand can cause trapping of sand updrift of the structures, within the entrance, or add cost to the project without achieving any additional benefit. With the exception of the dry beach portion, which is easily controlled to a fairly tight tolerance, it is more cost effective to establish volumetric distribution parameters for the portions of the fill that are inaccessible by ordinary land equipment or by bottom dumping by hopper dredge. These areas can be allowed to fill at the natural angle of repose of the material being pumped at the time. Control of fill amounts and distribution may be done with specifications that require minimum amounts of fill within a certain reach of beach, maybe 150 m or so. Interim fill sections within this segment should be required to have similar amounts of fill within a reasonable tolerance to allow for variations in the filling process.

In specific designs where the entire profile needs to be nourished during construction or particular placements of material are desired rather than hydraulic redistribution of the fill, these requirements may be met by utilizing bottom dumping by shallow-draft hopper dredges or by using a special-purpose spill barge or other pipeline handling arrangement.

Contractual language that details the requirements for monitoring, habitat preservation, or relocation of identified plant and animal life is a requirement for each contract, along with provisions to preserve public and private property from damages due to construction operations. Access to the beach for contractor's operations is requisite for any project. Additionally, the construction operations must be controlled to prevent most interference with the tourist trade and beach use. This can be accomplished readily by securing an area at the immediate fill site with approximately 500 to 600 m of beachfront working area, providing pedestrian access over pipelines, and intensive public education.

Public Access and Disturbance During Construction

The primary solution to the aggravations of the impacts of construction on the use and enjoyment of a beach is the knowledge that they will pass any given area on the beach within a short period of time. To ensure the credibility of this remedy, the project management must require a sufficient rate of progress with the fill and limit the area on the beach accessible to the contractor for construction operations at any given time. The manner in which this is to be accomplished must be a requirement of the specifications and the subject of an understanding between the owner's representative and the contractor prior to the start of the project.

Contractual Constraints

Project Schedule Requirements

The schedule for requirements on a beach nourishment project takes into account the protection offered (or recreation afforded) by the existing beach, construction interferences with the public during high-use periods, weather impacts on the cost of operations, impacts on the environment, and political timing with regard to funding cycles. Contractors choose equipment so as to produce the lowest unit cost and meet contractual requirements as defined economically. Low unit costs may be achieved with a costly daily expense over a short but highly productive period or a lower daily expense over a longer period.

Payment Items

Three items regarding pay structure are particularly important in beach replenishment projects. The first of these includes fair assessment and dealing with contractor risk due to weather impacts. Contractors have the ability to assess risk for average weather patterns but would be able to negotiate lower prices if some risk sharing with the owner is formulated. A second item relates to completed but unaccepted beach fill. Often requirements for acceptance of fill sections do not realistically evaluate contractor work in place prior to storm events. A third item is the designation of pay templates for the fill. Stringent requirements for slope dimensions in areas where the contractor cannot grade without specialized equipment on unrealistic slope designs lead to higher prices for "loss factor" contingencies or unfair payment for useful fill in place. Volumetric tolerances below the surf zone should be reasonable.

Dredging Industry Considerations

In addition to the effects of all these factors on the cost of a project from the contractor's viewpoint, there are some situations that may be more relevant to beach nourishment projects accomplished by dredging than to building or highway construction. Dredging in most cases, and certainly in the case of offshore borrow sites, is accomplished by large individual pieces of equipment that each cost millions or tens of millions of dollars. Coupled with this high capital investment is a relatively low yearly use, which may be on the order of 6 to 8 months for all types of navigation channel maintenance and construction dredging and generally 6 months or less for beach nourishment projects. This low utilization is a result of the construction issues discussed previously, as well as the number of available plants of these types in the United States today. There are at least nine major cutter-hydraulic dredges and eight major trailing-suction hopper dredges in the U.S. fleet today, as well as two barge-tug combinations that could perform offshore work. These two factors result in a high daily cost of equipment for beach nourishment projects. The cost of marine insurance for equipment, insurance requirements for dredging personnel, and recent increases in liability for environmentally sensitive situations further add to the cost of dredging operations.

The U.S. dredging industry has further experienced recent consolidation of existing companies and entrance into the beach nourishment area by companies that previously did not perform this type of work. Additionally, the continual retrofitting and construction of new plants have resulted in the possibility of four or more companies bidding in the beach nourishment marketplace for the various types of projects. This number could easily double if projects using material from protected waters are considered.

Although this appears to present a favorable climate for the cost of beach projects, the general nature of these projects and their high cost force owners (who are generally public bodies) to look for areas in which to implement savings. The greatest risks to contractors on these projects are the variable and somewhat unknown nature of the material being dredged and the unpredictable nature of the weather. Owners and engineers can mitigate the material factors by ensuring performance of a detailed and comprehensive prebid soils investigation. This could take the form of payment of a standby rate for periods of bad weather in which the plant could not work or payment for a portion or all of the costs associated with the interim demobilization and remobilization surrounding major storm events. To level the playing field and ensure a proper degree of effort on the contractor's part, these parameters would need to be expressed in terms of absolute sea conditions or wind forces rather than general terms describing the dredge's ability to work or its productive work hours.

Another cost factor may be the volatility of costs for emergency work or cycles of maintenance conducted earlier than planned. It is obviously to the owner's advantage to be able to decline to contract the work if the prices at bid time are considered unreasonable. To protect this option, consideration should be given to the early performance of maintenance cycles before they become truly emergency in nature. Another possible solution to the increased cost of emergency work is a state, regional, or federal organization of contracts that provide for yearly maintenance work to be done. The specific assignment of work would be made according to the need at a time nearer to the time of dredging than is possible with the present lengthy prework planning period.

Future Needs

In order to serve the requirements of an expanding beach nourishment marketplace, the following developments will be critical to the U.S. dredging industry.

Greater Efficiency in Offshore Conditions

As with the development of the offshore energy industry, the dredging market will demand greater productivity throughout larger ranges of weather conditions than at present. Development of more single-purpose offshore hull forms, more flexible and heavy-duty moorings, and more material delivery systems are presently evolving and will develop at a more rapid pace as the economics of beach material delivery grows. It is likely that much of this technology will evolve from offshore experience gained by energy companies and be adapted to dredging equipment.

Ability to Mine Deeper Sand Deposits and Deliver Farther

Larger equipment supporting longer dredge ladders or remote active dragheads will be developed as borrowing of farther offshore deposits becomes economical. Higher-head pumping systems that use more sophisticated booster control will enable delivery of sand from farther offshore borrow sites.

Long-Distance Transport of Material

Although long-term source estimates of sand and gravel resources in the U.S. exclusive economic zone are in the billions of cubic meters, localized shortages (particularly in the Florida and Gulf coast regions) may make the importation of beach fill material from relatively long distances an economic feasibility. This concept may also see fruition if the public becomes willing to pay for this methodology as a compromise to environmental considerations in some regions.

The transport distance for disposal of dredged material presently reaches roundtrips exceeding 160 km when carried to some U.S. Environmental Protection Agency-designated ocean disposal sites. This is accomplished in the $9.00 / m^3 range, including the dredging, albeit at small daily quantities of about 4,500 m^3. This type of relatively local transport could be accommodated with large hopper barges or dump scows in today's beach nourishment market. Rehandling and placement costs would increase the cost.

To become productive using this concept, bulk carriers of the type used to transport coal, ore, or grain internationally would be utilized. In addition to the freight charges, mining and loading costs, as well as unloading and placement costs on the receiving end, would be included. One concept would be to outfit the carriers so that the sand cargo could be deposited in underwater stockpiles strategically placed to allow redistribution via cutter-suction or hopper dredge as needed.

Project Quality Control

Having discussed the multitude of steps necessary to bring a beach nourishment project to construction, the owner must ensure proper construction technique with the following quality control measures:

- detailed pre- and postfill surveys, with sufficient extensions past closure depth;
- daily samples of fill material and grain-size distribution analysis;
- records of borrow site excavation coverage on a daily basis and calculation of gross quantities removed;
- detailed calculations of fill volume within and without pay tolerances; and
- records of contractor equipment used, hours worked, payrolls, and fuel consumption.

Alternative Construction Concepts

As additions to the presently considered beach nourishment concepts and techniques, the following ideas may have some merit.

Regional Project Design

Coastal segments, geological features, or other natural separations often fail to coincide with political boundaries. The concept of regionalization, although extremely difficult to implement, is as valid for beach replenishment as it is for water resource usage, infrastructure maintenance, and solid waste disposal. A larger coastline segment for a project may yield advantages in design, economies of scale, and savings in maintenance costs through contract efficiencies. Regional plans may also be more effective in attracting national funding sources.

Stockpiling and Redistributing Navigation Dredging Material

Present limitations on the use of navigation dredging for beach replenishment often require unwieldy coordination between the navigation project and the beach owner. An alternative way of assigning costs may be to allow navigation projects to stockpile material in close proximity to beach fill areas for later redistribution by the locality instead of mandating one continuous process from navigation project to beach fill.

Storm Emergency Fleet

Based loosely on other federal programs for private hopper dredges, it may be desirable that certain contract requirements be preprocessed for a core of emergency response equipment to facilitate protective rebuilding after natural disasters have decimated beaches and dune systems, and left people and property at risk.

Sand Bypass Systems

The use of sand bypassing systems was described in general terms in Chapter 4. The amount of sand to be bypassed is established by the natural coastal processes in the region. The quantity needed for beach nourishment may be greater than the amount trapped in the entrance channel and harbor, in which case bypassing only this amount will not be sufficient to adequately maintain the downdrift beaches. The system designed to bypass the sand depends upon the quantity to be bypassed, wave climate, tidal characteristics, the size and layout of the entrance channel and harbor, how often maintenance dredging is required, how often nourishment is needed, and the times of the year that bypassing will be permitted (due to environmental and multiple-use requirements). The system that is best for maintenance dredging may not be the optimum one for beach nourishment, and vice versa, but the system chosen must be adequate for both functions. Because of the complex relationships among wave dimensions and directional characteristics, water levels, and the transport and deposition of sand, a system that is optimum for normal use may be overwhelmed during some storms. The system used may well have to be modified based on experience.

Several different systems have been designed and used that may be appropriate at a specific site: mobile dredges in the harbor entrance (Santa Cruz, California); movable dredge in the lee of a detached breakwater forming the updrift sand trap (Channel Islands Harbor and Port Hueneme, California); movable dredge within an entrance using a weir jetty on the updrift side (Hillsborough Inlet, Florida); fixed pump with dredge mounted on a movable boom (South Lake Worth Inlet, Florida); a series of fixed jet pump-crater units mounted on a pier normal to the beach on the updrift side (Nerang River Entrance, Queensland, Australia); and a jet pump (eductor) mounted on a movable crane, with main water supply and booster pumps in a fixed building (Indian River Inlet, Delaware). These and other installations and their operational performance are described in *Sand Bypassing System, Engineering and Design Manual* (USACE, 1991), which provides guidance for the design and evaluation of sand bypassing systems.

The following information is needed to plan a project based on quantitative data:

- a statement of the problem;
- sand sources and sinks and sand characteristics in the littoral cell;
- background erosion and accretion rates and the reasons for them;
- wave climate, including directions—measured or hindcast;
- tide data and calculations of flood- and ebb-tide sand transport characteristics;
- calculations and observations of alongshore transport of sand;
- cross-shore movement of sand by waves and tidal currents;
- estimates of sand transport into the entrance or harbor, ebb-tide shoal, and external sand trap if one is a part of the project;
- loss of sand to the offshore caused by structures;
- sand budget, areal and temporal, based on calculations and observations of accretion at nearby structures, such as groins or jetties;
- storm surge climate;
- calculation of wave, water level, and sand movement during severe storms to evaluate system component safety;
- identification and mapping of habitats;
- effect of system on biological communities;
- effect of pumping and deposition of sand on biological communities, on other uses, and on public safety; and
- calculation of downdrift changes with time for several scenarios of sand budget and placement schedules.

After the above information has been obtained or estimated, a system may be designed. Some details on layouts, pumps, and other mechanical components are available in the USACE design manual (USACE, 1991).

REFERENCES

BEB. 1958. Behavior of Beach Fill and Borrow Area at Harrison County, Mississippi. Technical Memorandum No. 107. Washington, D.C.: Beach Erosion Board, U.S. Army Corps of Engineers.

Beachler, K. E., and S. H. Higgins. 1992. Hollywood/Hallandale, building Florida's beaches in the 1990's. Shore and Beach 60(3):15-22.

Bodge, K. R., and E. J. Olsen. 1992. Aragonite beachfill at Fisher Island, Florida. Shore and Beach 69(1):3-8.

Cunningham, R. T. 1966. Evaluation of Bahamian oolitic aragonite sand for Florida beach nourishment. Shore and Beach 34(1):18-21.

Dean, R. G. 1987. Coastal sediment processes: toward engineering solutions. Pp. 1-24 in Proceedings of Coastal Sediments '87, Specialty Conference on Advances in Understanding of Coastal Sediment Processes, Vol. 1. New York: American Society of Civil Engineers.

Domurat, G. W. 1987. Beach nourishment: a working solution. Shore and Beach 55(3-4):92-95.

Dornhelm, R. B. 1995. The Coney Island public beach and boardwalk improvement of 1923. Shore and Beach 63(1):7-11.

Egense, A. K., and C. J. Sonu. 1987. Assessment of beach nourishment methodologies. Pp. 4421-4433 in Coastal Zone '87. New York: American Society of Civil Engineers.

Farley, P. P. 1923. Coney Island public beach and boardwalk improvements. Paper 136. The Municipal Engineers Journal 9(4).

Flick, R. E. 1993. The myth and reality of Southern California beaches. Shore and Beach 61(3):3-13.

Galster, R. W., and M. L. Schwartz. 1990. Ediz Hook—a case history of coastal erosion and rehabilitation. Journal of Coastal Research, Artificial Beaches 6(Special Issue):103-113.

Gee, H. C. 1965. Beach nourishment from offshore sources. Journal of Waterways and Harbors Division 91(WW3):1-5.

Grosskopf, W. G., and D. K. Stauble. 1993. Atlantic coast of Maryland (Ocean City) shoreline protection plan. Shore and Beach 61(1):3-7.

Herron, W. J. 1987. Sand replenishment in Southern California. Shore and Beach 56(3-4):87-91.

Leidersdorf, C. B., R. C. Hollar, and G. Woodell. 1994. Human intervention with the beaches of Santa Monica Bay, California. Shore and Beach 62(3):29-38.

Meisburger, E. P., and S. J. Williams. 1981. Use of Vibratory Coring Samplers for Sediment Surveys. Coastal Engineering Technical Aid 81-9. Fort Belvoir, Va.: Coastal Engineering Research Center, U.S. Army Corps of Engineers.

Monroe, F. F. 1969. Oolitic Aragonite and Quartz Sand: Laboratory Comparison Under Wave Action. Miscellaneous Paper No. 1-69. Washington, D.C.: Coastal Engineering Research Center, U.S. Army Corps of Engineers.

Nordstrom, K. F., J. R. Allen, D. J. Sherman, and N. P. Psuty. 1979. Management considerations for beach nourishment at Sandy Hook, New Jersey. Coastal Engineering 2:215-236.

Rouch, F., and B. Bellessort. 1990. Man-made beaches more than 20 years on. Pp. 2394-2401 in Proceedings of the 22nd Coastal Engineering Conference, Vol. 3. New York: American Society of Civil Engineers.

Tourman, L. 1968. The Creation of an Artificial Beach in Larvatto Bay-Monte Carlo, Principality of Monaco. Pp. 558-569 in Proceedings of the 11th Conference on Coastal Engineering. New York: American Society of Civil Engineers.

USACE. 1991. Sand Bypassing System, Engineering and Design Manual. Engineering and Design Manual No. EM 1110-2-1616. Washington, D.C.: U.S. Army Corps of Engineers.

USACE. 1994. Shoreline Protection and Beach Nourishment Projects of the U.S. Army Corps of Engineers. IWR Report 94-PS-1. Fort Belvoir, Va.: Institute of Water Resources, Water Resources Support Center, U.S. Army Corps of Engineers.

Watts, G. M. 1963. Behavior of offshore borrow zones in beach fill operations. Pp. 17-24 in International Association for Hydraulic Research Tenth Congress, Vol. 1. London: International Association for Hydraulic Research.

Weggel, J. R., and R. M. Sorensen. 1991. Performance of the 1986 Atlantic City, New Jersey, beach nourishment project. Shore and Beach 59(3):29-36.

Wiegel, R. L. 1959. Sand bypassing at Santa Barbara, California. Journal of Waterways and Harbors Division 85(WW2):1-30.

Wiegel, R. L. 1964. Oceanographical Engineering. Englewood Cliffs, N.J.: Prentice-Hall.

Wiegel, R. L. 1992. Dade County, Florida, beach nourishment and hurricane surge protection. Shore and Beach 60(4):2-28.

Wiegel, R. L. 1993. Artificial beach construction with sand/gravel made by crushing rock. Shore and Beach 61(4):28-29.

Wiegel, R. L. 1994. Ocean beach nourishment on the USA Pacific coast. Shore and Beach 62(1):11-36.

G

Physical Processes Monitoring

Monitoring the physical elements of beach nourishment projects provides a means for determining a project's actual performance versus its predicted performance. Monitoring also provides data needed to identify and correct any problems associated with the project and to help guide future renourishment programs.

Physical processes monitoring is undertaken to determine whether a beach nourishment project is performing successfully or whether it is time to renourish. The monitoring of physical processes is undertaken more often than biological or economic monitoring. The physical processes monitored are usually those that:

- move sand alongshore,
- move sand normal to the shore, or
- cause elevated water levels.

Measurements may include both the forces that move sand and the response of the beach to these forces. However, many physical processes monitoring programs address only the response of a beach to these forces—for example, *beach profile changes* and *shoreline recession*. Important forces include waves and currents. Beach responses include the transport and redistribution of sand by wave-induced alongshore currents and seasonal and storm-caused beach profile changes—that is, onshore and offshore sand movement.

The decision to renourish a beach needs to be based on the occurrence of a predefined set of site conditions that a monitoring program is capable of providing. These might include:

- recession of the "average" shoreline to a predefined line,
- loss of a specified fraction of the sand volume placed in an area,
- occurrence of local erosional hot spots that seriously jeopardize upland development of the project itself, or
- a combination of these conditions.

If *shoreline recession* is the trigger, normal seasonal beach profile variations must be taken into account.

Renourishment criteria need to be chosen with a planned factor of safety, so that upland development and the project do not become vulnerable to the effects of storms of less-than-design criteria during the necessary planning, engineering, and mobilization period that precedes construction. For example, renourishment might be triggered when the shoreline recedes to the point where it is projected that, on average, it will no longer provide adequate protection against the design storm in the next year or two. This example presumes that the project includes advanced fill to provide a cushion against loss of design integrity.

Designing a monitoring program that will meet the preceding objectives requires the use of local physical conditions to characterize the range of conditions that might be encountered at the project site. These local conditions would include wave climate, currents, wind conditions, and other physical factors. Data for these conditions are generally available as a result of the design process.

PURPOSES OF MONITORING

Monitoring can be undertaken for various purposes. These principally include *operational* and *performance* monitoring. Operational monitoring is undertaken to implement and maintain a project. It can be as simple as a periodic site inspection or can involve the collection of quantitative data on which to base decisions to

- renourish,
- repair structures, or
- take other remedial action to prevent economic loss or damage.

Operational monitoring includes both prestorm and poststorm monitoring. Performance monitoring is undertaken to develop information and procedures for design verification and for lessons that may be applied in the design of future projects. It involves systematic data collection to develop information useful for the design of future projects or to validate the design methodology used on a given project. One purpose of performance monitoring is to understand fundamental coastal processes and how they influence beach nourishment project performance—for example, to understand how a project impacts adjacent areas as sand is moved along and across the shore.

Computer models and other analytical models used for beach nourishment project design and sediment budget analyses form the framework for performance monitoring programs. Monitoring must measure those forces included in the models that move sediments as well as the beach's response to those forces— that is, waves, currents, and beach profiles. Performance monitoring can provide feedback to the design process by testing design assumptions. It can lead to the development of new design procedures. Performance monitoring might also provide additional data on the physical environment at a project site that were not available at the time of the design.

PHASES OF MONITORING

Monitoring has three basic phases: preconstruction, construction, and postconstruction monitoring.

Preconstruction monitoring acquires regional and site-specific data for design and for baseline data against which project-caused changes can be measured. It involves the collection of data about the physical environment that describe regional and site-specific processes and includes collecting data for design. The physical data needed include measurement of waves, currents, water levels, beach profiles, and meteorological conditions.

Construction monitoring might be undertaken to verify payment to a contractor, to ensure quality control, to obtain as-built information or to document construction practices and how they affect project performance. It involves collecting data on how a project was actually built, how much sand was actually placed, and where it was placed. Such monitoring is conducted in order to pay a contractor or to ensure quality control and to keep track of what materials were actually used (e.g., size characteristics of the sand actually placed on the beach). The objectives of quality control during construction include ensuring that the specified quantity of sand is received and that the sand meets the desired design-size distribution.

Postconstruction monitoring involves the systematic collection of data after construction is complete to study the project's performance. Data are gathered on how a project is performing with respect to design objectives or to make operational decisions such as when to renourish or repair structures. Postconstruction monitoring seeks to answer the basic question: Is the project functioning as intended?

SCALE AND DURATION OF MONITORING PROGRAMS

A simple monitoring program might involve only periodic inspections to determine the width of the protective beach at various locations within a project to determine if renourishment or other corrective action is required. Profile surveys determine the disposition of the sand placed in the project area and establish

---

BOX G-1
Beach Nourishment Monitoring, Ocean City, Maryland

Stauble and Kraus (1993) and Stauble et al. (1993) describe a monitoring program at Ocean City, Maryland. Ocean City is located on Fenwick Island, a barrier island that extends southward from where it connects with the mainland north of the Maryland-Delaware border. The beach nourishment project is bounded on the south by Ocean City Inlet and on the north by the Maryland-Delaware border. The project was extended northward through the town of Fenwick Island, Delaware, by the state of Delaware. Initially, in the summer of 1988, the state of Maryland placed 2.1 million m^3 of sand to form a recreational beach. The U.S. Army Corps of Engineers subsequently placed 2.9 million m^3 for shore protection. The shore protection fill was placed in two stages, between June and September 1990 (from the inlet to about 100th Street) and between June and August 1991 (from 100th Street to the Maryland-Delaware border). The center third of the project was monitored to determine the fate of the sand in response to storms. In addition to tracking project performance, the purpose of the monitoring included research. The monitored portion of the project extends from 37th Street in the south to 103rd Street in the north. Twelve profile lines were surveyed approximately quarterly between 1988 and 1993. Profile lines were surveyed seaward a distance 300 m from the shoreline using a survey sled. Additional surveys were conducted following several severe storms. Wave and water- level data were initially obtained from two nondirectional gauges located about 1 km offshore at a depth of 10 m. These gauges were located approximately off 10th and 80th streets. They were later replaced with directional wave-gauge arrays. Sediment samples were taken along the profile lines at times when profile surveys were made.

---

the volume of sand remaining on the beach per unit length of beach. Hot spots— areas of localized erosion—can be identified from visual inspection and quantified from profile surveys.

Because of the dynamic nature of beach nourishment projects, both short- and long-term monitoring programs are needed. Short-term impacts are defined as those that occur during construction and those that persist for a few days or weeks following construction, but that are not discernable after several months. Long-term impacts are those that persist on the order of months to years. Short-term monitoring is needed to assess near-term performance and any design and placement adjustments that may be needed to accommodate site-specific conditions that deviate from design parameters. Long-term monitoring consists of systematic collection of physical data needed to support assessment of project performance and to guide the renourishment program.

PHYSICAL PROCESSES MONITORING

Monitoring the physical processes and their effects relevant to a beach nourishment project needs to be done within the framework of a sediment budget for

---

BOX G-2
Beach Nourishment Monitoring, Perdido Key, Florida

Work (1993) describes beach nourishment monitoring at Perdido Key, Florida, where, between November 1989 and June 1990, 4.1 million m^3 of sand were placed along 7.6 km of beach to widen the beach by an average of 140 m. During later phases of the nourishment, sand was placed offshore to form a berm. Perdido Key is a barrier island along Florida's "panhandle" coast of the Gulf of Mexico. The project is bounded on the east by Pensacola Pass. The purpose of monitoring was to quantify coastal processes at the site, including the forces that move sediments, to verify the design procedures and thus the performance of the project. Consequently, the monitoring was for research purposes as well as project evaluation. The monitoring project was developed to determine the disposition of the sand in the project in response to waves and currents and to monitor the movement of the offshore berm constructed as profile nourishment.

Monitoring included surveys of 33 beach profiles seaward to a depth 4 to 5 m below National Geodetic Vertical Datum (NGVD). Profiles were surveyed every 3 or 4 months starting in 1990 following an initial base condition survey in 1989, about a year before the project was completed. (There were nine profile surveys in 3 years.) The profile lines coincide with lines established by the Florida Department of Natural Resources. In addition, four bathymetric surveys of the offshore area were made. Two directional wave gauges were installed, and supplemental tide data were obtained. Meteorological data were obtained from a coastal station located on Perdido Key. Photographs of the project were taken whenever profile surveys were conducted. Six or seven sand samples were taken across each profile line during six of the nine profile surveys.

---

the project area and adjacent areas. A sediment budget expresses the principle of conservation of sand: sand is neither created nor destroyed. Sand lost from one area is gained by another. A sediment budget seeks to answer questions such as:

- What is the initial distribution of sediment within the project?
- Where is it going?
- At what rate?
- How much is being lost from the project?
- How is it redistributed within the project?
- What processes move the sand?
- What physical characteristics of the sand must be known to quantitatively define the sediment budget?
- What have the historical rates of erosion been?

A sediment budget requires that all sediment sources and sinks in the study area be identified. Regional sand sources, in addition to beach nourishment, might include rivers, local bluff erosion, and sand transport into an area from adjacent areas. Sinks include ebb- and flood-tide shoals associated with tidal inlets, wind transport into back bay areas, losses to offshore canyons, and sand movement out of an area by alongshore or offshore transport.

The spatial extent of the sediment budget and the time period for which it is constructed determine the kind and amount of data to be collected. When the time period for which the sediment budget is being developed (the averaging period) is on the order of months or years, the sediment budget is generally based on long-term data. The conservation of sand principle can also be applied to time periods of several hours or days in order to develop numerical computer models of sand transport, which can be used to predict shoreline changes and onshore-offshore transport. Numerical models of coastal processes are, in fact, the limiting case of sediment budget equations constructed for an infinitesimally small time interval and subsequently integrated over time. Numerical models apply knowledge of coastal processes to predicting sand movement within and out of a beach nourishment project.

Previous History of a Project Area and Adjacent Areas

The history of events and coastal projects along a reach of beach may simply be anecdotal or may involve quantitative documented data on earlier nourishment projects and on other natural and man-made changes. Data can be regional or site specific. Background information, among other things, needs to include:

- historical erosion rates,
- relative changes and trends in sea level,
- astronomical tides,
- storm surges,
- local anthropogenic impacts,
- statistical descriptions of the wave environment and storm frequency, and
- documented information on wave climate.

Beach Profiles

Beach profiles provide basic data on the volume and location of sand within and adjacent to beach nourishment projects. Profiles are simply measurements of elevation along a line across the subaerial and subaqueous beach extending from the dune offshore into deep water. Profile lines along which elevations are measured are usually established perpendicular to the shoreline. As shoreline orientation changes, however, the relative alignment of profile lines may change. Profile surveys spaced in time can be used to determine the movement of the sand along the profile as well as along the shoreline. Also, beach nourishment projects often benefit beaches outside the project area or are affected by conditions adjacent to the project. It is often necessary to look outside the immediate project boundaries,

**BOX G-3
Beach Nourishment Monitoring,
Hilton Head Island, South Carolina**

Bodge et al. (1993) describe a monitoring program at Hilton Head, South Carolina. Hilton Head is located along the southern South Carolina coast, bounded on the north by Port Royal Sound and on the south by Calibogue Sound. Approximately 1.8 million m^3 of sand was placed along 10,700 m of beach near the center of Hilton Head Island between May and August 1990. Monitoring included surveys of 32 profile lines. The profile lines are part of an ongoing beach monitoring program sponsored by the town of Hilton Head Island. They have been surveyed at least semiannually since 1986. Surveys extended about 300 m seaward of the shoreline to a depth of 3 m. Sand samples were obtained both before and following construction and in the borrow area. No wave data were collected as a part of the monitoring program. The nourished area extends from Profile 13 in the south to Profile 27 in the north, covering about one-half of Hilton Head's ocean shoreline. Profiles 1 through 12 and 28 through 32 are located south and north of the nourished area, respectively, and are used to track movement of project sand to adjacent beaches.

and profile lines may need to be established on beaches adjacent to the project area as well as on project beaches.

Factors to be considered in establishing profile survey lines include:

- profile spacing,
- profile length,
- frequency of surveys,
- surveying procedures available,
- required accuracy, and
- application of the data to make operational decisions or to develop a sediment budget or mathematical model.

Spacing between adjacent profile lines is dictated by the expected changes with distance along a beach. If changes occur over short distances, as they might on beaches with structures, profiles must be spaced close together to accurately define volumetric changes. If spaced too far apart, profiles will not accurately define erosion or accretion on the beach. For example, between structures in a groin field, at least two and preferably three profile lines are needed; on long reaches of relatively straight beaches, profiles may be more widely spaced. Profiles also need to be spaced closer to each other near the ends of nourishment projects to monitor end losses. Profiles outside of the project area need to be located in a manner so as to permit determination of how much sand is gained by adjacent beaches at the expense of the project.

The length and accuracy of a profile line determine whether cross-shore coastal processes can be quantified. Ideally, profiles would start at the upper part of the beach landward of where wave action and erosion occur (at the toe of the dune) and extend offshore to at least the depth of closure. Profile changes occur infrequently seaward of the depth of closure (Hallermeier, 1981). (A fixed depth of closure is difficult to define. It must be defined in a statistical sense given the local wave climate and offshore profile. While phenomena other than large, long-period waves might move sand seaward of the closure depth, for practical purposes closure depth is determined by the wave environment.) Profiles can be divided into subaerial and subaqueous components. Often the two components are surveyed at different times, since different survey techniques are often used. The problem is to match the two surveys where they traverse the same area across the surf zone—a region where bathymetric changes occur frequently and rapidly. Subaerial profiles can be surveyed by using standard leveling techniques. Subaqueous surveys can be obtained by lead-line sounding or by using an acoustic fathometer. However, the best profiling systems can traverse the surf zone from the subaerial beach to the closure depth without interruption. For example, a survey sled with a graduated mast towed from offshore across the surf zone onto the dry beach provides such a system (Langley, 1992). Grosskopf and Kraus (1994) recommend that a system composed of a sea sled capable of traversing the surf zone and a total-station surveying system be used wherever possible to survey profiles (see Figure G-1). They show that errors in determining offshore and surf-zone elevations are small using this technique and that measurements are more reproducible. This in turn leads to better estimates of sand volumes lost and gained across the profiles and to better determinations of the fate of nourishment sand. Other systems capable of traversing the surf zone and producing accurate surveys include sophisticated mobile survey stations like the "CRAB" (see Figure G-2).

Profile surveys must be spaced close enough in time to define seasonal profile changes, beach response to storms, and long-term profile evolution. Survey frequency might also change during a monitoring program with more frequent surveys taken shortly after construction when changes are rapid and less frequent surveys taken later when changes are slower. Initially, profile surveys need to be made at least quarterly to document typical seasonal variations. When experience is gained, less frequent surveys might suffice.

In addition to scheduled profile surveys, the effects of storms on beach profiles need to be monitored. This might require special mobilization after storms to conduct beach surveys. Ideally both pre- and poststorm surveys need to be obtained. However, prestorm surveys are difficult to obtain because sufficient advance mobilization time often is not available. Poststorm surveys need to be obtained as soon as is practical after each significant storm in order to record the storm's effects. Changes following the first significant storm of a season will bring about the most dramatic profile changes; subsequent storms, unless more

FIGURE G-1   Sea sled for measuring beach profiles from the dry beach through the surf zone to depth of closure.

FIGURE G-2   Coastal Research Amphibious Buggy (CRAB), a sophisticated mobile survey station used to profile the seabed from the dune through the surf zone out to a water depth of 10 m.

> **BOX G-4**
> **Beach Nourishment Monitoring, Indian Rocks Beach, Florida**
>
> Creaser et al. (1993) describe the monitoring program at Indian Rocks Beach, Florida. Indian Rocks Beach is located on Sand Key along the west coast of Florida near Tampa. Sand Key is a barrier island about 25 km long. The shoreline on Sand Key is convex seaward, and Indian Rocks Beach is located just north of the center of the island. Approximately 1.1 million m^3 of sand was placed along 4 km of coast creating an average berm width of 65 m. Thirty-four profile lines, spaced an average of 150 m apart, were surveyed monthly to a depth of -1.5 m NGVD. The profile lines are along ranges established by the Florida Department of Natural Resources. Twenty-eight of the profiles are within the nourished area; two are north of the nourished area and four are south. Surveys were made by using a total station with a reflecting prism affixed to a stadia rod. Wave data were obtained from a U.S. Geological Survey gauge offshore of the project at a depth of 4 m. Meteorological data, including wind speed, direction, and atmospheric pressure, were obtained from the Tampa airport.

severe than preceding storms or preceded by an extended period of beach building, will cause less dramatic profile changes.

Beach profile data are usually analyzed by comparing two profiles taken at the same location at different times to determine changes during the intervening time. The area between the two profiles represents the volumetric change per unit of shoreline length during that period. A similar analysis of a nearby profile line allows the volume change between the two profile stations to be computed. The volume lost or gained is the average of the two end-area changes multiplied by the distance between the stations. The accuracy of the computed area change at a given station depends on the accuracy of the profile data. The accuracy of volume computations depends on the distance between the two stations, the accuracy of the individual profiles, and whether the two profiles adequately characterize the beach conditions between them. Beach profile errors are not cumulative, and an error made during one survey affects only that survey and possibly only a portion of the profile. Volume calculations made using erroneous profile data lead to errors in estimating volume changes, but those errors can be corrected by subsequent surveys. Where shoreline orientation and processes do not change much along a beach, profile lines can be spaced farther apart and still adequately describe beach conditions. For beaches that change their orientation with distance, closely spaced profiles are necessary.

More detailed analyses can quantify changes above, below, or between given contour lines. For example, subaerial beach changes can be quantified by computing profile changes above the mean sea level (MSL) contour. In addition to volume calculations, shoreline movement in the period between two surveys can be determined from profile data. The distance from a fixed baseline to any given shoreline contour—the mean high-water, mean sea-level, or mean low-water contour—can be found from each survey.

Waves

Waves produce the most important forces that move sand in the littoral zone. Consequently, wave data are important in any performance-type monitoring program. Wave-induced alongshore currents move sand along shore. Changing wave heights and periods continuously move sand onshore and offshore toward an elusive equilibrium.

Data on wave height, period, and direction are needed in order to estimate potential alongshore transport rates; heights and periods alone are insufficient. Wave data can be obtained by direct measurement or by using mathematical relationships that transform meteorological data such as atmospheric pressure fields or wind data into wave heights, periods, and directions. The U.S. Army Corps of Engineers (USACE) Wave Information Study used atmospheric pressure data and wind data to hindcast historical wave information, including heights, periods, and directions, for the Atlantic, Gulf of Mexico, Pacific, and Great Lakes coastal waters. (See, for example, Jensen, 1983, and Hubertz et al., 1993.) If wave conditions are known at an offshore location, they must be transformed to the project site by shoaling and refraction analyses. An advantage of direct wave measurement is that its characteristics can be obtained in the vicinity of the nourishment project and would require little or no transformation to obtain conditions at the project site. A disadvantage is that local wave measurements may not apply to distant parts of a project because of local bathymetric differences.

There are many types of wave gauges. They include surface-piercing gauges (e.g., Baylor gauge), pressure gauges, combined pressure gauges with biaxial current meters, accelerometer buoys, and inverted echo sounders. Each has inherent advantages and disadvantages (NRC, 1989). Multiple-gauge arrays can be used to measure wave direction. Direction can also be determined by slope arrays of pressure gauges in shallow water and tilt buoys in deep water. Directional wave gauge systems frequently experience operational problems and are generally expensive to operate and maintain. Their advantage is their ability to accurately measure concurrent time histories of wave height, period, and direction (and water level if so configured) and report the data in near real time when cabled to shore. The USACE routinely uses directional wave gauges to collect wave data for project studies. Another alternative is to couple a normal wave gauge to obtain wave heights and periods with detailed hindcasts to obtain direction.

Visual wave and nearshore current observations can provide estimates of nearshore wave height, period, and direction; however, data are often biased toward low heights (observers do not want to visit the beach during storms), and directional estimates are at best poor. An example of a visual wave observation program is the Littoral Environmental Observation Program, which was operated by the USACE for a number of years (Schneider, 1981). Wave data are analyzed to obtain significant wave height, period, and, when possible, direction.

Complex wave gauge arrays or other systems are usually necessary to determine wave direction; consequently, wave direction is not often obtained in beach nourishment monitoring programs. Alternatively, wave direction may be inferred from local wind direction for locally generated seas; however, distantly generated swell may not be traveling in the same direction as local winds. If waves have not been generated by local winds, wave direction and wind direction can differ significantly.

Wave measurement systems need to be selected in view of any special conditions that exist at monitoring sites, such as unusually long period wave components, bimodal spectra, salinity, water depths, or tidal range.

Currents

Nearshore currents are not typically measured as part of beach nourishment monitoring except for research purposes. If measured, nearshore currents are likely to be used to estimate potential alongshore sand transport rates. For example, alongshore current measurements obtained by using the USACE's Littoral Environmental Observation Program procedures (Schneider, 1981) can be used to estimate alongshore sand transport rates (Walton, 1980). Usually, however, alongshore currents are computed from wave height, period, and direction.

In addition to alongshore currents caused by waves, other nearshore currents can provide a mechanism for moving sand into, within, and out of beach nourishment projects. Tidal currents might be important in causing end losses from a nourishment project. Beach nourishment projects located near tidal inlets can be affected by flood and ebb currents; however, tidal currents at inlets are rarely measured during typical beach nourishment monitoring programs. For research purposes, they might be measured to determine the tidal prism entering an inlet and to estimate how much sand is removed from the littoral system and trapped by the inlet. Wind-driven nearshore currents are generally less important.

Current speed and direction can be measured by deploying fixed recording current meters; however, spatial variations in current speed and direction cannot be obtained without installing an array of expensive meters. Other techniques for measuring current speed and direction track floating drogues using standard surveying techniques. Also, dye patches in the water can be tracked using Littoral Environmental Observation-type procedures (Schneider, 1981) or photographed to determine current speed and direction. This latter technique is not useful for long-term or routine monitoring but provides data for only a limited space and time.

Water Levels

Information on water levels during storms is important for performance monitoring to validate the design procedures used to predict dune erosion and flood damage. Astronomical tides are predicted and water levels are measured routinely by the National Oceanic and Atmospheric Administration's (NOAA) National Ocean Survey at stations located around the U.S. coastline (NOAA, 1993). Meteorological or storm tides constitute that portion of the measured water-level record not explained by predicted astronomical tides. Generally, these deviations from predicted tides are due mostly to wind stresses on the water surface and to atmospheric pressure (including the "ship wave" effect in shallow water caused by rapidly moving pressure systems) and Coriolis setup. Storm- and astronomical-tide levels combine to allow waves to act higher up on a beach profile and result in flooding and beach and dune erosion during storms. They are, therefore, very important in evaluating the response of a beach nourishment project to a given storm. At some tide-recording stations, periods of records extend back more than 100 years. Water-level data are available from NOAA for sites near most beach nourishment projects in the United States. For stations with long records, data on relative sea-level changes can also be obtained (Hicks, 1983). Water-level data are also a natural byproduct of using pressure gauges to measure nearshore waves if care is taken to preserve the mean water-level data.

Sediment Characteristics

Important sediment characteristics include mineralogy, specific gravity, specific surface, mean grain size, grain size distribution, grain shape, and settling velocity (Smith, 1992). The primary parameter in determining the response of a beach profile to waves and currents is the settling velocity. The effects of many of the other parameters are included through their influence on the sand's settling velocity. Information on these characteristics is needed for

- sand in borrow areas,
- sand on a beach prior to beach nourishment (native sand), and
- sand actually placed on a beach by truck or from a dredge's discharge line.

Spatial differences in sediment characteristics may also be important. For example, the distribution of mean grain size along the beach profile and along a beach can be important, since different grain sizes are moved at different rates by waves and currents. Coarser grains tend to accumulate in the surf zone.

Temporal changes in sediment characteristics may also occur on a beach as a result of wave winnowing processes. Consequently, a sediment monitoring program may require periodic resampling to determine such changes.

Structures

Coastal structures contribute to the performance of beach nourishment projects by trapping sand in alongshore transport, reorienting the local shoreline with respect to prevailing incident waves, sheltering the shoreline, and slowing the loss of sand. Alternatively, some long structures can speed the offshore loss of sand by altering local current patterns. The types of structures present in a project area are important. They can include

- single groins,
- multiple groins (a groin field),
- terminal groins,
- seawalls,
- bulkheads,
- revetments, and
- nearshore breakwaters.

In order to acquire sufficient data for analysis, monitoring programs must identify

- the types of structures present;
- how they are constructed;
- their planform, orientation, spacing, and height;
- their effect on waves and currents;
- their permeability to waves and sand; and
- their effect on the stability of the beach nourishment project.

The effects of structures on the stability of a beach nourishment project can vary over the project's lifetime. As sand erodes, the structures may become more and more exposed to waves and currents, and their beneficial or detrimental effects may be enhanced. The location and spacing of structures dictate the spacing of beach profiles needed to obtain accurate volumetric beach changes.

Borrow Areas

Borrow areas need to be monitored to quantify physical changes; however, they are often not monitored at all. Prior to construction, borrow areas need to be sampled to determine whether proper-sized sand is available. Following construction, infilling of the borrow area needs to be monitored to determine the characteristics of the material that accumulates and the rate of filling. If the same borrow area is intended for reuse as a sand source, monitoring needs to establish if there is sufficient sand available for future use.

Special Studies

It may often be useful to conduct certain special studies in conjunction with beach nourishment monitoring. Examples of special studies might include hydraulic or sedimentation measurements at tidal inlets; sand tracer studies to determine dispersal patterns for sediments along beaches, onshore and offshore, and into inlets; dye studies to monitor unusual current patterns in the vicinity of coastal structures; and evaluations of new dredging and nearshore disposal techniques. For example, studies using naturally occurring materials as tracers as well as dyed or radioactively tagged native sand have been used to identify the source of sediments and to monitor their movement in the littoral zone. Other special studies (perhaps more correctly classified as field experiments) might be conceived and carried out to quantify unique conditions associated with specific beach nourishment projects. Such special studies are usually in the realm of research.

Global Positioning Systems

The establishment and availability of global positioning systems (GPSs) in recent years have revolutionized terrestrial surveying. GPS systems use signals from three or more satellites to determine the horizontal and vertical positions of a point on the earth's surface to within about 4 in. Defense applications can achieve such accuracy in real time; however, commercial applications must rely on data available only after a survey has been conducted to correct readings if such accuracy is desired. Lesser accuracy on the order of 5 to 10 m can be obtained in real time, if needed, for commercial applications using differential GPS (DGPS) equipment. Real-time measurements are generally not needed for beach nourishment project monitoring, so GPS does not, at present, offer advantages over standard surveying techniques for measurements like profile surveys. In the future, however, as costs decline, accuracy improves, and DGPS is more widely adopted, it may prove to be an economical system for surveying nourishment projects.

DGPS has other applications, however, that impact the construction and monitoring of beach nourishment projects. It can be used to locate equipment such as wave gauge arrays installed on the ocean bottom and to position cutterhead and hopper dredges to excavate in tightly defined borrow areas.

Geographical Information Systems

In recent years geographical information systems have come into prominence for storing, displaying, and analyzing spatial data of all types. These systems have been used for marine resource management (Friel and Haddad, 1992) and may provide a convenient way of storing and analyzing monitoring data obtained from beach nourishment projects.

Photographic Documentation

Photographs can be used to graphically document the performance of a beach nourishment project. Photographs are inexpensive, are easy to obtain, and can be used to picture conditions in areas between profile lines and at times between scheduled surveys. Ground-level photographs taken at the same location, in the same direction, and at various times of the year provide a quick indication of the changes within a project.

Time-lapse photography has been used to document beach changes. Depending on the time between photographs, time-lapse photography can document changes over a tidal cycle, resulting from storms, or over a season. Periodic controlled vertical aerial photography can provide data on changes in the location of the shoreline and, using standard photogrammetric methods, can provide data on changes in the topography of the subaerial beach.

Videotape can supplement regular photography and can also be used to document project conditions and performance before, during, and after storms. Prestorm video can be obtained quickly when a storm is predicted. A small airplane or helicopter can be used as a platform from which to videotape conditions over long stretches of coastline in a short period of time.

THIRD-PARTY MONITORING

In some instances, it may be advisable for monitoring to be done by a disinterested third party who can objectively evaluate the project's performance. This might be done in cases where a project, or some element of a project, is controversial and its sponsor or the public wants an independent evaluation of its performance. However, the objectives, scope, required accuracy, frequency of data collection, and how the data will be analyzed must be carefully defined in view of the project's objectives and expectations. Definitions of what constitutes successful performance need to be agreed upon prior to third-party monitoring of controversial projects.

REFERENCES

Bodge, K. E., E. J. Olsen, and C. G. Creed. 1993. Performance of beach nourishment at Hilton Head Island, South Carolina. In: Beach Nourishment Engineering and Management Considerations, Coastal Zone '93, New Orleans, Louisiana. New York: American Society of Civil Engineers.

Creaser, G. J., R. A. Davis, Jr., and J. Haines. 1993. Relationship between wave climate and performance of a recently nourished beach, Indian Rocks Beach, Pinellas County, Florida. In: Proceedings of Beach Nourishment Engineering and Management Considerations, Coastal Zone '93, New Orleans, Louisiana. New York: American Society of Civil Engineers.

Friel, C., and K. Haddad. 1992. GIS brings new outlook to Florida Keys marine resources manage-
    ment. GIS World 5(9).
Grosskopf, W. G., and N. C. Kraus. 1994. Guidelines for surveying beach nourishment projects.
    Shore and Beach 62(2):9-16.
Hallermeier, R. J. 1981. Seaward Limit of Significant Sand Transport by Waves: An Annual Zona-
    tion for Seasonal Profiles. Coastal Engineering Technical Aid No. CETA 81-2. Fort Belvoir,
    Va.: Coastal Engineering Research Center, U.S. Army Corps of Engineers.
Hicks, S. 1983. Sea Level Variations for the United States, 1855-1980. Washington, D.C.: National
    Oceanic and Atmospheric Administration.
Hubertz, J. M., R. M. Brooks, W. A. Brandon, and B. A. Tracy. 1993. Hindcast Wave Information
    for the U.S. Atlantic Coast. WIS Report 30. Vicksburg, Miss.: Coastal Engineering Research
    Center, U.S. Army Waterways Experiment Station, U.S. Army Corps of Engineers.
Jensen, R. E. 1983. Atlantic Coast Hindcast, Shallow-Water Significant Wave Information. WIS
    Report 9. Vicksburg, Miss.: Coastal Engineering Research Center, U.S. Army Waterways Ex-
    periment Station, U.S. Army Corps of Engineers.
Langley, T. 1992. Sea sled surveying through the surf zone. Shore and Beach 60(2):15-19.
NOAA. 1993. Tide Tables for the East Coast of North and South America. National Ocean Survey,
    National Oceanic and Atmospheric Administration. Washington, D.C.: U.S. Department of
    Commerce.
NRC. 1989. Measuring and Understanding Coastal Processes for Engineering Purposes. Marine
    Board, Commission on Engineering and Technical Systems, National Research Council. Wash-
    ington, D.C.: National Academy Press.
Schneider, C. 1981. The Littoral Environmental Observation (LEO) Data Collection Program. CETA
    81-5. Fort Belvoir, Va.: Coastal Engineering Research Center, U.S. Army Corps of Engineers.
Smith, A. W. S. 1992. Description of beach sands. Shore and Beach 60(3):23-30.
Stauble, D. K., and N. C. Kraus. 1993. Project performance: Ocean City, Maryland, beach nourish-
    ment. In: Proceedings of Beach Nourishment Engineering and Management Considerations,
    Coastal Zone '93, New Orleans, Louisiana. New York: American Society of Civil Engineers.
Stauble, D. K., A. W. Garcia, N. C. Kraus, W. G. Grosskopf, and G. P. Bass. 1993. Beach Nourish-
    ment Project Response and Design Evaluation: Ocean City, Maryland, Report 1, 1988-1992.
    Technical Report CERC-93-13. Vicksburg, Miss.: Coastal Engineering Research Center, U.S.
    Army Waterways Experiment Station, U.S. Army Corps of Engineers.
Walton, T. L. 1980. Computation of Longshore Energy Flux Using LEO Current Observations.
    CETA 80-3. Fort Belvoir, Va.: Coastal Engineering Research Center, U.S. Army Waterways
    Experiment Station, U.S. Army Corps of Engineers.
Work, P. A. 1993. Monitoring the evolution of a beach nourishment project. Pp. 57-70 in D. K.
    Stauble and N. C. Kraus, eds., Proceedings of Beach Nourishment Engineering and Manage-
    ment Considerations. New York: American Society of Civil Engineers.

H
U.S. Army Corps of Engineers Design Criteria

Historically, the design of coastal defense projects has been based on the specifications of a design storm. For urban coastal areas, protection was designed either for the standard project hurricane as defined by the National Weather Service or some other rare event. In the latter case, this was often the storm (hurricane) of record in the area of interest, with the peak surge elevation transferred to the project site and adjusted to coincide with high tide. Frequency of exceedance determinations, when a tide gauge was not available in or near the area of interest, were innovative, highly variable from locale to locale, and lacked a scientific basis.

Early beach fills were frequently designed to protect against erosion and to provide recreation. In such cases, coastal flood protection was not claimed. Most damages prevented were from mitigation of the effects of long-term erosion. Berms were generally 50 to 100 ft wide, as determined by the severity of historical events. Some berm widths were set to optimize the recreation benefits, as long as the historical shoreline was not exceeded, because most benefits were derived from enhanced recreation. The Water Resources Development Act of 1986 replaced the project purpose of beach erosion control with coastal storm damage reduction and recreation.

After the March 1962 northeaster that devastated much of the East coast shorefront areas, Joseph M. Caldwell, a U.S. Army Corps of Engineers (USACE) engineer, designed a dune and berm cross-section based on results of experiments conducted by using a large wave tank located at the Beach Erosion Board laboratory (predecessor of the Coastal Engineering Research Center) in Washington, D.C. The "Caldwell section" was used to design the protection of coasts for some time thereafter. These were the first uses of berms and artificial dunes as sacrificial shore protection measures.

The USACE currently uses a range of approaches for developing a set of storm events to evaluate design features. This change in design approach was part of the USACE's response to the national economic requirements of the *Economic and Environmental Principles for Water and Related Land Resources Implementation Studies* that were approved by President Reagan in 1983 (Schmidt, 1994; see Appendix B). The selected approach is based on project scope, availability of data, and level of resources. In the simplest case, hypothetical or historically based surges that represent a limited combination of storm parameters are scaled to define a set of storm events. Recurrence relationships are then obtained from existing elevation frequency curves. A more comprehensive design procedure is normally undertaken for large-scale projects. The prescribed procedure is to use numerical models of physical processes and statistical procedures. Historical storm events are used to define a representative storm training set. The beach's response to each event is determined by numerical models. Statistical procedures are then used to compute frequency relationships and associated error bands for the design parameters of interest and for storm damages. This more rigorous approach can be used to generate continuous frequency-of-occurrence relationships for any parameter in the design evaluation process, as well as to provide error-band input for risk-based design.

The current prescribed practice of the USACE is to use a set of storm events with a range of return periods to evaluate the cost effectiveness of design alternatives. Optimization of the net benefits for an area necessitates evaluation of a range of protection alternatives to determine their costs and the damage reduction benefits that each alternative would produce. The degree of protection, or storm damage reduction, that would be produced by each alternative can be evaluated for a series of storm events with return periods ranging from relatively frequent events (5-year return period or less) to extremely rare occurrences (500-year return period). The amount of damage likely to be produced by this range of storms with a beach nourishment project in place can be compared with the expected damage without the project, with the difference in potential damages representing the expected reduction in damages attributable to the particular design alternative being evaluated. The reduction in potential average annual damages plus the incidental average annual recreational benefits associated with the alternative represents the total annual benefits produced by the alternative. Net benefits for this plan are computed by determining the difference in the annual cost necessary to construct and maintain the alternative and its total annual benefits. This same procedure is then used to assess the other design alternatives being considered for a particular beach nourishment project. Protection plans can range from simple beach fills of varying widths to combined fills having both artificial dunes and berms. The singular plan that produces the maximum difference in net benefits is designated as the National Economic Development plan.

The cost associated with constructing and maintaining this plan establishes the maximum extent of federal cost sharing available for the project area. The result of this plan formulation process is that the plan does not provide protection for a particular storm. Rather, it is capable in varying degrees of reducing damages associated with essentially all storms (Jarrett, 1994; see Appendix B).

For coastal protection projects, design alternatives can include variations in berm width, berm height, and dune height and the inclusion of fixed structures. Under the USACE's prescribed procedure, the defined storm events are supposed to be chosen to reflect realistic combinations of various parameters descriptive of historical storm events that have impacted the location of interest. For tropical events, the storms need to define the range of durations, maximum winds, radius of maximum winds, pressure deficits, storm track, and other factors. For extratropical events, appropriate descriptors include the range of durations, hydrograph shapes, and maximum winds. Frequency relationships are then assigned to the set of storms.

Recurrence relationships are no longer directly assigned to a storm. They are assigned to some measurable characteristic or result of the storm such as maximum surge height. In cases such as beach recession, factors such as stage hydrograph shape and wave characteristics determine the extent of recession. Because storms are characterized by multiple properties, the set-of-storm-events concept is the preferred approach for analysis and is considered by the USACE to be more useable and realistic than the single design storm method. This approach recognizes the beneficial effects a project will have during storm events that have parameters exceeding those that produce zero or minimal damage as well as the probability that such events will occur.

I

Excerpts from Federal Laws Pertaining to Placement of Sand from Channel Maintenance Projects on Beaches

PUBLIC LAW 94-587
WATER RESOURCES DEVELOPMENT ACT OF 1976

Section 145. The Secretary of the Army, acting through the Chief of Engineers, is authorized upon request of the State, to place on the beaches of such State, beach-quality sand, which has been dredged in constructing and maintaining navigation inlets and channels adjacent to such beaches, if the Secretary deems such action to be in the public interest and upon payment of the increased cost thereof above the cost required for alternative methods of disposing of such sand.

PUBLIC LAW 99-662
WATER RESOURCES DEVELOPMENT ACT OF 1986

Section 933. Cost sharing for disposal of material on beaches. Section 145 of the Water Resources Development Act of 1976 (33 U.S.C. 426) is amended by inserting "by such State of 50 percent" after "upon payment."

PUBLIC LAW 100-676
WATER RESOURCES DEVELOPMENT ACT OF 1988

Section 35. Placement of dredged beach quality sand on beaches. Section 145 of the Water Resources Development Act of 1976 (33 U.S.C. 426) is amended by adding at the end thereof the following new sentence: "In carrying out this section, the Secretary shall give consideration to the State's schedule for providing its share of funds for placing such sand on the beaches of such State and shall, to the maximum extent practicable, accommodate such schedule."

PUBLIC LAW 102-580
WATER RESOURCES DEVELOPMENT ACT OF 1992

Section 207. Cost-sharing for disposal of dredged material on beaches. Section 145 of the Water Resources Development Act of 1976 (33 U.S.C. 426) is amended by striking the last sentence and inserting the following new sentences: "At the request of the State, the Secretary may enter into an agreement with a political subdivision of the State to place sand on the beaches of the political subdivision of the State under the same terms and conditions required in first sentence of this section; except that the political subdivision shall be responsible for providing any payments required under such sentence in lieu of the State. In carrying out this section the Secretary shall give consideration to the schedule of the State, or the schedule of the responsible political subdivision of the requesting State, for providing its share of funds for placing such sand on the beaches of the State or the political subdivision and shall, to the maximum extent practicable, accommodate such schedule."

SECTION 145 OF PUBLIC LAW 94-587 (AS AMENDED)

The Secretary of the Army, acting through the Chief of Engineers, is authorized upon request of the State, to place on the beaches of such State beach-quality sand which has been dredged in constructing and maintaining navigation inlets and channels adjacent to such beaches, if the Secretary deems such action to be in the public interest and upon payment by such State of 50 percent of the increased cost thereof above the cost required for alternative methods of disposing of such sand. At the request of the State, the Secretary may enter into an agreement with a political subdivision of the State to place sand on the beaches of the political subdivision of the State under the same terms and conditions required in the first sentence of this section in lieu of the State. In carrying out this section, the Secretary shall give consideration to the schedule of the State, or the schedule of the responsible political subdivision of the requesting State, for providing its share of funds for placing such sand on the beaches of the State or political subdivision and shall, to the maximum extent practicable, accommodate such schedule.

Index

A

Abandonment
  of nourishment project, 12, 120-121
  of shore buildings, 17, 27-28
Accountability, 13, 104-105
Accretion of sediment
  design considerations, 141-142
  recommendations for research, 157
Adjacent areas
  considerations in project site
    selection, 145
  in cost-benefit analysis, 5, 47-48, 153
  effects of hard structures in
    nourishment projects, 89-91
  in project and program planning, 8,
    31, 148
  property values, 47-48, 138, 257-258,
    262-263
  See also Spreading losses
Adjustable structures, 90
Advanced fill, 8, 102, 142, 193, 194,
  200-201, 212-213
Alaska, 179
Alongshore spreading. *See* Sediment
  transport; Spreading losses

Amenity values, 47-48, 258
Arctic coast, 22
Army Corps of Engineers, U.S.
    (USACE)
  Beach Erosion Board, 59
  Coastal Engineering Research Board,
    59
  Coastal Engineering Research Center,
    59, 100, 193
  contracting for technical services, 9,
    150
  coordination of navigation projects
    and shore protection projects, 39
  cost-benefit analysis methodology, 5,
    45, 47, 137, 152-154, 251-252,
    260-262
  credentialing of coastal engineers,
    105
  current shore protection strategies, 60
  design procedures and standards, 6,
    102-103, 191, 311-313
  evaluation of nontraditional devices,
    12, 145
  evolution of shore protection
    strategies, 59, 311-312
  FEMA and, 73

C

flood, 13, 18, 154, 156. *See also*
National Flood Insurance Program
risk assessment, 41
Interior, U.S. Department of, 19, 147
See also Minerals Management
Service
International comparison, 25
spending for beach protection, 15
Interval between renourishments
accuracy of projections, 54
cost of fixed structures and, 144
first renourishment, 7, 142
as measure of project performance,
43
performance predictions, 83
public awareness, 146
risk analysis, 229-230
statistical modeling, 235
Italy, 225

J

Japan, 15

L

Land-use plans, 49, 263
Land values, 14
Laws and regulations
affecting beach nourishment projects,
43
NOAA authorities, 61
project planning process, 39-40
USACE authority, 59-60
on use of dredged sand from
navigation projects, 314-315
on use of fixed structures, 11, 18,
143-145
valuation of environmental effects, 48
See also specific legislation
Licensing of engineers, 105
Littoral Environment Observation
Program, 305
Local conditions
baseline profile, 87, 129, 134, 296

design considerations, 6, 94, 141,
142, 143, 295
distribution of project benefits and,
45
history of site, 299
implications for dredging operations,
284-285
measurement of project success and,
41-42
potential settings for nourishment
projects, 88
preconstruction monitoring, 129, 296
predictability of project performance
affected by, 94-95
project formulation for, 32-33
Long-term considerations
accreditation of nourishment projects
as hazard-reducing, 74-75, 79-80
in beach nourishment program, 9
biological resource degradation, 10
climate shifts, 23, 40
construction standards for shore
buildings, 76-78
in cost-benefit analysis, 50-51
cost projections, 53-54
environmental effects of dredging,
115, 118-120
federal agency coordination, 79-80
measures of project success, 149-150
placement of sand, 32-34
in project design, 189
project monitoring, 297
public awareness and understanding
of, 38, 53
research and development needs in
dredging industry, 288-289
restoration of abandoned projects,
120-121
sand placement technique, 32-34
sea-level rise, 213
social effects of projects, 252-253,
263-264
socioeconomic factors, 23

of effects of fixed structures, 11
elements of campaign for, 38, 53-55
initial sediment losses after
  nourishment, 36-37, 208
interest in shoreline protection, 14
of National Flood Insurance Program,
  67-68
participation in project planning, 7,
  28-29, 141
project costs, 53-54, 55
project performance and, 2, 34-38, 55
recommendations for, 141, 146-147
survey of, 34-36, 137-138
Public Law *71-520,* 58-59
Public Law *94-587,* 315

R

Rainfall, 41
Reconnaissance study, 29
Recreation
  contingent valuation of, 255
  as factor in cost-benefit analysis, 4-5,
    46, 52, 137-138, 152, 153, 199-
    200, 255, 258, 261-262
  monitoring, 137-138
  travel cost valuation of, 255
  valuation in USACE cost-benefit
    analysis, 47, 251-252
  value of beaches for, 1, 14-15
Research activities
  Geological Survey, U.S., 68-70
  Minerals Management Service, 71
  USACE, 59
Research needs
  coastal processes, 10-11, 156-157
  correlation of closure with depth of
    closure, 87
  cost-benefit distribution, 139
  for decision-making, 10-11
  design and prediction methodologies,
    6, 10-11, 157
  directional wave data, 10, 157
  evaluation of nontraditional projects,
    12, 144-145

for National Flood Insurance Program
  planning basis, 65-66
for policy making, 17
recommendations, 156-157
Revetments/seawalls/bulkheads, 16,
  183-185, 196-198, 222-225. *See
  also* Fixed structures
Risk analysis/assessment
  current practyice, 41
  data needs, 227, 234
  in design process, 227-229
  elements of, 226-227
  FEMA evaluation of nourishment
    projects, 64-65, 78
  FEMA flood hazard surveys, 64
  public understanding of project risks,
    34-36
  relevance to nourishment projects,
    226
  simulation techniques, 228, 233-235
  storm-related, 229-231
River and Harbor Act of 1968, 59-60
Rivers as sand sources, 270

S

Safety factors in project design, 6, 142
Sand bypass operation, 8-9, 145
  definition, 24
  design of, 214, 215, 290-292
  nature of, 99-100
  navigation projects and, 104
  need for, 213
  as source of sand for nourishment,
    100-101, 270
  systems for, 214-215, 291
Sand-tight jetties, 221-222
Sand volume
  accuracy of predictions, 83
  advanced-fill design, 200-201, 212-
    213
  calculating nourishment quantity, 6,
    194-195
  design determinants, 194-198, 203-
    204, 212